Basics of Group Counseling and Psychotherapy

AN INTRODUCTORY GUIDE

Second Edition

Jerrold Lee Shapiro, Lawrence Stephen Peltz,
and Susan Bernadett-Shapiro

Bassim Hamadeh, CEO and Publisher
Leah Sheets, Associate Editor
Alia Bales, Associate Production Editor
Jess Estrella, Senior Graphic Designer
Alexa Lucido, Licensing Coordinator
Don Kesner, Interior Designer
Natalie Piccotti, Senior Marketing Manager
Kassie Graves, Vice President of Editorial
Jamie Giganti, Director of Academic Publishing

ISBN: 978-1-5165-3250-6 (pbk) / 978-1-5165-3251-3 (br)

Basics of Group Counseling and Psychotherapy

AN INTRODUCTORY GUIDE

Second Edition

Dedication

To our grandchildren: William Myer, Lydia Jean and Evelyn Kate

JLS & STBS

To my wife and partner in life, Cathy: you are my everything. And to our grandchildren: Shelby Lee, Evan Joseph, Lily Jane and Piper Annette

LSP

And to the hundreds of graduate students in our group classes at the University of Hawaii and Santa Clara University. They have made our efforts in group training more than worthwhile and carry the torch as group counselors and therapists.

Brief Table of Contents

Detailed Table of Contents

Introduction to this Edition

This text and manual is an updated iteration of our earlier book on brief group treatment (Shapiro, Peltz, & Bernadett-Shapiro, 1998). It has been revised and updated to account for changes since the beginning of the 21st century.

The authors of this text have been counselors and psychotherapists for decades. During those years, group counseling and psychotherapy have been a significant aspect of our work. Dr. Shapiro did his first group as an intern at the VA outpatient clinic in Boston in 1965, Dr. Peltz has been actively doing groups since the mid-1970s, and Dr. Bernadett-Shapiro since the 1980s. We have been teaching introductory and advanced classes in group counseling and therapy and leading training groups throughout those years. Characteristically we have been involved as leaders, members or supervisors of between 15 and 20 groups annually.

In those years, we have developed a series of methods for graduate students in mental health fields to learn about group process and the basics of leading groups designed for personal change. These methods have been taught to masters and doctoral level students in our graduate programs with continual refinements.

This text offers the best we can offer in terms of how a new trainee or counselor new to group treatment can learn how to understand what is going on in her/his groups, what interventions are most likely to be effective, and when to make those interventions,

The book focuses primarily on brief closed groups. Characteristically, the term *brief treatment* or time-limited (MacKenzie, 1990) refers to groups that last somewhere between 20–30 hours in length or about 2–3 months in duration. Although we discuss the open-ended, changing membership outpatient groups that are still popular in some clinical settings today, the bulk of the process and outcome evidence derives from groups with stable membership and are relatively short term.

Like most clinical training, reading a book will not make for a well-trained clinician. This is intended as a start to competent, effective clinical work with groups. It is expected that training, which is described in detail in the text, must include membership in a group, understanding of how different theories address group counseling and psychotherapy and co-leadership of at least two to three groups under direct supervision.

There is no "one-size-fits-all" effective approach to counseling and therapy. Each client and each group brings unique experiences, values, traits, and needs to each group. Effective counseling and therapy require group leaders to understand these from client perspectives and to adjust interventions based on what best suits the clients and the ability to discern the best timing for interventions.

This introductory text provides a psychological GPS of sorts to help leaders with the timing of interventions. We will describe in detail the normal, natural trajectory of groups of all kinds and identify those that do not fit into the progression. Based on the group process, we recommend particular interventions be made at specific junctures in the group. One example of the failure to do this is for group leaders to attempt to make therapeutic recommendations when the group is in the earliest forming stages. Such therapeutic endeavors delivered at this time characteristically fall on deaf ears. However, the very same interventions made when the group and individual members are ready and receptive are usually far more impactful.

In all of the groups discussed in this book, diversity of background, culture, ethnicity, values, and so on, is usually a great benefit. By contrast, groups whose members have wildly diverse levels of ego strength, and psychological pathology are very likely to fail.

The work in this book is best when readers have a concurrent or prior experience as members of a training group, experiential lab group, counseling group, or the like. We also recommend the use of task groups for projects in this class as a way to underscore similarities and differences in group process across types of groups.

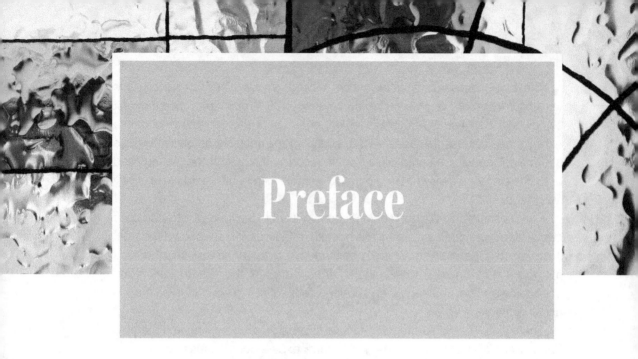

Preface

This text represents its authors' long professional and personal association. The three of us met and worked at the University of Hawaii during the 1970s: Dr. Peltz in counseling psychology in 1973 and Dr. Bernadett-Shapiro in the graduate nursing program in 1978. Our professional and personal collaboration has continued to the present. I have provided this personal account to explain these frameworks and their impact on our work.

I have been involved in the practice of group therapy, group counseling, and growth groups since 1965. Curiously, my interest in groups and other multiperson therapies did not begin auspiciously.

As a graduate student intern in 1965, my first exposure to groups was a "current events group" that met several days a week at the VA Outpatient Center in Boston. The group was used essentially as a holding area for male patients (primarily with dual diagnosis or ambulatory schizophrenic diagnoses) and was charged with "getting the men to talk about current events." The predominant therapeutic tool was the morning edition of the *Boston Globe.* Although I was never convinced that any learning or meaningful discussion about current events ever occurred, something interesting happened over the 3-month duration of our group. Despite no apparent lessening of the patients' symptoms, attendance was fairly stable, and I grew to like several of the group members. Meanwhile, two floors away, a psychologist and social worker held a discharge planning group that I was allowed to observe through a two-way mirror. Members of this group seemed to experience rapid, marked amelioration of their symptoms. My longing to do similar work remained unrequited during that training. I had similar experiences in internships at Downey VA Medical Center in Illinois and again at the Boston VA Outpatient Center in 1966.

As in intern at Hawaii State Hospital in Kaneohe in 1966 and 1967, I was given my first "therapy" group. At that time, it was common practice in psychology to provide interns with patients *they could not possibly harm.* This group met on Monday, Wednesday, and Friday morning from 7:45 to 9:15. The members were six men of Japanese descent, all of whom were diagnosed "chronic undifferentiated schizophrenic." The shortest hospitalization stay of any of the members was 19 years. My supervisor observed all sessions of this group from behind the ubiquitous two-way mirror, and we discussed the sessions immediately after they ended. I have three very clear memories of this group: (1) the discrepancy between my initial tolerance for silence (approximately 23 nanoseconds) and that of the patients (approximately 23 hours); (2) my never discovering whether three of the patients spoke any English, pidgin English, or Japanese (my co-therapist was a Japanese-speaking psychiatric nurse); and (3) my undying gratitude for the federal government's mandate that most holidays were to be observed on Mondays or Fridays.

A second group, which I co-led with a very talented senior social worker during my intern year, was a Tuesday-Thursday afternoon group of acting-out adolescents. It is no small wonder to me that, for the next three decades, this background led me to devote much of my clinical and research interest to group processes. Between 1965 and 2017, I was directly involved with more than 700 growth, therapy, counseling, and industry groups as a leader, member, researcher, supervisor, and consultant. Since 1969, as a fully time professor, I have also taught courses and developed vertically integrated training programs in group counseling and therapy in graduate programs in New York, Hawaii, and California—most recently at Santa Clara University.

All this involvement has convinced me that group treatment should be the cornerstone of any major mental health treatment program. I believe there are many advantages of group treatment that go far beyond the obvious economic benefits. Research and clinical writings also support this contention. I am also aware of the most unfortunate continuing aspect of group leadership in institutional, organizational, and treatment centers: *Very few of the people who lead groups are formally trained in group process.* Many group leaders are well-trained individual counselors or therapists who have been assigned to groups without completing even one course or supervised practicum in group work. Even with the best intentions, such leaders tend to do individual therapy with an audience rather than use the most powerful and dramatic effects of group process and influence.

This book is based on a crucial supposition: *Group leaders must be aware of group process.* The book represents an attempt to provide a road map for graduate students and new group leaders. However, it is not an attempt to chart every street, road, or lane. The point of view presented here is my belief that interventions in any successful group (or any other type of treatment) depend a great deal on timing. If I don't know where the group is at any given moment, I am far more likely to take wrong turns in my attempt to get where I want to go.

The inexorable generic process provided in this book is designed to serve the leader as a signpost and reference map. It is as theory-free and objectively descriptive as my colleagues and I could make it. We have spent many hours observing and consulting with leaders whose perspectives are widely divergent; the process described gives substantial attention to their approaches.

Our personal approaches to counseling, therapy, or task groups are closely related. Dr. Bernadett-Shapiro's primary orientation is object relations. Both Dr. Peltz and I describe ourselves as existential, with his approaches tending toward the American cognitive end of that realm and mine tending toward the European dynamic end. We all are informed by systems approaches. We are sure that the illumination shed by our varying perspectives will leave important areas of the landscape in shadows. Certainly leaders of groups with widely different theories, goals, and populations may have to adapt portions of the process for their maximal personal use.

We apologize for the fervency with which some of this book was written. The apparent certainty we exude is not intended to sell something to the unwary. Rather, it expresses the enthusiasm of practitioners who have embraced group process for 50 years and extol its virtues as an old friend and lover. Even after all these years and hundreds of groups, each of us enters each new group with anticipation, excitement, and hope. We are all active clinicians, currently leading brief treatment groups. Dr. Bernadett-Shapiro has taught group leadership at two universities and is the consultant-supervisor for the experiential groups in the graduate counseling psychology program at Santa Clara University. Dr. Peltz is co-leading couples groups and adult groups, and he and I regularly co-lead men's groups in the community. As part of my work as a faculty member at Santa Clara University, I direct group training and teach introductory and advanced group classes throughout the academic year.

Although much of this book was written for our students in counseling and clinical psychology and in social work, we hope that experienced group practitioners will also find something new in it or remember an older precept of value that has drifted away.

As you read this text, you may notice that many of the references may seem dated. Wherever possible, we have used the most comprehensive source. Thus, many of the outcome research references date back to the 1970s, a time of great interest in and prolific research on group outcome and process. We refer to several recent studies that have added to our knowledge of group therapy and counseling. However, when a recent study primarily replicates older data or observations, we have chosen to cite the primary source to honor the pioneering work in the field.

We would like to acknowledge many wonderful people who have guided our learning about group therapy and counseling over the years. In particular, we want to thank all of our students in the group training classes and advanced leader training programs at the University of Hawaii Counseling Program (1970–1978), School of Professional Nursing and Social Work (1976–1981), and Santa Clara University (1982–present). Many of these students have become professional group leaders and teachers, and we take great pride in our small part in their success.

We also want to express our thanks to Acquisition Editor, Kassie Graves and the editorial and production staff at Cognella for their faith in this project and wonderful assistance in making this book a reality.

Jerrold Lee Shapiro, Ph.D.

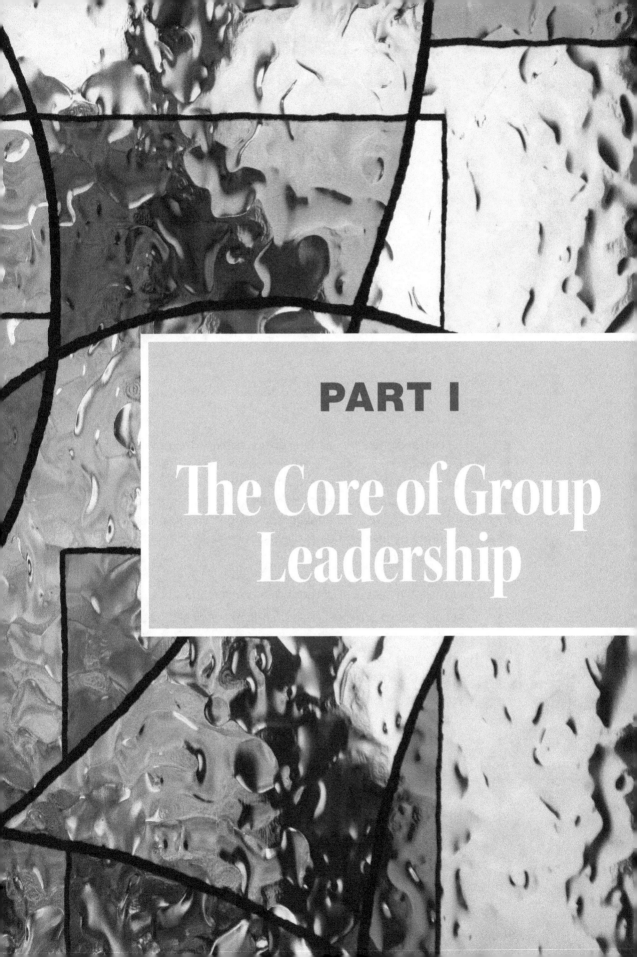

PART I

The Core of Group Leadership

CHAPTER 1

An Introduction to Brief, Closed Groups

This text is designed for leaders of counseling, therapy, and growth groups who wish to bring a time-honored, proven, effective, ethical approach to treatment groups in an era in which cost containment and economic concerns are regarded at least as important as therapeutic and ethical considerations. The therapeutic approach is based on assumptions that are supported by research data, clinical observations, and the economics of modern health care.

- Groups are the treatment of choice in a brief therapy model.
- Treatment groups are most effective if they are closed, short term, and process-centered.
- Thematic groups with somewhat homogenous membership will be most effective in the short term.
- When groups are led properly, there is a generic, predictable developmental process.
- Multiperson treatments such as groups require different therapist skills than individual modalities.
- Training in group methods is necessary for effective treatment.

These assumptions provide the backdrop and the *raison d'etre* for this text.

Groups as the Treatment of Choice

In a special edition of the *Journal of Specialists in Group Work*, Shapiro and Bernadett-Shapiro (1985) argued that the beginning of the 21st century would be marked by extensive growth in group treatments. Since then, experts commenting on managed care treatments such as Budman (1992), Budman and Gurman (1988), and Norcross, Alford, and DiMichele (1992) have echoed that forecast. In the most recent Delphi Poll of experts in the field (Norcross, Pfund, & Prochaska, 2013), group therapy and short-term treatment are listed in the top eight areas expected to increase in the decade 2013–2022.

Although we believe that group treatment will be prominent in the future, we acknowledge its long and successful past. Since the turn of the 20th century, and Pratt's (1906; 1907; 1908; 1911) early attempts at alternative (group) treatment for tuberculosis patients, groups have been used for virtually every patient population known (cf. Delucia-Waack, Kalodner, & Riva, 2014; Lubin & Lubin, 1987). Throughout this century, the use of groups and research on their effectiveness has varied as each major type of mental health treatment (medical, psychotherapy, family therapy, group therapy) have had periods of ascendancy and periods of relative disinterest from the bulk of practitioners. At the present time, primarily because of financial considerations, medical-biological treatments are ascending in popularity as are group counseling and psychotherapy approaches.

The unique advantages of group treatment include the following:

Cost
Research (i.e., Barlow, 2014; Burlingame, Fuhriman, & Mosier, 2003; Burlingame & Krogel, 2005; Shapiro, 1978, 2010) has indicated that group psychotherapy has been as successful as each other form of treatment in comparable or shorter time periods. Economics however, are not the sole advantage of group treatment.

Connectedness
Groups provide opportunities for socialization, a sense of shared experience, and a corresponding reduction of feelings of isolation. Many groups also lead to continuing care by way of postgroup support systems.

Reality Testing
The group environment provides opportunities for learning and practicing new behaviors in a setting that more closely resembles the "real world." Feedback from other members will be different from the reactions of an individual therapist whose contract is to understand the client from the client's personal perspective. In addition, feedback may occur in real time instead of delayed experiences between sessions.

Vicarious Learning

In a group, each member has the opportunity to learn by observation of others. For many people, learning is best accomplished when one is not on "the hot seat." Members may work through their own personal issues by witnessing the struggles and successes of others.

Minimization of Pathology

Not all of the therapy that occurs in a group comes from the leader. Much help is offered by members to each other. When someone receives assistance from another who is "just a member like me," the receiver sees that his or her problems are not impossibly serious or unmanageable. The result may be development of a more positive and hopeful outlook.

Altruism

A common source of problems for individuals seeking mental health treatment involves low self-esteem. When members act benevolently toward their peers or provide insight or caring for other group members, they normally feel quite good about seeing the results of their efforts and about the act of helping itself. Feelings of altruism are incompatible with low self-esteem. A group setting in which one member can assist another offers a certain enhancement of self-esteem.

Experimentation

Group members are encouraged to experiment with novel behaviors and reactions and motivated to request feedback within a nurturing environment. The group is a setting in which members might rehearse new behaviors and/or get advance reactions to an anticipated event without the risk inherent in the event itself. They may then adjust their behavior accordingly in preparing for the real occasion.

Dilution of Transference Relationships

Although the primary and most powerful transference occurs between group members and group leaders, there is inevitable projection onto other members of the group as well. This shift allows all members to be more aware of such projections and eases working through of problems because the intensity is somewhat distributed throughout the group.

Universality

One of the most impactful experience of group is the growing understanding that everyone has problems, secrets, shame in their past, and struggles. As group members see the figurative skeletons in others' closets, they get a more realistic perspective on how personal struggles are not unique. In the face of this information, their sense of isolation and feelings of being singularly pathological are minimized.

Short-Term Groups

Evaluating outcome research on time-limited groups is complicated by a host of factors: not the least of these is defining *brief treatment*. Many terms are used by different authors, Corey, Corey, and Corey (2014) and Yalom and Lecsz (2005) use the terms "brief group counseling" and "brief group therapy." MacKenzie (1993) called his groups "time-managed" and "time-limited" group psycho-therapy. Budman (1992) used the more specific term, "time-effective" treatment, and Forsyth (2010) and Corey (2015) have called it "brief group work." We prefer "brief group treatment," which was used in our first edition (1998), and that is the term that will be used in this text.

Exactly what constitutes a label of "brief" is also a little unclear. Koss and Butcher (1986) considered brief treatment to involve groups that met for fewer than 25 sessions. Budman, Demby, and Randall (1980) used 15 session groups. Shapiro (1978) and his colleagues (Diamond & Shapiro, 1973; Shapiro & Diamond, 1972) reported on 30-hour groups and on 20-hour groups (six 2-hour sessions and one 8-hour marathon). Foulds (1971) and many other group leaders who practice in university settings (i.e., Corey et al., 2010; Shechtman & Toren, 2009) ran groups for an academic semester or quarter.

Reviewers of the time-limited group literature (Budman, Simeone, Reilly, & Demby, 1994; Dies, 1992a) conclude that these groups, when led by experienced professionals, are effective in alleviating symptomatology and fostering growth. In comparison with waiting list control groups, time-limited group members show significant improvement (i.e., Piper, McCallum, & Hassan, 1992). However, Piper et al. have also indicated that such groups may not be as powerful or comprehen-sive as longer term therapies or individual work of equal duration. A complicating factor for empirical comparisons is the experience of leaders; oftentimes groups in outcome studies are regularly led by trainees or inexprinces group therapists (Shapiro, 2010).

It is important to recognize that brief groups are not simply abbreviated forms of long-term groups. They have different goals and these are more clearly delin-eated. The format may also be different. Among the differences for brief treatment groups in this text are the following:

- Closed enrollment. The same members enter and leave the group together.
- Predetermined beginning and termination.
- Less than 6 months in duration (Cuijpers, van Straten, & Warmerdam, 2008; Hanson, Lambert, & Forman, 2002; Horowitz & Garber, 2006; Shapiro et al., 1998; Stice, Rohde, Seeley, & Gau, 2008).
- Limited, clearly set goals.
- Process oriented with a here-and-now focus.

- Predictable epigenetic trajectory.

- Often members have some identifiable commonality and the groups may have a specific theme (i.e., Drum & Knott, 2009).

- Professional leaders (co-leaders strongly recommended) (Shapiro, 2010; Shapiro et al., 1998).

- Screening for fit and level of ego strength is essential.

The upshot of these multiple criteria is that brief treatment groups must *be carefully geared to specific limited goals, conducted by trained professional leaders, and structured to maximize factors such as cohesion, altruism, and the other unique group treatment advantages by employing a process focus.*

Closed, Short-Term, Process-Oriented Groups

Many leaders prefer ongoing groups in which members enter and leave as is personally appropriate (i.e., Yalom, 1995; Yalom & Lescz, 2005). Arguments that this more closely simulates real life are undeniably compelling. As members enter and depart the group, individuals have the opportunity to work with their personal issues of separation and individuation, fears of intimacy, dependency and rejection. They can weigh their own considerations about when "it is time." Certainly such groups have a valuable place in therapy.

However, there are also compelling advantages of groups beginning and closing together, such as the time involved in incorporating a new member or the adjustment to the loss of an senior one. In open groups with each change in the group population, there is an inevitable regression to earlier stages of group process. Because the developmental process (trajectory) is a core component in group effectiveness, interruptions of the process may inhibit the natural unfolding of the group progress and hence its impact. In a brief therapy environment, the team-oriented synergy of a closed group is particularly healing.

The focus on process (content within context) is particularly central to group members' learning about themselves and their impact on others. A process focus provides a developmental psychological map of the interpersonal terrain. With this as a guide, the leaders may highlight more clearly the current reality of the group and the impact of individuals within that framework. A focus on process also trains individuals to explore the context and consequences of their actions as well as the content and apparent motivation. More than that, a *process focus* creates a unique setting for personal learning. A frequently disconcerting fact in the life of parents and teachers is that our children and students learn only when they are ready to learn. Repetitions alone, even those with the most compelling multimedia delivery systems are insufficient if the receiver is unprepared. A process focus sets the stage for learning in two ways: (1) It provides a focus on self and on the here and now interactions between self and others, eliminating distractions, and (2) because it is socially unusual it adds a certain amount of functional anxiety and vigilance that facilitates learning.

Thematic/Relatively Homogeneous Groups

For short-term treatment, group members must be able to affiliate with each other fairly quickly. Doing so is easier when they feel commonalities between their abilities and needs and those of their peers. The most important homogeneity in a group is levels of ego strength or its converse, levels of pathology. Although groups have been shown to be effective with almost every level of pathology, they are overly affected by discrepancies. To a large degree, the most pathological individual in a group has the greatest influence in restricting the group's trajectory. It is analogous to the reality that the weakest link has a greater impact on the overall strength of the chain. Thus a group of persons with acute concerns are best not mixed with clients whose problems are chronic.

Content themes are of value for both attracting members to work on a predictable concern and also for centering the discussion around consensual issues. Broad themes in which each member sees part of himself or herself within the purview of the group are most effective. A theme is best utilized as a catalyst to group formation and development rather than as a definition or defense of member personalities.

Predictable Developmental Process

The first several chapters of this text are dedicated entirely to an observable process model. The model has emerged from 25 years of research and clinical work (Shapiro, 1978). It coordinates well with the work of other researchers and clinicians (i.e., Corey, 1990, 2014; Foulds & Hannigan, 1976). A four-phase, 30-stage model is detailed. Leaders are trained to observe the natural development of the group process. Effective interventions are tied directly to specific points in the evolving process trajectory. For example, different leadership actions are necessary when the group is in Phase II (Transition) or Phase III (Treatment) than when it is in Phase IV (Termination). Leadership challenges and the methodology to effectively employ them for the group's benefit are necessary to provide the transition to treatment. Premature attempts to intervene therapeutically and directly before these challenges emerge, may actually deter the group process.

Group Treatment, Individual Treatment, and Family Treatment

Group treatment requires a number of unique skills that are different from those necessary in individual or family modalities. Of particular note is the sophisticated ability to intervene at three different levels: intrapsychic, dyadic, and group. In individual work, the latter two are somewhat irrelevant except in addressing the transference or personal therapist-client interactions.

In couple or family therapy, the therapist must be aware of the system that exists between the clients outside of the therapy hour. Interventions are best geared to addressing this ongoing system. In group, the system that develops is only present during the group itself. Each individual is best served if he or she receives from the group interactions important personal information that is transferable to life outside the group. Yalom and Lecsz (2005) describe the group as a microcosm of the individual's interpersonal world. More colorfully, Tillich (1973) suggests that everyone significant, "your mother, your father, your brother, your sister, your cousins, your dog, your cat are all available in the group." In this way the group mirrors interactions within a member's family and social milieu.

Training in Multiperson Therapies

Although formal group treatment has an almost century-long history, the majority of group leaders today are still primarily or solely trained in individual and infrequently, family therapy methods. This book is primarily designed for those who are beginning schooling or practice in group treatment. It is no substitute for a rigorous training program or supervised experience. A model of minimal training requirements and basic skills are provided (Chapter 7).

Some Realities of Modern Health Care

Since the late 1980s, the health care crisis in America has been addressed increasingly by an economic model (DeLeon, VandenBos, & Bulatoa, 1991). Health maintenance organizations (HMOs) promise cost containment, and full health care from womb to tomb in return for a moderate regular premium and spreading risk across large populations. The dollars saved, however, may come at a high price. Members of such an insurance plan normally have less discretion about the type of treatment they may receive for any given ailment and to some extent, whether their plans will authorize any treatment at all. The bottom line for any business such as an HMO is the difference between dollars received in premiums and the expenses incurred from providing treatment. Maintaining and growing profit margins often means restricting and limiting "expensive" care and procedures.

In the United States, the Affordable Care Act (2010), often referred to as "Obama Care," has made inroads in correcting some of these deficiencies. As this is written, it remains in place, but more than 50 unsuccessful efforts to repeal it have occurred and each "replace" plan has been far more economic than focused on health care. Alternative plans would sharply reduce overall coverage and mental health coverage in particular. To the extent that mental health services are truncated in the future, certain treatments will be favored or prescribed. The preferred treatments are medication and time-limited group therapy. In some European countries, such as Germany and England, the mode of therapy that is covered by national health service plans is characteristically limited to cognitive behavior therapy.

It is a harsh reality that mental health is not a high priority in such systems. Like other "lower status" medical specialties (e.g., pediatrics, obstetrics), practitioners have had to fight for the diminishing pot of dollars available. As a result, the quality of care inevitably suffers. Indeed, rewards in the form of bonuses and promotions are commonly given on the expense end of the equation rather than the care end. "Successful" providers are those whose computer track record shows that they see clients for the fewest sessions. Saving money by withholding treatment is often cherished within managed care. Primary care physicians or triage personnel receive bonuses for referring the fewest patients to expensive treatment.

Far more detrimental is the subtle withholding of treatment that occurs when clients for group therapy are assigned to a waiting list for several months, before an opening may occur. Several lawsuits have been filed against major providers who actually have lengthy waiting lists and little actual group therapy available. These organizations have been successfully sued for "care delayed, care denied," using the long waits in place of treatment (Levin, 2015; NUHW, 2014; Pfeifer & Terhune, 2016).

Managed Care and Group Treatment

What are the implications of this for your practice? Your clients may be resentful in group because they were denied more costly individual psychotherapy or counseling. They may exhibit more pathology because less severe "problems in living" including family and marital issues are addressed at the primary care physician level and not referred or may not be covered by the insurance plan. They will be less likely to be "YAWVIS"[1] patients; more likely to have personality disorder diagnoses, borderline personality traits, or defensive structures. You may have more patients taking psychotropic medication in group therapy. As a group leader, you may have less ability to effectively screen your clients.

---

1   YAWVIS is an acronym for the traditional patients who get the most care and highest interest from practitioners. These patients are young, attractive, wealthy, verbal, intelligent, and sexy

Dealing in such brief treatments with groups of patients having such a wide range of needs requires adjustments to your normal practice or leadership style. Normally, when time is short, the natural tendency for a leader is to speed up in an attempt to cover everything before time expires. Unfortunately, accelerating treatment in counseling and therapy frequently has a paradoxical effect. Increasing pressure to find solutions is routinely met with greater resistance to change.

This paradox is a prime reason to use a process-oriented model. With this model, patient resistance is coalesced and dealt with ontologically. By viewing resistance as an important part of the "readiness-to-learn" phenomenon in group, the process model actually increases the pace at which members approach desired outcomes by judicious moderating speed at certain crucial junctures, early in the group. By focusing directly, and in predetermined ways, on the developmental stages of resistance, group members who are beginning from a point of lower motivation have more of an opportunity to become open to healing.

It is important to understand that whatever theory or techniques that you customarily use will be effective with some segment of the population in your groups. The process model is designed as a substrate on which your particular theoretical perspective may be maximally effective. With this foundation, psychodynamic, behavioral, humanistic and psychoeducational groups can all be enhanced.

In too much of the literature, these theories are juxtaposed as competing approaches. By contrast, the current approach was designed by observing the commonalities of successful groups of every type. Similarities are most dominant early in the group process. In the treatment phase of the group, the different approaches demonstrate clear distinctions. Thus a Gestalt-oriented leader and a cognitive behavioral leader will seem to share more commonalities in approach in the transition phase and far less during the treatment phase.

The ensuing brief treatment model is sensitive to cost containment, is adjustable across theoretical orientations, and is likely to maintain quality care at least within appropriately defined limits.

Summary

Group psychotherapy is a modality particularly well suited to emerging needs within mental health delivery systems for informed and proficient care. The group context encourages individuals to explore the consequences of their actions as well as the meaning and underlying motivation. A group process model is proposed as an efficient means of participant learning and behavioral change.

Leadership training in group process is essential. The most effective leadership interventions are tied to this predictable model of developmental generic group process. In addition, the leader must attend to three levels of process and intervention: intrapsychic, interpersonal, and group level.

Certain participant and treatment variables have been shown to optimize group treatment outcomes. The ideal group is closed, time-limited, homogeneous, and process-focused. Groups with specific limited goals, led by trained professional leaders using interventions geared to increase cohesion, appropriate self-disclosure and altruism amongst members are most productive.

CHAPTER 2

Group Process Phase I: Preparation and Orientation

Stage 1:   **Determination of Group Goals and Population**

Stage 2:   **Leader Announces Group Logistics**

Stage 3:   **Members Apply for the Group**

Stage 4:   **Screening**

"While I know each group is unique, I frequently
have a sense of déjà vu in every group I lead."

This casual lunch time comment between two group therapists in Hawaii one day in 1970 spurred a 25-year intensive study of groups, beginning with a survey of local and national experts on group process. The results of the survey and of group leadership literature indicates that experienced group leaders see distinct differences in their groups as well as commonalities that make them all appear similar.

Group Commonalities and Differences

This seeming contradiction is present in all forms of therapy to some extent. Most theorists point to communalities in recommended treatment approaches while stressing the individuality of every patient. Nowhere is the apparent incongruity so poignantly expressed as in group therapy.

How Are Groups Different?

Yalom and Lecsz (2005) among others, note the seeming infinite variety of content issues and problems addressed in groups. Specific material discussed, therapeutic interventions, and conflict resolution are unique to each group. Because each group is comprised of several different personalities at a particular period of time, singularity of expression and novel experiences are to be expected.

How Are Groups the Same?

Despite the variance in specific content and content themes between groups, the *process*, or pattern of interaction, within different groups is remarkably similar. In an effective and successful group, certain stages normally occur in a reliable sequence.

Stages of Group Models

As Table 2.1 shows, several authors have described predictable stages in group development—developmental schema in which successive stages are built on completion of previous ones. As early as 1936, Wender described four such stages for patients in neoanalytic group therapy. His process description included, (1) intellectualization, (2) transference between patients, (3) catharsis, and (4) group interest as patients moved through emotional difficulties to emerge with effective interest in their social sphere and society in general.

Battegay (1989) working with a compatible framework 53 years later, formulated a very similar five-stage developmental sequence: (1) exploratory contact, (2) regression, (3) catharsis, (4) insight, and (5) social learning. Battegay clearly states that such stages may well be limited to *closed, long-term, analytically oriented groups*.

Table 2.1 Several Conceptions of Predictable Group Stages

Author and Date	Stage 1	Stage 2	Stage 3	Stage 4	Stage 5	Stage 6
Wender, 1936	Intellectualization	Transference between patients	Catharsis	Group interest, social interest		
Dreikurs, 1951	Establishment of relations	Interpretation of dynamics	Gaining understanding	Reorientation		
Schutz, 1973	Inclusion	Control	Affection			
Tuckman, 1965 Tuckman & Jensen, 1977	Forming	Storming	Norming	Performing	Adjourning	
Shapiro, 1978	Introduction	Learning the rules	Therapy proper	Termination		
Henry, 1981	Initiating	Convening	Formation	Conflict	Maintenance	Termination
Dies, 1985	Preparation	Early group sessions	Transition	Working	Termination	
Corey & Corey, 1987	Initial stage	Transition	Working	Ending		
Battegay, 1989	Exploratory contact	Regression	Catharsis	Insight	Social learning	
MacKenzie, 1990	Engagement	Differentiation	Working	Termination		
Yalom, 1995	Orientation, hesitant participation, search for similarities, search for meaning, and dependency	Conflict, dominance, rebellion	Cohesiveness			

Dreikurs (1951), employing an Adlerian perspective, focused more on the educative process in groups. He perceived four stages: (1) establishment of relations, (2) interpretation of dynamics, (3) patients gaining understanding, and (4) reorientation.

Tuckman (1965) and Tuckman and Jenson (1977) colorfully described five stages as (1) forming, (2) storming, (3) norming, (4) performing, and (5) adjourning. Schutz (1973), whose work was more centered on growth groups, described "an inevitable sequence" of three stages: (1) inclusion, (2) control, and (3) affection. Members work through their conflicts of belonging to the group, establishing and maintaining their roles in the group pecking order, and explore their closeness to other members.

Yalom (2005), in the latest revision of his classic group psychotherapy text, sees an *initial stage* characterized by orientation, hesitant participation, search for similarities, search for meaning, and dependency. This is followed by the *second stage* characterized by conflict, dominance, and rebellion. The *third stage* for Yalom involves the development of cohesiveness.

These are markedly similar to Schutz's formulations. However, Yalom describes several qualifying factors that can dramatically affect his indicated sequence: leadership qualities, patient qualities, additions to and deletions from membership, attendance, and so on. Yalom also suggests that discrete stages can be described reliably only early in a group's development. As a group develops over time and subgrouping occurs, groups become more unique. One crucial factor in Yalom's model is that it is based almost entirely on open-ended groups. Authors whose research is on closed groups are able to describe an extended process because of the essential progressive nature of their groups.

Shapiro (1978), describing a core group process for both therapy and encounter groups, formulated four inevitable process phases: (1) introduction, (2) learning the rules, (3) therapy proper, and (4) termination (transfer of training).

Corey, Corey, and Corey (2014) using a similar paradigm, based on their own considerable work with closed groups in a college population, described (1) an initial stage, (2) a transition stage, (3) a working stage, and (4) an ending stage. MacKenzie (1990) calls his stages (1) engagement, (2) differentiation, (3) working, and (4) termination.

The chronological process analysis presented in this text conforms to the whole group model espoused by Corey and Corey (1987), Fiebert (1963), MacKenzie (1990), and Shapiro (1978). Clearly, open-ended groups such as those described by Yalom will conform to this model only to the extent that there is stable membership over time. There is no question that predictability of process diminishes as membership changes.

Group process in closed groups is presented in four interlocking phases. Each phase is comprised of a number of identifiable stages and tasks. The four phases are as follows:

    I. Preparation

    II. Transition

    III. Intervention (Working or Treatment)

    IV. Termination

The process presented is descriptive of a *well-screened, optimally functioning, time-limited, closed group, led by an accomplished leader with therapeutically viable clients in a counseling, therapy, growth, or encounter format.*

This process is envisioned as both *inevitable* and *ideal*. It is inevitable in the sense that successful completion of each previous stage is considered prerequisite to engaging in and coping with subsequent stages. To some extent, however, this model is also an ideal. Many groups fail to complete all the stages. Hence, one aspect of the success of any group can be measured by progress through the process sequence prior to the termination.

Value of Predictable Process

Group leadership shifts with group process. Leadership behaviors that are effective at one stage in a group are often deleterious at other stages. It is axiomatic that group members such as patients in psychotherapy need to know where they are and the extent of their resources prior to developing new life paths. Thus in the words of a recent group participant, "If I don't know where I am when I start out, in an hour I could be two hours from my desired destination." It is essential that an effective group leader appraise the lay of the land before heading off to explore new directions. All change-based interventions described in this text are geared precisely to the existing process in the group.

The following process analysis represents the results of 20 years of the senior author's research of group treatment and leadership and more than 50 years of personally leading, supervising, and observing groups and group leaders in a host of clinical settings. It is designed as a map to get the novice group leader to the right neighborhood. The unique streets, roads, lanes, and blind alleys must be individually discovered.

Despite best efforts to remain eclectic, any such formulation will represent several biases in theory, perception, and description. It behooves the reader to use this process formulation as a guide that must be adapted to personally relevant theories and populations. Differences in approaches to specific populations are described in the final part of the book. The primary theory that underscores this work is a *dynamically oriented existential-humanistic psychotherapy*. Therapists with related theories (i.e., Gestalt, psychodynamic and object relations) will have little difficulty applying the principles. A greater bridge may need to be constructed to accommodate behaviorally based or psychoeducational theories. However, the core principles and process are claimed to be universal. Divergences between approaches will occur primarily in Phase III (treatment), where specific interventions will be more differentially based in the practitioner's theory.

Phase I: Preparation
Stage 1: Determination of Group Goals and Population

A group begins as a concept. Leaders normally respond to an identified need in a particular community. Once the need is recognized, and a group intervention chosen, the leaders must then reach the target population with information and enticement to apply for inclusion in the group. Establishing and maintaining a productive treatment group is no easy task, especially in a private practice setting. Careful planning and effective, ethical marketing are essential.

Within a managed care or capitated environment, the needs of the patients will by necessity be assessed by an agent of the responsible third-party payer. Leaders may be establishing groups based on needs or mandates of patients' coverages and economic demands as well as their clinical needs. The inherent ethical concerns will have to be addressed continually, both with potential group members and with the preferred provider organization (PPO), health maintenance organization (HMO), or insurer (cf., Rosenberg & Zimet, 1995).

For example, a particular HMO or PPO might cover its insured for substance abuse but not for marital difficulties. Under other circumstances a group might be free to focus on both or either. In a limiting environment, the treatment may have to be focused primarily on the importance of substance abuse in family discord and membership may be restricted by use of diagnostic codes that involve drug or alcohol problems.

Among the multitude of factors that will influence the group membership makeup are cost, location, time of day, length and number of sessions, leader characteristics and credentials, population, cultural factors, and the desired mix of clients. Only when these factors are carefully evaluated can the leader move to an invitation for members to apply. Each logistic criterion set by a leader will narrow the range of applicants and the heterogeneity among members.

Fees. The fee charged for group sessions will have a powerful impact on membership. Some fees are clearly too high for many potential patients. By contrast, some fees will be too low to draw certain populations.

Fees can range widely in a given area. A brief informal survey in the San Francisco Bay area conducted by the senior author in 2016–2017 revealed that average fees for outpatient fee-for-service groups were between $30.00 and $40.00 per hour/per patient. A typical 90-minute group session, with one or two leaders, cost $45.00 to $80.00. Most recent surveys indicate that groups for adolescents or children have slightly lower fees. Many such groups require monthly commitments of members or charge for the entire group (i.e., 10 sessions) at the outset. Members of a PPO or with providers with a capitated contract might be required to make a fixed copayment, with the leader billing a preset amount to the insurer or subcapitated organization for the balance.

In the San Francisco survey, lower fees were normally reported for groups conducted in church, school, or community settings. Several groups conducted in community agencies used subsidized sliding scales that ran from $1.00 to $15.00 per session. HMOs and employee assistance programs (EAPs) offered specific theme groups for members at nominal (if any) out-of-pocket cost.

Many group leaders have found to their surprise that fee setting is quite peculiar. High fees will eliminate certain portions of the population, but very low fee or "free" groups will do the same thing. As one potential participant at a free clinic stated, "if it's free, it ain't worth nothin'." A curious trait of American society seems to be the perception that something that is free is not as good as things that cost a lot. One way to solve the dilemma of offering groups to people who cannot afford to pay for treatment is to make the group have an *apparent* price. Thus for one series of "free" groups at a community mental health center, patients were required to pay 50 cents per session. However, each member was given 50 cents worth of bus tokens at the end of each session. The groups had far higher attendance than comparable "free" groups.

Setting fees may be complex for a professional. If the fee is not determined by the referring entity such as a clinic or managed care organization, several factors must be balanced. Among these are the therapists' experience and training, customary rates in the region, and needs and resources of the client population as well as the therapists' need for income.

In private practice, determination of fees is often arithmetic. If the leaders each need to be compensated $100/hour for their time, two leaders and a two-hour session means that they must bring in $400 per group session. Thus if there are 8 members, each would pay $50/session ($25/hour).

Figure 2.1 Phases and Stages of Normal Group Process

Phase I: Preparation

Stage 1: Determination of Group Goals and Population

Stage 2: Leader Announces Group Logistics

Stage 3: Members Apply for the Group

Stage 4: Screening

Phase II: Transition

Stage 5: Leader Specifies Ground Rules

Stage 6: Introductions

Stage 7: The Initial (Short) Silence

Stage 8: The Short Silence Is Broken

Stage 9: Discussion of There-and-Then Topic

Stage 10: Natural Death of Discussion

Stage 11: The Long Silence

Stage 12: Members' First Sortie

Stage 13: Opening of the Discussion

Stage 14: Group Leader Focuses on Here-and-Now Process

Stage 15: Debriefing the Leadership Tests: Focus on Feelings

Stage 16: Leader Encourages the Expression of Emotion

Phase III: Treatment (Working; Intervention)

Stage 17: Internal Focus

Stage 18: Norms Are Solidified

Stage 19: Minority Members Identified; Inclusion Revisited

Stage 20: Intensity Increases

Stage 21: Leader Employs Therapeutic Skills

Stage 22: Problem-Solving Orientation Practiced

Stage 23: Expression of Feelings about the Process and the Group

Phase IV: Termination

Stage 24: Leader Announces Imminent End of Group Time

Stage 25: Invitation to Work

Stage 26: A Trust Boost

Stage 27: Transfer of Training

Stage 28A: Good and Welfare

Stage 28B: Closing Ceremonies

Stage 29: Leader's Closing

Stage 30: Aloha

Location. The most common locations for groups are community agencies, clinics and hospitals, churches, schools and colleges, private offices, and hotel meeting rooms. The specific group meeting site should be consistent with the desired participants.

The specific site for a group meeting will dramatically influence group composition. Some people are so uncomfortable with various settings, they would not consider attending any meeting in these places. Community agencies, for example, will attract some folks and repel others. A neighborhood community center might limit the number of applications from people who want anonymity, or who live in different neighborhoods.

Distance and travel time are also significant factors in the viability of a particular group setting. Many groups seem to be set around the early evening hours. Getting across town at these times in most major cities can be a traffic nightmare. Distance and commute time make up one factor, but this is not the sole determinant of participation. In Honolulu, a group held at the Kalihi community center (a poorer neighborhood) would not draw many potential group members from nearby more affluent Aiea or Pacific Heights. Almost every community has districts that are threatening to people from other locales. These discomforts range from fears about physical safety to a sense of estrangement with folks from different cultures or socioeconomic strata. For example, a group held in poorer neighborhoods on the south side of Chicago would have a completely different composition from that of a group held in a wealthy northern suburb such as Winnetka. Similarly, a university setting may be very comfortable and familiar for college graduates, but much less so for those who do not have college experience. Some potential members will avoid a church meeting place because of the denomination. Others will feel safer because of the presumed sanction of a religious setting.

Another factor is that some members prefer a group that is distant from their home or work sites to better safeguard confidentiality. Others prefer the close proximity to reduce travel time. Often within EAP programs, the work site is proffered and flex time provided by the employer. This arrangement will obviously suit some potential members better than others.

Time of Sessions. In some ways, the time of the session can be the most critical factor in enrollment. It must be acceptable to the desired population. Groups that meet in the morning are very unlikely to draw many working people. Similarly dinner hour groups will be less attractive to members with families and Saturday evening groups are anathema to "singles." For many years, group leaders who wanted male participants traditionally avoided Monday evenings in the fall on the premise that they would not forego "Monday Night Football." By contrast, it was an especially desired time for "women's groups." Groups for young mothers may be held successfully during the middle of the day if they provide a playroom and child care. In general, most therapists hold group meetings in the late afternoon or early evening.

Some HMOs or agencies only offer groups during normal office hours or on a single weekday evening. Patients who cannot attend at designated times are simply discouraged. Because they are compensated by the number of people under contract or for regular staff salaries, rather than for services rendered, it may be economically beneficial for some organizational providers to restrict times available. This is the opposite of a consumer-oriented private practice situation.

Group leaders must also consider their own diurnal energy levels. Some leaders have their best energy for group work in the evening whereas others are fading at this time. Co-leaders of marathon groups often try to compensate their own periods of highest energy with their partner's lower times.

Length of Group Meetings. The total number of sessions and extent to which groups are open or closed also affect potential participation. Some members will choose a closed group with a predictable fixed number of sessions; others prefer the flexibility of the open environment. Closed groups that have more than 10 to 12 sessions (or 30 hours) may be too much of an initial commitment for some potential members. Open groups may also appear foreboding in length. Some people will be threatened by a group that appears too short to accomplish much without great intensity. In general, closed outpatient groups are commonly 6 to 20 sessions in length with the vast majority in the 10 to 12 session range.

Publicity. The manner in which members are sought is also a powerful factor in group success. Advertisements posted on telephone poles, social media electronic bulletin boards, or supermarket bulletin boards pull for different populations from those attracted by a professional note circulated among local individual therapists. Many clients are unwilling to commit their time or psyches to any methods that in any way sound unprofessional, yet an equal number shy away from the established health care provider in search of something more dramatic or unusual. It is incumbent on the leaders to predetermine which of these populations they wish to tap. Typically, groups that are oriented toward growth or education can be drawn with publicity that is more open and general. By contrast, therapy group members are more often referred by informed colleagues, other related professionals, such as primary care physicians, attorneys, or clergy, or by advertisements in medical centers.

Leader Characteristics and Credentials. Potential group members often show great interest in the qualifications of leaders. Some will be interested only in working with licensed professionals with advanced degrees. Some will be attracted to leaders with a particular theoretical approach. By contrast, people who are distrustful of traditional medicine may be attracted to "self-help" leaders who are themselves dealing with issues similar to the members.

In addition, cultural factors may be significant. Potential members will be reluctant to apply for inclusion in a group if they think the leader is unable to understand their ethnic or cultural concerns. For example, in a recent group offered for Japanese Americans whose parents were interred in camps during World War II, one leader had a Japanese surname and one had a European surname. It is doubtful that this group would have had as much success had the leader with the Japanese surname and appropriate cultural experience not been available.

One of the most successful and continuous group therapy programs in this country has been housed in the Vet Centers, an organization designed to assist Vietnam era veterans. One of the major advantages and appeals of such centers is the fact that they are staffed by veterans (combat and noncombat) as well as civilians.

Stage 2: Leader Announces Group Logistics

The announcement and statement of critical logistics is important in determining who will apply for the group and what may happen once it begins. Such factors as where and how the group is publicized; cost; meeting place; number of sessions and time of sessions; group goals; leader's reputation, theoretical background, and age; potential clients' perception of the professionalism and warmth of the leader will all substantially affect the subsequent group membership.

The following figures are examples of some characteristic announcements that have appeared in major cities around the United States. Names and identities or other distinguishing characteristics have been changed for professional reasons.

Figure 2.2 is an announcement for an awareness and movement group. It was advertised via flyers to people on a selected mailing list. An advertisement such as this is likely to draw such participants as students in mental health-related professions, mental health professionals, dancers, and other college-educated, somewhat sophisticated, middle-class working people. It is unlikely to draw severely disturbed or poverty-level participants. Members of such a group (in the encounter/workshop format) would typically be functioning adequately and would be interested in experimenting with growth activities.

Figure 2.2 Sample Group Announcement (Smith and Jones)

A Weekend Workshop

Awareness and Movement

Led by Bill Jones, Ph.D., and Jean Smith, M.A.

Bill is a certified clinical psychologist and a Gestalt therapist. He has been practicing psychotherapy for over 10 years in his community. He is also on the Ethics Committee of the State Mental Health Board and works as a program developer for the state's mental health services.

Jean is an advanced practitioner in Rolfing and a dance and yoga instructor. She teaches creative movement and has done substancial work in integrating movement techniques.

We will work with the group to help members integrate the different components of their beings. Through a series of movement exercises and individual and group work, members will have an opportunity to come to a better understanding of self and of the body as a source of energy and expression.

Dates: February 6 & 7, 2018

Schedule: Friday, February 6, 8–11 P.M.
Saturday, February 7, 10 A.M.–6 P.M.

Fee: $45.00; students $35.00

Location: Central Church
6245 Halekulani Lane
Honolulu, Hawaii 96823

Dr. Van Wheeler, whose announcement appears in Figure 2.3 is clearly positioning herself to attract a wealthy clientele. Cost, location, and presentation all are geared to eliminate patients and students in the middle and lower socioeconomic levels. Although this therapist is offering what seems to be similar to Smith and Jones (Figure 2.2), a very different participant is likely to apply for her group.

Figure 2.3 Sample Group Announcement (Van Wheeler)

Dr. Elizabeth Van Wheeler, B.A., M.Sc., M.D., Ed.D.,

is happy to announce an

AWARENESS WORKSHOP

Dr. Van Wheeler was educated at Oxford and Paris and
is a lifetime member of the International Socioanalytic Association.
This workshop will use a variety of techniques, especially
movement and body awareness, to reintroduce and
help reintegrate body energy and self.
Members will become in touch with and learn new ways to
express themselves.

Membership is very limited

Date: February 3, 2018, Friday, 7–10 P.M.
            February 4, 2018, Saturday, 10 A.M.–6 P.M.

Fee: $750.00. Catered lunch for Saturday is included.

Location: Penthouse, Hilton Hotel

A flyer-type advertisement (Figure 2.4) for group members appeared on university campus bulletin boards. It is unlikely that Guru Rakar will compete for the same populations that Dr. Van Wheeler (Figure 2.3) will attract.

Another quite different means of inviting members is with memoranda such as the one in Figure 2.5. This figure and the next four announcements are also for professionals, but they are presented in different ways. Figure 2.6 announces an entire season of scheduled groups developed by a group therapy center. In Figure 2.7, an individual psychotherapist establishes the relocation of her practice by announcing two new groups to her colleagues, asking for referrals.

Figure 2.8 is a notice of a group developed for and by psychotherapists. The last announcement (Figure 2.8) is a request for referrals from the director of a state mental health clinic.

Figure 2.4 Sample Group Announcement (Guru Shana Rakar)

A WEEKEND OF TRUTH THROUGH MOVEMENT ENERGY

"COME INTO KNOWING"

The Peninsula Dynamic Spiritual Learning Center presents a weekend group experience with the renowed Guru Shana Rakar, recently returned from India, and his assistants Sandy Beach and Elaine Nixon, B.A. The guru will work with individuals in attaining knowledge in a group setting to enhance knowledge of self and of one's own inner strengths.

Cost: $50.00/one person; $80.00/couple
Time: Sunrise to sunset, Saturday, February 3, 2018
Place: Behind Green Chapel

FIGURE 2.5 Sample Group Announcement (Quincy Mental Health Clinic)

MEMORANDUM

March 19, 2017

TO: Selected Psychotherapists in Private Practice
         Selected Psychotherapists in State Mental Health Centers
FROM: Quincy Mental Health Clinic
Re: Referrals of Nonpsychotic Patients to an interpersonal skills group

This is to inform you that Drs. Joe Smith and Elaine Brown will be conducting weekly group therapy sessions on Tuesday evenings, 7–10 P.M., commencing May 1, 2018 for 12 consecutive Tuesday evenings. The group membership will consist of 8–10 patients who are diagnosed with neurotic or situational adjustment problems. The focus of this group is interpersonal, and it is seen as an excellent adjunct to ongoing individual therapy. If you have any nonpsychotic, "Axis I" patients that you feel would benefit from this group, referrals will be accepted and appreciated. Sessions will cost $20.00 per participant per session. Sliding scale applies.

We will screen all members carefully for "goodness of fit" in the groups. Please contact Joe and Elaine at QMHC (617) 555–9590.

FIGURE 2.6 Sample Group Announcement (Kentucky)

THE KENTUCKY CENTER FOR GROUP THERAPY
Proudly Announces its lineup of groups for the Winter 2017 Season

MEN'S GROUP FOR MALES 21+ . Led by Martin Reilly, Ph.D. and Bill Bernstein, MSW. This group will meet on Thursday evenings from 7:30–9:30 for 10 weeks. The themes for the Winter groups are friendship, communication and work/home life balance.

WOMEN'S GROUP FOR FEMALES 21+. Led by Maggie Cotton Ph.D. and Jen Cohen, Ph.D. This group will meet on Wednesday evenings from 7:30–9:30 for 10 weeks. The themes for the Winter groups are balancing work, relationships and home life, assertiveness and communication skill building.

FRIDAY NIGHT COUPLES GROUP FOR MARRIED AND COMMITTED COUPLES will continue for another term. There is space for 2 or three new couples in this ongoing group. The group focuses on communication within and between couples, issues of security and freedom and stresses male-female dialogue. The group meetings are from 7:30 to 9:30 for ten weeks and are led by Drs. Myra and Will Stone.

THERAPISTS' GROWTH/SUPERVISION GROUP WILL BE OPEN THIS WINTER FOR 4–6 NEW MEMBERS. This group which meets from noon to 2:pm on Fridays accepts licensed therapists in any discipline who wish to explore transference/counter-transference issues and professional/personal concerns. The leaders Martin Weiss, Ph.D. and Cindy Swarz, M.D. work from a Psychodynamic framework.

ANXIETY AND PHOBIA GROUP FOR ADULTS will begin on January 9 and run for 8 consecutive Mondays at 2:30 pm–4:30 pm. Dr. Cecily Brown will be leading this group.

All groups meet in our second floor Group room, Ste. 200, 2222 Bardstown,

PROFESSIONALS AND REFERRALS ARE WELCOME TO ALL OF THESE GROUPS.

PLEASE CALL OR FAX 555-5000 TO SCHEDULE A SCREENING INTERVIEW OR FOR FURTHER INFORMATION.

Figure 2.7 Sample Group Announcement (Karple)

Sandra A. Karple, Ph. D.
Individual & Group
Psychotherapy Offices in Palo
Alto and San Francisco (415)
555-4414
Member, American Group Psychotherapy Association,
Northern California Group Psychotherapy Society
Advanced Certification: Maritime Society of Group Psychotherapy

Dear Colleague,

I am announcing the relocation of my private practice, with the following two groups beginning in January. I would appreciate referrals of appropriate clients.

Women with eating disorders

An eating disorder is a symptom associated with issues intertwined with female psychological development. This group will provide an environment in which members can focus on.

(1)   Origins of problem eating vis-a-vis feelings of powerlessness in her family of origin or society in general

(2)   Food as a means to express unconscious and/or unspoken needs

(3)   The promotion and practice of strategies for enhanced self-care in a caring, protective environment

Meets on Friday mornings 7:30 to 9:00 A.M.

Psychotherapy Group for Women

This group is a resource for women who wish to explore issues of identity; family dynamics; and relationships with friends, work associates, and society-at-large.

Meets on Wednesday evenings 6:30–8:00 P.M.

I will personally meet individually with prospective members to assess whether the group will be an appropriate resource for change and growth.

The monthly fee for each group is $160.00. There is no charge for the screening interview; Membership is limited to 8 participants.

I have been a licensed Clinical Psychologist in Pennsylvania and California for 8 years. My research on the psychology of women has been published in professional journals.

I welcome further contact from you.

Figure 2.8 Sample Group Announcement (Anderson and Ellman)

PSYCHOTHERAPY GROUP

Psychotherapy has often been called
"the impossible profession."
The required awareness of our internal processes
and of our effects on others adds demands
to already emotionally stressful work.

We believe that group therapy with colleagues
provides a valuable arena for growth and support
and a potential antidote to therapist burnout.

Catharine Anderson has been a group therapist for
25 years and has directed and led training
groups and Institutes.

Jack Ellman has been a group therapist for
forty years and has been a training supervisor for experienced therapists.

Openings are available In our
psychotherapists' group which meets
Wednesdays at 1–2:30 pm.

Please call
Catharine Anderson, LCSW 312 555-4464 or
Jack Ellman, Ph.D. 312 555-4466

720 Sheridan, Suite 207, Chicago, IL

FOR PSYCHOTHERAPISTS

Figure 2.9 Sample Group Announcement (State Mental Health Clinic)

June 1, 2013
INTRADEPARTMENTAL MEMO

To: All Therapists
From: Director, State Mental Health Clinic
Re: Available Spaces in Couples Groups

This fall two of our psychology interns and two psychiatric residents will be leading couples groups in the evenings. There will be one resident and one intern co-leading groups on Tuesday and Wednesday evenings. The groups are designed to help couples in conflict learn more effective communication patterns and to help reduce our waiting list rolls. Please make referrals directly to Dr. Hong, intern training coordinator. We will need at least 8 couples to fill both groups. All costs will be covered by my office, and services to patients are free. I trust you will consider need as one factor in selection.

Semi-Voluntary Groups. In a managed care environment or in certain geographical areas in which choice is limited, members may be offered a particular group or a small choice of available groups. The following example (Figure 2.10) is from a large managed care operation in a metropolitan area. It is an internal note to the triage personnel regarding patient intake.

Figure 2.10 Sample Internal Memo (Available Groups)

Directions to Triage Nurse

After medication options are considered and patients have medication consults if necessary, it is strongly encouraged that they be referred to the outpatient group network in the system. Please refer to your Group Openings Worksheet published each week by The Center. Please note that group treatment is far less costly than individual outpatient treatment. It is also better for most of our patients.

July Group Schedule: All adult patients who work or reside in Cachement Area One should be referred to the outpatient group conducted by Millie Greenstock, M.S.W. The group leader for patients in Cachement Area Two are to be referred to Mark Willow, M.F.T.. The group leader for Cachement Area Three is Juanita Lopez, Ph.D. Patients who live or work in Cachement Area Four should be given a choice of the most convenient group session. No groups will be started in Area 4 until Sept. 15. Any patient wishing a different group location or time is free to choose one, but "group hopping" will not be possible.

Specialty Populations: Patients with addiction problems are to be referred to local 12 step programs and the groups for recovering addicts. Grace Lee, M.S.W. will be conducting a group for recovering addicts in the Southern Region on Saturday mornings. Either Bob Wilson, M.D. or Maggie Kane, M.D. will be doing the Wed. evening addiction group. No members who are currently "using" are appropriate for these groups. They are designed as post-detox groups.

The *Adult Children of Alcoholics group* will be available in August at the central office. Contact Marie for scheduling. The group therapist will be named.

The *singles group* is also taking referrals this month. Contact Dr. Bernal at 555-5465. A new Men's group will be available in August and Dr. Farraday is accepting members now. Finally, the women's groups are being led by Dr. Clark (Southern Area). Felicia Roll and Candy Martinez are doing the central region group.

All referrals are to be made directly to the group leader.

Other managed care providers used similar referral systems. In one local HMO, for example, group therapy is continuous. All patients are assigned for a specified number of sessions to a large group run by staff members, who rotate into and out of the group. When one group reaches 15 members, a second is started. The group goals are assessment and treatment. Patient are not offered any other outpatient treatment save medication.

Finally, a third managed care system provides a menu of services for clients. These clients, in consultation with their primary care physician or mental health triage personnel may choose a theme group (addiction; adult children of alcoholics (ACA); past trauma; stress management; women's issues; couples; etc.) or a general ongoing outpatient group.

Because these groups are all part of the same network and are administratively and financially linked, screening differs from that in unrestricted outpatient environments. Patients who wish to use their prepaid insurance coverage often do not have as wide an assortment of choices for group or individual forms of treatment. Similarly, practitioners are more likely to accept a wider range of clients in a group, because they have "a right" to treatment, according to the list of benefits in their medical insurance coverage.

Alternatively, a therapist who is a full-time employee of an HMO and who is not subject to profit sharing or bonus pressure, may be more circumspect in including a member in a particular group than an outpatient therapist who is "hungry" for patients.

Involuntary Groups. A major factor in the composition of groups is the extent to which they are voluntary. In the groups advertised above, group membership was by application and selection. Such is not always the case. Figures 2.11 and 2.12 offer two examples of an involuntary group assignment. These introductions to group membership carry with them potentially destructive elements.

Figure 2.11 Notice of Mandatory Attendance Groups (Parents of Schoolchildren)

Dear Mr. & Mrs. White:

Your son/daughter has been reported to the school principal repeatedly for smoking in the school lavatories. In lieu of punishment, he/she has been assigned to a group guidance session with Miss Young, the school counselor. The sessions will occur every Monday, Wednesday, and Friday from 10–11 am. We have found that these sessions are helpful to students and do reduce future infractions of school policies. Attendance is mandatory for one month with your consent. If you accept these terms, please complete and sign the attached permission slip.

If you would prefer to discuss this matter with me personally, please call for an appointment.

Sincerely,

Candace Edwards, Principal

Figure 2.12 Notice of Mandatory Attendance Groups (Inmates)

MEMO

To: Inmates, Black, White, Brown, Green, Redd.
        Charlestown Penitentiary
From: J.E.M. Cauliflower, Warden JEMC

You have been assigned to group therapy with psychology interns S. Johnson and J. Jackson. The group commences 0900 Wednesday, May 1 and will terminate at 1030. The group will last for 15 weeks or until your release. It is expected that you will learn social skills necessary upon your upcoming release from this center. On-time attendance is mandatory.

The membership of institutional groups, such as those for hospitalized patients, the military, prisoners, students, graduate students, business or management representatives, or court-directed participants is frequently by assignment rather than choice. In these cases, a primary leadership responsibility is to address effectively the resentment and resistance that members often bring to the group. Completing any real therapeutic work will be difficult until the group members are at least nominal volunteers. The probability for positive results are slight unless members are at least willing to see what they could achieve in an involuntary or mandatory group.

Stage 3: Members Apply for the Group

Application for group membership can take several forms. Potential members can personally apply by telephone, online, by completing a form and sending or bringing it to the growth center, mental health clinic, or leader. They may also approach the group by referral from appropriate sources, such as other therapists, physicians, clergy, parents, schools, former clients, or family members.

It is essential that leaders and members are clear at this stage that members are *making application* to the group. There is no guarantee of participation. Of course, mandatory groups may guarantee attendance, if not full participation.

Stage 4: Screening

Screening is one of the most critical components of the entire group process. A poorly screened group is assuredly one with extra handicaps. Some screening errors can be so serious as to almost guarantee failure. Selection for inclusion is most often made by the leaders or the institution sponsoring the group, although Vander Kolk (1985) notes that occasionally members are involved in, or make, the decision. In open, higher functioning groups, members who are added may well have to pass some screening by continuing members. Lifton (1966) and Hansen, Warner, and Smith (1980) provide guidelines for timing and approaches to such additions.

There are differences in populations and goals between growth and therapy groups. Potential members must therefore be screened accordingly. Mixing psychotherapy patients and growth-oriented clients will limit the learning of both. Group progress is often dependent on—sometimes unconscious—agreements or compromises about the type of material, the psychological language system the group will use, and the goals it will pursue. The sooner these agreements can be made, the further the group can progress in the allotted time. A group with widely divergent goals cannot make these agreements readily and will spend an inordinate amount of time in Phase II (transition), leaving far less group time actually to work on change.

In some ways, the group's progress is most limited by the pathology of the lowest functioning member. A poor mix of members can render progress beyond the earliest stages of group laborious and painful. Indeed, inadequate screening is the most likely cause for a group to get bogged down or produce casualties.

When one considers the significant ramifications of ineffective screening, this stage is curiously minimized by counselors, therapists, and group leaders. Screening errors are most probable when leaders are too eager to fill their groups, when they underestimate psychopathology (especially in growth-oriented groups), or when they overestimate the effectiveness of natural screening of the marketplace. The 2007 Best Practices Guidelines of the Association of Specialists in Group Work (Thomas & Pender, 2008) recommend individual pre-screening interviews by the leaders of the group. The (1988) Guidelines of the American Association for Counseling and Development requires member counselors to "screen prospective group members, especially when the emphasis is on self-awareness and growth through self-awareness. [The group leader] must maintain an awareness of the group members' compatibility throughout the life of the group." (p. 3)

Capuzzi, Gross, and Stauffer (2010), Carroll and Wiggins (1990), Corey (2015), Rutan, Stone & Shay (2014), Shapiro (1978), and Yalom and Lescz (2005) are among the authors who have underscored the primacy of screening for effective groups. They assert that an improper mix of members is the most likely cause for a group to get bogged down or produce casualties. They have identified two major screening questions for group:

1. Is this group appropriate for the client?
2. Is the client appropriate for this group?

Homogeneity or Heterogeneity? Some leaders favor homogeneous membership to emphasize shared experiences, understanding, and altruism and to instill hope by providing encouraging examples of success within the group setting. Others favor heterogeneous membership for its diverse feedback possibilities, higher levels of interest, and models of novel approaches to problem solving.

Many questions arise regarding this issue:

- Should people with different problems be in the same group?
- Do you have to personally share a particular problem to fully understand the emotional ramifications of that problem?
- Should members who know each other previously (e.g., from work, school, neighborhood) be in the same group? What are the implications of a prior acquaintance for the involved members? What are the implications for the members who do not know anyone in the group from past association?

- What are the ramifications of loss of confidentiality in EAP groups offered in the workplace?

- What is the appropriate age range for members? What age groups fit together and which don't?

- When do you include both genders and when do you have independent men's groups and women's groups?

- Should people with addictions be in groups with nonaddicted peers? Which diagnostic categories are best kept apart?

With the increasing growth of "12-step" groups, based on the Alcoholics Anonymous self-help model and a host of other self-help programs, there are a large number of group participants who have certain experiences that lead to expectations of a group with a designated leader. Groups that are geared to a 12-step model and consistent with its philosophical underpinnings can accommodate such members quite successfully. However, mixed groups with alternative theoretical perspectives may not fare as well. The time required to reindoctrinate all members to a novel method of group work, and a new psychological language system could drastically reduce time and ability to proceed through the normal trajectory of group process. By contrast, some members with prior experience in 12-step meetings and individual therapy often adapt quickly and utilize well what a group has to offer.

Ego Strength. As a rule of thumb, the most salient screening question has to do with a potential member's ego strength (the obverse of pathology). Generally, heterogeneous membership with regard to anamnestic information is desired. People of different ages, races, cultures, and walks of life often become a very productive group. However, the group is best served when members are roughly similar in ego strength. People with roughly equivalent levels of pathology will work together better than groups with wide-ranging differences. Thus, a mix of people whose needs for support and growth differ dramatically will work less well. One example of this occurred in an outpatient clinic. In a single group of eight members, diagnoses of members included schizophrenia, bipolar disorder, borderline personality, adjustment disorder, dysthymia, and posttraumatic stress disorder. By the third session, only three members had come to all three sessions. In such a group, the neediest person would most control the direction of the process.

Isolates. Another screening issue involves group isolates. Common examples of isolates in a group include one person of a different gender, a person addicted to alcohol or drugs in a group in which addiction is not a core issue, an individual isolated by a wide age gap, and so on.

A 17-year-old high school senior, Suzanne, was referred to the senior author after 2 years in a particularly trying group therapy experience. This group, led by a locally well-known therapist, consisted of nine members—the teenager and four couples aged 29 to 45 who were having marital problems. Suzanne simply did not belong in this married couples group. Not only did she misunderstand many of the conflicts between the couples, but she emerged with an especially pessimistic view of marriage and heterosexual relationships. Subsequent consultation with the group therapist confirmed that in his opinion, Suzanne did not "get much out of the group," and several of the other members were reticent to discuss some of their sexual problems "in front of a 17-year-old child." This was a clear case of poor or absent screening based on the simplistic notion that because all nine of these people could benefit from group treatment, they could function well together.

In another situation, an experienced group trainer was asked to consult on a "block" in an ongoing women's awareness group in a small community. He reported,

> As a male I was surprised to receive this request and reticent to accept. This surprise was minor by comparison to the shock I experienced on entering the group room. In addition to four single women (Mary, Kathy, Ann, Peggy) and three married women (Martha, Linda, Sandy), there was another group member by the name of Edward. Ed was a social worker, the former husband of Linda and Kathy and the current lover of Peggy. The rationale of the group was that since Ed was so much being discussed in the group, it seemed only fair to have him present. The block in this women's awareness group was that, dynamically, the group process centered around a man. I recommended an immediate "Ed-ectomy." He and I left the group together to the relief and benefit of all concerned.

More Severe Pathology. Potential group members with personality disorders (formerly referred to as Axis II) can be very well accommodated in groups that are specifically geared to their developmental relationship needs (i.e., Finn and Shakir, 1990). Similarly, groups are commonly employed for treatment of patients with psychotic and severe addiction problems. The crucial screening factor is the limitation to relatively homogenous membership and a generally longer time frame for the group to function.

Poor Alignment of Population, Goals, and Resources. Screening difficulties based on the presence of isolates are easier to foresee than differences based on symbiotic pathological systems, level or type of problem to be discussed, or readiness and motivation for the group experience. In groups with heterogeneous membership held in an outpatient setting, several types of members can be extremely counterproductive for group progress. Brain-damaged individuals, people on the severe end of the autistic spectrum, severely psychotic (especially withdrawn and paranoid) patients, psychopathic individuals, individuals currently abusing drugs or alcohol, suicidal clients, and very assaultive patients are all bad risks in an outpatient group and have no place at all in growth groups. Not only will these members gain little or even regress personally, but they will also severely limit the benefits accrued by other members of the group. These clinical observations have long been confirmed in the group therapy literature by Slavson (1951), Yalom (1970), Rosenbaum and Hartley (1962), and Corsini and Lundin (1955). Certainly any members whose pathology would lead them to be insensitive, or in extreme instances, to prey on other members are poor risks (Dinkmeyer & Muro, 1971).

Symbiotic Combinations. Certain combinations of group members also can cause grief for the group leader and inhibit the group process, particularly in growth groups, where the group contract often has no allusion to pathology. People who have outside-of-group relationships (particularly secret ones) may be a problem. Vander Kolk (1985) and Capuzzi, Gross, and Stauffer (2010) also indicate the potential dangers of mixing suicidal patients of different levels of lethality. Another potentially disruptive combination involves a person who uses hysteric or borderline defenses and an authoritarian personality type who tends to avoid intimacy by "protecting" (fathering, mothering) others.

An example of this predicament occurred during introductions in an intern-led training group for graduate students in a mental health graduate program. Three members of the group had already given their names and described their personal expectations when a fourth said, "My name is Christine. … I don't know If I should be here. … I get scared easy and I'm afraid of you two especially (she indicated two of the men in the group). When people start getting upset and emotional I freak out. I even tried suicide three times."

Immediately, Dan, one of the men in the group, responded in a crisp, booming voice, "Well, you don't have to worry here, sweets, anyone who tries to get you upset will have to answer to me first." During his response he extended his index finger in an arc pointing toward each member of the group. This symbiotic relationship interrupted group process for several sessions.

Whenever other group members began to discuss anything emotionally, Christine would begin to shake, cower, and express a need to run from the room. Dan would then respond by verbally intimidating the person who was expressing the high levels of emotion. In this way, the principals allowed one another to express the feelings that they were personally unable to express directly. Christine never had to deal with her "unacceptable" anger, and Dan never had to deal with his anger-covered fear. They effectively kept the group from getting to deeper (more frightening) levels of interaction.

The co-leaders had their hands very full with this relationship until the fourth session of the group. At that meeting, a breakthrough occurred when Christine tried to provoke the group by being absent after having been seen in the hall outside the group room minutes earlier. Without her presence, the group leaders progressed swiftly to confront members' feelings of being threatened by her fragility, and by Dan's intimidation. By the next meeting, when she returned, Dan had sufficient courage to refuse to save her from her anxiety. Only then could the group move forward.

The Extra-Group Relationship. Another combination of members that causes great difficulties is two members who have had a serious prior relationship. This is especially powerful when the group is composed of others who do not know one another well. The case of Denise and Billy provides a classic example.

The "singles" group was designed to help people learn to relate more comfortably and effectively to members of the opposite sex. Because of this theme, there was a prerequisite that members did not know each other beforehand.

As the group progressed, it became clear that each time Billy spoke, Denise made the next statement and "put him down as a 'typical male.'" Similarly, whenever Denise spoke, Billy accused her of "being sexually provocative, but denying it verbally." The other group members and leaders confronted them several times with this pattern, with no apparent behavior change.

Their interaction become so dominant that the group leader finally confronted them with the following statement: "You two sound like a married couple deciding to get a divorce and wanting to gain some measure of revenge." This was followed by a pregnant silence during which both Denise and Billy got very pale. Finally, they admitted that they *had* been married for 4 years. The group continued only after they agreed to drop out and seek individual psychotherapy.

Secret Motivations. One other type of person that makes group work especially complex is the person who has "something to sell." These individuals come to groups essentially to convince others to join with them in some belief system or value. They are either sufficiently insecure, well-defended, or convinced enough of their own righteousness to be unaccepting of other members' values, beliefs, or language systems. Recent converts to religious, spiritual, or pop psychology sects can frequently spend much of the group's time attempting to induce the group to accept verbatim their own elitist, myopic approach to understanding their experience and their own singular jargon. In the process, they reject all others as unsophisticated or insensitive. Such members often seduce other members and unsuspecting leaders into expending vast amounts of time attempting to "work with them and be fair."

Denny was one such participant in an otherwise high-functioning outpatient group of helpers in mental health fields. He was a supportive and contributing member of the group for several sessions. In the fifth group meeting, a question of an unwanted pregnancy came up in the group. Marion, volunteered that several years ago, she had an abortion that entailed making a very painful and difficult decision. While she was weeping, Denny became increasingly agitated, finally bursting out of the room screaming at her, "anyone who has murdered a child should be put to death herself! After he left, the group turned its attention to supporting Marion. When a group member leaves the group in anger, it is good practice to have one of the leaders attend to the exiting member while the other leader debriefs with the group.

At the next group meeting, he arrived with "right-to-life" literature replete with graphic pictures and railed at the group and at Marion in particular for a lengthy period before the leaders finally demanded that he stop, whereupon he again left the session. His belief and feelings about abortion (although not his position on the death sentence policy) was likely shared by others in the group. What made his group participation problematic was his vehemence, his unwillingness to consider others' opinions or feelings, and his "judge, jury, and executioner" stance. He literally shouted down others who tried to support Marion or discuss the unwanted pregnancy with the man who originally brought it up for discussion. The leaders, admittedly caught off guard by this series of actions, permitted it to progress far beyond what might be appropriate or healthy for the group. In unexpected circumstances such as this, leaders must be ready to jump in quickly to mediate and manage conflicts when they begin to escalate.

The Cost of Inadequate Screening. This screening stage of group process is critically important in setting group tone and eliminating unnecessary problems. Errors of omission and of commission come back to haunt group leaders in a variety of ways. Poor screening can seriously limit group outcome. A leader who attempts to do bargain basement screening will pay for it several times over during the life of the group.

One example of incomplete screening will make this point clear (Shapiro, 1978). Nine members were enrolled in a one-day marathon group in 1973. On the last day before the group was to meet, one co-leader was talking casually to a colleague regarding his disappointment about the lack of a tenth group member. The colleague replied that he had a person on his waiting list, suggesting that the co-leader call her. Because it was so late, a very brief, inadequate telephone screening was done. Tina, a mental health professional, seemed motivated and pleasant on the phone, and was invited to come to the group the following day. The co-leader wrote,

> I rationalized: There's not enough time to do a personal in-office screening; she was "screened" by a colleague; she's been on a waiting list for a group, so she couldn't be in urgent need of help; she's a professional person in a mental health profession. These justifications were used in the absence of the typical appropriate face-to-face interview.

Tina was the fourth member to introduce herself in the group the next day. Her speech was exceptionally fast and pressured, and her eyes seemed to glaze and defocus every few seconds. The following is a short excerpt of her 8-minute self-introduction:

> Well, my name is Tina, but it isn't really Tina that's only since it happened, before that it was different but really the same—Sally or Rudy but that was before the man-husband-father rolled over the kids with the steam roller-crusher-flat but not really only but they were dead but I didn't so now they cry but it seems no he didn't exist—they are. God punishes them but I save-savior-saved. ... (p. 76)

During this introduction the other group members appeared terrified and seemed to be trying to enlarge the size of the group room by pressing their backs against the walls of the room. The other group co-leader had a look of shock, surprise, and what could be most kindly described as a "How could you do this to me?" look on his face. "I personally had the customary countenance of a person who has recently been kicked in the stomach by a horse."

Once Tina was through with her introduction, and before the remaining members introduced themselves, the leaders called a break and contacted a colleague. They arranged for emergency treatment and reconvened the rather shaken group members once she had departed. The group wrestled with Tina's pathology for approximately two hours before they were able to refocus on their own personal concerns.

Screening Members into the Group. Screening can be best employed for inclusion rather than exclusion (i.e., Yalom, 1995) and necessitates finding a good mix of people: similar enough to understand one another, yet different enough to be able to learn innovative viewpoints, behaviors, and solutions to problems from one another. One or two appropriate members can bridge a gap between two otherwise discrete subgroups of people within a single group. Group membership also needs to coincide with the ability and level of functioning of the leaders. Groups simply cannot progress beyond the leaders' ability to effectively cope with any particular level of process.

One example of screening in members with special abilities to bridge gaps occurred in a recent outpatient couples group. There were three couples ready for the group: a married couple in their mid-20s with two small children; an unmarried couple without children in their mid-20s; a couple in their late 30s with a blended family. The leaders added a couple in their 30s with no children and a couple approaching 40 with two young children from the current marriage and two adolescents from her prior marriage. These two last couples helped provide additional support and connections between members.

In a group conducted in a local church, the counselor added two recovering alcoholic members to a group whose prior enrollees were parents of children who were abusing alcohol and nondrinkers who had excessive emotional dependence on institutional authorities.

Members may also be screened in to a group to fill out the age range or balance other characteristics. A group consisting of five members in their 20s and 30s and one aged 55 has a potential isolate, but adding a few members in their 40s could minimize that possibility. Similarly, in a group of graduate counseling students, two males were added to balance a group of five women and two other men.

In the screening process there are foci on potential client's demographic information:

1. personal goals for the group,
2. previous individual and group therapy,
3. psychological strengths, and
4. psychological weaknesses.

The screening interview form, shown in Figure 2.13 is the one we commonly use. It is not necessarily appropriate for any particular group setting, but may be used as a model. No legal ruling has been made regarding use of this form.

Figure 2.13 Screening Interview Form

SCREENING INTERVIEW FOR GROUPS

Jerrold Lee Shapiro, Ph.D., ABMP OHANA Family Therapy Institute

THIS IS A GENERIC MODEL.

PLEASE ADJUST FOR SPECIFIC GROUPS AS APPROPRIATE

PART 1

To be completed by Group Leader prior to interview.

TYPE OF GROUP: Therapy _____   Growth _____   Counseling _____   Other _____

POPULATION: _____

DATES & TIMES FOR GROUP MEETINGS: _____

SPECIAL CONSIDERATIONS:* _____

* specific population requirements etc.

PART 2

To be completed by Group Leader while interviewing prospective Members.

NAME: _____   Sex _____

ADDRESS: _____

PHONE: (___) _____   AGE: _____   RELATIONSHIP STATUS _____

ETHNICITY/CULTURE/GENDER ID:

FOR THERAPY GROUPS: Detail results of Psychological Assessment and/or Mental Status Exam.

Viability for Group Treatment?

FOR ALL GROUPS:

1. How did you hear about this group? (referral source or ?)
2. Reasons for applying for group.
3. Describe prior counseling/therapy experience. (Situation & evaluation) Individual, group.
4. Any current psychiatric, or medical conditions and treatment>
5. Relevant medical history (some leaders prefer a medical history check list)
6. Alcohol and drug history (any dependence/addiction etc)
7. Relationship/sexual history (especially interpersonal difficulties)
8. Any particular problems with the law?
9. To what extent is your current situation a crisis?
10. Some estimate of self-esteem (i.e., How satisfied are you with the way you are? What do you need to change?)
11. When things become anxiety producing do you tend to become more quiet or more talkative? (examples)
12. What role do fate, luck or chance play in making your life what it is?
13. Do you tend to trust others quickly or slowly?
14. What do you hope to get out of this group?
15. What do you expect to get out of this group?
16. Is there a particular best way for others to relate to you? (example)

When Applicants are Excluded. We try as best as possible to provide a brief consultation and referral for those for whom the group will not be optimal. It is not simply a matter of "hiring" and rejecting. There is a professional responsibility to offer possible referrals to those who are not invited to join the group.

For example, a group leader may give the following statement to someone who is not right for the group:

> As we spoke, I realized that this particular group would not provide what you described you were seeking. There is another group/individual/family therapy that seems like it is better suited to your stated goals. Here is the name and contact information of the counselor/therapist, that I'd recommend.

The Other Side of Screening. The other major role in screening is education. In addition to addressing inclusion and exclusion for a particular group, it is important to prepare and orient members, helping to establish realistic goals, explore expectations, risks and rights, describe and decrease any unwarranted anxiety about participating in the group. This allows both members and leaders to make a more informed decision about inclusion in the group and provides the leader with helpful information that may be used during the group.

One of the major components of screening is to introduce members' rights and responsibilities during the group. These will brought up again during the group introduction in Phase II.

Among the rights for all prospective members is a statement of purpose, a description of format procedures and ground rules, a chance for a pregroup interview, such as the screening interview.

In addition, members must be informed of their rights once the group actually begins. The most important is the *right to leave* or quit entirely. In involuntary situations, there may be consequences for premature exiting. Other rights are that what they disclose will be held in *confidence* (to the extent of legal and ethical restrictions). Confidentiality can be tricky in groups, because other members may not hold the same honor for confidentiality as the professional leaders. Other rights include, *freedom to use the group resources*, *freedom from coercion*, and *competent, ethical* leadership.

Pregroup Preparation. Prior to the first actual group meeting, some leaders prefer a pregroup meeting for orientation and preparation. Egan (1976) who conducted "human relations training" groups from a skills training perspective, preferred a structured approach with considerable training to orient members for maximum work in the group once it actually begins. Corey (1990) focusing primarily on university level counseling groups, favors a fairly elaborate preparatory session in which the leader explores with the members their "expectations, fears, goals and misconceptions; the basics of group process; psychological risks associated with group membership and ways of minimizing them; the values and limitations of groups; guidelines for getting the most from the group experience; and the necessity of confidentiality" (p. 93).

Corey also uses this "initial session" for extended screening and obtaining a commitment to continued membership. In these sessions, he discusses with participants the importance of their own preparation for group work; stresses the importance of their personal level of investment; examines with members their reasons for being in the group, expectations, hopes, and fears about participating; and helps them better crystallize their personal life issues and level of disclosure. In addition he impresses members with the importance of keeping a journal and of thinking between sessions about what they wish to address.

At least one controlled research effort established the value of a preparatory session in increasing subsequent member interpersonal interactions (Yalom, Houts, Newell, & Rand, 1979). The authors also claimed that patients' faith in the process improved, maximizing any potential placebo effects. Yalom (1985) later described a fairly extensive preparation including an exploration of misconceptions and expectations; description of his existential theory of group work; prediction of stumbling blocks; discussions of trust, self-disclosure, extra-group socialization, confidentiality and goals; exploration of risks inherent in group therapy; and an examination of how members can best grow from the experience. Vinogradov and Yalom (1990) particularly encourage the use of such sessions to reduce negative expectations.

In their review of pregroup participation, Orlinsky and Howard (1986) concluded that a majority of studies strongly favor role preparation procedures as measured by self-reports of members, observers and leaders and paper and pencil indices. However, Piper and Perrault (1989) were less enthusiastic about the value of pregroup training in their subsequent review of outcome measures. They indicated that the cost in time for any benefits was minimal. In general, if the group leaders are more comfortable with a "prepped group," it is probably worth doing.

Whether pregroup sessions or instructions are employed or not, the screening and preparation end with the first session of the group. Once the logistics are set and group members screened, Phase I of the group process is complete. When the group convenes, Phase II begins.

At Santa Clara University, a handout (Figure 2.14) is mailed to counseling psychology graduate students, prior to the initial session of their mandatory training groups.

Figure 2.14 Pregroup Instructions

LAB GROUP INSTRUCTIONS (revised 01/13/2016)

Please read the following information carefully. If there are any questions that your group leaders cannot answer please contact Dr. xxx.

CPSY 221 is a *required* non-graded (Cr/NC), 1.5 unit *laboratory* component of the CPSY 219 class (the course on group theory/process). The materials from the lab group are needed to complete class requirements for CPSY 219. *You cannot take the 219 class without the lab.*

The groups serve several functions and it is important that you understand these. First and foremost, the lab group experience is designed to enhance your understanding of group process in an experiential manner. Second, if you plan to do group counseling in the future, it is important that you understand what it is like to be a member of a group and to focus on your personal experience in the here-and-now environment of a training group. It is customary in mental health training programs to have this experiential component while learning about group leadership. Finally, it is the intent of the faculty that you have the opportunity to become aware of personal aspects of yourselves that are likely to impact on your training and future counseling. We hope that you will be as open and honest about your personal self *as you feel appropriate* in these group settings. Lab groups, like all training groups, may well be useful personally, but they are NOT therapy groups for you. It is not a place to "spill one's guts," or to try to resolve long standing personality issues that stem from childhood trauma.

Limitations of Privacy. These groups are designed to be private and the faculty of the program will not be privy to any content discussed in the group with several mandatory exceptions. The first exception to student privacy in the lab pertains to **potential harm to self, others, or property, child abuse, or elder abuse**. All faculty and thus the lab group leaders are mandated to make a report to the SCU title IX office any **sexual harassment and sexual violence** involving a student and any other SCU community member and must report to the office of student life any **unlawful harassment or discrimination** based on race, color, national origin, ancestry, sex, sexual orientation, age, religious creed, physical or mental disability, medical condition as defined by California law, marital status, citizenship status, gender identity, gender expression, genetic information, or other status protected by law.

In addition, if there is concern about potential for danger to self or others, all faculty, including lab group leaders may report a **distressed or distressing student** to the office of student life. The office of student life would follow up with the student to ensure that they are made aware of all available resources. Finally, all faculty, including lab group leaders who reasonably believe that a student is exhibiting **behavior that is unprofessional** and/or that the student is in need of faculty evaluation or intervention, will complete and send a form which is sent to the Chairperson of the department. **All of these exceptions to student privacy apply to all classes at SCU, the lab groups are no different. The lab groups are not psychotherapy and do not have the full protection of confidentiality that is present in psychotherapy.**

To enhance the privacy of the group content, we hire licensed group leaders from the community who do not teach academic classes in the program. There are also advanced student co-leaders and all groups are supervised by another professional. Student identity is protected during supervision.

Although the leaders and faculty will do all they can to maintain privacy, it is incumbent on you as an individual to use common sense and good judgment about what you choose to talk about in group. In addition, it is even more essential that each of you also be very careful about keeping the privacy of your fellow members.

It is important to recognize the difference between the content of an individual's personal descriptions and the reactions to such a revelation. For example, if a group member were to disclose that she is "receiving psychotherapy for an eating disorder," that communication (the content) is protected. However, if in reaction to her disclosure a person, another group member emotionally attacks, ridicules or is abusive towards her, that behavior *is not necessarily protected*.

For a group leader, such judgmentalism and abuse may indicate that a person has some personal work to do before becoming a professional counselor. In this case, the group leader may make a report to the faculty for a review of the student. **This is both a very rare occurrence and is the same procedure that the faculty follow if such behavior emerges in any class in the program.**

Extended Privacy. There are additional requirements imposed on group members and the co-leaders which are more typical in a training setting than a clinical setting. First, protecting members privacy continues beyond the end of the group through the duration of the student's experience at Santa Clara. (Explanation: while you are a student here, the group member who revealed he/she was a "receiving psychotherapy for an eating disorder" must have that communication protected while she remains in the program, while you remain in the program, and into the future).

Secondly, extended privacy means extreme awareness to third party sensitivity. For example, if I were to tell a third party that a Samoan guy in my group said something, I would be identifying him even without giving his name—it is far different from saying "one person in my group told me that I seemed too kind to others and not taking care of myself enough." The latter disclosure is about you as a person and the identifying information does not risk anyone else's privacy. If a reasonable person can put two and two together and identify a person, you have violated the original person's privacy. This may seem like a burden at first, but when you think about it, it is an important professional standard and responsibility.

The other concern is that it is likely that members of your group, and the co-leader, to whom you have revealed personal information, may well be in classes with you during this term or later. This makes the protection of privacy more sensitive.

It is our experience that privacy is rarely violated. If such a violation were to occur, it may be unintentional or accidental. However, if it is violated by clear lack of responsibility on the person's part [or an innate tendency to gossip], it is grounds for losing one's license once you have become a professional and it is also grounds to question your ability to succeed in this field.

Academic and Therapeutic. Many programs make personal therapy a mandatory part of graduate student training. The CPSY faculty has decided to strongly recommend personal therapy, but not to require it. The lab groups are not a substitute for personal therapy.

They offer a necessary opportunity to understand in a fuller way what it is like to be a member rather than a leader of a group. This is an essential part of training and we expect you to learn a great deal from it. Group experiences in which members work with their own emotional, cognitive, and value-based reactions are generally seen as an integral part of any graduate training in human services work. Often students remember the work in groups with peers as the most meaningful of all graduate school experiences. We hope that you will use the group in this way and gain a great deal from your participation.

Thus, your lab group may be therapeutic and self-revelatory, but it is not psychotherapy and does not have the protection of confidentiality offered in psychotherapy. The lab groups, like all training groups, presume psychological adequacy. There is an expectation for example, that the people in this group are not significantly pathological, i.e. that they are essentially "healthy" and may be expected to do things typical "clients" might not ,be expected to do. For example, you will be expected to accept the termination of the group at 6 weeks without a need to be weaned away from this encounter in a more "therapeutically" planned manner. Secondly, you need to attend the meetings, because attendance is required (even though if you were a client you might simply skip this week because you needed to "resist" important psychological issues that you were gradually beginning to confront), etc. These points of divergence between what is academic and what is therapeutic may get confusing. When in doubt, assume that you are in an academic setting and that you are attempting (for the purposes of clinical training and

experience) to simulate the therapeutic milieu. The closer you get to your personal thoughts and feelings in the group, the better the learning experiences; the more you try to act and feel like an active participant rather than an observer, the better the group will be for both yourself and the other members. The more you trust in your leader and the therapeutic process (rather than be a grade-conscious student), the better will be your experience. Remember, if you attend and participate, your grade will be "Credit." **You will not be graded on any content!**

ATTENDANCE

Attendance is required! There are a few reasons, the most important of which is simply that everyone in the group becomes a "significant other" as time progresses. When one or two significant others are absent, the whole group suffers from it, loses pace over it, slows down, needs to recover, etc. To more fully experience the processes of change and evolution of a group (packed into six weeks) we need to count on each other's presence.

Groups meet for six 2-hour, weekly sessions. There will also be a one 8-hour marathon session generally between the 4th and 5th session. Students must attend the marathon and are expected at all sessions. A single absence may be excused by the group leader. Missing more than one session or the marathon will require repetition of the lab group and has implications for your completing the work in CPSY 219.

If you think that you may have to miss group once in the quarter, and you know of that scheduled event in advance ... please defer enrollment in CPSY 221 and CPSY 219 to a subsequent quarter. Look at your schedule and sign up for this lab group only if you are sure you will be able to make these meetings.

PLEASE NOTE:

You will be asked to participate at a level appropriate to your own personality style and demands of the field (i.e., there is a difference between being an introvert or shy and a clear indication that you are only passing time with no intention of being a group member).

Requirements

Students must keep a journal of their reactions during the group sessions. These journals will be used to complete assignments in the CPSY 219 course. The journals are best done right after the group meetings, You will *not* be able to take notes during sessions.

It is important to keep the journal accurately and to hold on to the journal until you have to fulfil requirements in the Group course. **PLEASE NOTE: YOU WILL NOT BE REQUIRED TO TURN IN ANY PART OF THE JOURNAL UNLESS YOU DECIDE IT IS APPROPRIATE.** During the group course, you will be asked to compare your group with the theoretical models and process presented.

The journal during the laboratory pre-group should include three components:

1. Entries from each session in which the events of the session are described.
2. Your feelings about and during those events. Remember that feelings are emotional reactions.
3. Your thoughts about these events and the session. Include perceptions of your fellow members and the leaders.

FAQ's

How should I behave in Group? What is expected? What should I avoid doing? I've just started the program, and I don't know what is expected of me.

Answers to these questions are not easy. However, there are some positive attitudes that make group work and that make you have a better experience. Think about adopting them and try to be reasonably experimental.

1) Be careful about your expectations. These groups are *not* in-depth psychotherapy such as personal individual psychotherapy. They focus more on interactions and on interpersonal issues that can reasonably be addressed in the 7 sessions. They are also not like classes. The group leaders will not structure the groups like a class. The members will have to create much of the structure and to build it with increasing trust during the group.

2) Be courageous and as time goes on, try to "give" the group some personal issues you might not otherwise talk about. If you do communicate about these issues, you will probably be quite surprised how effectively the group treats them and/or you with them.

3) Try to take **small experimental** "risks." Share your feelings, perceptions and reflections push your personal boundaries of self-growth.

4) Assume your feelings have validity. If you feel something about someone in the group, try to put that into words that communicate and get those feelings out. Rather than call the person an SOB, maybe you can describe what is occurring to you internally. Try it.

5) Listen to feedback you are getting. Watch how others listen to feedback they are getting.

6) Give feedback. Be forthcoming.

7) Things to avoid if you can:

   a. avoid "intellectualizing" too much; try to stay at a feeling level as much as you can.

   b. avoid absolutes. If someone tells you that "storytelling" is bad or "asking questions" is bad, forget these absolutes. Too much storytelling is bad. Too much question-asking is bad. Too much confrontation is bad. Too much kindness and reassurance are bad, too. Look for a nice balance and help steer the course of the group as if it were a great space ship which needed frequent mid-course corrections to properly get it to its destination.

   c. avoid withholding: the group will get nowhere if you deny others your reactions. Leaders and fellow members won't know what you are withholding; they won't know you very well if you do, and you'll feel alienated from the process and the group if you hold back too much.

8) Be aware of yourself. Are you talking too much, dominating too much, talking too little, being too much of one thing? Are you always in the role of helper? How are others seeing you? Seek feedback and try out novel behaviors.

Finally, if you have been in individual, family or group therapy before, or been in growth groups, you may have a great deal of experience. ... try to recapture your innocence; try not to fall into the role of healer-helper-therapist, but try, once again, to embrace opportunities for growth and find the person within, who is struggling with issues. Concentrate on "being a member".

As the group progresses and matures, your skills as a listener and helper, even some of your interventions, will be encouraged and will even come spontaneously to you, and we will all profit from them. Entering the group with an attitude of being an auxiliary, stand-by-therapist on-call does disservice to the growth of the group. Similarly, assuming that you are above personal concerns and that you are in a group with others who are less fortunate does a disservice to both you and the other members. For the 20 hours of group time, be a group member and let the opportunities to "lead" or help or try out some interventions present themselves. Don't compete with the leader or co-leader. It just inhibits the group and minimizes your personal learning in the group.

SUMMARY of Lab Group Information

The lab group (221) is part of the CPSY 219 class. ATTENDANCE IS REQUIRED

Although you must protect the privacy of members, the lab groups are not psychotherapy and do not have the confidentiality of psychotherapy. You must keep a JOURNAL (for use in CPSY 219).

Summary

Similar to human development in general, each group is both unique and shares universal process and stages. The authors use four stages of group process: preparation, transition, therapy (working), and termination.

The preparation (orientation) stage includes determination of group goals, population, logistics, and screening criteria. The logistics of the group will follow rationally and depend on the specific goals and population. Screening group members involves finding a therapeutic fit between member and group. Ego strength is identified as the most salient screening factor in the creation of a therapeutic group. Screening is both an inclusive and an exclusive process as the leaders attempt to bring together people who are similar enough to be able to empathize yet different enough to expand their repertoire of problem-solving behaviors.

CHAPTER 3

Group Process Phase II: Transition

It's not about *making* the horse drink. It's about giving the horse a salt lick on the way to the trough.

The predominant task of Phase II (transition) is to prepare the group members for treatment or intervention. It is natural for members to be fearful of new experiences and threats to the status quo in their lives. As much as they may want their lives to be different, they are expected to be resistant to change. The core function of the transition period is to make the upcoming treatment more palatable and user-friendly. During this group phase, members are encouraged to build trust and confidence in themselves and the other members, develop group cohesion, learn group norms, find their role in the group as it develops, reduce anxiety about personal introspection and revelation, and become a bit more experimental. Effective leaders facilitate this by allowing the natural group process to unfold and helping members understand, and come to grips with their internal feelings and certain inevitable dilemmas that emerge (i.e., Dies & Dies, 1993). During this period, the leaders must provide support and encouragement for the members' struggles and growth. They also help the group members learn how to focus on the here-and-now process in the group.

The early stages of group process have some therapeutic value, but their greatest impact is in the members learning the language, foci, ethics, and process of the group. These stages can be quite lengthy, taking several sessions, or quite brief, as with a group consisting of graduate students enrolled in a class focusing on group process. During this stage, members need to feel included and believe that the group will offer them something.

The transition period has often been described as dominated by struggle. Corey and Corey (1982) write,

> Before groups progress to a working stage, they typically go through a transitional phase. During this phase, groups are generally characterized by anxiety, defensiveness, resistance, the struggle for control, inter-member conflict, conflicts with or challenges to the leader, and various patterns of problem behaviors (p. 121).

McKenzie (1987) characterizes this period as one of rebellion and struggle for differentiation, emphasizing issues of control, dominance, and anger. Members question how well they fit in the group, whether the confidentiality is real and what will happen if they disagree with others.

The period can be frustrating, especially to novice group leaders. The frustration arises when leaders are impatient to get on with the business of therapy and behavior change. Some leaders also are very uncomfortable when the anxiety of members gets turned toward the leaders as challenges. Some writers are far more sanguine about the vagaries of this group phase. For example, Schutz (1973) focused primarily on inclusion and belonging and on finding one's place on the group hierarchy. Dies and Dies (1993) wrote of a natural unfolding in which members share what they have in common, building trust and then testing the leaders. Many authors (i.e., Yalom & Lescz, 2005) note the significance of developing cohesion during this phase.

According to Shapiro, Peltz, and Bernadett-Shapiro (1998), two specific major tests of leadership must take place:

1. discovering the limits of the leader's skill, emotional strength, and competence (the group's ceiling) and

2. becoming aware of matters beyond the group's abilities (the group's floor).

The extent to which these matters are managed and resolved will substantively determine the extent of work that can be addressed later in treatment phase of the group.

Leaders' roles during transition are to provide support and encouragement for members' struggles and growth. When leaders demonstrate comfort in the face of members' struggles and challenges and redirect attention to a here and now focus, members are more able to face more directly their challenges and fears of change. Shapiro (2010) argues that the extent to which the leadership passes these tests determines the extent of treatment possible later.

Early Observations

A perceptive group leader can glean a great deal from pregroup behavior. Do members linger outside the group room or come directly in? Do they speak to others socially or keep to themselves? Are they early, on time, or late? How have they dressed for the group? Where do they sit? Do they continue to chat after the group leader announces the commencement of the group?

No leader will make final or absolute judgments about group members based on such nonverbal behavior, but the group leader can develop hypotheses that can be subsequently tested as the group process unfolds. For example, the leader may make tentative assumptions about members, based on where they sit in the group. Typically, participants tend to sit next to people from whom they feel support, across from people to whom they're attracted, and at right angles to people who seem threatening. Such observations can help a group leader make early estimates of interpersonal reactivity and comfort between members.

If you make the heuristic assumption that people do not choose their seat accidentally, you can formulate hypotheses readily regarding members' feelings of affinity or expectations of support. These assumptions may be used later, in orchestrating dyadic interactions between members. For example, when Sarah described considerable anxiety about speaking in the group, the leader turned to Darrell who was sitting next to her and asked him whether he shared Sarah's anxiety. His statement that he was also anxious helped normalize Sarah's experience and reduce her anxiety to more manageable levels. The fact that they had chosen to sit in adjacent seats made the leader's choice of Darrell a safer bet for a supportive reply.

Darrell's actual answer in this case is not crucial for Sarah. Support could be generated even if Darrell had indicated no anxiety. The leader could then acknowledge the difference each of them was experiencing and throw the anxiety question to other group members. In this way, there is acknowledgment and support regardless of one's unique response to the situation.

Stage 5: Leader Specifies Ground Rules

Setting the Tone

The entire tone for the group may be set by the leader's introductory remarks. The manner in which the group leader presents herself and the ground rules will be the first cue members have for learning how to behave and talk in the group. One of the most critical factors to be determined is the level of anxiety that will be employed. It seems clear that as the level of ambiguity (or the lack of structure) increases, anxiety increases, and this affects the level of performance. Figure 3.1 illustrates the relationship of performance and anxiety.

Figure 3.1 The Relationship Between Performance and Anxiety

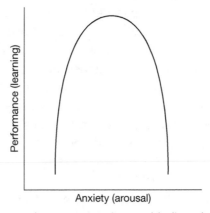

In most of American culture, anxiety is roughly linearly related to ambiguity. As can be seen in Figure 3.2, as ambiguity rises, so does anxiety. Conversely, when the opposite of ambiguity's (structure), increases, anxiety decreases commensurately.

Figure 3.2 A Rough Estimate of the Relationship of Ambiguity and Anxiety

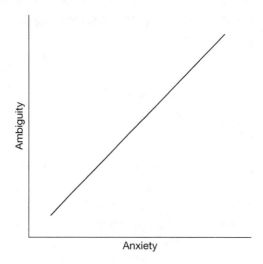

The group leader can effectively manage the level of anxiety in the group setting by maintaining control over the amount of structure present in the group at any one time. We know that optimal learning in any setting occurs when anxiety is at moderate levels. Therefore, a group leader can enhance the effectiveness of the group process by maintaining levels of structure that engender moderate levels of anxiety. When members of the group appear too anxious to be productive, the leader can add structure to bring the anxiety down to more productive levels. Conversely, when there is too little arousal in the group, the leader can reduce the amount of structure. This is most easily done by making it clear to members that they are to do something, but providing few cues as to what specifically is expected. In the vernacular, members can then get "psyched up" in the session.

Specifying Ground Rules

Each group and each group leader will have certain idiosyncratic rules and preferences about group participation. The specifics of such instructions seem less important than the level of structure they convey. Therapy groups, children's groups, and classroom groups generally have more restrictive and structured ground rules than do encounter, T-, and growth-oriented groups. Some representative ground rules are included in the sample introduction given below:

> **SUSAN (CO-LEADER):** Hello, my name is Susan. I'll be co-leading this group with Jerry (indicates co-leader). Our goal in this group is for open, honest communication between members. We will stress becoming aware of and expressing feelings because that's something we all share and understand. We will

be focusing a great deal on the "here and now," or what's going on within this group in the present, because we can all look at that much more effectively than we can a "there and then" memory. We will also work toward congruence in integrating thoughts and feelings.

Needless to say, "here-and-now" feelings about "there-and-then" events are very much grist for our group mill. Jerry, would you like to add anything?

JERRY (CO-LEADER 2): Thanks, Susan. I'd like to begin by underscoring what Susan has already said. I'd also like to bring up a few other ground rules. First and foremost is confidentiality— what is said in this group must remain within the group. If something really important happens to you in the group we encourage you to bring that back home to important people: spouses, family, friends, individual therapists, and others, but we ask you not to share anyone else's words or experience or to identify anyone else. Any questions, so far? (pauses) A second form of confidentiality involves the question of whether or not members of the group can meet outside of the group—say over coffee—and discuss group events. How do you feel about that?

If desired, discussion follows until a group decision is reached or it seems clear that one will not be reached at this time. Many leaders including Yalom (1990) presume that the members will inevitably talk outside of the group. They request that whatever conversations occur are subsequently shared with the group during sessions.

Some group leaders do not leave this up to the group. They set a rule that whatever is said in the group is sacrosanct and is not to be discussed outside of group, including among members.

JERRY: Another ground rule for this group has to do with the expectancies that people often bring into the group with them. Unlike popular magazine articles or other sensationalized accounts, there will be no nudity, sexual touching, or violence within this group. Smoking is not allowed and ask that you not eat or drink during the session. [These two rules are optional and clearly depend on leader's preferences.] Please also do not come to future sessions drunk, high, or stoned.

Let us add that if you do not wish to do something or talk about something, all you need say is "I don't want to do or talk about that," and we won't push you, nor will we allow the group to push you. However, if you say "I can't"—generally an avoidant reaction—we'll gently nudge you.

Are there any questions?

SUSAN: Two additional points. This is a place for you to bring up and discuss things that are bothering you. It's a safe place to take risks and talk about your real concerns.

Finally, you've probably noticed the video (audio) equipment in the room. These sessions will all be recorded.[1] The recordings will only be available to members and leaders in the group. Their purpose is to help us better understand and remember what went on in the session. The video of each session is only kept until the next session. Any questions, comments, issues?

Even in this short opening, several ground rules are established, and yet the level of ambiguity is still high. Briefly, these rules were initiated: first names used; leaders identified; co-leadership equality established; open, honest communication stated as goal; focus on feelings stated; expression of feelings stressed; here and now defined; taking one's experience home suggested; confidentiality identified as foremost group rule; no nudity, sexual touching, or violence; no smoking; no eating; and no one to attend while drunk, high, or stoned. In addition, members were cautioned to say they *won't* talk about something, not *can't* talk about it. They were told the group could discuss issues and make group decisions, and that they should bring up their own problems. Despite all this information, the group members' anxiety is likely to be somewhat high because they really do not specifically know what is expected of them personally.

A much less structured, less common in this century, yet still extant, opening for encounter groups leads to a very different level of anxiety: "Hello, my name is George and this is my co-leader, Pam. The only rules for this group are that there'll be no violence or sex. Who would like to begin?"

This minimal structure normally will produce greater levels of anxiety for group members. For that reason, such limited directions are deemed insufficient even for growth groups consisting of higher functioning members. Clients who can tolerate higher levels of tension are best served by some predictable structure and a focus of attention on the anxiety they do experience. It is essential that the level of structure and anxiety be group specific and balanced to produce maximal growth possible for the members.

---

1   Recording sessions with written permission is most common in training and growth groups and least common in therapy groups. It clearly depends on a leaders' preference as to whether any recording takes place and how the tapes are used.

In theme-centered and psychoeducational groups, ground rules are nec-essarily more specific. Often, handouts or reading assignments are provided for members' discussion. The leader may begin with a structured exercise that is related to the group theme or composition. For example, in a couples group, each couple may be asked to describe how they happened to get together. This is an endeavor that normally is not unique, focuses on happier days and is enjoyable to most couples. The leader may then follow with a suggestion that each couple present together discussions of what and when things changed. Vastly greater structure may also be employed as in the following two examples.

> **BOB (LEADER):** Hello, My name is Bob. I am a Gestalt therapist and this will be a Gestalt group. As I mentioned to you in the interview sessions, I like to work with one member at a time, individually. I use the "hot seat," with which many of you may be familiar. When any of you is ready, the hot seat is available. I will work intensively with you and your concerns, if I am able to do so at that time. While you have the hot seat, I ask that others refrain from commenting unless absolutely necessary.
>
> When you take the hot seat, I expect you to focus on the totality of your experience at the moment—what you are expe-riencing, feeling, thinking and so on. I will ask you to focus on many nonverbal aspects of your ongoing experience. Gestalt therapy works to find integration, a whole that is greater than the individual parts of experience. The goal here is for you to come to your senses as a way of fully living your life. I'll fill you in on more theory later. Let's begin the group now. Who would like to be the first to take the hot seat?"

In this example, members may well have great anxiety about being in the hot seat, but the rules are crystal clear. There is little anxiety for a member who determines that he will not be taking that special seat. The high level of structure gives members a sense that they have control over what will be expected of them, and an ability to limit the depths of the unknown. Behaviorally oriented psychoeducational groups also have a greater amount of structure:

> **SANDRA (CO-LEADER):** Hello. Welcome to the group. As we discussed in the pregroup sessions, each of you has come to the group wanting to become more confident in your rela-tionships. As you know, confidence is built slowly, success by success. This group will provide each of you the opportunity to

have successes in relationships and to learn how to continue a positive pattern in your relationships. Mark could you continue.

MARK (CO-LEADER): Thank you Sandra. First of all I want to tell you that I am a graduate of a group like this. I never believed I could lead a group, yet here I am. So if I could build my confidence, anybody can.

Each of our 12 sessions will have a theme and a series of exercises for all of us to practice and progressively work toward a more confident self. The more you can bring yourself to try new behaviors, the more feedback you can get and the more progress you will make. We will not embarrass you, nor will we criticize your attempts. You will be given honest feedback as to what works well and what could be improved. All of us will make practical suggestions to help you.

SANDRA: Two more things. Nobody will be forced to try anything. It's up to you how much you choose to do or how far you would like to go. We'll just help you and give you the opportunity to learn in a safe setting. Secondly, there will be homework that we will ask you to do each week. Some of it will be easy; some may be a little difficult. All of the homework will be similar to the practicing we do in the group.

To begin now, I'd like each of you to introduce yourself. Tell your name, describe what brought you to this group, and say what greater confidence will do for you. Turning to her right, she continued, "Would you be willing to begin? What is your name?"

This highly structured group introduction is geared for low ambiguity, low anxiety, and greater leader influence on process.

Regardless of the specific introduction, as the rules are given by the group leaders, the level of ambiguity and hence the level of anxiety are set. In this way, a basic tone for the group is determined: the less structure, the more ambiguity, the more anxiety, and the greatest amount of freedom for members. The leaders must balance security and freedom for members by considering the population, members' needs, and their ego strength.

Stage 6: Introductions

Each member of the group is asked to introduce himself or herself. The three most important components of this process are *entry, becoming accustomed to sharing information about oneself,* and *open communications of expectancies.*

Leaders frequently ask members to give their names, describe what they hope to gain from their group participation, and state what they fear might happen in the group. Such an introduction allows members to enter the group by participating verbally. Generally, providing this information is relatively nonthreatening, as members have already rehearsed it during the screening procedure and in their heads when thinking about the group. Talking on instruction, about fears and expectancies is also excellent basic training for later group participation. Hence, from the outset, the leader's expectation that members will discuss such things in the group is being made clear and members begin practicing.

One interesting phenomenon that occurs in many groups is that members are so busy rehearsing what they'll say when their own turn comes that they do not "hear" the names or introductions of other members who precede them. Often the first member to introduce himself learns the most about the other members. In pointing this out, the leader begins to establish the principle that the main topic for discussion is members' behavior within the group.

It is important to finish the whole round of introductions before any major issues are allowed to develop. Frequently, a group member has been thinking about a problem and waiting to share it for so long that simply giving his name is a cue for a rush of affect and a plea for assistance. The leader's task is to help everyone become at least nominally included in the group before any issues occur that could shut members out. One example of this, already cited, was that of Tina, the improperly screened member.

Another less bizarre example occurred in a training group led by two supervised student group leaders. One of the leaders introduced himself (the fifth person to do so), and a member who had also introduced himself began engaging the leader in a fairly intense manner—asking for help, advice, and so on. The leader mistakenly began to do therapy, and this piece of process lasted almost an hour of the 2-hour session.

During this time the group members who had not yet been introduced and the other co-leader maintained a watchful, anxious silence. Only after this "therapy" ended were they able to join the group. Not only did they report feeling like outsiders, but they also said they felt like latecomers to the group. Furthermore, the co-leader who was left out felt that her effectiveness as an equal co-leader had been permanently diminished. Her status as a leader was in fact lower than his for several sessions, even though she was the more experienced of the two.

Sometimes, not everyone is present during the initial introductions. This is obviously true in groups with open membership or an open membership period. Some groups employ an inner (active) circle and an outer (observer) circle. Other groups such as the advanced training groups led by Shapiro and Peltz have a rotation of two members operating video cameras at all times. It is essential that any originally unincluded members are provided an opportunity to introduce themselves as soon as they enter the inner group circle. In the training groups with the video camera operators, the leaders ask that they leave their camera in their turn and partake of the introductions along with the other members.

Stage 7: The Initial (Short) Silence

After introductions have been completed, members typically turn to the leader with expectancies that he or she will provide some structure. Depending on the group population and goals, the leaders may establish a particular agenda. For example, in a group of individuals suffering from severe anxiety or phobias, she may begin by asking people to focus on current anxiety in the group: "We are all here to help reduce anxiety, so let's begin by going around the room and putting your current anxiety on a scale from 1 to 10 with 10 being the highest."

Once members do this, she may ask them each in turn what might reduce the scaled score one notch and what would likely increase it by one notch. By providing this structure, even though it focuses directly on the experience of anxiety, most group members will notice that their anxiety in the group becomes slightly more moderate.

In all groups, whether or not there is a theme or common need, the leaders usually titrate the level of structure to the level of anxiety present. Some anxiety facilitates movement and growth. Too much anxiety will be ineffective.

Most often, when the members turn toward the leaders with anticipation that they will provide some structure, the leaders look back at the members. When the leaders do not fulfil the members' expectations, anxiety tends to increase and a short silence ensues. This silence lasts typically less than two minutes.

Stage 8: Short Silence Is Broken

For leader-centered groups, in which responsibility for change rests with the group leaders, the silence will probably be ended by a leader suggestion for some type of group activity. This may be a structured exercise, reflection on the group theme, some type of warm-up technique, or a request for an agenda.

Most counseling, therapy, and growth groups are member-centered and process-oriented. In these groups, it is important to impress upon members that they are responsible for their personal changes. The leader will normally refrain from ending the short silence as a way of underscoring that this group is designed for experiential learning by members. In member-centered groups, the short silence typically is ended by one or more members in one of the following ways:

1. Request for information.
2. Demand for leader structure.
3. Expression of frustration or discomfort.
4. Nonverbal signs of anxiety.

In our culture, silence in a group setting that is not precipitated by a special request for it (e.g., "Let us pray") or by particular situational demands (e.g., library, funeral parlor) tends to be anxiety provoking. The ending of this short silence appears to be an attempt to eliminate this increasing anxiety.

It is important to note that for novice group leaders, whose anxiety about leading the group is often high at this point, this short silence can seem subjectively like it lasted only microseconds or was hours long. The biggest temptation is to deal with one's own anxiety by adding external structure with a group exercise or internally by quietly meditating. Far more fruitful is the ability to observe what is happening in the group.

Request for Information

Because the silence is ended as a way of reducing the anxiety provoked by its existence, the manner of its termination often appears less than rational. Requests for information can run the gamut from "Tell me what to do now" to "What do you think of the situation in the Middle East?" to "Can the Giants catch the Dodgers this year?" One fascinating instance occurred in a group led by a woman therapist whose husband was a locally famous therapist and whose father-in-law was an internationally known author. The request for information proceeded as follows:

> MEMBER 1: You said you last name was _____? Was your husband in the paper last week?
>
> **THERAPIST:** Uh, huh.
>
> MEMBER 2: Are you related to _____ (father-in-law)? Oh, wow. I've read a lot of his stuff.
>
> MEMBER 3: Me too, he's brilliant.
>
> MEMBER 4: Well, his philosophies are intriguing from a Western point of view, but hardly complete when considering Eastern approaches.

This request for information served the function of reducing the anxiety and distracting the group from its primary *here-and-now* focus and attendant anxiety. Because such *there-and-then* discussions are unlikely to be fruitful in the long term, the leader needs to be careful not to encourage their continuance. However, the therapist is able to garner valuable diagnostic information about members' styles of responding and the methods each uses to manage anxiety, even from this brief, early episode.

In groups where there is an out-of-group assignment such as journal keeping or assigned homework, the request for information usually centers around the extra group task. Some typical examples are the following:

- "In this journal do we have to remember everything in the group? Wouldn't it be better if we took notes during the meetings?"
- "Do we have to turn in the journals? The whole journal or parts? Do you want it typed? Do we just email it to you or bring it in?"
- "Are you both on staff here?"
- "What happens if we can't get all the assignments in on time?"

Demands for Leader Structure

Sometimes members' anxiety is expressed in apparently discrepant demands for leader action. Frequently they consist of such comments as follows:

- "OK, you're the leader, what do we do now?"
- "Do you have any starting (ice-breaking) exercises? I hear that's a good way to start a group."
- "What are you going to do now?"
- "Well are we just going to sit here?"

One impressive example of this occurred during a human relations training workshop with administrators from a community college. The actual length of this short silence was approximately *90 seconds* and was broken with the following:

- Member 1: "Look, I just can't stay here all day. I've got work to do."
- Member 2: "Time is money."
- Member 3: "What's the matter with you?"
- Member 4: "Look if *you* don't want to *teach this class*, one of us can."

Each of these statements, directed at the leader, was uttered with increased intensity. Incredible as it may seem, 4 years after this 90-second silence, one group member recalled his experience of the entire group as the "agony of nobody never saying nothing."

Expression of Frustration or Discomfort

In some groups the anxiety is expressed directly as in the following:

- "I just can't stand it when it's so quiet."
- "Somebody say something!"
- "I'm starting to sweat and my heart is thumping and I feel really shaky and hot."

Nonverbal Expressions of Anxiety

Some of the common ways that members express anxiety without words include tremulous shaking, constant shifting of positions, leg jiggling, crying, giggling, dropping or spilling something, whispering something to another member, and humming or whistling.

It is important for the leader to recognize the discomfort and use that recognition to begin orienting members to focus on their internal experience. There is no formula for this. Each leader and theory has a different way of reflecting back to the clients what is being heard. Here is one leader turning the focus back to the group: "It seems like not knowing what we should be doing is uncomfortable. I wonder what is disquieting about this situation."

It is also a time for leaders to be making mental notes about the members' different abilities to contain and use their anxiety, and to notice coalitions, support, and antagonisms already present in the group. *It is not a time to make the group safer by "fixing the anxiety problem"* (Bernard & McKenzie, 1994).

Stage 9: Discussion of There-and-Then Topic

Once the silence is broken, members of the group will frequently pick up any topic for discussion with a there-and-then (rather than here-and-now) focus. This discussion of some external communality seems to be

1. an effort to stimulate group activity,
2. a hedge against another (painful) silence, and
3. an early attempt to establish a sense of belonging in the group.

The topic is frequently interesting and most often safe, objective, and something the majority of members can share. This is especially true for groups who have out-of-group activities in common and, of course, natural groups.

This there-and-then discussion of apparently irrelevant topics demarcates a time that is both difficult and rich for therapists. During these conversations it is imperative that the group leader *not* become involved in the *content* of the discussion. No matter how interesting the topic, the leaders' task at this juncture is primarily diagnostic. The therapist may make a few *process* comments during this stage, but by far the most important task for the group leader is to observe the group members developing their "pecking order" and establishing their various roles in the group.

The best way for the leader to facilitate the group is by making process comments. In one 2017 group for example, the members were heatedly discussing the Trump presidency. When asked for her opinion, the leader intervened by commenting, "This group has found a topic that includes most members and is apparently safe at this time."

Another approach is to simply describe what has been occurring in more objective terms. Thus rather than getting involved in the content, the leader indicates that the most interesting topic for exploration is what is occurring in the room, without indicating her or his own perspectives: "I am aware that Paul and Shana have very strong negative feelings. Robbie seems to have mixed feelings and others have not yet expressed an opinion."

If the leader does not get embroiled in the content of the there-and-then topic and hence does not keep it alive, this conversation will die a natural death.

Stage 10: Natural Death of Discussion

After a time, members begin to drop out of the there-and-then discussion. Perhaps boredom, perhaps by hearing the process comments of the leader, or perhaps the anxiety is lowered enough to facilitate movement to less safe (more here-and-now) topics. In any case, the discussion pales and finally terminates. In some groups of highly anxious, highly verbal people, the group therapist may have to be gently directive in terminating this discussion, especially if group time is limited. Normally, leader references to group process will be sufficient to encourage the demise of this discussion.

Stage 11: The Long Silence

With the death of the there-and-then discussion, a longer period of silence often commences. Members now have some sense of what they are not supposed to discuss, but they are unclear regarding the kind of work that is possible in this group. The silence can last from 30 seconds to a few minutes to (in rare cases) more than an hour, depending on the leaders' orientation, theory, personal tolerance for ambiguity, and the level of members' ego strength. The period is characterized by nervous fidgeting, lack of eye contact, avoidance of physical contact, maintenance of social distance, and increasing anxiety.

Some group leaders will break this silence as certain optimal levels of anxiety are attained. They may, for example, comment at the group level by giving voice to the anxiety present in the room, or they may focus on an individual member or piece of process. Others will rely on group members to end the long silence. Some leaders argue that if the therapist ends the silence, group members will learn to rely on her or him to continue to do so in the future. This is a responsibility they prefer to leave with group members. These leaders are most likely to hold to that standard in long-term depth-oriented groups, groups with experienced members or mental health professionals, or high-level growth groups. They may take the time of the silence to observe the members' nonverbal behaviors for later use in the therapy phase of the group process.

By contrast, leaders of groups with completely inexperienced group members, groups with severe time limitations, or themes that are not benefitted by the silence find it best to terminate the silence as a way to keep the anxiety from becoming dysfunctionally high. They then help the group focus on the anxiety that such silence arouses, and help members to increase their self-observation.

In the short-term groups mandated by managed care coverage, the silence may seem to leaders as an inordinately slow or obtuse way to get members to learn how to focus internally and be more fully present. Many leaders in such groups will terminate the silence by requesting that a particular member refocus on a personal matter, or to ask the group members in general to consider how they would like to attain their stated goals in the group. One leader of theme-centered groups often asks how the current silence fits with the theme.

Why Silence?

The use of silence and ambiguity in a group setting has been one of the most misunderstood and misused aspects of group treatment. Clearly, it may have quite wide-ranging results. To create a group in which members will gain optimally from each progressive group stage the leader must prepare the members for the next stage of the group process. However, to be effective, the leader must not do everything for the members of the group. Like a good parent, the leader's task is to let the members experiment and sometimes stumble in the learning process. However, it is always a good idea to take appropriate safety precautions to avoid having those under your care fall on their heads.

To be effective, the silence in a group needs to serve as a clear indication to members that each of them is responsible for their own anxiety and how they accommodate it. The leader wants to send a message that the members are capable and do not need to be bailed out. Normally, a well-timed silence gets that message across effectively and expeditiously. However, in a group in which members are not yet prepared to exercise some rudimentary responsibility for their own feelings, a lengthy silence may be both premature and detrimental.

What this means to the practitioner is that the silence is a valuable tool in the group. Like all tools it can be used effectively or ineffectively. To effect or proliferate a silence without a specific process or therapeutic goal in mind is inappropriate. In using ambiguity, leaders are advised to consider the members' sophistication, ego strength, readiness, timing of interventions, and leaders' tolerance.

Leader Anxiety. Because silence in a group setting is anxiety producing, it is imperative for group therapists to discover their personal tolerances for such anxiety and to work to increase their thresholds for silence. Lengthy silences can be very difficult for leaders to withstand and can have dramatic effects on members. Shapiro (1978) described the longest silence in his personal group leadership career:

> I was co-leading a one-day marathon group with _____.
> Since most of the group members knew me already, it was
> agreed that my co-leader would take the lead during the early
> phases of the group. ... The silence lasted for 46 minutes and
> 22 seconds (but who was counting?), punctuated only once by
> one member of the group remarking after 21 minutes, "I bought
> a Toyota yesterday." ... The laughter release was immense for
> most of the members and myself. (My co-leader took the oppor-
> tunity to slowly swing the toothpick in the lower right corner of
> his mouth all the way over to the lower left). ... After the entire si-
> lence, one woman began to discuss a very serious problem and
> the group really took off from there. ... There couldn't have been
> another 20-second silence for the duration of the 15 hours. ... It
> seemed almost as if nobody was going to risk another massive
> silence like the last one. ... In retrospect it was one of the most
> powerful groups I've ever been involved in. Most members used
> the experience to make decisions they wanted to make, and the
> transfer of training was immense. ... Sometimes I think a large
> part of the power of that group was the members' working on
> real problems out of fear of another silence occurring as painful
> as the first (p. 87).

Had Shapiro been doing the group alone or with another co-leader, he would
likely have terminated the silence at a point where he could be less anxious or
bored. The most important guideline for new group leaders is that your tolerance
for anxiety may be the best guide for your effectiveness. Sometimes, it is best
to structure for yourself to be most effective. Bottom line: no clients need an
overanxious counselor.

When Silence Doesn't Equal Anxiety. Silence is not always a generator
of anxiety. In almost every group, there are members who use the quiet to "center" themselves, rid themselves of daily stress and pressure, or just cherish the
moment of respite from a preschooler's or boss's ostensibly endless questions
or demands. These members may welcome the very silence that others find
painful and difficult. Discussions that break and process the silence may result in
members facing some of the intrinsic differences that exist in the group.

One Rule of Thumb. In deciding how long to maintain a silence, leaders must
first be aware of their personal level of psychological comfort with a given silence.
Once they are clear that the silence is not pushing their own personal limits of
tolerance, they would do well to monitor the members' nonverbal behavior. As
a general rule, it is unimportant to break a silence when the first member shows
anxiety by psychologically leaving the room. However, about the time that the
second or third member seems to be "spacing out" as a way to control his or her

level of anxiety, it is wise for a leader to intervene by asking an individual who is sitting adjacent to this member to describe what he is feeling. In a "singles" group of people in their 20s and 30s, the following interchange occurred:

After discussing the "bar and hook-up scene" for a lengthy time, the discussion drifted away into silence. In less than a minute, Mark had left his body in the room, but not his consciousness. A few minutes later, Sallie became more physically agitated and seemed to be getting ready to shut down as well. Sallie was sitting between Jim and Louise.

> **LARRY (Leader 1):** (Noticing Sallie's agitation) Jim, What's happening with you right now?
>
> JIM: I am really feeling anxious. I don't like this quiet.
>
> **LARRY:** So this is troubling for you. How about you Sallie?
>
> SALLIE: I am really anxious. I do not care for the silent treatment. It's the way my mother used to punish me. She would just ignore me. It's also what my old boyfriend did. He'd get icy cold and completely quiet and I was supposed to figure out what to do.

Sallie was brought back to the room by the leader's intervention with Jim. She was not singled out at a time when she was showing clear signs of agitation. She was very ready to talk about her anxiety once the silence was broken. She also provided some important information about her needs and issues in this group.

It is not important that the called upon member has a "right" answer. What might have occurred if the leader had addressed Louise instead of Jim?

> **LARRY (Leader 1):** (Noticing Sallie's agitation) Louise, What's happening with you right now?
>
> LOUISE: I am just feeling the peace and quiet. This is the first moment I've had to meditate and focus on myself. It's great.
>
> **LARRY:** So I've just managed to interrupt your moment of tranquility. Do others also need the time to come to quiescence? How is the silence for you, Sallie?
>
> SALLIE: I am really anxious. I hate silence. It's the way my mother used to punish me. She would just ignore me. It's also what my old boyfriend did. He'd get icy cold and completely quiet and I was supposed to figure out what to do.

Such an intervention has several advantages. It elicits information from several members (Jim, Sallie, Louise). It sets an expectation that the leader will ask members about their feelings in the here and now. It also gives Sallie an opening to talk about her fears without being singled out or put on a hot seat at a time when she is showing so much anxiety nonverbally.

Stage 12: Members' First Sortie

Whether the leader encourages a participant to speak or a member volunteers, one member will express himself or herself in an attempt to define his or her role in the group. The member can do this by the following:

1. Asking for group help in problem solving.
2. Asking for group attention.
3. Trying to win the affection of the group or of a particular member or leader.
4. Meeting some perceived group expectancies.
5. Obtaining leadership of the group.

It is axiomatic in systems theory (e.g., Haley, 1963) that each time members of the group speak, they are simultaneously conveying information and defining or redefining the relationships between themselves and other members of the group at that moment. In a recent group, Sandra talked about her feelings and then asked Fred to describe his reaction to what she said. In so doing, she was conveying information and asking a question. *She also redefined the relationship between herself and Fred* and perhaps other members of the group. In essence, she established that she had a right to share information about herself, that she had a right to ask questions of Fred and an expectation that he respond to what she had said. Fred's response, "I felt very sad when you were talking," gave her a content answer to her question and by its occurrence, conveyed his agreement to her assumptions about their relationship.

This concept seems quite applicable to the silence breaker in a group. Frequently the person who speaks first and thus terminates the long silence predisposes the other group members and leaders to perceive him or her in a particular way. For example, the person may be defined as the identified patient: "Well, I've got this big problem I need help with," or nonverbally, he or she may indicate a desire for group attention by crying, flirting, sighing, fainting, getting up and moving around, and so on. Of course, verbal expressions of almost any type will also call group attention to the speaker. In addition to requesting group help in solving a problem, a member might ask the group to share in other feelings he or she may be experiencing. A group member may express comfort or discomfort with the silence and look to other members for confirmation or support:

- "I really get uptight when it's so quiet."

- "I wish someone would say something."
- "Wow, this is the first relaxing moment I've had all day."
- "Is this what's supposed to happen?"

Such interactions can help determine a member's role in the group, gain attention, meet perceived expectancies, or win affection from the group or a particular member. Indeed, a moderate amount of problem sharing at this stage may win a member the role of "star" patient and potentially exempt him or her from subsequent pressures to work in greater depth in the treatment phase of the group.

Introduction to the Leadership Challenge

One common pattern following the silence breaking is an early form of what is commonly referred to as a *leadership challenge*. This event, which occurs almost universally in growth groups and frequently in therapy groups, often occurs at this point in the group process.

The leadership challenge is a crucial and mandatory component of group process. Until the group confronts the ability of the leader to withstand adversity and personal discomfort, members will have difficulty trusting the leaders' abilities to handle the members' serious personal dilemmas, problems, and concerns. A leader who acts defensively and ignores or attacks a member who issues a challenge is an unlikely source of support for members' most sensitive feelings.

If the challenge is to occur at this point in the group process, it is normally characterized by questions regarding the leader's competence, training, background, or methods regarding how the group may proceed:

- "Exactly how many groups have you actually led?" (Typically asked only of novice leaders.)
- "Are you a psychologist or a real doctor or what?"
- "How old are you?"
- "Well, if nothing is going to happen, why don't you (directed to the leader) suggest a technique or exercise? If you don't know any, I could suggest a few. … I hate wasting time like this, why don't we try … ?"

Another example, spoken angrily and forcefully, might be the following:
- "Okay, let's get this show on the road, obviously they (addressed to leaders) aren't going to do anything. Why don't we elect a chairman to bring up topics or something?"

In addition to being delivered at high volume, it may be expressed with very blue language including wide use of the "f-bomb." Unless the leader is prepared to deal with this, the group can become rooted at this stage for an excessive time. Leadership challenges as crucial tests are addressed later in this chapter.

If the leader does not succumb to the pressure to be the expected authority figure by instituting the requested action (exercise, explanation, etc.) and responds instead to the process extant in the group, other members may begin to respond to the silence-breaking member. An understanding begins to emerge that members will be responsible for their own growth and change.

A leader may at this point focus on the process of the individual member: "So you would like me to structure this situation by suggesting topics for discussion. Is there a particular topic that you would like to discuss?"

The focus may also be on the group: "John is expressing some discomfort at the silence. What are other people feeling?"

Note that it is usually preferable to ask *which* emotion is being experienced to help focus the members on their internal reactions. The use of the word *how* (are you feeling?) commonly elicits the automatic reaction, "Fine, how are you?" — much less fruitful therapeutically. Of course, the leader may decide to remain silent.

Our experience is that in the situation where a new group leader is asked how many groups has he or she done previously or their age, it is often useful to respond directly before looking for the members' motivation.

Kim, a 29-year-old MFT intern was co-leading a group in an agency with a more experienced, older Caucasian male. She is Korean American, petite, and looks young for her age. The following interaction occurred in her very first group.

> MEMBER: (Directed to Kim) You seem very young. Exactly how many groups have you done before?
>
> **KIM (LEADER):** Actually, this is my first group. Is that of concern for you?
>
> MEMBER: Well, I was hoping for someone with a lot more experience and maturity.
>
> **KIM:** Well, if there is something important I miss about you, please don't hesitate to let me know. Is there something you think I won't understand that you could say now?

Here, Kim, is validating the member's expressed concern without being caught in trying to defend or protect her own ego. In this way, the member can choose to discuss something about which he is concerned, or at least learn that his questions about her competence will not harm the group. She is modeling honesty and a willingness to engage.

The situation could have been made significantly worse if she had responded defensively, such as asserting, "I am old enough," or "I am well-trained to do this group." It would also have been a long-term negative if her more experienced co-leader had jumped in to protect her. Had he done that, he would be confirming the member's perception that she wasn't to be considered a co-leader.

Stage 13: Opening of the Discussion

If a more extensive leadership challenge is not instituted here, or if the members are relatively comfortable with the way the leader responds, the first member's personal disclosures will help encourage others to risk entering the group discussion.

As soon as the first member breaks the speaking barrier, other members also let their thoughts and reactions be heard. Sometimes, rather judgmental reactions ensue with other members agreeing with the statements of the first speaker or being critical. Occasionally, criticism for breaking the silence is leveled. In other groups, the attempt to win attention is rejected or the problem that has been brought up maybe viewed as inappropriate.

During all this discussion, the leader must not join in or take sides. His or her task is to use this interaction to train the group participants to begin to explore the process of their group. Ultimately, members will be responsible for instituting discussions and examining their internal processes that govern the way they interact.

Stage 14: Group Leader Focuses on Here-and-Now Process

While the entire interchange regarding the first speaker's communication unfolds, the leader must continually focus the group's attention on the ongoing process. Instead of joining in on the discussion of the presented issue, the leader-therapist must make statements that answer the unasked question: "What's going on between us, at this time, in this room?"

Two sample leaders' interactions at this point might be the following:

- "What I'm aware of is that Greg was saying he was dissatisfied with what was happening and requesting that the leaders put in an exercise. Then Joan and Marie expressed their anger with him for doing that and pointed out that they didn't want to do an exercise."

- "I saw Greg asking for help with his problem of inadvertently somehow getting people angry with him, and now it seems like Joan and Marie are angry with him. Seems like whatever you do on the outside to get people angry is happening right here. I wonder what's going on?"

Similar leader interactions, all focusing on the here and now, continue throughout this period of the group. In essence, the group members are being trained to scrutinize their behavior *as it occurs in real time*. Changes will be more likely once members receive feedback on the impact and consequences of this behavior from their fellow members and the leaders.

As the leader continues to make here-and-now process comments, members begin to open up or "unfreeze" some of their less threatening, but still important, concerns.

The Two Major Tests of Leadership

As the group begins to open up, the potential for greater depth and vulnerability increases. Before progressing to these more sensitive areas, members must develop greater trust for each other and especially for the leaders. One way to establish greater security is to be more fully aware of the potential limits in a situation.

In every group, two limits of the group leaders' skills must be ascertained: an estimate of their strengths (how much they can handle) and an estimate of the limitations (what is outside the group's capacity). Often the establishment of weaknesses come first. Please be aware that the order of these two tests is variable.

The First Leadership Challenge: Setting the Floor

A common challenge to the leader is the "unsolvable problem." This problem occurs in some form in every change-oriented group and in most task groups. It provides an opportunity for the group to experience the leader's work with a seemingly important yet relatively "safe" topic. After all, a leader's failure to help with a problem that is not solvable is ultimately not very threatening.

The test of the floor usually begins when one member begins to talk about a personal problem (frequently a marital or relationship problem) that occurs outside the group, yet presumably affects his interactions in the group as well. The presentation of the problem and accompanying indecision about what to do are lengthy, time-consuming, and frequently accompanied by sadness, crying, anger, frustration, or fearfulness. Often the problem area—marriage, separation, divorce, parenting, affairs, sexual inadequacies, aggression, substance abuse— is one that affects or interests many group members. A spirited discussion ensues, with the presenter discussing the problem and expressing feelings with increasing detail.

As the discussion continues, other group members attempt to help by giving advice, recommending alternative solutions, and offering guidance, assistance, and support. Frequently members will share their own similar experiences, expressing how they handled or mishandled similar situations in their own lives. This advice is freely offered and usually presented with caring, concern, and support for the individual, but it falls on seemingly deaf ears.

All Suggestions Fail to Resolve the Problem (the classic "yes, but." response). Despite the concern, support, and caring with which the advice is offered, it is all rejected. The problem is maintained in full force even in the face of a wealth of alternative suggestions. This is reflected by:

1. A failure to move on—the patient holds on to the problem and the discussion of it.

2. A lack of change in the expression of feelings. This member's affect remains the same, despite the input or ostensible catharsis.

3. Active rejection of or disagreement with the advice. The problem presenter refuses to accept that the problem could be solved.

The following vignette excerpted from a training group illustrates this process:

> MARTY: I wonder if it's okay to talk about this problem I'm having with my wife.
>
> **LEADERS:** (Nonverbal signal to go ahead.)
>
> MARTY: Well, I don't even know where to start—my marriage is really bad now. I don't know, it was, you know, good for a while, but now ... it's like I don't know anymore. ... seems like she's angry at me all the time and I'm angry at her all the time. ... just dread going home even. ... really feel guilty about that (nonverbal signs of sadness, frustration).
>
> VAL: How long has it been like this?
>
> MARTY: Almost 2 years.
>
> VAL: Have you done anything about it?
>
> MARTY: I feel like I'm at my wits' end ... like I've tried everything ... nothing seems to work.
>
> SUE: You know I went thru that for 6 years before I finally got a divorce. Have you thought about that?

MARTY: I think about it all the time, but then I think I just haven't tried hard enough. You know, I always believed that if I really worked at it, I could be married to anyone ...

MEL: That sounds self-defeating to me.

SUE: Yeah, when do you know you've tried enough? I went back and forth like that for years before I finally walked out one day—never to return.

MARTY: Well, you know I've thought about divorce, but I've just been brought up to think divorce is wrong ... failure.

FLO: You know, when George and I had problems like that, we had a baby—that really changed our lives for the better.

MEL: Whoa, that seems like it'd really compound the problem if things didn't get better.

MARTY: I always wanted kids, but now I'm afraid of being even more entrapped. Maybe I just ought to drop it, nothing seems to help.

VAL: What about counseling?

MARTY: She won't go ... she says that since I'm a counselor professionally ... me and the counselor would just gang up on her.

PETER: What about your minister, or a friend of the family that she trusts?

MARTY: That's a good idea, but she's really a loner, you know, I don't think she'd trust anyone.

SUE: It just seems like nothing will work ... really frustrating.

MARTY: Yeah, I feel like that too, but I keep hoping and believing there must be some way out of this mess.

SUE: Do you do anything together, maybe if you took up a hobby or a class together.

MARTY: You know, I thought that was it too. We took this aerobics class together, and I really got into it even though it was her suggestion. But then she began resenting my being better than her and dropped the course, so I dropped it too. I was only doing it to be with her.

This interaction continued in this vein for approximately 20 minutes.

PETER: (After a silence) I'm really frustrated.

GAIL (Leader 1): (Addressing a member who appears bored) Sandy, where are you?

SANDY: Bored and frustrated.

JOHN: Me too, I just feel guilty saying it, but there's no way to help him.

CLIFF (Leader 2): What I see happening here is Marty presenting a real problem, many people offering advice and the advice being rejected, and several people becoming frustrated and feeling helpless.

Leader Refers to Group Process. The leaders' role in this example was to focus on group interaction and describe the group process. If we keep in mind the importance of this piece of group process, the reasons for their behavior is clear. In terms of group process, the leaders must pass a test: They must demonstrate to the group the kinds of problems they cannot fix. The problem is unsolvable in this group context and serves the group by remaining so. If the leader gets involved in advice giving or doing therapy with the help-rejecting complainer, this stage can be maintained indefinitely.

It is important for the leader to wait until the group members become frustrated, bored, or angry before pointing out the help-rejecting nature of this interaction. Thus the leader's job at this stage is to be patient; then, at the optimal time, he or she is to describe the process as Cliff did in the example above: presentation of the problem, several offers of advice, a rejection of the advice, a lack of resolution, and an emergent group sense of frustration.

Leaders can also use this piece of group process to underscore the importance of congruence between verbal and nonverbal expression of the issue. Despite its evident seriousness, and personal nature, the "unsolvable" problem is often presented in a detached, summarized, analytical fashion. In one group, a member talked about his rejection by his parents and twin sister following his public coming out as gay. Although his feelings about this rejection would seem noteworthy, most of his presentation involved analysis of how they were victims of social pressures and prejudice. He said he felt it was an understandably defensive reaction on the part of his twin, since, he psychologized, "if he were really emotionally female, then she must be afraid of her own masculine tendencies."

HERB: … I think my sister is truly afraid of her own homosexuality.

WILL: What are you afraid of?

HERB: Nothing. I've already come out. … She's just headed for trouble unless she comes to grips with her inner psyche.

MARTHA: Maybe she doesn't have any homosexual feelings. I don't, and I don't think that makes me screwed up.

SALLIE: I've never had sexual attraction, for other women, but I sure am turned on by men (directed at the male co-leader … an issue that was to become dominant a short time later).

HERB: Well, I think if she looked deeper she'd see that she's repressed all those feelings.

MARTHA: So you think I've repressed mine also. (Herb was silent at this point, but he had an expression on his face that could have been translated, "If the shoe fits, wear it.")

ARLENE (Leader 1): Martha, what are you feeling now?

MARTHA: Well, he just basically called me a lesbian.

ARLENE: So, you're feeling …

MARTHA: I'm pissed at Herb. He as much said that everyone's either a "homo" and knows it or they're "homo" and repressed it.

ROGER (Leader 2): Herb, what do you hear Martha saying?

HERB: Oh, she's just uptight.

ROGER: What do you hear in her anger at you?

HERB: She's threatened and feeling scared of her inner tendencies.

ROGER: What are you feeling?

HERB: Oh, I know where she's at, I was there once too.

ROGER: What are you feeling?

HERB: Oh, well, what she's ea …

ROGER: WHAT ARE YOU FEELING?

HERB: I don't know. I'm pissed at you for jumping at me like this.

ROGER: Good. I am pressuring you and I'd be angry too if I was on the receiving end. What are you feeling toward Martha?

HERB: Mad, I hate words like "homo" and "queer".

ROGER She put you down.

HERB: Yeah.

ROGER: What's happening now?

HERB: I don't know.

ROGER: Focus on your body, what feelings come up?

HERB: Funny feeling in my stomach. …

ROGER: What emotion do you usually feel in your stomach?

HERB: When I'm afraid.

ROGER: Afraid of?

HERB: The group won't accept me, because I'm gay.

ROGER: Anyone in particular?

HERB: Joe … (indicating a young male in group).

JOE: Wow, that really scares me.

ARLENE: How so?

JOE: Yeah, I really don't know how to take that.

ARLENE: I can see you're shaking.

JOE: Well, I'd like to be close to Herb, but it really scares me to think of sexual …

ARLENE: Can you tell Herb what kind of feelings you're experiencing and what limits you have?

JOE: Yeah.

ARLENE: Go ahead.

Notice how both leaders consistently focus on the here-and-now group process and on feelings. The group has come a long way—from discussing Herb's twin sister and her purported problems of repression (outside of the group), to the impact of a relationship between two males when one has described himself as gay. It is too early in the group process for the group members to stay with this intense level of interaction for very long. However, such pieces of process occur regularly during this time period. The leaders' refocusing the problem—from speculation about someone who is outside of the group to members' feelings in the group room—provides the group with valuable information about what the leaders can and cannot do. It becomes more evident that the leaders and the group cannot do much about people who are not present unless they impact within-group interactions and they can work effectively with what occurs in the group per se.

The most important leader virtue during this time is patience. The leader can focus on the presenting individual and request feelings only after the discussion has progressed long enough for most members to have some feelings about the presenter and the problem.

Typically this is a long, drawn-out, difficult procedure, but the leader's interventions are designed to assist members in identifying, clarifying, and understanding their emotions as primary motivators of behavior. Leaders will ask members to describe and pay attention to their emotions as a way to keep a here-and-now focus in the group. Remember, this is not a time for treatment; the leaders job is to train the members to be maximally available for the treatment they will receive later in the group. There is tremendous pressure for group leaders in short-term groups to hurry through this stage and get to the "really important" treatment phase. However, pushing the members at this point usually will have a paradoxical effect. They will work more efficiently when they are more fully trusting of the group leadership and the other members and the group limits. It is best to encourage these types of tests to occur and to work with them, rather than to treat them as a barrier to some subsequent work presumed more important. The leadership test is the primary work at this stage.

Novice leaders often ask how to distinguish between unsolvable problems and more workable requests for assistance. In addition to clues in the content of the expressed concern, there are three parameters common to the "unsolvable" problem.

1. Normally, the problem occurs outside of the group and involves others who are not present.
2. It has a long history.
3. There is some discrepancy between the intensity of the problem and the amount of emotion displayed in the group.

Problems with content clues include requests for miraculous cures:

- In one group a woman tearfully indicated to the group that she wanted an amputated limb to be restored and healthy.
- A man wanted the group to convince his ex-wife to come back to him 8 years after their divorce.
- A 12-year-old wanted to have a deceased grandmother returned to life.
- A college sophomore wanted better food at the dormitory.
- A woman wanted the group to get help for her husband's alcoholism.

Discrepancies between expressed affect and content of the predicament are also frequently an obvious sign of the "unsolvable" problem.

- In an outpatient group, a woman spoke of the recent sudden death of her husband, as if she was describing his going to the corner to buy a loaf of bread.
- In a military group, a young airman spoke unemotionally about a "dear John" letter from his wife, while other men in the group were tearful at his description.
- A 50-year-old administrator talked about being "laid off" from a job for incompetence after 27 years with the same company, yet complained only about "age discrimination."
- A graduate student in a training group spoke with anger about her husband for not being more understanding about her infidelity.

Such detached discussions of issues that would seem traumatic are cues for the therapist to attend to group process or to focus on the missing *affective* components in the here-and-now.

The Second Leadership Challenge: Finding the Ceiling

The second challenge for leaders (although not necessarily in that order) represents the group's testing the leaders' strengths. During this leadership challenge, leaders will be pushed to set limits on members' behavior. By setting these limits, a leader provides structure, and consequently reduces anxiety in the group. Until the leaders pass a test demonstrating their ability to handle a difficult challenge, the members will be less trusting and treatment will be less effective.

The direct leadership challenge is a most threatening time for leaders; especially those who are novices in group treatment. For this reason, many leaders attempt to avoid or deny the challenges that do occur. Such avoidance will create fertile ground for additional challenges, decrease trust in the leaders' abilities to help members; and effectively place limits on potential growth in the treatment phase of the group. In some groups, failure to pass the "ceiling test" might mean the group stays in transition and never actually enters the treatment phase.

This leadership challenge may occur around the silences or at any time during the group. If it is resolved when it first occurs, it may not recur. However, many leaders report that some small leadership challenge may be part of every session as a test that the group remains a safe place for members' vulnerability. It is common for members trust to be most shaky just before the group enters into greater emotional depth. When this occurs, the members challenge the leader to reassure them by demonstrating that she or he can handle whatever psychological issue may be forthcoming.

Leadership challenges that occur during the latter stages of the transition phase of the group are often quite strong, especially when they are the last step before the group moves into the treatment phase. The strength of the challenge often symbolically represents the level of members' security needs. These challenges take two forms, each requiring slightly different responses:

1. Attacks on the group leader as an authority figure.
2. Personal or ad hominem attacks.

As a rule of thumb, leaders generally respond as authorities when they are challenged as authorities, and personally when the challenge is personal. This is mitigated, of course, by their personal values, abilities, and theory.

Challenges to Leader as Authority Figure. Prior to trusting any authority figure, individuals need to be reassured that the authority will use his or her power fairly and protectively. The group members will find ways of challenging a leader to prove that the group will be a safe place. The challenges to leaders' authority can come in myriad ways.

Questions about the leaders' experience, competency, age, training, background, or methods are commonplace, as are requests for the leaders to take an active role in setting an agenda for the meeting. By facing up to and dealing with the challenge, a leader shows she or he can handle attacks, demonstrates that expressions of negative feelings are not necessarily wrong or inappropriate, and shows that individuals will not be rejected for expressing their anger or fears. The leader should indicate, however, that members will be asked to express their fear directly rather than through the cover of anger.

When leaders' authority is challenged, they should respond from the position of authority. They should treat the challenge as resistance. They then should interpret, reflect, and encourage the expression, examination, and exploration of the intrapsychic basis of the member discontent and discomfort over the lack of customary leadership.

In response to a demand that the leader do something to give her direction, one member asserted, "A proper leader would have an agenda and a direction for us. How are we to possibly do it right without any plan or method?" The leader replied, "I understand that you would like me to be more directive. Tell me about your discomfort with the apparent lack of structure?" The response invited the member to begin to explore personal reactions and influences. The following interaction ensued:

> DEBBIE: Dammit. I asked you for direction and you just threw it back on me. I don't know what to do. That's why I politely asked you to do your job. You are the one getting paid for this aren't you?
>
> **KATE (LEADER):** I do understand that you would like me to structure this situation much more for you. What makes not knowing what's happening so much of concern?
>
> DEBBIE: Yes! It is important. I paid good money for this and now I have to do all my work and all yours also.
>
> **KATE:** Focus on your work. What would you like to have happen for you right now?
>
> DEBBIE: I don't know what I want. I just know that I'm upset.
>
> **KATE:** There's good reason for that upset. I am apparently not living up to your expectations, and you are quite upset because of a lack of direction. Where else in your life do you feel similarly?
>
> DEBBIE: I don't feel this way anywhere else. I keep things in control.
>
> **KATE:** That must take a lot of energy. So this is a unique situation for you.
>
> DEBBIE: Yes!
>
> **KATE:** What would happen if you experimented by seeing what Debbie is like without the structure?

> DEBBIE: I could do that by myself.
>
> **KATE:** Yes you probably could. Are you willing to try it now? Just take a moment to focus on what's inside you rather than what I am doing or not doing.

Defensive responses by the leader will normally lead to exacerbations of the test. For example, if Kate had responded to Debbie's challenge by taking it personally or responding at the same level, the challenge might have been intensified or gone underground to emerge in greater vehemence later. The next example demonstrates a defensive response:

> DEBBIE: Dammit. I asked you for direction and you just threw it back on me. I don't know what to do. That's why I politely asked you to do your job. You are the one getting paid for this aren't you?
>
> **KATE (LEADER):** I don't particularly like your tone. If you are prone to anger, you might want to explore your needs to deal with that and to project it onto authority figures.
>
> DEBBIE: I just want you to do your job. I don't want to sit around and waste time.
>
> KARL: Yeah. I agree with Debbie. Why don't you suggest some way that we can get this show on the road.
>
> **KATE:** Karl. Please wait. Now Debbie, where outside do you get so angry? Who are you really angry with? Is it all authority figures, perhaps someone from your past? Your parents?
>
> DEBBIE: No. It's just you. You're the "teacher" here. I thought you'd present something for us to work on. I don't have any issue with my parents.

Debbie might maintain her combative stance, or she might be defeated, but the group leader has so far informed the group that there is little maneuvering room here. In a sense, the "floor" and "ceiling" are quite close together. Future tests of leadership, perhaps more vehement ones, are inevitable if the group is to move into any realistic treatment.

Another way for leaders to handle the problem is the approach favored by Bernadett-Shapiro. Her method has the following three components:

Crystallizing the Resistance. Utilizing the catalyst[2] leadership role on an intrapsychic level, the leader focuses on and clarifies the expression of anger.

Working with the Anxiety. When the initial leadership challenge occurs, the anxiety level in the group rises significantly. As the leader remains in control in the face of the anger, the anxiety in the group begins to subside. At this juncture, the leader uses the environmental manipulator role (see Chapter 6) to decrease anxiety in the group by adding structure (requesting feelings and perceptions from others in the group). This normally elicits a combination of criticism and support for the leader.

Working Through. The leader then connects members at an interpersonal level to assist the group members discuss their different reactions with each other. The ability to contain these feelings and give the group an experience of safety in the face of negative emotions sets the ceiling in the group. Members now know how far they can go into exploring difficult emotional matters with this leader. They also begin to understand that they can agree to disagree without the occurrence of disasters. In this way, the original challenge to the leader evolves into a challenge the group may solve collaboratively.

Dr. Bernadett-Shapiro notes that this process may have to be repeated during a single session or over several sessions during the transition phase.

Personal Challenges to Leader. Sometimes the challenges are directed not toward the leader's authority as much as to the leaders' person. These questions attack a leaders' character more than his or her abilities as a leader. They may take many forms, but all seem to be related to some form of active transference.

- One man in a group accused the leader of doing the group only for the money, suggesting he had no interest in group members.

- In groups of professionals, frequently a member believes that he would be a better leader than the person actually leading the group.

- A woman accused a male group leader of rejecting her by the way he looked at her and accused him of refusing to acknowledge the obvious sexual attraction between them.

- In another group the same leader was criticized for looking at a woman in the group with what one member described as "bedroom eyes."

- In a mandatory group, leaders were verbally attacked for "forcing" inmates—of an institution into their group, against their will.

The leader's personal appearance or office may also be frequent targets.

---

2   In later chapters, five key roles of leadership will be defined and explicated. In addition to serving as group catalyst, leaders also are orchestrators, information disseminators, environmental manipulators, and participants.

- In one group, a leader was chastised for being overweight, and told that if he couldn't take care of his personal life he could never be helpful to a member.

- One female leader was asked repeatedly how old she was and then informed that she was too young to understand mature adults' problems.

- In one group of parents, the leader was repeatedly informed that having children's drawings on the wall was "unprofessional" in a setting for adults.

Leaders need to be able to respond to these challenges, and confront the challenger in a beneficial way. Leaders who are too sensitive about such personal matters should take care to work them through at least to the point that they can use the challenge therapeutically. In general, certain groups and group members seem able to ferret out a personal weakness with the unerring precision of a laser beam. These include clients who are manic (bipolar disorder), have borderline personalities, or who are adolescents.

How will a leader deal with a personal challenge? The general rule of thumb is to respond personally. However, the group reins need to be temporarily handed over if the leader is to work with the challenges most effectively. *Having someone to take over and guide the interaction when such situations arise is one of the primary advantages of having a co-leader in the group.* If there is a co-leader, as is strongly recommended in this text, a leader might either indicate nonverbally to the co-leader to take over, or to make a statement such as, "I want to respond to you personally, but it would be inappropriate to do so in the role of leader. Russ (indicating the co-leader) would you be willing to be in charge of the process while Debbie and I talk about these concerns?"

The challenged leader then will directly respond to the member in question. In one group for example, a member refused to do an exercise suggested by the leader, and indicated that she was refusing because she "felt" the leader was "not a real person." After temporarily stepping into the membership role, the leader began to talk directly with that member:

> **JOANN (LEADER):** What is it about me that seems so unreal to you?
>
> CHLOE: Everything about you. You just are always asking questions? "How are you feeling?", "Go with that!", "What does that remind you of?" Well, what are YOU feeling.
>
> **JOANN:** Well, Right now I'm feeling anxious in the face of your anger (directly expressing her here-and-now experience).

TONY (CO-LEADER): Cami, you seem surprised by JoAnn's answer. What's going on inside for you?

In a group of group therapists, the leader was angrily challenged by a member at the beginning of the second session:

BILL: You know I am just sick of this shit. You don't seem to realize who is in this group, and you're jerking us around with this elementary nonsense. Either get with the program or get out, I am sick and tired of wasting my time with an amateur. ...

MICHAEL (LEADER): (After glancing at the co-leader and indicating nonverbally that she should assume sole leadership for a while.) You really seem enraged at me. What am I doing that's bringing up such strong feelings?

BILL: Well that's the point you stupid asshole. You don't even know how inept you are. (He followed this with a vituperative outburst of barely contained rage, peppered with questions about the leader's parentage and making several derogatory Oedipal references in less of a literary than a street-language hyphenated format.)

MICHAEL: (In an angry voice) You know Bill, I am not willing to have you dump like this. If you have an issue with me let's deal with it if not, back off. I am really angry at what seems like an unprovoked attack on my character.

BILL: Unprovoked! You ask for it just by the way you sit there ... so uptight and arrogant.

PEGGY (CO-LEADER): Bill you seem absolutely enraged at Michael. What do you want from him at this time?

Although Bill continued his outpourings of feelings, dismissing Peggy as well, the rest of the group was able to view his behavior as unreasonable and came to the support of the leaders, confident that they were strong enough to stand up to even such an extraordinarily powerful challenge.

Much later in the group, during the treatment phase, the issue of Bill's anger at Michael reemerged. This time the group was prepared for it. They had sufficient trust in the leadership, and far less fear of conflict in general to be totally disconcerted by the attack. By then, the group had a history of resolving conflicts. At that time, Bill was able to describe his attraction for Peggy, and his inaccurate assumption that she and Michael were involved sexually. With the group's help, he was able to become aware of both his process of making assumptions and self-inciting internal process as well as a primitive (and self-defeating) method of aggressive confrontation.

However, at the time of the initial challenge neither of the co-leaders had any sense of what was going on inside Bill. They could only deal with the personal attack in a personal way. Michael, to whom the challenge was directed, responded initially by requesting that Bill focus on his anger, and subsequently with a direct expression of his own anger. Peggy appropriately maintained the leadership by orchestrating the conflict.

If there is no co-leader, the leader may ask a member to play the mediating role during the conflict temporarily. Although this is not optimal, one positive side effect is to indicate to the group that they have the resources in the membership to deal with difficult and unsettling interchanges. Secondly, the member who is chosen normally has quite an ego-building experience.

In some groups, no member could be expected to fill that bill. In such groups, the leader must play multiple roles simultaneously: supporting the challenging member's attack, dealing with and expressing her personal feelings at the time, interpreting what is going on for the group, and monitoring the other members.

Most group leaders have developed the skill to do this over time, or they focus solely on the principal goal of the leadership challenge test: giving the group members a sense of how much she can tolerate—providing a ceiling. Remember, leadership challenges are to be embraced rather than avoided! The successful resolution of leadership challenges allows the group to enter treatment successfully.

Two Final Points Regarding Leadership Challenges. Normally, the leadership is challenged in a way that is manageable. Challenges are usually by members of the same sex as the leader and at a level at which the leader is not out of her depth. The (unconscious) goal of the challenge is for the group to find leader strength so that they can establish a safety zone. It is not about defeating the leader. In fact, despite our considerable fears, the group will not allow the leader to be overthrown. Nobody would know what to expect in such a situation. It is simply not safe for the members to allow a revolution or a coup.

Stage 15: Debriefing the Leadership Tests: Focus on Feelings

After the leader has focused on the here-and-now feelings and identified the feelings of helplessness, anger, and frustration, group members begin to express a variety of emotions. They may express frustration about the situation, anxiety about talking, fear that the group really cannot help anyone, anger at the leader for not being a good therapist (as indicated by the inability to cure the problems of the help-rejecting complainer), fear at becoming a target of a member's or leader's anger, empathy with other members, boredom, and pressure to bring up their own problems. This emotional expression must be supported.

Stage 16: Leader Encourages the Expression of Emotion

No matter how negative the verbally expressed emotion may be for the leader, he or she must support its expression. Members must learn that the group is a safe place to say even difficult things. The leader's encouragement of the discussion of affect is crucial for the development of group trust (Rogers, 1969) and cohesion (Yalom, 1995, 2005)—two central components of the therapeutic outcome of the group process.

At this point the final major group norm is established: the open honest expression of feelings. This marks the end of Phase II. Members now know what it takes to be a group member. They still need to practice these skills and to try them on for comfort and suitability, but by this stage in the group process all the information as to what's expected of members is available. The group is now prepared to proceed to the business of change.

Transition to Treatment

The successful resolution of the two tests of leadership marshals in the treatment phase of the Group. At this point four group process norms are established: (1) a focus on here and now; (2) a focus on feelings; (3) an open expression of feelings (and personal thoughts); and (4) an avoidance of judgments of others in the group. These norms will occur within the range of trust determined by the leadership tests.

However, some additional transition may occur, especially if the tests come early, or after some particularly deep therapeutic or emotional work. Members will need to reassure themselves that the group remains a safe place. Smaller leadership challenges may occur throughout the group. Some groups seem to mark every progress in the group with an additional (albeit less intense) test of the group floor or ceiling. When members are particularly anxious, or when the membership includes individuals with "borderline" personality types or borderline defense structures, leadership challenges may occur even during termination.

The group may stray from a process orientation from time to time when the anxiety level rises in the room. Whenever these events occur, the leader's job is to refocus the group's attention on the process, to encourage them to focus on and to express their feelings.

How It's Supposed to Go Versus Real Life

Readers should recognize that each of the stages is depicted as if it occurs discretely in the actual group process. A text must present them this way for descriptive purposes. In the real-life group situation, however, the movement from stage to stage is less clear-cut. Often stages need to be repeated, and because a group is working on Stage 11 during a given session there is no guarantee that it will begin the next session at Stage 11 or 12. Indeed, it may regress to Stage 9 or 10. Furthermore, some members may persist through subsequent stages in displaying behaviors customary at earlier stages. Similar to other changes involving people, the distinctions between stages are often less discrete in an actual group than are the broader-based phases of group process.

Summary

The second stage of group process is the transition stage that normally occurs during the first one-third of a time-limited group. In this phase of the group process members learn to trust themselves, the leaders, and other members in the group. Members learn how to help one another by sharing their personal feelings and experiences with each other. Each member must preserve personal boundaries while participating in intrapsychic, interpersonal, and group level dialogue.

The transition stage requires the leader to actively embrace challenge and conflict within the group to demonstrate safety and boundaries for treatment. Successful negotiation of the two major tests of leadership—establishing the leader's skill and competence and recognizing that there are matters beyond the leaders abilities—results in cohesion and development of an environment that encourages members to confront intrapsychic and interpersonal change.

CHAPTER 4

Phase III: Treatment

To be effective, group leaders must have the therapeutic abilities and timing to help move members into useful insights and behavior change. Leaders' skillfulness during the treatment (Phase III) and termination (Phase IV) phases will determine whether the group members are to derive any lasting therapeutic benefit from the experience.

Much has been written about the "instant intimacy" of the here-and-now group. Such intimacy has certain therapeutic as well as growth value, but it is only the means to an end if the group is truly designed for relatively permanent life impact. The professional leader understands that group members must be prepared to learn, before they can learn. As described earlier, several hours of group time are spent to prime members for the therapy to follow. At the conclusion of the last chapter, we noted the members' readiness for the treatment available in group therapy once they have learned the group norms and have begun to operate within the purview of these norms. In short, once the group members are comfortable within the tested parameters and levels of trust of a group and are willing to be open to change in the here and now, they are prepared to learn how to make desired adjustments in their lives at home.

Learning in group therapy occurs just as it does in all other settings. It is essential for the group leader to provide an environment in which members may safely experiment with new behavior and learn by trial and error, receiving immediate feedback and encouragement for desired behaviors. Members must be allowed opportunities to gain insight and understanding and to experience vicarious learning through the behavior of others by identification and imitation. They must also be able to explore their personal expectations and test these under conditions in which they are assured of honest feedback. Often, confronting the discrepancies between what is expected and what actually occurs provides members with essential insight and motivation for change.

The Paradoxical Environment: Higher Intensity, Lower Danger

A curious aspect of the group environment is that it is both safer than other contexts and simultaneously more anxiety provoking. In a well-functioning group, the emotional intensity is often artificially high. Much of this intensity—and also much of the group members' learning—is a result of members' experimentation with new behaviors and thoughts in a situation that limits the consequences of such trial-and-error learning. For example, group members may experiment with expressing their fears without concern for the repercussions of such admissions. They may learn from other members' feedback how much expressed fear they can handle and how it can be expressed effectively.

This is quite different from other situations. In a work environment, for instance, direct expressions of any emotion, particularly fear, sadness, or anger, may well be unacceptable. The ramifications of such "emotional outbursts" could be severe. However, by becoming *aware* of the fear through the group and receiving feedback from other members, an individual might find an effective way to express or otherwise deal with his or her experienced affect in other settings.

The group is uniquely designed to allow people to have emotional experiences and to learn *during* the experience. The intensity created in group sessions actually creates opportunities for members to wrestle with difficult issues and interactions and to observe themselves while they are reacting.

In the description of the group process to follow, notice how group members participate in each other's problem solving and in giving and receiving reinforcement. Under these circumstances, learning is enhanced both in amount and in speed of acquisition. The group's reputation as a "psychological pressure cooker"—a place where behavior change can occur more rapidly than in normal social situations, with less loss of energy—is well earned.

Solvable Problems

Remember Marty, the "help-rejecting complainer" with the unsolvable problem with his wife in Phase II? Let's look at how Marty might deal with the same issue during the treatment phase of the group.

MARTY: I wonder if it'd be okay to talk about this problem I'm having with my wife.

LEADERS: (Nonverbal signal to go ahead.)

MARTY: Well, I feel really stuck. We are not getting along at all, and I am just not sure what I am doing to keep the conflict going. I'm afraid that I started a fight last weekend for no-good reason. It makes me worry a lot.

GAIL (CO-LEADER): What would lead you to do that?

MARTY: This feels embarrassing, but I think it was a time when we could have been close, and I got anxious.

VAL: That's really sad.

MARTY: Yeah, It's almost like I don't want it to work, but I really think I do.

VAL: Sometimes I think my husband picks fights with me when he's afraid of something or needs to be more in control.

SUE: I do that.

MARTY: You pick fights?

SUE: Sometimes, I know I'm being unreasonable, but I just press matters until it ends in a fight.

CLIFF (CO-LEADER): Marty, why do you think you picked this particular fight? What was going on?

MARTY: Well, it was Saturday night and we were free. The kids were off with my in-laws and we had planned a nice dinner. Then her sister called just as I was finishing the special meal I was preparing and Linda just talked to her for a long time. I just got more and more burned. I thought the meal would dry out and I just got more pissed off by the minute. When she got off the phone, I started in with provocative comments about her sister. I just kept ragging on her until she lost it. Blew the entire night.

CLIFF: So what made you wonder about your motives?

MARTY: Well, Linda didn't know that the meal was done and I didn't tell her. I just assumed she should know. I also knew she is very sensitive about her family and as much as she rags on them, I know I shouldn't.

CLIFF: So what advantage did the fight have for you? It sounds like the consequence of your actions was distance instead of closeness. Could that have been an unconscious goal?

MARTY: You know, I hate when you do that (smiling and looking down). That's what bugs me! This is very embarrassing. I even knew when I did it that I could ruin the evening. I think I was so afraid that I'd get my hopes up for a great romantic evening and sexual fulfillment for a change and if it didn't happen I'd feel rejected. So, I just made sure it wouldn't happen.

CLIFF: It was worse to take the risk of rejection than to arrange for the rejection under your own control.

MARTY: That sounds dumb, but true.

MEL: If I were Linda, I'd be really frustrated.

MARTY: She is. The thing is that she is really trying now. She has her stuff too and she's not that easy to live with at times, but just because she has an open gas tank doesn't mean I have to light matches and drop them around.

GAIL: Sue, You're having a strong reaction right now.

SUE: Well it's two things. I do the same thing to my boyfriend. I pick fights to test his loyalty and how much crap he'll put up with to make him prove he loves me.

GAIL: … and the second?

SUE: I was wondering if Marty had done that to me at the beginning of this session.

GAIL: Do you want to ask him?

SUE: Did you pick a fight with me about the directions because you wanted to push me away? I felt really pushed away.

MARTY: I did. I find you very attractive and I need to focus on my marriage now, so I tried to make you less appealing by making you wrong.

The leaders were then able to get Sue and Marty to work on the interaction in the group. Once they learned how to resolve such issues in better ways in the group, they were asked to refocus on the back home relationships.

This interaction is quite different in tone, trust, and openness than the earlier one. What are the differences and what makes it possible? For one thing, the group is not discussing Marty's wife's problems. She is not in the group. The therapy will be with Marty and his personal fears and ambivalence that interfere with his intimacy with his relationships. Marty is taking personal responsibility by focusing internally on behaviors and feelings that he may change. Secondly members of the group are talking about their own similarities and reactions, rather than trying to provide an obvious solution to a purported problem. They are joining with him rather than directing him. Third, everyone is talking about her or his own personal feelings. Fourth, the leaders' interactions are invitations for Marty and others to explore at increasingly deeper levels. Finally, the issue is brought into the group by focusing on a here-and-now interaction between Marty and Sue: an interaction that may be understood and resolved in the present. This is the ground for quick, true, and insightful problem solving.

Stage 17: Internal Focus

During the treatment phase members focus much more internally. Instead of looking for others to blame for their current difficulties, they focus more directly on their own responsibility and potential personal changes. Marty knows that his wife has some part in the marital problem, but here he is attending to the things over which he has some control—his own contribution.

Although this exploration is potentially embarrassing, he has more faith in his abilities to make changes because he has developed trust in the group. He shares "closet skeletons" with his fellow members and is willing to discuss matters that he will not talk about otherwise. More than anything else, members can begin to interact differently in this group phase, because they trust the leaders. The leaders' abilities are more proven; they have passed the tests of leadership; and the range of issues that are appropriate for the group to address are established.

Stage 18: Norms Are Solidified

Throughout the treatment phase of the group, members become involved in the expression and interchange of feelings about their concerns. They use the theoretical language system of the leaders more consistently and focus on the here-and-now process of the group. They expose more of their deeper feelings and experiment with them—with one another, and with the leaders. Increasingly, members abide by the group rules, eventually incorporating items into a common language and becoming, for the most part, unaware of the uniqueness of these forms of communication. An example of this type of communication is the following:

JANICE: Rob, I sense that something is bothering you.

ROB: What makes you say that?

JANICE: Well, I guess I'm picking up on your nonverbals.

ANDY: Yeah, I've noticed you kind of moving around a lot and looking uncomfortable, especially when Sally was talking.

LINDA (Leader 1): What are you experiencing, Rob?

ROB: Well, it's like everyone is ganging up on me and trying to get me on the hot seat.

LINDA: And you're feeling?

ROB: I'm not ready to be on the spot.

JANICE: You are uncomfortable about something, but you want to bring it up at your own speed.

ROB: Yeah, Is that okay? (Directed to male co-leader who has not yet spoken.)

KEVIN (Leader 2): It's okay with me for you to wait, but I do hope you'll feel free to share it when it's important to you.

ROB: Well there is something that I could bring up, but I don't know how to get started (looking toward Kevin).

KEVIN: And of course it's harder if someone else is calling you out and setting a potential timeline.

JANICE: You know Rob, I wasn't trying to pressure you so much as to say, I'm interested in what is going on for you.

KEVIN: What's that like to hear what Janice is saying?

ROB: I guess I know you aren't pressuring me and I do care that you are open to me. It's just hard to talk about something that I feel so shameful about …

(Silence for about a minute.)

ROB: So you know how in the bible it says how you are supposed to honor your father and mother? Well I've been living a lie with them about my dope use and my live-in girlfriend.

KEVIN: What part of that is most troubling and shameful?

ROB: I like to think of myself as someone with a lot of integrity. I don't feel like I am living that way now. I haven't mentioned this in the group before either; like I am hiding part of myself from important people.

Stage 19: Minority Members Identified; Inclusion Revisited

As the members grow closer, some clearly have not participated verbally in the group. They are identified by the other members or the leader and a request is made for their participation.

Leaders can check in with quiet members briefly each meeting, yet for more extensive verbal participation, most leaders allow the group members to recognize and invite participation from these minority members. The reasoning is that there is generally less threat in an invitation from fellow members than in a request from the leader. These heretofore nonparticipatory members are assumed to have remained on the fringe of the group because of their fears of being more involved. A request for participation by the leader could aggravate the fear and paradoxically make it more difficult for members to enter verbally. An important exception to this suggestion is related to the time left in the group. If time remaining is short, the leader must recognize these less verbal members and request their thoughts and feelings.

No matter who brings up the issue of less participation, a discussion about inclusion ensues. The majority group members discuss and analyze the "nonparticipation" of these minority members and the effects of such "nonparticipation" on them. A typical discussion follows:

> FRED: Hey, you know Rita, Gayle, and Herb haven't said anything in weeks. I wonder if you're bored or something.
>
> HERB: I'm not bored.
>
> SHEILA: I think it's cultural, you know, I mean … Rita and Gayle are Asian, like me and I think they tend to be more reserved (said smilingly and caringly at Rita and Gayle, who are sitting together).
>
> GAYLE: I think that's true, nobody in my family talks much. But Rita and I talk outside. I just don't have anything to say.
>
> FRED: Well, I think it's unfair, I unloaded all my vulnerability and you know me, but I just don't know you at all.
>
> KIM (Leader 1): Sounds like it's important for you to have them talk more.
>
> FRED: Yeah, right. I've talked about some pretty deep stuff and I don't know if I can trust them.
>
> M.J. (Leader 2): Tell them!
>
> FRED: I don't trust any of you (looking directly at Herb).

KIM: What would you like from Herb?

FRED: I want you (to Herb) to stop judging me and "dissing" me in your mind.

HERB: I don't know what "dissing" means, but I'm not judging you.

SANDRA: Well, I feel judged too, it's like I say something and you just look at me and I think it's disapproval.

M.J.: Herb, what are you feeling now?

This dialogue may continue for some time, but its course will be altered slightly.

Not only do Fred and Sandra's feelings deserve attention, but it is also necessary to consider the feelings of Herb, Gayle, and Rita. Hence the group leaders must deal with the following:

1. Inclusion of the three members.
2. The three members' fear of verbal participation.
3. Needs for approval expressed by at least two of the previously participating members.
4. Acceptance of alternative styles of communication.
5. Feelings of anger from Gayle and Rita at having been lumped into a "culturally different" category, instead of having their current silent behavior accepted.
6. Leaders' own feelings of inadequacy and desire for every member to have a positive experience in the group.

During this stage, an invitation is extended to the minority members to enter or choose to participate minimally. With guidance by the group leaders, the minority members will enter the group as verbal participants; negotiate with the group for their inclusion, albeit as quiet members; attack the members; withdraw from the group altogether; or remain nonverbal.

A member may enter the group verbally in a variety of ways. In one classic example of this, a woman member was asked why she was so quiet. She replied, "Nobody asked me anything." Another member immediately asked her, "Is there anything you'd like to share with us?" Her reply (Example 1) was the following:

> Well, yes, I have so much to share. I don't know where to start.
> … I guess the biggest thing is that I'm deathly afraid this group
> will end. … It's the most important thing in my life. You're the only
> people I've allowed myself to care for since my husband died
> nine months ago.

At this point her eyes became moist and she found it difficult to continue talking. With group support, she was at center stage in the group for almost an hour.

An example of negotiation occurred in the same group. Almost as soon as the previous piece of process was terminated, another "quiet" member said (Example 2):

> I also feel the group is important, but I feel very uncomfortable sharing things when they're happening. I've always been introverted. I'm not bored at all. I feel like I've been emotionally involved each minute … like when Joe was talking about the operation and losing his arm, I just put myself in his place and imagined the pain and fear and felt incomplete and ugly, and when Marie talked about the mess with her husband, I just knew I had to go home and talk to my husband. We had a good talk, but I don't know what's gonna happen to us. Oh, when Joanie talked about having an affair, I felt all the excitement and all the guilt. It's just hard for me to just open up, but I really feel a part of this group.

Both of these members found easy acceptance and described feeling more included.

If minority members choose to attack, several avenues are open: defensive protestations of how many things they did say; distraction techniques, such as "Well, I'd *really* like to know what's going on with Pete"; or confrontation. One extraordinary event occurred in a group of mental health professionals. A person who had a master's degree and 10 years' experience with counseling and casework responded to a request for his participation like this (Example 3):

> Damn right, I haven't said anything. I thought this was a high-level group and you people have all been acting like freaks or patients. Jesus, you all have problems and share things like feelings that are best kept to oneself. You're a bunch of sickies or fugitives from the sixties. I don't want to associate with you and surely wouldn't tell you a thing about me. I mean, how could you help me, I'm much healthier than all of you.

Then addressing one of the leaders, he continued:

> I'm really surprised at you for letting this go on. A competent leader wouldn't allow a member to be attacked like I have been. I'd leave now if I didn't have to show on my timesheet that I'd been here.

Shortly thereafter this individual withdrew from the group and ultimately from the mental health field. The group experience allowed him to feel so different from other counselors and therapists that he was able to get into a different and more appropriate profession.

Members may also simply state that they believe the request for their verbal participation is an excessive demand and indicate that they wish to withdraw; some may do so. Other members may not respond verbally to the request and may simply remain silent.

If the minority group members become verbal and do join in, as in the first example above, they are invariably accepted into full membership and receive a great deal of support from the other members. If, however, they reject the group and want to withdraw, the group may elect to allow them to, or request that they stay. If the member attacks (Example 3), the group may choose to fight, allow the person entry into the group, or ostracize the attacker, disallowing his inclusion. If the member negotiates (Example 2), the group will negotiate also. Group members may honor the individual's preference to stay quiet, but ask him to try to express more for the sake of other members, or make a deal that he need not talk unless asked a specific question, in which case he will try to respond verbally. In situations where the nonverbal member is *emotionally* engaged in the group, as in Example 2, the likelihood is high that he or she will be given total acceptance. However, if the nonverbal negotiating member is emotionally, as well as verbally, out of touch with the other group members, he or she may well be rejected or excluded.

No matter what decisions the group makes, the leaders must respond to the range of emotions released at this time. Such feelings as fear of abandonment, insecurity, belonging, loneliness, isolation, communion, paranoia, fear, and anger all emerge. Members must recognize and work on these feelings until they reach some understanding and resolution. It is important to explore with majority members, their personal needs to have others participate as they do. The issue may be less about the minority member's quiet, than a reflection of majority member's insecurity and the meaning they ascribe to others who do not agree with them.

Revisiting this inclusion issue is the last major stumbling block to the therapeutic group process. Once these conflicts are resolved, the group can turn its attention freely to any personal or interpersonal problem and work toward solutions.

Levels of Therapeutic Intervention

During the treatment phase of the group, the leaders encourage the continuation and deepening of the developing group norms. As group members become increasingly comfortable with the care from the group environment and learn the most effective ways to tap into those resources, the therapy expands and deepens. A major advantage of group treatment is that it allows for flexibility and multimodal pathways to the members' goals.

Normally throughout this period, the leaders intervene at three different levels of interaction: intrapsychic; dyadic/interpersonal; and group.

The Intrapsychic level. At the intrapsychic level, group counselors and therapists encourage members to focus more internally, to examine their unconscious motivation, personal patterns, emotions, and historical reactions. For example, the leader might say, "John, your anger right now seems familiar. What do you sense is the basis of that?" or "Where do you have this reaction outside of group?" The intrapsychic level will resemble individual treatment with an audience. Sometimes the fact that this exploration is witnessed makes it more potent.

The Dyadic/Interpersonal level. The leader highlights interactions and inter-relationships between members. She or he also connects the needs of some members with the resources available from others. This focus helps members explore their impact on others and observe their reactions to other members in the group. The leader might intervene by highlighting an interaction between two members, "John, would you tell Lisa what she is doing right now that is being helpful to you?" or "Jake, it probably sounds like Mary is reading your mail out loud." Often, this type of interaction resembles some of the work one would see in couples treatment or mediation.

The Group Level. At the group level, the leader asks questions of, or makes suggestions to, the group membership as a whole. She may, for example, check the general group mood or level of anxiety. For example, "John is saying that he's feeling upset and angry at the way the group is progressing. Where are the rest of you on that?"; "What are others feeling right now?"; or "Perhaps we could take a few moments and reflect on the group coming to an end in only three weeks."

Each level has obvious advantages and disadvantages. The intrapsychic offers the greatest depth of emotional processing and repair. However, it is limited by the relevance of one person's work to others in the group. Too much intrapsychic work in a group can lead to an atmosphere where a member "takes a ticket and waits for my turn."

Group-level work offers the greatest breadth and provides more simultaneous group work: every member works at the same level. It is limited because at the group level, depth is circumscribed by the member who is working at the most surface level. Uncovering of unconscious material is minimal.

Group-level comments or queries reinforce the identity and belonging of group members. This sense of connection enhances cohesion, providing fertile ground for the safety necessary for psychological growth.

The dyadic level allows for some members to work together at the same level, broadening the deeper work to more members, but the leader must keep the members connected and the depth and the generalization of such interactions are both moderate.

In a maximally effective group, leaders will employ all these levels of treatment. Their choices will be determined by the existing process, the group goals and the leaders' theoretical orientations. For example, when one member begins to out-pace the group depth, it is usually helpful to limit this member's sense of isolation by encouraging the other group members to try similar, personally appropriate explorations. If two members share certain concerns, it is usually of great value to have them explore together. In theme-oriented groups, personal gains are often underscored as examples of success, encouraging hope in other members who are still struggling. Instilling hope is a major factor in psychotherapeutic change (i.e., Frank, 1961).

Multiple Roles of Leadership

In addition to the levels of intervention, there are different roles that leaders play to enhance group development and effectiveness in the therapy. While members are learning and using the group norms, the leader will be a resource for information dissemination; at the same time, she must act as a catalyst, cajoling and igniting expressions of feelings. She may also be a major source of reinforcement and support for members as they express their here-and-now feelings. To some extent, the leader serves as a model of appropriate behaviors.

It is also the leader's job to orchestrate the group. In this role, the leader encourages and controls the relative give and take among members, attempt-ing to bring the needs of one member into coordination with the resources of other members. The multiple roles of leadership are extensively examined in Chapter 6.

Stage 20: Intensity Increases

As the group becomes more comfortable using the specialized language, ther-apeutic approach and topics of group discussion, members expose more and more of the normally hidden parts of their personalities and their more important personal concerns. In return, they receive acceptance, reactions, and caring from the leader and fellow members. In this way, growing group trust and cohesion empowers members to expose progressively deeper aspects of themselves. In groups where the goal is rapid behavior change and symptom amelioration, the intensity increases as members experiment with alternative behaviors and reactions with group support.

As the depth of the discussion increases, there is a contiguous increase in the frequency and intensity of expressed emotion. Members begin describing a multitude of life events and their reactions to them. Often such descriptions are heavily laden with affect. With the encouragement of the leader, and to some extent, the other members, individuals are urged to describe emotionally charged events in detail and to share their present feelings regarding these events. As members express and explore these feelings, intensity increases commensurately, with higher levels of arousal. Anger is expressed in a loud voice or yelling, hurt is accompanied with signs of sadness such as tears, and fear can be seen with trembling lips, shaking, and "frightened" glances.

For the most part, the leader and other group members will support the expressors in displaying their affect in this way. This support naturally engenders further similar expressions. During these emotional manifestations the leader must employ a multitude of therapeutic skills.

Note that as levels of emotional expression intensify, other group members may become frightened. It is imperative that the group leader support these members and give them permission to express their own anxiety while encouraging the continuing display of high levels of affect by those engaged in the action. Each group has limits for allowable levels of intensity. The group leader must be aware of these limits and keep the level of arousal within them. The leader wants to allow for enough anxiety for optimal learning, but not so much as to cause disruption of such learning. Thus, in some groups, dramatic displays of high levels of emotion are acceptable, whereas in other groups, a quieter, more subdued acknowledgment of shared feelings is appropriate to foster the same amounts of learning.

It is important to recognize the difference between "real" or existential anxiety and neurotic anxiety. Real anxiety involves facing the fears of the unknown, taking appropriate risks, facing up to life's limits, and so on. Clients are best served when therapists explore these anxieties with caring, support, and understanding. The group leaders can hold out an offer for members to try small experiments in the group.

By contrast, neurotic anxiety manifests itself by avoidance of the real concerns and operates internally to preserve the status quo, even if it is painful or deleterious to better functioning. Neurotic anxiety is often addressed best with mild confrontation, geared to the manner of the patient's style. Thus if a group member is cognitively oriented, the confrontation may be to challenge the thinking, before focusing on emotions. If he or she is emotionally oriented, questions about the level of affective pain that results from avoidance, addressed from an emotional perspective is more effective.

In a group of adults with social anxiety, the following occurred. Max, describing another recent failure on a dating site began with his concerns about finding a partner.

> MAX: I tried a new dating site last weekend. It's one where people just swipe right or left to indicate if they are interested in

you. So I swiped right (I'm interested) on about seven or eight ladies and none of them chose me.

CARMEN: That sounds depressing. I've never had much luck on those dating sites. I wondered if it was my picture or my name or what, but even when I do get a chance to have coffee with someone, it usually ends up empty. Actually, I can't seem to remember if you are supposed to swipe left or right.

MAX: Yeah. I am so sure that nobody would want me. I don't even post a picture; just an icon (neurotic anxiety—not risking being rejected for his appearance).

ELENA (Leader 1): I understand that not being chosen would be very painful and I know from past meetings that you say that you take rejection and envision it for the rest of your life.

MAX: Yeah. That's what I did on Sunday and Monday this week.

ELENA: I'm also aware that by not posting your actual picture, you make it much harder for someone to choose you.

SADIE: I don't know about others, but I'd be very hesitant to click yes if I didn't see a picture. It's like I'd be worried about what an unknown person might want from me. I mean. I don't try the "meet-a-mate.com" things often, because of some bad experiences, but I just want to see a picture for first impressions. A friend of mine once tried to meet someone with no picture and it was a teen, posing as a 30-something.

CARY: Besides, Max. I think you are reasonably good looking. It's not like your picture would be repulsive.

ELENA: (Turning it back to Max and trying to find the existential anxiety.) So Max, what are you hearing?

MAX: That I should have posted my picture.

ELENA: But if you had, you might get rejected for who you are instead of your method of presentation. What would it be like if you got rejected with your picture?

MAX: Worse, then there would be no hope.

ELENA: Then you'd be faced with loneliness, isolation, forever alone?

MAX: Yeah.

ELENA: So the risk is huge and the method of keeping it less is to be less effective on a dating site. I have a bigger question for you. What would happen if someone clicked that they did want to meet you? What would you have to face then?

MAX: I don't think I ever consider that option.

SADIE: Well I know for me that would be worse. If I got to know the person and then was dumped, it'd be like a real rejection, not just a virtual thing.

MARV (Leader 2): Sounds like you may have some experience with that.

The ensuing discussion in the group was around self-defeat as an option to actual loss and ultimately each person facing to some extent the risks of being selected and of being rejected.

When to Lower Emotional Intensity

So far, the discussion has concerned the typical group, where levels of affect must be increased. In certain treatment groups, however, the group leader must operate in diametrically opposite ways. In groups of "acting-out" patients, teenagers adjudged delinquent, or inmates in prisons for example, learning frequently can occur only if the level of affect is substantially decreased. In a group of violent prison inmates, the leader customarily spends several sessions teaching group members how to respond at lower levels of aggression. In one such group (Shapiro, 1978), each time the intensity of emotional expression began to increase, a mediating response was interposed. Members were encouraged and trained to discriminate between several levels of anger and to respond to them differently. Most important, they were instructed to consider the consequences of their actions before expressing these feelings physically, as opposed to their prior customary mode of acting spontaneously and suffering subsequent reactions. In this group of inmates, the level of affect displayed was controlled, just as it is in most groups. The major difference was that encouragement was given for lower levels of expression.

The important point is for the group leader to operate within meaningful levels of arousal. Levels of intensity that allow members to be uncomfortable with their own current functioning and open to learning new behaviors must be determined by the psychological characteristics of the membership, as well as leadership style and abilities. Only within these limits can successful treatment occur.

Stage 21: Leader Employs Therapeutic Skills

Each accomplished group therapist has a variety of skills and techniques designed to assist group members to change behaviors and attitudes. Whatever their theoretical background, psychotherapists have two aligned goals: insight and behavior change (in the order accommodated by their theories). Most therapeutic endeavors involve (1) discussion of problems and feelings, (2) reconstruction of the problems in some viable theoretical framework, (3) exploration of possible solutions, (4) attempts at new solutions or conflict resolution, (5) feedback on attempts, (6) individual reactions, (7) refinement, and (8) adjustments to back-home solutions. The therapists' tools in accomplishing these are predominantly verbal. Therapists listen, summarize, analyze, provide feedback, encourage commitments and contracts, offer suggestions, and provide support.

During this stage of the group, many individual therapy skills are utilized. Role playing, role reversals, psychodrama, focusing, sensory awareness exercises, systematic desensitization, guided fantasy, empty-chair conversations, and myriad related techniques may be employed, depending on the individual members' receptivity and the therapist's armamentarium of interventions. Individual, depth psychotherapy techniques are also employed, suggestions are made, information or analysis is provided; informal hypnotherapy or other one-to-one work is done in front of the group.

In all these therapeutic endeavors, relationship building is primary and *timing* is essential. As with every professional skill, sequence and timing play a major role. Many of us have watched a baseball player with a "picture-book' swing. When he swings a bat, it looks ideal. However, if he cannot apply this ideal swing at the precise moment, the ball crosses the plate, he is destined to a minor league career. Similar concerns for timing must be observed by therapists; the best-planned, most elaborate intervention can be valueless unless the members are ready to receive it.

One of the most common mistakes made by novice therapists is to verbalize an analysis or understanding of the group process prematurely. Group leaders are trained in theory and are focusing on group process, but most of the members are not; therefore, the leaders are likely to comprehend process much earlier than the members. If they go ahead and blurt out what they see, members will honestly not understand what the therapists are addressing and will reject it, or they will simply appear not to have heard it at all. The therapist must delay any interpretation and intervention until the group is emotionally and cognitively prepared to hear them. Those seemingly "divinely inspired" (off-the-wall) dramatic interpretations that seem to work so well in movies and videos about therapy are much less likely to be effective in a real-life group.

Whose Theory Is No. 1?

Virtually every major counseling and therapy theory has been used in, and adapted to, groups. Each has been successful with certain client populations. Two factors are germane in determining the success of any singular therapeutic approach:

1.   It must be appropriate for the group leader. Her theory must be consistent with her basic values and way of being in the world.

2. There must be a close match between the leaders' theory and the clients' "theories"[1]

Stage 22: Problem-solving Orientation Practiced

Whatever the theoretical orientation of the leader, the problem-solving stage is the prime time for members to work fruitfully on their concerns. They have resolved the issues of inclusion. They know how to belong and feel some ownership over the group. They have become accustomed to each other's personal styles, and the differences in the group as well as the commonalities. They have had to struggle together and face a great deal of adversity. As a result of their common struggle, they have become very close. They have shared more intimate parts of themselves than they normally do and hence have a deep sense of trust in the other members.

Within this context, problem solving in both intrapsychic and interpersonal realms can be accomplished effectively. At this time, real, present, meaningful concerns are shared and dealt with by the group. Because the level of interpersonal trust is so high, members do not reject one another's help, as they might have done earlier in the group; rather they seek it actively. Members frequently attempt to solve problems together and confront each other honestly and with caring. Interpersonal conflicts between members of the group are discussed with greater understanding of each person's position and concerns. Suggestions for change are encouraged and attempted with far less defensiveness than in other situations.

In the course of Stages 21 and 22 most members verbally participate in the group activity. These members will ask for and offer help and assistance. They will form close emotional ties with the other members and develop the levels of trust and cohesion that lead to a real sense of intimacy. Such intimacy enhances subsequent behavior change.

During this period, the group is truly a therapeutic milieu. If the leader has successfully negotiated the earlier tasks and stages, members are prepared to promote each other's growth. The group functions as a whole to help each member. One member may be confrontive; another supportive; yet another may offer an alternative frame of reference or share a similar experience. In this manner,

---

1   Describing clients' theories is unusual, but it is a crucial piece of understanding that is neglected by most writers in the psychological literature. It seems clear that clients, like therapists, have a point of view about what makes for change and how they will personally change. Clients who work best with behavior first are much more likely to get help in behavioral modes, whereas those who believe in understanding before action will respond far better to more analytic approaches. Creating a good match and somewhat coordinated values between therapists and patients maximizes the impact of the therapy (Shapiro, 2016b).

group members move comfortably between helper and client roles, becoming therapeutic for one another. The leader orchestrates this process and offers occasional interpretations and guidance.

In short, this is the stage of the group that members hoped for when they entered. Indeed, at this point in an effective encounter (growth) group, members through their own illuminative journey can sometimes contribute to the leaders' personal growth. This is also the stage of therapeutic group process that is so rudely cut off by termination.

A Note About Stages 21 and 22

To discuss Stages 21 and 22 as we have the other stages may be somewhat misleading. Although they represent only two points in the entire group process, they typically last longer than all the others. In an effective long-term group, fully 40% of the entire group time will be consumed during this part of the therapeutic phase.

In shorter term groups and (third-party payer) mandated brief groups, the work that takes place in these two stages is particularly significant. These groups are "results oriented" and centered on crisis solutions, focused behavior change and symptom amelioration. In such a group, approximately 20% to 30% of the total time may be dedicated to these two stages. Many leaders, in an ill-advised attempt to maximize gains in a short-term group will rush to get to these stages. Unfortunately, these stages are effective *only when the prior stages have successfully been completed*. Without surmounting the challenges of the prior stages, particularly the tests of leadership in the transition phase, the members will not be as successful in these true problem solving stages.

In short, there is a natural developmental process that must unfold. Without this group childhood and adolescence, there will not be a successful group adulthood.

Stage 23: Expression of Feelings About the Process and the Group

In the most effective groups, members actually do more than learn transferable skills. They also experience some "real time" learning as well. In these most successful groups, the members discuss their emotions, experiences, perceptions, and so on, as they are occurring in the groups. Thus, Tim is able to learn about himself as he is in the group as well as being able to reflect on the group process after he takes his group experience home. This is an exceptionally powerful form of learning.

TIM: ... so it just keeps on happening. As soon as I get really close to a woman and let my real self out, she finds another way of rejecting me.

DANNY: Yeah. It's like they tell you they want your true feelings, and then when you give them the real feelings, they think you're a baby who's asking for a mother.

ELYSA (LEADER): So the two of you can share this frustration with women.

TIM: I wish I could find just one woman who didn't play games all the time.

ELYSA: There are women in here. Do you feel them playing games?

TIM: Well. In here it's different. We're all here as people to help one another. It's different than dating.

KAREN: I'm not sure it's that different, Tim. I know I play some dating games, because I need to make the situation safer, but I am also reticent to tell you how I feel about you in here. I just stay quiet instead.

ELYSA: Are you offering that feedback now?

KAREN: If Tim wants it, I suppose I'd be willing.

ELYSA: Tim?

TIM: Okay.

KAREN: This may be unfair to you, but when you opened up before, you seemed so intense. It's like more than I can handle at one time. I'd like to get to know you a piece at a time, but not all at once.

ELYSA: So you want Tim to share his feelings, but when he does, he's too intense? Or is it that you only want certain feelings?

TIM: It's because I get nervous. When I start feeling vulnerable, I want to back off and shut up, but I also want her to like me. So I plunge ahead, against my own best judgment. And once I get going I can't seem to shut myself off. I keep waiting for some kind of reaction and the woman just shrinks back and then withdraws completely.

ELYSA: Would you be willing to tell Karen what you were feeling toward her right now?

TIM: (Hesitantly) I'm threatened by your rejection and I don't know how to get out of it. I know you haven't actually rejected me yet, but I fear it's coming. … To be completely truthful, I like you, and that's why the rejection would be worse.

KAREN: (Hesitantly) I find you attractive also, and I'm afraid of you rejecting me or your overrunning me.

ELYSA: How could he "overrun" you in here?

KAREN: By not giving me time to go at my speed. He seems to be either "on" or "off" full power. I am not that way. I need to go slow and in moderation.

ELYSA: Tim, what do you think of that feedback?

TIM: Karen, that is really helpful. I know I do that out of group as well. I would like to go at a speed with you that is mutually satisfactory. Would you be willing to let me know if I start to go too fast? I will also try to watch it, but the more feedback in here the better. … (Turning to Elysa) I am really feeling anxious now.

Elysa then turned to an intrapsychic mode from the dyadic to help him explore the anxiety in greater depth.

During this time, the work that Tim and Karen (and other group members, vicariously) are doing with each other is on the "front lines." Any changes in Tim's feelings and behavior here are assimilated and tested in the present. The learning is quite intense and often long-standing. This is the most unusual opportunity afforded by group counseling or therapy: to be able to try out novel behaviors, test limits, and get feedback in real time. The group serves as "cultural island"—a special milieu in which each of these participants has a right to expect feedback from several individuals and an opportunity to experiment without the repercussions likely in normal environments.

This stage and these phenomena are the goal of most group leaders, although a group does not have to reach this level of functioning to be successful. However, for those that do, the rewards are magnified. Even so, when the group does reach this stage, it probably will not sustain this level of interaction for long. For one thing, the anxiety that accompanies such authentic communication will grow and the group will regress periodically to earlier stages in reaction. In addition, this stage is always truncated by termination.

Summary

The treatment phase that occurs approximately at the halfway point in a time-limited group, should perhaps be thought of as the phase of concentrated learning.

Four group norms are established during the treatment phase: (1) a focus on here and now, (2) a focus on feelings, (3) an open expression of feelings and thoughts, and (4) an avoidance of judging others in the group. As the group moves to deeper levels of sharing, minority members (members who have not participated on par with other members) are identified. The decision and/or ability of these members to participate both verbally and nonverbally with feelings and cognitions often determines the level of intimacy the group is able to attain. Having learned in earlier stages the importance of sharing their own experiences and feelings, members of the group serve as psychological resources for each other during this period.

During the treatment phase the therapist is primarily a catalyst of intrapsychic learning and an orchestrator of interpersonal learning. Theoretically informed understanding and exploration of intrapsychic, interpersonal, and group level process is the backdrop for effectively timed interventions by the leader. In the optimally lead group, members are able to learn from their exploration and experimentation, from the experiences and perspective of other members, and from the theoretical understanding and explanation of the leader.

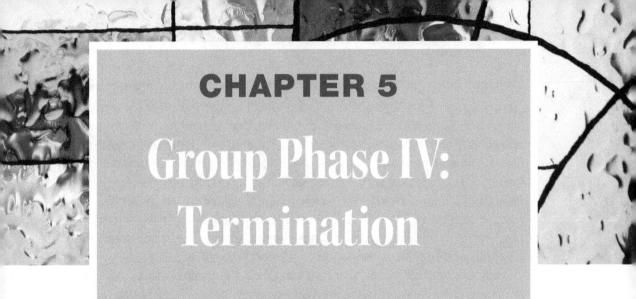

CHAPTER 5

Group Phase IV: Termination

Termination as an Unnatural Occurrence

Prior to Phase IV, entry into each succeeding stage was prompted by completion of significant processes of its predecessor. In closed brief treatment groups, stages of termination are determined by a different criterion. The length of the group was set before the group ever began, and the group must end at the appointed time. Very often, this timing seems intrusive, inconvenient, and clearly insensitive to the developmental stages of group process.

Termination of a group, is not simply an acknowledgment that the allotted time has ended. This phase of the group is as important for group success as screening, transition, or treatment. Yet as Gazda (1989) writes, "all too often group leaders neglect this phase of group work and termination of the group is abrupt and without much processing of termination issues" (p. 307). Toseland and Rivas (1984) note a variety of tasks associated with termination including, maintaining and generalizing change effects, promoting individual functioning of members, helping members with their feelings about ending the group (and other life endings), future planning, making referrals, and evaluation. Jacobs, Schimmel, Masson, and Harvill (2016) include reviewing and summarizing, assessing members' growth, finishing business, implementing change, providing feedback, handling good-byes, and planning for continuing problem resolution.

Naturally, much of this work occurs throughout the group sessions, however, termination is the time that members most poignantly confront their feelings about loss, ending of relationships, and future planning. It is also during termination that the crucial process of *transfer of training* must become paramount.

Transfer of Training

Of all the skills group leaders must possess, none are more important than those that assist members to transfer the group learning to their back-home situations. Meaningful evaluation of group outcome must be based on the clients' out-of-group lives. Any group that eschews the significance of the links between in-group and out-of-group experiences will be little more than a pastime. Training excellent members, whose greatest successes are limited to the group setting, is simply insufficient.

These situations are obviously less problematic in natural groups than in formed groups. In family counseling, couples groups, and groups formed of members from some existing work or community organization, the back-home environment is, to some extent, in the treatment group. Transfer of training occurs during group sessions and between sessions. The group goes home as a unit and continues the work that occurred in session. However, even in these natural groups, termination is a significant event and the leader must focus on skills and cognitions from the group sessions that will have enduring impact.

Some authors recommend a "plan of action" as a part of termination (i.e., Vander Kolk, 1985). Corey (1990) recommends a more cognitive behavioral orientation to this period, focusing on behaviors, goals and methods of evaluation. Kottler (1982) underscores the significance of effective transfer of training to decrease dependency on the group.

Obstacles to Effective Termination

Based on years of clinical observation, we believe that termination is unquestionably the part of group therapy that leaders do most poorly. There are several obvious reasons for this, including

1. the leaders' personal resistance to terminating,
2. the leaders' own needs for reassurance, and
3. a lack of training in closing.

Personal Resistance

"Hello" usually indicates the beginning of a relationship and of untapped potential. "Good bye" is the end. In every good-bye there is the symbol of the inevitable final parting. No wonder many of us have developed far better social skills for greeting than departing.[1] Although the ultimate role of all counselors and therapists is obsolescence, we share the difficulty in terminating relationships that have been emotionally intense and meaningful.

In a termination of a group, the leaders will often experience a sense of loss and personal sadness. It is not unusual for group leaders to be struck with a sense of personal loneliness after a group ends. As one group therapist journaled,

> I was looking forward to this group ending. It was a chance to have Wednesday evenings free again for a while. … A chance to care better for myself and take care of things that were hanging. … (yet) I felt my impending sense of loss the last 3 weeks and I found myself wanting more rather than less contact with a few members. Then the last night after they left and I was cleaning up the room, straightening the chairs. I heard them laughing outside the room as they walked together to the parking lot. … I confess, I peeked out the window and saw them hugging. I thought of my empty apartment, and wanted to go out there and join them for their post-group-beer and pizza. It really hurt that they were together and I was alone. It was all I could do to not re-join them. … I wonder if I had been avoiding closing the group for weeks. …"

---

1   It is interesting that cultures that see beginnings and endings more naturally as a part of existence use the same term for hello and good bye (e.g., the Hebrew word "shalom" also stands for "peace," and the Hawaiian term "aloha" also stands for "love").

Leaders may attempt to avoid their own fears of loss by unconsciously engaging in behaviors that prolong their role in their clients' lives. One method to avert such feelings is to ignore the impending termination of the group. Another is to create greater dependence on the group or leaders unconsciously by failing to properly refocus the members' attention to their out-of-group existence. This behavior commonly results when leaders demonstrate a lack of persistence when members underplay the significance of the impending termination. Some leaders may even postpone discussion about the group's ending until the final group meeting.

Reassurance

In the business of human services, evaluation of one's personal impact is problematic. Results are neither obvious nor immediate. Here are common questions group leaders might ask:

- When do I know if I have done enough?
- How can I be sure that I have done the best that I can for each member of the group?
- When is my job really complete?

Because long-term outcomes are rarely known by the end of a group, leaders must look for other criteria by which to judge the success of their work. Often the yardsticks that are used are internal ones. Such measures are subject to all of the personal doubts, concerns, and misperceptions that a counselor or therapist might have.

Unconscious needs for personal nurturance are often an important motivator for health care workers. Many of us in the helping professions are attracted to our fields because of personal experiences and needs. To the extent that we are unaware of these personal drives, we are susceptible to low self-esteem. Unsure of ourselves, we seek reassurance partially by providing for others. This can make us somewhat dependent on the success of our group members. Such unconscious needs for personal reassurance that we have been successful may make group termination seem like our own personal final exam. Avoidance of this test by procrastination is understandable, if deleterious.

A Lack of Training

This third point—lack of training—requires special attention. No one would respect a plumber who could clear a clogged drain but could not reconnect the pipes, a mechanic who could take an automobile engine apart but could not put it back together, or a surgeon who could open up a patient but could not close the wound: "The operation was a success but the patient died" is simply not acceptable. Yet we tolerate the analogous situation in group therapists.

In the first place, few graduate programs and predoctoral internships in the United States provide sufficient classwork and supervised practice to meet minimal criteria (Markus and King, 2003). Shapiro (2001) indicated that the modal number of required group therapy classes in clinical psychology, counseling psychology, and psychiatry resident programs nationally is zero. It is commonplace only in masters-level programs to offer a single class in groups. Many programs simply train students in individual and/or family therapy and expect them to learn group leadership by generalization. This may be akin to asking an orthopedic surgeon to do neural surgery and explains somewhat the pull for new graduates to focus more on psychoeducation than process groups. Summarizing extant group training programs, Brown (2010) called for uniform standards and establishment of basic competencies for group leaders.

Second, in most clinical training graduate programs, opening skills for all forms of therapy or counseling are stressed to the minimization of middle or closing stages. Students frequently complain that they finish their training before they learn how to engage in those most critical closing or transfer of training skills.[2] Of course, the quarter or semester system does not lend itself easily to continuing with cases from beginning to end. Professors can much more easily demonstrate opening and treatment techniques than termination. The only way to truly understand the full termination process is to follow a group (couple, family, or individual) through the entire course of treatment.

Practica and internship field placements are better suited to such training, but today's caseloads often preclude sufficient individual supervision. Indeed, for many agencies, the interns provide the bulk of the service to the clients. Professional staff, often cut to minimal levels, are relegated to administrative roles, fund raising, and supervision of a large group of such interns.

Termination Proper

Most therapists acknowledge that termination begins with the first session. Whitaker (1982), for example, speaking about family therapy, comments that his use of a clipboard and note taking at the very first session is a way of underscoring the boundary between the therapist and the patient that will not be crossed. This, he believes, allows the patients to begin the separation process even as they begin to attach. Similarly, behavior therapists remind us that transfer of training must be a primary focus of the treatment from the earliest contact and contract. Although group leaders disagree about the exact timing for leadership attention

---

2   Normally students from a behaviorally oriented program, or one in which behavioral techniques are readily available, are better schooled in the transfer of training and evaluation skills.

to termination, most agree that between one-third to one-fifth of the total group time will likely be spent in this phase.

Although regard for the members' use of group experiences for their home lives should be ongoing throughout a group, termination is the phase in which such concerns become salient. In addition, during this phase the leader must bring the group to conclusion and effect an appropriate parting.

Stage 24: Leader Announces Imminent End of Group Time

Termination officially begins when the leader verbally announces the number of hours left in the group. This initial announcement should be made when approximately 30% to 40% of the group time remains. The first announcement typically is made at the beginning of a session (or at an appropriate gap in marathon): "I think it's important for us to keep in mind that we only have three more sessions to go after tonight" or "Well we're more than halfway through our group time. It may be of value to think about issues that you may want to bring up in the remaining time."

In an unconscious acknowledgment to the difficulty of ending, this first announcement rarely has a noticeable effect on the group members; indeed, it seems to pass by almost virtually unheard. The second such announcement may have only a slightly greater impact. This second notice of the imminent termination is often accompanied by a request for members to think about any unfinished business.

Although the immediate impact of the leader's announcement is not readily visible, members may begin to respond to it after a short period of time. Normally, one member begins to talk about a concern with, or fear of, the group ending, and not having enough time to deal with all the problems he wishes to discuss. This allows the leader to encourage members to begin focusing on the termination process and the impact of loss, both within the group and upon their lives outside the group in days and years to come.

Stage 25: Invitation to Work

Once members begin to discuss their feelings about the group's ending, the leader invites them to consider and share any unfinished business or problems. Members who have heretofore been reticent to discuss their own concerns and who have spent most of their group time helping others often accept the leaders' invitation. This is commonly accompanied by some pressure from the other members.

Two forms of unfinished business are frequently discussed at this time: problems that members have in their outside-of-group lives, and problems between members of the group that are still unresolved. In a recent group, one member chose this time to talk about his living with his parents at age 35 and his fears that other members would have treated him differently throughout the group had they known earlier. In the same group, two of the women worked on their seemingly interminable competition with one another.

This stage, like many of the others can be quite time-consuming. It is imperative that the leader provide enough time for such issues to emerge and be addressed.

Stage 26: A Trust Boost

At this late stage of the group, trust among members would be expected to be high and it usually is. However, if members are to navigate through the straits of transfer of training and departure, the highest levels of trust and cohesion are beneficial.

This trust can be enhanced in several ways. Two of the most straightforward methods have worked best for us. The first is pointing out to the group that the last few hours will be hard on everyone, and each person will need a great deal of support. This statement is followed by a request that members be therapeutic for each other. In addition to reducing competition between members, this method encourages them to be altruistic and experience the ego building that accompanies helping others. Altruism is truly antithetical to low self-esteem.

A second straightforward technique asks members to share something new with the group: "Something that is important to you in your life, but which you've had no reason to bring up here as yet." The major advantages of this technique are that it allows members to present a fuller picture of themselves and helps them better coordinate their lives outside of the group with their behavior inside the group.

Sometimes a member will produce very surprising pieces of information. In addition to important clinical issues such as a history of abuse, negative personal matters, relationship problems, and so on, members also disclose aspects of their personality that have been absent in group interaction. One member in a group revealed that she was the local "Ronald McDonald" clown. A dour appearing fellow who worked as an engineer, talked about his notable sense of humor and avocation as a stand-up comedian. Another member talked of her years of service as a nun and of her struggles to stay with or to leave the order.

SARAH: I know I've been taking up the group's time talking about whether to leave the order. I so appreciate all of this support.

JOHN (Leader 1): You know, Sarah, I'm really glad that you're letting it in. If you're willing to go a little deeper into what you just said, I'm hearing two things and would like to share them with you (after a short pause he continues).

SARAH: I don't know what I could have said that would have such significance but sure, I'd like to know.

JOHN: Well it's subtle but I think it's important. You mentioned using up the group's time. Of course, you deserve to get all that you can in the time remaining. I'm just wondering if you're having some feelings about the group ending. I'm also aware of your appreciation of the support you're receiving. Would you be willing to take a minute to imagine the weeks to come and how you will take that support with you? Perhaps other members can take a minute for themselves to consider this as well.

No matter which trust- and cohesion-building methods are employed, the members need to be prepared to bring their group learning back home.

Stage 27: Transfer of Training

The competent group leader has consistently stressed that members make a connection between the group and their outside environments throughout the group sessions. Whenever members have dealt with any complex issue, the leaders have requested that they experiment with any group-engendered recommendations in their back-home environment. Consistent inferences are made to how group learning can be attempted in real-life situations. During this late group stage, however, the leaders must require each member to make much more direct connections between the group work and the home environment.

Each group member is requested to provide answers to these four questions:

1. What have you learned about yourself that is new in this group?
2. What else? (sometimes repeated several times)
3. What will you now do with this new knowledge?
4. How will you do it specifically?

Some typical answers have included the following content:

Well, I guess what I've learned is how I control other people by my sickness. ... it's hard and ... you know ... scary ... but I realize that I've been acting crazy for so long, I'm not sure I can act any other way. I guess I know that my wife likes it when I act this way—that also seems weird. What am I going to do? Well, I want to try to make it as a not crazy person. ... me and my wife need to go into therapy. I also need to stop screwing up on the job. I know when I'm gonna act crazy. ... I can just keep off my job on those days. It's okay 'cause it only happens on full and new moons—so two days a month sick leave. ... ha, ha (group joins in this joke). I think I can make it especially if we see Dr. _____.

The following familiar response came from a military officer:

You know what I've learned here? It's easy ... being right all the time isn't all it's cracked up to be. I've spent my whole life believing that if I was right everything would be so perfect, so I did it ... top of my class, service academy, two masters degrees ... beautiful wife. What I learned here is how lonely I am and what I'll do is be more damn human and less a damn computer. Maybe my kids will even stop viewing me as a mountain or something. I've never felt as good as I have in here ... it's like I've got a new lease on life. I plan to go home, get my wife, and take off to this place I know ... no, wait ... I'll just tell her I miss and love her and let her decide what we'll do (group applauds).

The therapist asks, *"What else?"*

Delegate! Delegate! Delegate! I've got to let the troops in my shop do more. They all rely on me, and that's fine for me, 'cause I do the job best. But it really doesn't do much for their initiative ... they really are good. I don't need to be the golden boy all the time.

Not all such reports are so positive, and sometimes much therapeutic work is necessary to help the members make the transfer. The following example is presented verbatim from a tape of a group of middle managers of a large engineering firm. The client, Patrick, is 42 years old and has been with the firm for almost 15 years. He is a good-looking, sturdy individual who could easily pass for a man in his early 30s. He has a friendly smile, but during the group many other members said that often when he smiled he looked angry.

GARY (Leader 1): Patrick, what have you learned new in the group?

PAT: Well, I guess I finally learned how to deal with problems openly and honestly.

GARY: How do you mean?

PAT: Well, when problems come up, I'm going to be careful to pay attention to my feelings now.

GARY: How will you do that?

PAT: Well, like I really need to talk to my boss.

GARY: For example?

PAT: Well, I think the shop could really run better with a few alterations.

JOE: Like what?

PAT: Well, lots of things, I don't know, just I want to talk to him, get some things off my chest.

CHANDRA (Leader 2): Pat, let's role play. Who here could play your boss?

PAT: Charley.

CHANDRA: Okay, Charley, will you?

CHARLEY: Sure.

GARY: Pat, set the stage. Where? When? How?

PAT: Oh, I don't know.

CHANDRA: Try!

PAT: Okay, Monday morning as soon as he comes in, I'm going to go up to his office and tell him I need to talk.

CHANDRA: Tell your boss! (Gesturing toward Charley).

PAT: Sam (that's his name), you know we've worked together for 12 years now and until this weekend I never admitted to myself how you've really fucked up this company. I mean I'm so pissed at you … you were really an asshole about that long-time customer.

This speech went on for almost 4 minutes. As soon as it terminated, Charley looked up and said, "Patrick, you're fired." Patrick looked as if he'd been punched in the stomach. He was speechless, hurt, and confused, but he admitted that Charley had played the boss's role accurately. He kept saying how different it was in the group.

The role playing and rehearsal that followed actually took almost 70 minutes. During this time Patrick and Charley did 11 "takes" of the role playing until Patrick had a solution that the members agreed would work. The final decision was for Patrick to see his boss over their regular coffee later in the week and talk about his ideas for changes, without criticizing or calling Sam's parentage into question. We can add that this solution worked so well that Patrick is now Sam's partner in their own spin-off business. Had the group leader not pressed Patrick to reveal and try out his plan, the result could have been a disaster.

So it is with all groups. Unless transfer of training is carefully and seriously administered, much of the total effectiveness of the group will be mitigated. Transfer thus is of great import in augmenting the positive effects in the group and quite significantly, in preventing casualties.

In some groups, a member may bring up a significant issue so late in the group that processing them is impossible. It is conceivable that only the pressure of termination may lead to the disclosure or conversely, that bringing it up with so little time remaining indicates the member's ambivalence and resistance to dealing with the issue and with the group ending.

Leaders need to tread the thin line between being sensitive to the person, the enormity of his or her concerns and keeping to the timetable. It can be difficult setting limits about what aspects of the issue are possible to address given time limitations. Members may avoid closure and ask to extend the group time. Usually, members and the group as a whole can be guided toward closure, using the resistance to ending as a vehicle to a soft landing, rather than attempting to enforce compliance.

The following is a transcript from a group of adults dealing with social anxiety:

> Connie: I have something I want to tell everyone that I've been holding back. (Looking to the leaders for assent. When the leader nodded she continued.) I am starting radiation right after the group ends. They found a tumor in my head, but not my brain.

Several members of the group made audible gasps and the dialogue continued.

> **MARK (Leader 1):** My goodness, Connie, that sounds very scary.
>
> CONNIE: I guess it is. The docs said I probably won't need chemo and as long as it doesn't grow and impact my brain, I won't need surgery.
>
> MELANIE: I am so sorry that you are going to go through all this. I had in situ breast cancer when I was 35 and I was terrified. My husband freaked when I thought I would lose the breast, but I had a lumpectomy and radiation and it's been in remission for 12 years now.

GRACE: (Weeping) My mom and my oldest sister both had breast cancer and it took their lives.

WILL: Yeah, my mom too. It is so scary. I wish you had told us sooner so we could offer you some support.

MARK: Connie what are you hearing from the group?

CONNIE: That they are very supportive and they care and that they wish I had brought it up sooner.

MARK: What do you think about that?

CONNIE: I'm not sure why.

LATASHA (Leader 2): It seems like you are very ambivalent about whether you want to discuss it in here. What can we do to help, even in the short time we have remaining?

CONNIE: I know we have to quit. I just wanted people to know … Could I call people here to check in when the radiation begins. (Many are nodding.)

LATASHA: You can certainly call Mark or me and it looks like many others are nodding that they'd be available.

CONNIE: Thank you (crying now). I didn't want to drop this on all of you.

WILL: You are the one who has to deal with cancer. Don't worry about it being an imposition on us … me!

MARK: Are you getting what you wanted from this? How can you make it work for support from others?

Stage 28: Good and Welfare

After each member has worked on the issue of his or her own personal use of the group experience, members and leaders often share their overall impressions of the group. Frequently, valuable positive feedback is shared and feelings about ending the group are explored. Often the leaders share many of their own personal feelings and observations.[3] This stage is often tearful and sensitive; it prepares the group for the leaders' final elements.

---

3   Such explorations are dependent on the leaders' values and theories. Often the reason given for leaders who become more personal at this time is to reduce the therapeutic transference and projections that have accompanied their roles during the earlier sessions. Of course, such a diminution of distance is anathema to those who espouse more classical analytic or behavioral theories.

Stage 28(A): Closing Ceremonies

Some group leaders use a closing ritual as a symbolic way to mark termination. These ceremonies may help reify the process of leaving the group and reentering normal life. Ceremonies may be simple or elaborate.

One organization that has used ceremonies effectively is the Vet Center. This organization, which has provided "reintegration" groups for thousands of Vietnam era veterans, has been responsible for many group innovations. The ceremonies used often focus on the members leaving the war behind and reentering "life in the world." Some examples include writing reactions to the past on a board or strips of paper and then burning them, and leaving or destroying painful artifacts of the war such as uniforms, medals, or letters. Symbolic ways of alleviating guilt for past actions that emerge in the group have been used very successfully. Shapiro (2016a) described one particularly powerful reaction of one Vietnam era veteran in making some peace with his memories of a buddy lost in combat by connecting with the family of the lost soldier and sharing the medals he received.

Groups with a religious or spiritual theme also commonly close with a ceremony or prayer. This can be very meaningful for members and help enhance the gains from the group. Leaders must be careful in such prayers however, if the group contains a mix of members from different religions. In a recent group at a Jesuit university, two members had to overcome their discomfort when the leader automatically closed her prayer with the words "in the name of the Father, the Son and the Holy Spirit." There was no negative intent, and no real harm was done, but the ceremony would have been more sensitive and effective if all members of the group were Roman Catholic or if more general terms requesting God's attention and support were used.

Some group leaders are uncomfortable with ceremonies and avoid them altogether. When ceremonial closings are held, they must be appropriate for all group members. Often encounter group ceremonies such as mandatory group hugs, or other physical contact, can make members sufficiently uncomfortable that the impact of the group experience as a whole is diminished.

Stage 29: Leader's Closing

All leaders close a group in their own characteristic way. Some prefer lengthy reviews and progress reports for each member. Others prefer to describe their impressions of the group as a whole, or possibly their personal feelings about closing.

If the leader gives a closing speech, it normally contains two elements: to give each member adequate feedback from the leader's point of view, and to provide a potential referral source for follow-up work. Some leaders keep their closing remarks short; others try to provide evaluative feedback to each member of the group regarding each one's relative strengths and challenges with reference to the issues discussed in the group. Here is one part of such a statement:

> Jeanie, I see you as a remarkably competent young woman with a great number of strengths to work yourself through this divorce decision you've made. I am concerned that there's a danger of your fear inducing you to quickly find another man to replace Len as a way of not testing those strengths.

> The leader also has the responsibility to address issues that may not have been fully developed in the group and are likely come to full fruition after termination.

This does not mean that the leader does follow-up therapy with each member. It is important, however, for the leader to be available for consultation and referral, at least for issues that are group-engendered. Our personal experience is that such an offer is not abused by group members. A follow-up offer for referral is not very time-consuming, and it is ethically essential. It can go a long way in helping to prevent group casualties. Equally important ethically is that leaders not use this as a way to create a need for their personal services or to expand their private practice businesses. In general, referrals to specialists or other professionals is advised. If referrals to the group have been made from other therapists, the leaders will do their best to encourage the members to return to, or continue their work with those individual therapists.

If group leaders do have individual clients in the group or if they will take an occasional client from group into individual therapy, it is important to have a prohibition against discussing group specifics and especially about other members during individual sessions. Although this may constitute a dual relationship, it is not unethical per se (see Chapter 8). It can be tricky, but with carefully chosen clients, limited circumstances, and awareness of potential conflicts, it can work.

When the consultation is offered, the group session officially terminates, occasionally with some physical contact such as hugging or holding hands.

Stage 30: Aloha

After the last session ends, members often tend to linger and extend nostalgic alohas, often sharing phone numbers and making plans for future contact. It is not unusual for members to get together without the leader after the group terminates. Shapiro (1978) recalled a couples group he led in 1969–1970.

> We met on Tuesday nights from 7 to 10. There were four couples in the group, three of whom really wanted to stay together. The

> group ended in April 1970, and to this day those three couples
> still get together every Tuesday night. They formed a mixed
> doubles bowling team in a local league. … done well, too—last
> Christmas (1975), they sent me a picture of the four trophies they
> had won last year. They not only got their relationships together,
> but they developed a workable mutual support system that goes
> far beyond any therapy. (p. 112)

Annual cards from the members of that group came until 1980. At least to that time, they were still meeting on Tuesday evenings.

The entire group process is an arduous journey, but a group that makes it all the way can reap a bountiful harvest for its members (and leaders). Every group does not make the entire journey, however. Often a group will have progressed through only half of the stages before termination must begin. Such a group can be of value in and of itself, and members can accrue a number of benefits.

The phases discussed above comprise an attainable goal, not a bare minimum. The goal pertains exclusively to *closed* groups, however. Groups with open membership progress past Phase II only when the membership is stable over an extended time. This is because as each new member is added to the group, earlier phases are reinstituted to benefit and to reestablish members' roles and inclusion.

To help keep the group process moving forward, some leaders have the current group members indoctrinate new members. With appropriate screening for consistent ego strength and a short period of assistance from senior members, the group may then move ahead with minimal regression to earlier group stages. This is a common practice in outpatient groups in private practice, where closed groups are difficult to create.

In addition, groups within institutions often have an open "intake" group for all admitted patients on an open ward. A poster with group rules is displayed and ongoing patients introduce the rules and purpose of the group as they orient new members, perhaps daily. This works best if the therapeutic milieu in the hospital supports and honors the group as an integral component of overall treatment.

Termination in Open Groups

Termination has here-to-fore been discussed with regard to closed groups in which all the group members begin and end the group experience at the same time. This text is particularly geared to such groups. The advantage of these groups is that the whole group progresses through the termination steps together. The disadvantage is that because of the mutual termination, it does not simulate well the normal life experience of individuals leaving important people and being left by them.

In open groups, members join and leave when doing so is personally appropriate. At any group session, some members will be dealing with issues of inclusion and others with treatment and some with feelings of rejection and loss as a member will be leaving. Several issues must be considered by the group leader.

Fair Warning

A customary ground rule in open groups for members to give notice that they intend to leave and then remain for a predetermined number of sessions prior to their departure from the group. This policy exists (1) to insure that other members will have the opportunity to work on any unfinished business with the departing person and not be confronted with a sudden unexplained absence; (2) to allow sufficient time for the member to prepare emotionally for the termination; (3) to allow the leaders to assist the leaving member with transfer of training; (4) to make referrals; (5) to provide an opportunity for members who tend to avoid problems by flight to confront their discomfort, rather than to act out of it; and (6) to allow the leaders sufficient time to screen and prepare potential new members to join the ongoing group.

Changes in the Group "System"

Leaders must be aware that any changes in the group membership will affect the group chemistry. Whenever a member enters or leaves the group, the group must reform into a new configuration. Alliances change; support systems are altered; and power in the group may shift. At this point, the group process will frequently regress to earlier stages of group development to reintegrate and restructure. Feelings about inclusion, exclusion, and abandonment commonly will emerge for many remaining members.

Perhaps the exiting member was intimidating. The group will now be able to move ahead will less fear. Perhaps she was a warm supportive member. The loss of that support may have to be compensated by other members. The leaders must be alert to the new integration of the group and adjust perceptions of members as well as the group process. Members will express new aspects of themselves as the group composition changes and both the quantity and quality of individuals' participation may shift.

Elicitation of Members Feelings About the Loss

Lewis (1978) points out the differences in affect that accompany task and educational groups versus growth-oriented and treatment-oriented groups. In the former, members are primarily focused on the goal and are likely to have a far less emotional experience when someone leaves—not unlike a person completing a class. By contrast, in growth or treatment groups in which members have been more self-disclosing, other members typically experience a feeling of loss when someone leaves the group. This feeling may well call up other separations in members' lives. Soon after a member terminates, the first major work that occurs in the group is on the topic of personal losses, perhaps dating back to childhood. A leader must allow for the open expression of all feelings as a member leaves. If remaining members do not have an opportunity and encouragement to discuss their reactions, they may attribute the person's departure to something they may have said or done.

Among the commonly expressed feelings are sadness, fear, anger, happiness, and relief. A member who feels relief or anger when someone is leaving may also be struck by secondary guilt feelings. This is all material to be processed (often referred to as "grist for the group mill"). Guilt may also be engendered if a member anticipates more personal time in the group because of one less member, especially if the departing person demanded a lot of group time. Unexpressed, this guilt may grow and diminish the benefit of the increased time and attention.

Early Terminations

Sometimes, a member may decide apparently suddenly to leave the group. It is important for these members to delineate carefully their thinking and decision making in the group. Often after a particularly deep or painful session a member may miss a week with little or no reason and then decide to terminate. Yalom (1995, 2005) also identifies as early terminators patients who have difficulty expressing gratitude or positive emotions. Conversely, patients who find terminations difficult in their life may well try to truncate the painful process by ending it prematurely. Patients may use the spectrum of defenses to leave the group. Among these is anger, often employed to punish the leader, particular group members, or the group as a whole by rejecting the entire endeavor. It is incumbent on group leaders to encourage members to terminate at a time when both they and the other members feel somewhat comfortable with the event. Group leaders also need to encourage a member who is attempting to escape from difficult emotions or interactions to stay until the discomfort has been sufficiently worked through and the termination is more natural. However, leaders must not try to hold on to patients after it is time to leave treatment. That is a clear ethical violation for all mental health professionals.

Sudden Termination. Sometimes members leave a group without any warning. In institutions, members who are discharged or transferred simply terminate by not showing up for a meeting. This may be particularly problematic for remaining members. They are caught between a desire to avoid talking about someone who is absent, worries that something they said or did caused the person to exit, and a host of unexpressed personal feelings of rejection.

When possible, leaders are advised to invite a member who is physically able to come to a final meeting to do so. In some cases, another member of the group may know how to contact the departed member to make such an invitation. For example, members of a hospital in-patient group may prefer to come back to their ongoing group after discharge than to join a new outpatient group.

There are, of course, situations where the departing member will not be able to attend. In military groups, sudden reassignments can relocate a member thousands of miles away by the next group session. In a prison group, nobody presumes that a former inmate who was unexpectedly released would come back into the prison for a group meeting. Indeed, if he were paroled, he could be legally barred from returning and associating with convicted felons. In such cases, remaining members may wish to discuss their feelings by writing to the person who exited. It may or may not be prudent to actually mail such letters.

Finally, a group member may die while a group is ongoing. Serious attention must be paid to mourning and unrealistic fears that the group or a particular member was responsible for the death.

Ultimately, the goal of termination is to maximize the impact of the group experience for all members. Transfer of training, reminders of attention to feelings, and a final chance to practice the group skills all serve members after the group is concluded.

Follow Up

Some group leaders, especially those who work in institutional settings, schedule follow up sessions three to six months after the group termination. Advocates of these sessions (Corey & Corey, 1987; Corey, Corey, & Corey, 2014) believe that members will be motivated to make the changes they began in the group, knowing that the group will reconvene. A plan for future meetings also encourages members to support each other in the interim. In the follow-up session, members can discuss difficulties since the end of the group and seek help from fellow members, whom they trust. Many leaders also use these sessions to collect evaluative outcome data.

In closed groups, members may be invited back for a "graduates night." Toseland, Kabat, and Kemp (1983) use such sessions to review members commitment to maintaining changes, to remind members of life changes since the beginning of the group, and to have members support each other when there are difficulties in implementing group learning in real-life situations. There is also the probability of general support.

There are two potential downside risks to such sessions:

1. It may be inconvenient or impossible for all members to reconvene. The leaders must then decide whether to meet with only part of the original membership.

2. Knowing that there will be a follow-up meeting, some members may avoid dealing with effective termination at the end of the regular sessions. Instead of saying good bye, they may simply say *au revoir.*

For the leaders, such postgroup sessions involve metaphorically walking a tightrope. Introducing any new material for discussion, inducing the members to regroup, or in any way create a need for additional therapy, is inappropriate; yet therapists must be available for client needs, to make appropriate referrals, and to support continued learning and application of skills acquired in the group to the patients' independent life situation.

Summary

Termination seems to be an unnatural occurrence in the group process. It requires the leader to introduce, catalyze, and persistently focus the group's attention on the process of the group ending. In no other phase of the group is the leader called on as clearly to "lead" the group in acknowledging the crisis of its own finale and symbolic death.

A leader's personal style of termination can be the most important ingredient in the group's ability to face the end of its existence. As leaders, we have basically three styles of termination. Often, leaders tend to terminate too early or too late. It is important for leaders to be able to endure the complexities and intensities of being in the moment with our feelings and personal issues germane to termination.

The process of termination begins with the first session in a closed group when the leader delineates the parameters of the group and announces the ending date. From this beginning, the leader continues to keep members apprised of the approaching termination of each individual group session as well as the remaining number of group sessions. Members' heightened awareness of their thoughts and feelings about ending and loss makes the termination more poignant.

The two significant and profound goals of this phase of group are: saying good bye and redirecting members' work to their home lives. The extent of each member's satisfaction with his or her ability to apply the group learning to the real world is the measure of the group's success. Many an otherwise successful group has lost much of its therapeutic influence by ignoring or failing to face fully the tasks of termination.

Three specific tasks are pertinent to the termination phase: the trust boost, transfer of training, and closing rituals. In the trust boost, the leader must make a direct request for members to support one another during the often difficult termination process. In addition, members are often asked to disclose something new about themselves, enhancing intimacy and reducing transference by presenting a more complete personal picture.

Transfer of training is the *sine qua non* of group work. The leader must consistently stress a connection between group learning and its application to members' lives outside the group. Members are challenged to be specific and concrete in how they will make changes in their lives.

Closing rituals need to be specifically tailored to each unique group and ideally would grow naturally out of a particular group's themes and style. The expression of typical feelings of sadness, fear, anger, relief, and joy need to be encouraged and processed. A helpful strategy is to inform members explicitly that each new ending and loss is an opportunity to work through previous losses. Members may experience a corrective emotional experience regarding loss, separation, individuation, and the development of interdependence.

CHAPTER 6

The Group Leader

O f the many variables operating in group therapy, leadership effectiveness is probably the most crucial. Competent leadership involves mastery of a wide variety of skills and functions. This chapter investigates three major areas of leadership: leadership styles, multiple roles, and functions.

Group therapists vary widely in their training, background, theoretical orientation, personality, intentions, and conceptions of their roles and goals. Most individuals who practice group therapy today were trained in disciplines such as psychology, medicine, nursing, education, public health, substance abuse, or social work. Some are very well trained in group process and techniques. Unfortunately, they are a minority. Oftentimes, group leaders are more knowledgeable of individual or family therapy than of group work itself. Some have had no training in group process, group counseling, or therapy. Some may have had a single graduate-level class in group work. Others may have had course work or similar training, but little supervised experience in dealing with groups.

Leader Personality

Some group therapists are mild, gentle, and "low key." Others are forceful and assertive. Some have well-defined philosophies that their group work emulates and supports; others take a pragmatic approach to their work. Some strive for "improvement of personality," whereas others focus on "amerlioration of symptoms," or "behavior change." Some see themselves primarily as teachers who have something to contribute to the relatively passive group members. Others regard themselves as clarifiers or analyzers, and still others see themselves as enablers or catalysts who help members to find themselves.[1] There are group therapists who take a very modest view of their efforts and hope only to assist people in limited ways; others take the grander view that they can reconstruct a person's entire personality. One persuasive argument is that there are as many types of group therapy as there are group therapists (Corsini, 1957). Yalom (2005) concurs, envisioning a host of "group therapies," rather than a singular model.

Qualifications

Who is a group leader? Is it anyone who is doing counseling or therapy group work? Can only people within certain professions be so labeled? From a legal point of view, most states restrict the use of the terms *psychotherapy* and *group psychotherapy* to people with specific degrees and licenses. Normally, a particular credential is required, such as an M.D., Ph.D. or PSY.D. (clinical or counseling psychology), M.S.W., MFT (marital and family therapist), M.A. (counseling), or M.S. (psychiatric nursing). However, none of the 50 states nor any of the Canadian provinces restricts the use of such terms as *training group, growth group, human relations training, T-group, encounter group,* or *sensitivity group*. There is no regulation of "educators" engaging in "group education," psychoeducation programs," or "encounter classes." The term *counseling* has been determined to be so broad that it does not fall under the professional rubric. Thus almost any person can engage in "counseling" whereas professional, trained counselors may be limited in their applications. Such problems frequently lead to paradoxical and ridiculous situations because of different legislative guidelines for licensed professionals and unlicensed individuals.

For example, an individual who is trained in group therapy and holds a Ph.D. in clinical psychology but is prelicensed in psychology may not lead any counseling groups without supervision. However, a lay practitioner with no training or credentials, any member of the clergy, educator, salesperson, marketer, or surgeon may lead growth, training, "motivation," or "educational" groups without fear of legal consequences.

No evidence exists to indicate that members of any particular profession are superior group therapists. Psychiatrists are not necessarily more adept than teachers, nurses more effective than public health experts, psychologists better than counselors, or social workers superior to ministers. As early as 1952,

---

1   In the brief group treatment modalities featured in this text, the goals are necessarily more limited than in long-term therapy groups. It is crucial for leaders from any school of psychological thought to recognize the limitations of a brief focused group. Such groups may, and frequently do, activate members to make significant life changes, but the leaders are rarely able to be present for the full unfolding of such changes.

Spotnitz, a psychiatrist, noted, "A gifted lay individual psychologist or social worker may do much better work with certain groups than a physician who may lack intuitive understanding of the individual in the group or of group dynamics" (p. 86).

Not everyone has the capabilities to be a group therapist. Many professionals who are otherwise well trained, do not have the interest or the capacity to do this work, whereas others take to group therapy naturally and eagerly. Several graduate students who had little interest in groups found them fascinating after their first experiences as a group member and an introductory class. Handling treatment groups requires not only interest and technical knowledge, but also direct experience in dealing with common, difficult interpersonal situations. Such experience can best be acquired by supervised practice.

To some practitioners, group process, with its multiple interrelationships, complex transferences, and fast-paced action, may seem chaotic. To others, those very attributes—speed, lack of protracted periods of relative inactivity, opportunities to work with several people simultaneously, patients' access to vicarious learning, and general stimulation—are far less demanding than the patience and persistence required in individual psychotherapy.

For the most part, we expect marketplace factors to select out competent professionals in every field. In addition, in all mental health fields, licensees are required to practice only within the scope of their training. Normally, ethical professionals will engage in those endeavors in which they are well trained and likely to be successful.

However, two factors mitigate the efficiency of this market-based selection. In many agencies, economic demands have mandated that the majority of staff do group work, regardless of prior training. Even in the private sector, many otherwise ethical practitioners, disenfranchised by closed provider panels and diminishing numbers of available patients, may find that economic necessity entices them to stretch their belief in their abilities. They may well lead groups for which their training is inadequate. In addition, the tremendous increase in popularity of encounter methodologies spawned in the late 1960s and early 1970s encouraged the appearance of thousands of untrained, self-styled group facilitators. Often these self-proclaimed "gurus" led dramatic, exciting, exercise-laden, high-casualty groups (cf. Lakin, 1969; Yalom & Lieberman, 1971).

One of the most dangerous components of the encounter methodologies is that they provide any "leader" with a technology that can be used to incisively open up a group member, but few corresponding closing skills. The dangers to clients of often well meaning, but naive practitioners have been well known for years. As early as 1955, Hadden argued that too many unqualified people were entering the field of group therapy. Cooper and Mangham (1971), Dreyfus and Kremenliev (1970), Grotjahn (1971), Lakin (1972), Lieberman, Yalom, and Miles (1973), and Shapiro (1973) have all cautioned that the vast numbers of group leaders may be harmful and have suggested characteristics that constitute competent leadership.

The following discussion of the roles, functions, skills, ethics, and training necessary for effective group leadership is designed to provide guidelines for readers in evaluating their own abilities and those of others.

Characteristics of the Group Therapist

Are there certain characteristics or personality traits mandatory for effective group leadership? Are the skills of group therapy learned, or do they require a certain type of individual? In this section, these questions are explored from the historical, practical, and training perspectives.

Relatively early in the history of group psychotherapy, a question arose regarding the importance of the therapist's personality. In 1908, Pratt said, "Success depends on gaining the friendship and confidence of the members" (p. 1070). Pratt's (1934) theory of therapy was based on Dejerine's belief that, "Psychotherapy depends wholly and exclusively upon the beneficial influence of one person on another." A statement by Pfeffer, Friedland, and Wortis (1949) probably fairly represented opinion on the issue at that time: "As yet undefinable aspects of the therapist's personality may be more important for his results than the technique he says he uses" (p. 214). In a review of the research and clinical literature, Shapiro (2016a) described these "active ingredients" in detail.

In the late 1950s, Rogers (1961) identified several "core factors" for successful psychotherapy. These necessary "core factors" for personality change included *empathy, genuineness (congruence),* and *unconditional positive regard*. Soon thereafter, these therapeutic characteristics were studied across a host of diagnoses and situations (i.e., Barrett-Lennard, 1962; Truax and Mitchell, 1971).

In the 1960s, a series of studies by Carkhuff and Berenson (1967) and Truax and his colleagues (Truax, 1966, 1971; Truax & Carkhuff, 1967; Truax, Carkhuff, Wargo, & Kodman, 1966) identified several variables that distinguish effective from ineffective therapists in each area of endeavor. High-functioning levels of warmth, empathy, genuineness, and congruence were considered to be necessary conditions for success in group therapy as well as in individual work. These authors argued that these "personality traits" were trainable skills. Demonstration of this research with regard to individual counseling therapy is impressive. Since the early 1970s, counseling psychology graduate programs have almost universally included a basic course or microcounseling curriculum to train students in these "core counseling skills" (i.e., Ivey, 1990). Such training has been quite helpful in developing the students' necessary basic skills.

Although few direct applications to group therapy situations have been substantiated, it is reasonable to assume that the same skills provide a necessary core for group counselors. However, it is equally clear that mastery of such skills although necessary, is insufficient to guarantee success. Thus, the question of some optimal personality for the group therapist has as yet not been fully answered.

To determine what characteristics are common to effective group leaders, we may explore the character structure of successful therapists. We may describe who this person appears to be. Likely, such a leader will be described as kind, firm, considerate, compassionate, personally centered, and sensitive. Another approach is to explore the roles leaders play in the group. Although we would expect that the traits described here would be reflected in group leadership behavior, leaders may interact in ways that are distinct from individual counseling and psychotherapy. Group treatment focuses to a large extent on relationships between members and between leaders and members.

Although group counselors and psychotherapists vary greatly in values and personality, there are some commonalities among effective group leaders. A host of group leader trainers believe that these common traits can be learned.

Norcross (2011), summarizing literature on evidence-based relationships indicated that the most important variable in counseling and psychotherapy was the nature of relationships between therapist and clients. In group, this can be enhanced by therapeutic interactions and relationships among the members.

The Ideal Personality for a Group Therapist

Is there a generalized personality for effective group therapists? Do certain methods call for specific personalities? According to Slavson (1951), the therapist should be friendly, generous, tolerant, accepting, and *quiet*. Slavson may well have been describing an ideal personality in terms of the culture of his day. Others have presented somewhat different personality criteria for the therapist who works with groups. Grotjahn (1971), a psychoanalyst like Slavson, argues that a group therapist, "must be a man of all seasons. He must be reliable; he must invite trust and confidence." Other therapist qualities suggested by Grotjahn include honesty, sincerity, spontaneity, responsibility, courage, firmness, humor, fallibility, and the ability to perform skillfully.

Corey and Corey (1992), and Corey (2015) detailed several personal characteristics of effective group leadership: courage; willingness to model; presence; good will and caring; belief in the group process; openness; ability to cope with attacks; personal power; stamina; willingness to seek new experience; self-awareness; and a sense of humor and inventiveness.

Our own formulation of the major essential characteristics of the effective group therapist is similar: honesty, integrity, patience, courage, flexibility, warmth, empathy, intelligence, timing, and self-knowledge.

Honesty

"… and the truth shall set you free!" (John, 8:35) Truthfulness is an essential requirement of therapy. The therapist must at all times respond to the members with honest feedback. This is not to suggest, however, that he or she needs always to be open, blunt, or brutal. There are many situations in which our first thoughts are best kept personal. What is important is that when we do speak, it is with the truth as we know it.

If the group members are to change their negative patterns of communication, they need accurate information about the consequences of their behavior. Similarly, because honest communication is one of the avowed goals of groups, the leader must be a model of this behavior. Honesty cannot be learned from an untruthful source.

Integrity

Integrity does not lag far behind honesty. Group members need to know that the leader will adhere to an agreed-on code of ethics. The leader must interact with members with their interests in mind. Integrity provides a solid basis from which members may experiment, confident that the leader will respond appropriately.

Patience

Another essential quality is patience. The therapist must have a high tolerance for boredom, frustration, and delay. She must have the ability to proceed doggedly in the face of disappointments and failure under conditions that induce anxiety, anger, and unrest. Patience should be the result of a deep conviction, amounting to faith in oneself, in the group, in the method, in the ongoing process, and in the theory. The patient therapist combines a feeling of assurance, security, determination, confidence, and hopefulness about herself and others. She would do well to have a generally optimistic outlook on life.

Courage

Somewhat related to patience is courage. The leader must have the capacity to act on her convictions and remain unswayed by immediate events. She needs faith to hold on to them with great tenacity, to follow with determination her line of approach, and to meet and contain opposition in an accepting manner, even when it occasionally may be forceful or explosive. Courage is needed to penetrate, sometimes blindly, into new areas or to meet crises with aplomb. The therapist must have inward qualities of fortitude. One significant component of courage is for the leader to share both his inner reality as well as taking action. It is potentially powerful when the group leader lets the group know that he is frightened but nevertheless going ahead.

Flexibility

Courage does not mean rigidity. Although the therapist must hold onto basic principles with tenacity, she must nevertheless be able to modify tactics without changing goals. She needs extraordinary flexibility to move rapidly from topic to topic, emotion to emotion, person to person, while keeping a sense of the needs of the group as a whole. She must be sensitive to the needs of the group and of individuals, but she must also be alert to the demands of society, to the varied cultures of the members and to the desires of patients' families as well as to ethical issues.

Warmth

The ideal therapist is a warm person with a genuine liking for others, one who really wants to see others improve. He may have preferences among members, but he must value them equally as striving individuals who are seeking change. He must be ready to give of himself fully. He must be open to members as they are.

Empathy

Closely related to warmth is empathy. An effective group therapist must be able to put herself into the shoes of her patients. She must experience their emotions as if they were her own, and must be able to communicate this shared experience accurately and articulately to members. She does not judge others; rather she shares in members' fears, pain, anger, and joy. At the same time, she must keep touch with other reality considerations. In a sense, the group therapist walks with one foot in the shoe of another and one foot in her own shoe.

Intelligence

It is not necessary for the therapist to be the most intelligent individual in the room, but he must be able to learn fairly rapidly, to be flexible enough to view the group from a variety of perspectives, and to make some theoretical sense of the material of the group interactions. A leader who is limited in intelligence could effectively dampen higher level cognitive processing by the members.

Timing

There is no human endeavor that does not require timing for maximum effectiveness. The best leadership observations are worthless if the group members are not prepared to listen. To score regularly, the basketball player must fake so that his defender leaps first, then jump into the air and shoot at the apex of his own jump while his defender is coming down. Similarly, the therapist must help group members relax their defenses and prepare to work on conflict resolution. With any variations in sequence, the effects will not be maximized. If the basketball shooter does not cause his defender to jump earlier than he does himself, the flight of the ball might be terminated in his face instead of the basket. Similarly, the group leader must time interventions carefully for best results. A common timing problem is when a group leader intervenes without awareness of or attention to the process trajectory. In this way, a leader might try to jump prematurely into treatment, while the group is struggling with trust-building in the transition phase.

Self-Knowledge

Leaders don't have to be conflict free or completely self-actualizing; such a requirement would eliminate all current leaders. They must, however, be aware of their personal psychological strengths and weaknesses. Unless the leader is self-aware, there is an ever-present danger that her personal conflicts, inadequacies, and needs instead of those of the members, will guide group interventions. It is far better for a leader to acknowledge an incapacity or unwillingness to venture into certain difficult areas than unknowingly to grope ignorantly in the dark with patients, perhaps compounding their fears and conflicts. In Shakespeare's *Hamlet*, Polonius gives final advice to his son: "This above all, to thine own self be true; and it must follow as the night the day, thou canst not then be false to any man."

This list of qualities may appear overwhelming at first, but these characteristics are less permanent traits than aspirational evolving goals. Each of us grows more personally with experience as a group leader and maturity in our life.

Who is this "ideal" group therapist? Is he or she any more than the kind of friend or mate we all cherish? Can any person who has these qualities of honesty, integrity, patience, courage, flexibility, warmth, empathy, intelligence, timing, and self-awareness be a group leader? These may all be necessary conditions for effective group leadership, but they are not sufficient. In the next chapter we investigate the other characteristics—training and a code of ethics—and in effect take the reader inside the head of the group therapist during a session. Before doing so, there is one more important consideration for any therapist.

Personality and Method

Earlier, we observed that the method and theory a group therapist uses is a function of his or her personality and values. It is difficult to think of a really introverted therapist using psychodrama with any success, and it may be just as difficult for a truly extroverted, outgoing person to contain himself within the limits of the client-centered, nondirective approach.

The best method for any person is one that reflects his or her personal values and nature. There is no absolute hierarchy of methods. Pratt made his maximum contribution with the class method, Moreno with psychodrama, Rogers with person-centered therapy, and Dreikurs with family counseling. Even the thought of Freud attempting bioenergetics is enough to demonstrate how incongruous such a situation can be. It is important to remember that Freud's free association method, use of the couch, and sitting behind the patient emerged from his personal preferences and introvertive personality. We have direct evidence on this point from Freud himself, who said,

> I must, however, expressedly state that this technique (free association) has proved the only method suited to my individuality. I do not venture to deny that a physician quite differently constituted might feel impelled to adopt a different attitude to his patients and to the task before him (1924, p. 27).

Other therapists have made similar remarks. Spotnitz (1952), for example, says, "The personality of a therapist may determine whether the group has an active or passive type of therapy" (p. 87). Kline (1952) comments, "It is probable that the dynamics of different groups actually do differ radically with the personality of the therapist" (p. 113). Kline also gives a personal example:

> I have always emphasized that within limits the organization of the group and the role of the therapist should be dependent largely on the personality of the therapist himself, rather than on rigid techniques. This conviction was derived from my initial unsuccessful attempts to emulate the procedures of Dr. Paul Schilder..." (p. 113).

The therapist needs some freedom to follow his own judgment. No one can tell him how to do what he must do. As early as 1953, Powdermaker and Frank (1953) tried to get therapists to operate in a uniform way. Even though the therapists wished to follow this established pattern, they managed to make subtle changes, in each case making modifications suited to their own personalities. Even in studies of outcome of manualized treatments, differences between individual therapists are often evident.

This book is written in the spirit of freedom for the therapist to decide on their own methods. We hope that explicit examples of a variety of attitudes and methods will help therapists make a better choice among them or will help give therapists the courage to strike out on their own. There was only one Sigmund Freud, Fritz Perls, Virginia Satir, and Carl Rogers. Saul Scheidlinger (1994) reflecting on his six decades as a group therapist commented, "For many years I believed in the classic one true way—that of Father Freud. Then as I grew younger I began to realize that as the world was different and I was different, the group approaches were also best different."

When therapists learn from their predecessors and apply this learning in their own unique ways, it is a bonus. However, when they try to be Freud, Perls, Satir, Rogers, or take as *gospel* the perspective favored in this text for that matter, they are not only doomed to mediocracy, but they will appear overstressed, phony, and foolish in the endeavor.

Types of Leadership

Methods of group treatment and styles of leaders vary widely. Each leader brings unique skills, personality, beliefs, and values to the group. Similarly, each co-leader team is unique in its approach to any constellation of group members. For this reason, any formal classification system may do injustice to individual group leaders. However, to investigate and compare the types of leadership, it is useful to cluster leaders in some way. We have chosen two dimensions: theory of group psychotherapy and leadership focus.

The predominant theories of group psychotherapy are well represented in several texts: for comparative investigations of group leadership readers are encouraged to explore Corey (2015), Kaplan and Sadock (1983), Long (1988), Schaffer and Galinsky (1989), and Vander Kolk (1985). Most group leaders claim to be representatives of one of the following psychotherapeutic approaches: Adlerian, behavioral, cognitive, constructivist, eclectic, encounter, existential, Gestalt, integrative, person-centered-Rogerian, object relations, psychoanalytic, psychodrama, psychodynamic (general), psychoeducational, rational-emotive, self-help, Sullivanian, transactional analysis, or 12-step. Each of these approaches provides a template with which to focus and highlight leaders' attention on specific member behavior and interactions, methods for understanding and interpreting members' communication and needs, and guidelines for interventions. Each theory considers specific elements to be critical, so leadership behavior will be substantially different across the theories depending on their particular allegiance.

In addition to the substantive differences based on theoretical orientation, individual variations within methods can be significant. Thus, simply knowing that someone is "a Gestalt therapist" does not mean that person's approach is identical with that of the late Fritz Perls or James Simkins. In their classic study of encounter groups, Yalom and Lieberman (1971) concluded that "Gestalt" leaders produced the most and least casualties.

Students in the process of developing their preferences among theories should be warned that being a "Rogerian" does not make them the therapeutic equivalent of Carl Rogers. Individual differences are still the core of psychological practice, and ultimately each group member must be approached uniquely. In a sense, a therapist's theory provides eyeglasses or filters through which an apparently chaotic group process can be viewed systematically, understood, and acted on strategically.

These glasses do not remain constant throughout a therapeutic career. At different stages of life and experience, therapists often find themselves more attracted to one theory than another. Frequently, one's preferred mode of working is influenced by life events, maturation, and changes in values. Often best group counseling or therapy is influenced by recent fluctuations as well as basic enduring positions. For present purposes, we shall first examine differences between leadership styles, then commonalities.

Leadership Focus: A Continuum for Comparison

Leadership orientation is one dimension that can be used to highlight dissimilarities between group leaders. The two poles of this dimension are the *interpersonal* and *intrapsychic* (Figure 6.1). As with any continuum, the two ends represent extreme, low-frequency values while middle positions are more common. Individual leaders can be compared with regard to their relative positions on the continuum. Treatment effectiveness for specific groups may be explored with this orientation in mind.

Figure 6.1 The Leadership Continuum

Extreme Intrapsychic	Moderate Use of Both	Extreme Interpersonal

Intrapsychic Intrapersonal	Interpersonal
Leaders dealing with individual members	Leaders dealing with interactions between members
Group as stimulus situation to investigate individual	Group as situation to investigate interactions
Techniques that isolate individual	Techniques that isolate interactions
Therapist as source of therapeutic goals	Members as source of therapeutic goals
Historical focus	Here-and-now focus
Within-individual focus	Between-people focus
Leader ⟶ Therapist	Leader ⟶ Members
Unconscious determinants of behavior	Conscious determinants of behavior
Success = Individual's relationship with self	Success = Individual's relationship with other people

Dissimilarities between intrapsychic and interpersonal leaders can be viewed most easily by looking first at the extremes. The *strict intrapsychic leader*, for example, works with individual members of the group in a *one-to-one* fashion. Techniques are designed to *isolate the individual*. The group itself is seen as a stimulus situation within *which the individual* can be treated. Success in such a group is measured by the *relationship of each member to himself* (i.e., balance of cognitive, sensory, and perceptual systems; id, ego, and superego coordination; parent, adult, and child working interdependently, etc.).

A major *focus* of the group is on the barriers or *defenses* of an individual that prevent a member's full cognitive and emotional expression. Techniques are primarily designed to work directly with these barriers. The leader's role approaches that of an individual therapist with individual members. It is often active, directive, and frequently centered on *unconscious determinants* of behavior. This leader regularly employs a historical orientation. Such terms as "catharsis" and "working through" a transference relationship with the leader appropriately apply to this style of leadership. Classic psychoanalytic, Adlerian, and Gestalt-oriented leaders can most often be described by this side of the continuum.

The *strict interpersonal leader* addresses relationships between members. Dyadic interactions, communication between members and the group as a whole, and the relational consequences of behavior are highlighted. Techniques are designed to *isolate interactions* between members. The group provides a unique stimulus situation within which interactions between members can be explored. Success is measured by the *relationship of members* to one another. A primary focus in the group is on the *between-people barriers* that prevent full interpersonal interaction and intimacy. Treatment approaches utilize the simulation of real-life interactions possible in a group. Opportunities then exist for members to try out novel strategies and resolve interpersonal problems.

The leader's role is more orchestrative, commonly active but generally nondirective. The focus is a here-and-now or future viewpoint rather than historical one. In general, between-member rather than within-member concerns are customarily explored. Success might be measured by the ability of the group to function "without a leader." The group, not the individual is the center of attention.

Each extreme of this continuum offers valuable approaches to help members face and resolve dilemmas in their lives. However, adhering to either extreme will limit leaders' use of the opposite skills and fail to maximize some of the major benefits of group treatment, particularly in a brief format.

For this reason, most successful leaders use a combination of interpersonal and intrapsychic interventions. Different stages of a group call for shifting foci. In a typical group, an intrapsychic orientation predominates in the treatment phase, whereas an interpersonal mode is more evident during the transition phase. Of course, group goals and population will affect the relative use of each orientation.

Leaders proficient in both intrapsychic and interpersonal skills seem to have definite advantages. Frequently these abilities are consistent with greater training in group therapy.

What People Learn in Groups

Before comparing the interpersonal and intrapsychic styles, we should examine exactly what it is that people learn in groups. What behaviors do change? What are the expectations for a "successful" graduate of group treatment?

Learning to Learn. At first, members must learn how to be available for what the group has to offer. They are confronted with

- a new language system;
- a new way of looking at themselves and others;
- a new set of rules, mores, or group ethics;
- new behaviors that make for good group membership, which are frequently quite different from those that provide success in back-home situations;
- learning how to cope differentially with stress situations;
- learning how to cope more effectively with ambiguity and the minimization of status or roles that typically govern social interactions; and
- giving and receiving honest feedback.

The group in general, and the leader specifically, create an environment where all this learning can take place. In the process, most members experience anxiety, respond to it in their characteristic manner, and receive feedback from others about the impact and effectiveness of their particular anxiety-reducing strategies. Through such interactions, members learn how to separate their anxiety about the unknown from their fear of anxiety itself. This allows them to reduce their neurotic anxiety (fear of fear) and make informed decisions about how to experiment with their lives safely (cf. Frankl, 1963; Shapiro, 2016a; Yalom, 1980).

New Skills. In the process of exploring their anxiety and characteristic behaviors and experimenting with new behaviors, members acquire some new skills that transfer well to their lives outside of group.

- They learn how to reduce anxiety through self-expression.
- They may learn how to be less fearful when not in control.
- They learn to cope with and be less fearful of rejection.

- They may become more skilled in assertiveness when dealing with authority figures.

- They increase their ability to be empathic.

- They learn how to be more trusting and trustworthy.

- They learn to be more responsible for their own thoughts and behavior.

- They become increasingly comfortable living more in the present.

- They experience a greater sense of community with others.

- When they experience a typically anxiety-provoking experience, they respond more thoughtfully and less automatically.

- They become more adept and open to helping others (altruism) and of being helped.

- They become much better problem solvers.

Each of these skills has been well documented in the short-term group literature (see Coche, 1983; Corey, Corey & Corey, 2014; Diamond & Shapiro, 1973; Dies, 1979; Dies & MacKenzie, 1983; Erickson, 1975; McCallum & Piper, 1990; Nicholas, 1984; Parloff & Dies, 1977; Shapiro, 1978; Shapiro, Peltz, & Bernadett-Shapiro, 1998; Shapiro & Diamond, 1972).

Comparing Leaders' Roles and Skills

Leaders normally employ a variety of roles and skills. Two of the most critical components in generating the various types of group learning are the leader's capabilities as a *model* for appropriate group behavior and her enhanced power as a *dispenser of reinforcements*.

Despite protestations to the contrary by many group facilitators, therapists, and leaders, the group leader does lead. He or she plays several roles during the course of a group: catalyst, orchestrator, information disseminator, a model for sharing and communicating, reinforcer, and (sometimes) participant. Because of the nature of groups, creation of ambiguity, elimination of typical roles, anxiety, and so on, the therapist's behavior stands out as a beacon and a model of appropriateness in a unique environment. In addition, because the therapist is usually the only person in the room who knows what is expected in this ambiguous situation, his or her power and influence as a model and reinforcer are greatly enhanced.

In examining leadership orientation roles, keep in mind that in describing these leadership styles we are exploring for the benefit of clarity, therapists' orientations that are on the extremes of the continuum. Most individual leaders' orientations will fall somewhere between the two poles.

In the role of therapist, the intrapsychic leader models behaviors such as getting clients to confront and work with the divergent aspects of their personalities, probing, questioning, and interpreting past events, dreams, or unconscious determinants of behavior. These roles are hardly appropriate for members to adopt. Even if such behaviors were acceptable for members to behave this way in a group, it would be very inappropriate in their day-to-day lives. In fact, members exhibiting these types of behaviors in group are likely to be confronted with that most feared expletive—"You're acting like a therapist!"

Furthermore, members in a group with strict intrapsychic or highly charismatic leaders can learn to maximize rather than minimize problems. This is because problem solving occurs for the individual only with the assistance of a very potent, apparently "omniscient" professional group therapist. When this level of intervention is necessary, it tends to promote the notion of a greater level of pathology among members, one that requires highly skilled professional assistance to effect change. Indeed, strict intrapsychic leaders tend to make no distinction between therapy and growth groups; they may see the clientele of the latter groups as suffering from some relatively less severe level of neurotic conflicts. By contrast, help received from a fellow member in the group setting tends to minimize a member's sense of the scope of the problem and helps a person perceive himself as less sick and the problem as more workable.

When the intrapsychic leader works individually with members, others tend to "wait for their turn" to expose "their problem." At times, waiting may be difficult, nonspontaneous, unfruitful, or boring. When members are encouraged to interact with one another however, issues emerge spontaneously, without dependence on the leader, and with fuller ownership of feelings by members. They have not been pushed into anything they can subsequently dismiss as "the therapist's agenda." An additional danger from a leader with a strict intrapsychic approach is the ability to project his or her own intrapsychic conflicts onto the group members and (assuming similarity) help them resolve their conflicts.

If the leader is the sole therapeutic agent, the members do not have the altruistic experience of serving as therapeutic agents themselves. Thus they lose an experience that can be ego-building, self-satisfying, and have great potential for emotional growth. The total amount of sharing among members is also reduced, diminishing their value as reinforcers for one another.

Finally, studies on encounter group casualties (i.e., Lieberman, Yalom, & Miles, 1973) have demonstrated that the intrapsychically oriented, high charismatic leader is the most likely to produce casualties. The self-styled "guru" is impressive and develops many "groupies," proselytizers, and converts to his personal religion, but an approach that combines the depth intrapsychic approach with an interpersonal focus is more successful and potentially less dangerous for group members.

Like the extreme intrapsychic therapist, the strict interpersonal group therapist also has disadvantages. A leader who functions primarily as an interpersonal process commentator, bringing people together, and fading into the background is a poor model for problem solving, intrapsychic exploration interaction, psychological depth, and spontaneity. The group essentially is denied the special distance and expertise of a professional counselor. The pure interpersonal leader also has low value as a dispenser of reinforcement.

The accomplished leader is able to be both interpersonal and intrapsychic to varying degrees at different times with different members, and must be able to distinguish among these times. Some groups call for a more intrapsychic or interpersonal style throughout. Leaders best serve a group when they allow members to test their ability to develop both freedom and control, encourage their interaction and mutual help, and yet protect them from scapegoating or going too far astray in their experimentation. In this realm, successful leadership is similar to effective parenting. One needs to let children explore their world freely, while ensuring that the child is safe during the exploration.

Whether a leader leans more toward the interpersonal or intrapsychic is of less import than the congruity with the leader's personal values, beliefs, and ethics. For the novice group therapist, however, an interpersonal orientation is less dangerous than an intrapsychic one: the positive strengths of group members are more easily elicited by interpersonal group leaders as power and influence in the group are more widely dispersed.

Group therapists can be compared with one another by reference to their leadership orientation, but this is not an absolute scale by any means. It is presented as a means to cluster therapists and make generalizations about their "fit" with a particular patient group. Each style is appropriate with different populations of patients. With young children, severely disturbed individuals, and many institutionalized populations, for example, a more intrapsychic, leader-to-member orientation may be necessary. In higher functioning groups, a more interpersonal, member-to-member style may be the more productive orientation.

Depending on the extent to which the leader is oriented toward depth and personality restructuring or interpersonal skill development, each leader will fulfill the variety of leadership roles to varying degrees. The intrapsychic leader may put more effort and group time into the catalyst function than into orchestration. An interpersonal leader in an encounter group may actually participate in the group, not unlike a member might, whereas a more intrapsychic leader would not approach member-like behaviors except in the rarest circumstances.

The Multiple Roles of Group Leadership

Group leaders generally play five major roles in the course of the group process:

- Information disseminator
- Catalyst

- Orchestrator
- Model/participant
- Dispenser of reinforcement/environment manipulator

Each role continues throughout the process, but at certain times, each role has periods of primacy. The *timing* for heightened employment of a given role is often a major determinant of group outcomes.

The Group Leader as a Disseminator of Information

In the most traditional role for leaders of all groups, the leader provides information. The counselor, therapist, or mental health worker is an expert who shares his or her expertise with group members. In this sense, the group is similar to most physician-patient interactions or educational experiences, in which the leader is the teacher or expert and the members are students or supplicants. The leader presents a curriculum that he or she hopes will be acquired by the members. To be effective, this information must be individualized to the recipients' needs and motivational levels. The group leader must be aware of resources and content that relate to the group experience.

The information dissemination role attains primacy during two group phases. The first occurs early in the group process. During the preparation phase (Phase I), the leader presents members with a considerable amount of specific information about the group. This carries over into the first few stages of the transition phase (i.e., ground rules, beginning exercise). The second time for heightened use of this role is in the termination phase (Phase IV) of the group process. At this time, leaders may suggest follow-up work or providing specific suggestions for members.

Information dissemination must be done moderately. Overuse of this role can turn the group into a simulated lecture, hardly useful for the kinds of learning expected in a group. Underuse may also lead to wasteful lack of direction. In some cases a single piece of information can save large quantities of time and effort. The following "comical" event is presented verbatim:

> BOB: Lew, where's the bathroom?
>
> **LEW (LEADER):** You'd like to know where the bathroom is.
>
> BOB: Yeah, that's what I asked.
>
> **LEW:** You seem irritated.
>
> BOB: (Patronizingly) Lewis, where's the bathroom?
>
> **LEW:** You are upset with me, because I haven't told you where the bathroom is.
>
> BOB: (Angrily) WHERE'S THE BATHROOM?
>
> **LEW:** Now you sound angry.

> BOB: (With cold anger) If you don't tell me where the bathroom is right now I'm going to use your pant leg as a urinal.

At this point the "leader" produced a door key and instructions. Bob took the key and left. He did not return for four sessions.

Such evasive refusal to give information is atypical, but many leaders, trained to be wary of personal disclosure that will inhibit the development of appropriate transference, do balk at providing facts for members. It seems important that a group therapist know when to give information, how much to give, and what the implications are of giving or withholding specific information.

In addition to information regarding group procedures and helpful hints for members to use the group more effectively, leaders are sometimes asked for personal information by members. As a rule of thumb, it is more facilitative for leaders to attend to the process extant in the group than to disclose specific details about their lives. When leaders do share their personal reactions, it is generally more important for them to disclose their momentary in-group experience than particulars of their personal back-home lives. For example, it is more appropriate for a leader to share a feeling of sadness in the group than to detail a recent personal romantic failure.

The Group Leader as Catalyst

In the role of a catalyst the group therapist serves two functions: As a generator of excitement or spark plug for the group, and as a mover of the group to its critical point, leaders highlight and channel patterns of verbal and nonverbal communication within the group, acknowledge less obvious or nonverbal expressions of affect, request feelings, and aim the group in the direction of a present, here-and-now focus. The leader uses a cooperative rather than competitive mode of communication and urges participants to risk revealing their personal beliefs and feelings rather than challenging others. She is most responsive to group levels of arousal and group feelings that reflect members' concerns. Fiebert (1968), to whom credit is given for naming both the catalyst and orchestrator roles, says that the catalyst, "holds up a mirror to the group so that they can view their behavior, chides members for their superficiality, and urges them towards bonds of intimacy" (p. 935).

The catalyst role reaches its apex during Phases II and III of the group process, while members are learning how to be group members and are going through the therapeutic intervention stages. The more intrapsychic a leader, the more he or she will use the catalyst role. Most intrapsychic interventions use catalyst skills, often beginning by focusing on an individual member.

LEADER: Joseph, I notice that while Virgie was describing the events of last year, you were looking very anxious. Can you say what was happening for you?

JOSEPH: Well, it was heartbreaking to hear what she encountered.

LEADER: … and what did that bring up for you personally?

The leader is turning up the heat on Joseph and directing him to express his own feelings, based on what Virgie was describing. Other examples of the catalyst role may be found in certain therapeutic techniques such as the empty chair technique.

Overemployment of this role can have the effect of creating a group dependency. The members will consistently look to the leader to entertain and counsel them. They will not learn to become catalysts for one another.

Under use can also have negative effects. In a group where the leader shies away from the catalyst role, members may become confused, directionless, bored, or apathetic. They may also never learn the major foci of the group process and will not know what parts of their experience to discuss; their conversations may therefore wander aimlessly through the time allotted for group meetings. The level of arousal may be so low as to be unmotivating.

The following is a vignette from a group experience during the therapeutic phase, showing the leaders acting as catalysts. One member had just finished talking about her lack of interest in sex with her husband as a result of her ongoing affair with one of his friends. As the group was working with this problem, one of the leaders noticed another woman member's face was pale and she was showing general nonverbal signs of anxiety.

JERRY (Leader 1): Betsy, could you verbalize that?

BETSY: Huh … what … well …

JERRY: (Supporting) What Joan was talking about seems to be affecting you a great deal.

BETSY: I feel scared.

JERRY: About what?

BETSY: My husband seems disinterested in me lately, and I'm really scared.

SUSAN (Leader 2): What Joan said makes you wonder whether or not he's having an affair and that's why he's not interested in sex with you.

BETSY: (Tearfully) Yes!

> **SUSAN:** (After Betsy was somewhat consoled) Can you verbalize your feelings now?
>
> BETSY: I'm really scared that he found someone better, and I've been ignoring his coming home late at night.
>
> **JERRY:** You sound scared … and angry.
>
> BETSY: Yes I think I am angry, I was a virgin when we got married and never had the chance to explore like Joan.

At this point the leaders orchestrated the process and had Joan and Betsy talk together. Subsequently, they came back to Betsy more intrapsychically and allowed her to explore the relative reality of her fear and her long history of suspiciousness and jealousy. She was then able to probe her own desire for distance from her husband, ultimately concluding that her husband was more likely to be working late at the office and wanting more contact with her than he was to be involved with another woman. As she began to explore in group her general feelings of low self-esteem, specifically about intimate relationships, she did resolve to talk more openly with her husband.

The Group Leader as Orchestrator

The role of orchestrator shares precedence with the catalyst role during the two middle group phases. The leader mediates the communication between members of the group. The members begin to learn that they have the ability to help one another.

Orchestration involves connecting one member's needs with other members' resources. Leaders put members with problems in touch with members who share their difficulties and can assist in resolution. Rather than leading the discussion, the group leader assists it by asking questions, reflecting individuals' feelings, underlining considerations that are growth producing, and highlighting and interpreting communication patterns. The leader is particularly sensitive to nonverbal aspects of communication such as tones of voice, body language, kinetics, and discrepancies between verbal and nonverbal components of messages. However, as an orchestrator, she does not interpret these directly, as she does in the catalyst role. Instead, she observes patterns that indicate resources and alignments within the group, and connects members, based in part on these observations and in part on their expression of similar content.

Effective orchestration requires an ongoing understanding of group process. Appropriately administered, it will maximize group learning as it increases members' participation in problem solving. It is thus a most powerful mode of learning. Orchestration skills are particularly employed by leaders with interpersonal orientations. Perhaps the most crucial aspect of this role is that it is ultimately expendable. A major index of its success is obsolescence. When group members learn to communicate and connect with one another spontaneously, freely, and openly, they eliminate the need for the leader to manage or facilitate their interactions.

An example of orchestration occurred in a couples group, at the onset of the therapeutic phase. Sherry and Michael are a young married couple.

JOHN: (Addressing the leaders) You know, I think Michael and Sherry really are in a bad way.

GAIL (Leader 1): Tell them that. (*orchestrating*)

JOHN: You guys seem angry at each other every single session.

PAUL (Leader 2): You're concerned about them? (*catalyst*)

JOHN: Yeah, I'd like them to get it together more.

SHERRY: I feel okay.

MICHAEL: That's the problem: whenever I confront her she says, "Hey man, it's cool."

PEGGY: Sherry, it doesn't look okay to me.

PAUL: Sherry, what do you hear John saying? (*orchestrating*)

SHERRY: That he's upset.

PAUL: What was he saying … ?

SHERRY: Well, he says he's concerned, but it's more like a put down.

GAIL: So you feel … (*catalyst*)

SHERRY: Angry and unwilling.

PAUL: John, is that what you wanted? (*catalyst*)

JOHN: She just doesn't listen.

PAUL: What message did you want to give her? (*orchestrating*)

JOHN: That I do care and that I think she's denying and repressing.

PAUL: How could you say that (without the interpretation) so Sherry would hear it? (*orchestrating*)

JOHN: I could say, "Hey, I feel uneasy when you look angry."

GAIL: Try that. (*orchestrating*)

JOHN: Sherry, I get scared to talk to you when you and Michael are fighting and you seem so angry.

GAIL: Sherry, what do you hear him saying? (*orchestrating*)

SHERRY: When I'm angry it scares him.

GAIL: But when you're angry you're also scared.

SHERRY: (Nods and looks down.)

GAIL: Who in here would you like to know that you're scared, without having to tell them? (*orchestrating*)

SHERRY: Michael.

GAIL: How could you let him know? (*orchestrating*)

SHERRY: I don't know.

PAUL: Michael, what is your reaction to what Sherry is saying? (*orchestrating*)

The orchestration done by both leaders was facilitative in allowing Michael and Sherry to become more empathic with each other and to improve their communication. The leaders did not return until later to the other emerging issue: John's role and motivation. At this point the key issue was the couple's interaction and the exploration of how anxiety may come out looking like anger.

Overutilization of the orchestration role at the expense of other roles can eliminate the leader's special therapeutic expertise. In this case, the leader serves only as a conveyor/facilitator and not as a catalyst, information disseminator, model, or reinforcer. In such a situation, the highest level of functioning for the group is determined by group members rather than the leader. Because the group cannot surpass the functioning level of its participants, overuse of orchestration severely limits its effectiveness. Characteristically, this deficit occurs with an extreme interpersonal-style or novice leader.

Underemployment of the orchestration role also limits group effectiveness. Lack of orchestration reduces the impact members can have on one another, ameliorates altruism on the part of the members, and limits between-member learning. In a group with minimal orchestration, what is going on may resemble individual psychotherapy with an audience. This type of deficit is most likely to occur with a strict intrapsychic orientation or with an individual psychotherapist untrained in group dynamics.

The Group Leader as Model-Participant

A major component of most complex learning is imitation. In their role as models, leaders demonstrate how to share information and feelings and demonstrate authentic, honest communication in the here and now. The group leader needs to be flexible in applying values, open to new learning about himself, and able to show, by example, the process of learning how to learn. Leaders may also model spontaneity, genuine caring for others, sincerity, assertiveness, ability to express and contain anxiety, making "I" statements rather than "you" statements, and conflict resolution skills.

In an unstructured situation, participants will naturally attempt to reduce their anxiety by providing structure. A common tactic by which members accomplish this is to look to the authority figure for clues of appropriate (tension-reducing) behavior. It is here that most members begin to imitate leadership behaviors. Some obvious forms of this imitation are the adoption of the leader's theoretical language by members and the seemingly unconscious appropriation of the leader's nonverbal communication cues. One example of this occurred in a group led by a colleague who had a habit of rhythmically stroking her long hair during periods of silence and high tension. By the fourth week of the group all six female group members were occasionally stroking their own hair the same way. This was even true for one woman who had short hair and who in effect was stroking hair that would not be long for years!

These examples are an indication of external modeling. Although interesting, they are relatively impermanent and not meaningful as changes; they simply illustrate how rapidly and insidiously modeling occurs. An example of a more psychological form of modeling occurred in a therapy group where a member was describing relatively dispassionately the recent death of his father.

> HARVEY: So I had to fly out to the funeral ... that was a downer ... missed all my friends here.
>
> **MICHAEL (Leader 1):** You know, I hear a very sad-sounding message, but I don't see any emotion. (*catalyst*)
>
> MARION: Yeah, I can't even feel any sympathy for you.
>
> HARVEY: (Coldly) I wasn't asking for any.
>
> **LARRY (Leader 2):** Harvey, what was your dad like?
>
> HARVEY: He was okay, pretty cold, never really paid much attention to any of us. I don't really miss him ... but I feel like I should.
>
> **LARRY:** When someone is cold to me and I love them, it hurts a lot. (*model-participant*)
>
> MARION: I don't know, sometimes when someone is cold to me I just understand it's the way they are.
>
> **LARRY:** Like Harvey was to you just now. (*orchestrating*)
>
> MARION: Yeah. (then smiling, almost embarrassed) I do care for you Harv, and I don't like being shut out.
>
> HARVEY: It's just hard to get into those feelings.
>
> SARAH: Do you want to?
>
> HARVEY: Yes, but I'm not sure.
>
> **MICHAEL:** (With moist eyes) My father died 7 years ago and it still makes me very sad when I think of how I miss him. (*model-participant; catalyst*)
>
> HARVEY: (Looking at Michael) It's just so frustrating. There's so much I wanted to say and some of it is not nice at all ... (Here he began crying and opening himself initially to his grief.)

There is no question that the leader's empathy and willingness to share his own sadness played a huge role in helping this patient experience some of his necessary grief. If the group leader can be accepting, spontaneous, self-disclosing, encouraging of others to examine themselves, cooperative, intimate, expressive of feelings in a here-and-now context, and nondefensive, group members can imitate these behaviors. Bandura and Walters (1963) have shown that imitation learning is maximized when the model has high status and receives positive reinforcements for behavior. The group leader comfortably fits these criteria.

Overuse of the model-participant role can not only diminish its effectiveness but also reduce the value of all the other leadership roles. A leader who becomes, for all intents and purposes, a member of the group, can cause it to follow his personal agenda. In this way, the group members are used as therapists or sounding boards for the leader's own work, instead of the reverse. In addition, the level of self-disclosure by the leader can be either more superficial or deeper than that of members. Thus members may hasten to conform to the leader's level of self-disclosure and in the process lose their own. When this happens, and one individual is more responsible than others for setting a level, a greater artificiality results.

An example of overuse of this role occurred in a growth group.

> BOB: (To the leader) You know, I'm not sure I feel comfortable enough here to really talk about some things.
>
> **BRIAN (LEADER):** That really pisses me off. You've just got to take more responsibility for you.
>
> BOB: I'm trying to, I just feel punished and untrusting.
>
> **BRIAN:** Bullshit, you're trying to suck me in to begging you to "tell us" and then (in a mocking voice), "I've got something to tell you but I won't tell you what it is, nyah, nyah."
>
> BOB: (Angrily) Sounds like that's your problem, not mine.
>
> **BRIAN:** That puts me down, like I'm not listening, or not following your expectation of me as a leader.
>
> PAT: I think you're being a bit hard on Bob. Is this pushing one of your buttons?
>
> **BRIAN:** You may be right. I guess it's my struggle with authority and being a good leader.

He then proceeded to analyze vocally his own behavior in detail. Brian may have provided an example of self-disclosure to the group, but very much at Bob's expense. His solipsistic approach to the group will encourage members either toward being the leader's caretaker or to imitate his "me first" self-centered approach.

Underparticipation may also be detrimental to group process. When members see the leader engaging only in nonparticipatory roles, they are apt to imitate these behaviors. Such behavior on the part of members is inappropriate. Members are not encouraged to orchestrate and catalyze without self-disclosure. Indeed, they are often criticized by other members for doing so. If the leader does not model appropriate behaviors for members, his potency as a model will be diminished, and members may simply imitate the inappropriate behaviors.

The Group Leader as Dispenser of Reinforcement and Environment Manipulator

Because the group is an ambiguous situation, it is anxiety producing. We believe that certain moderate levels of anxiety must be present for optimal amounts of learning to occur. The group leader is in a position to create a group environment that maximizes growth and learning by controlling the extant level of anxiety. The most efficient way for the group leader to control the level of anxiety is to regulate the level of ambiguity. In much of Western culture, ambiguity and anxiety are related approximately linearly. The therapist can lower levels of anxiety by adding structure or add anxiety by reducing structure.

One manner of controlling structure is through judicious selective reinforcement. In a group setting, this can include such behaviors as head nodding, verbal acknowledgment, attention, or smiling. In providing this kind of acknowledgment, the leader lets members know that they are on the right track, that this is approved behavior, and that they should continue in this vein. Such reinforcement has double value. It helps members feel positively, and it helps reduce anxiety by structuring the situation. Conversely, the ambiguity anxiety can be increased by nonreinforcement from the leaders.

Leaders can cause group anxiety to fluctuate by other techniques. They can raise anxiety by calling attention to a specific group member's behavior or making expectant eye contact with one member. On the other hand, by making group-level interpretations (e.g., "Seems like we're all feeling uncomfortable now, but it's hard for anyone to change the situation"), leaders can lower anxiety. In one sense, much of the learning in a group setting can be viewed as a function of motivation produced by the leaders' control of group anxiety.

In dispensing reinforcement, the group leader does more than simply provide structure. She is a powerful model and respected authority figure in the group, whose approval is valued tremendously. Members quickly learn how to please the therapist by acting in accordance with her apparent desires. In the group setting, members are reinforced for openness, genuineness, honesty, hard work, self-disclosure, motivation to change, listening and responding to others, flexibility in application of values, acceptance of others, and so on. These abilities stand members in good stead outside the group setting as well.

Overmanipulation by the group leader will cause group members to mistrust her. If they construe the group leader as a somewhat inhuman dispenser of reinforcement, members will curry favor by producing reinforceable behaviors, without any commitment. This is similar to students "psyching out" what a teacher wants to hear or see on an exam and producing those bits of information on paper, while forgetting their content and meaning almost simultaneously. They may get the reward of high grades, but understanding of the material requires a different type of incorporation.

By contrast, underutilization of this role may produce a rather laissez-faire chaos. In this situation, the group can remain over- or understructured, and hence over- or underaroused, for long periods of time. In such an environment, learning takes place only minimally and by chance.

Information Systems of Group Leaders

To conduct a group successfully, leaders must play the several roles described earlier in the chapter: information disseminator, catalyst, orchestrator, model-participant, and dispenser of reinforcement. To do this they rely on basic skills to take in the information they need to intervene effectively. Above all, the leader must be perceptive and open to the multiple streams of data available in a group setting.

If individuals are to function effectively in multiple leadership roles, they must be able to incorporate and evaluate simultaneously several major sets of data. In a sense, the leader must operate as a multitrack recorder, receiving messages from five overlapping yet distinct sources, mixing these inputs, and then producing a single response. The leader must be sensitive to

1.   the verbal content of members' messages,
2.   nonverbal messages of members,
3.   the context in which the message occurs,
4.   his or her own feelings, and
5.   his or her theoretical understanding or interpretation of the group process.

To respond to the group members effectively, the leader must be able to incorporate all five inputs and decode them. With all these data, however, the leader can respond to only a fraction of the information received. What distinguishes the most effective leaders is related to *which fraction* the leader responds to and the *timing and relevance* of the intervention. This is a complex task involving each of the five data sources.

Content of Members' Messages
The most obvious source of data is what is being said by the members at a given time. The content of a message is simply the verbal component—the words—as

they would appear in written form. The content of a message is the precise statement made by the sender.

Two examples help clarify this data source. The first one is the following:

JIM: I really feel happy today.

The content of this message, "I really feel happy today," can be less believable if, for example, it is said in a loud tone of voice, through clenched teeth, or as the person is banging the door of the room as he exits. Even though the message is less believable, the content remains the same.

The content is the same in the following example, even though the total message may be interpreted otherwise:

SAM: Jim, you'd better sit down; I've got some really bad news.

JIM: I really feel happy today.

Here, the content "I really feel happy today" is the same as it was above, but the context alters the message considerably.

These examples show that the verbal content is only one component of the message received by a group leader. It is an important component, and leader need to be aware of what is being said.

Nonverbal Messages of Members

Communication is not entirely verbal. Tones of voice, body positions, body movement, relative distance between people, and eye contact all serve to qualify verbal messages, and they communicate in and of themselves. Normally, verbal and nonverbal components convey the same message. When they do, we hardly notice the nonverbal message. However, when the verbal and nonverbal components are discrepant, the receiver must recognize that the message is complex. What part of Jim's communication will we believe? He says, "I really feel happy today," in a loud tone of voice, through clenched teeth, banging the door. Choosing either the verbal "happiness" or the nonverbal "anger" will give us only a partial picture.

Similarly, in our culture, if one person says, "Have a taste of this pie, it's really delicious" to another, and winks one eye in the direction of a third person, an observer would expect collusion between the speaker and the third person and an unpleasant surprise for the pie taster. The verbal message is qualified by the nonverbal wink.

Most people in mental health fields, trained in nonverbal communication, have a tendency to give primacy to nonverbal meanings. Such cues as eye contact or lack of eye contact are taken to reflect emotional states or veracity. Movement toward an individual while conversing with him or her is interpreted as a desire to communicate, and a movement away is seen as the reverse. Keeping one's arms folded across the chest or sitting behind a barrier are generally interpreted as signs of defensiveness or a need for greater interpersonal distance. Nonverbal data are collected and analyzed even with reference to a person's physical location in the group; members tend to sit close to people they believe are supportive, across from people who attract them, and at right angles to people with whom they are not comfortable.

In receiving such nonverbal data, leaders must be cautious in their interpretations. If two distinctly different messages are received, assuming that one is correct and the other incorrect is generally a mistake. The very fact that here were two conflicting messages is the critical piece of information. This observation may be presented as feedback to the member or filed away by the leader for later use. Here is an example of feedback.

> KATHY: This group has helped me so much I feel like a new person.
>
> **NORMAN (Leader 1):** You're saying something that would seem so happy, yet you look sad when you're saying it.
>
> KATHY: Well, the group has helped me.
>
> **NORMAN:** But there's more that you need.
>
> KATHY: Yes.
>
> **NORMAN:** Would you like to share that?
>
> KATHY: (Smiling at Norman and Leaning forward) I'm not sure.
>
> **HARRIET (Leader 2):** You'd like to share, but you want Norman to ask you.
>
> KATHY: (Angrily) Why do you always have to psychologize us?
>
> **HARRIET:** This is between you and Norm and you resent my joining in.
>
> KATHY: (Looking at Norman) When I saw you on the bus yesterday, you didn't even notice me. I felt put down.
>
> **NORMAN:** I never saw you. Did you say hello?
>
> KATHY: I was embarrassed.

Both leaders in this example confronted Kathy with her "double messages" in the context of several other leadership interventions. This type of feedback, properly timed, can be remarkably effective. For the most part, however, leaders will confront a member like this only after they have seen similar behaviors or have developed enough understanding of the individual that their confrontation occurs *with a particular goal in mind.* In this case, both leaders were willing to work with Kathy on her transference feelings with them.

Nonverbal behaviors are an important source of input with reference to other aspects of group process, especially when they contradict verbal content.

Contextual Cues

No communication is delivered in a void. As Haley (1963) so clearly indicates, each message contains two components: information and a redefinition of the current relationship between the communicators. In a two-way communication, each message given by either party confirms the current definition of the relationship as symmetrical or complementary, or it is an attempt to redefine the relationship.

Understanding the nature of such communication in a two-person situation is difficult; understanding such communication in a multiperson (group) setting is a mammoth undertaking. If we follow this assumption, each time a group member communicates with any other member or leader he or she is in effect simultaneously defining his or her relationships with each other member and leader as well.

Whenever a person instigates a communication, the context in which this message is sent plays an important function. For example, it may be appropriate to say something at a baseball game that would be very inappropriate in a church. Whenever a member sends a message in a group, he or she does so with some awareness of the total context: frequently the statement is made strategically. Thus a member may say something to the leader as a way of presenting himself to another member. In the following example, the member was addressing the leader directly, but was much more interested in communicating to another member.

> PETER: I just think that if people are into each other, whatever they do is cool.
>
> BETTY: (Looking at Doris, a leader) What do you think about open marriage?
>
> **DORIS (Leader 1):** That sounds like something you have feelings or questions about. ...
>
> BETTY: You know, I think my husband's really old fashioned ... it's like he thinks that if I ever hook up with another guy I'd be ruined forever.
>
> HAROLD: Does he feel that he can screw around?
>
> BETTY: You mean double standard? No ... he's not interested (then turns to leader).
>
> Doris, what should I do if I feel turned on to someone and want to go with those feelings, but Herb (husband) would really flip out?

DORIS: Is there someone here you're attracted to now?

BETTY: (Embarrassed) That's not the issue. The issue is that he set the rule and he doesn't want to break it, but what if I do … ?

DORIS: Are you concerned about who makes the rules, or the consequences of violating them?

LEN: Why don't you do it and not tell him?

BETTY: But then if he found out. …

RHONDA (Leader 2): Which is your concern?

BETTY: I don't think it's fair.

RHONDA: Is there someone here you'd like to explore this with?

BETTY: (Looking down, and in a soft voice) Claude. (At this point Peter looked very disappointed.)

CLAUDE: Uh, oh, … um … I mean.

RHONDA: That surprises you?

CLAUDE: Yes.

DORIS: What about Peter?

Here both Betty and Peter blushed and proceeded to share some elaborate feelings they harbored for one another. Peter's general comment to the group was accurately perceived by Betty as an invitation, and Betty's comments to Doris were as much an acknowledgment of Peter's invitation as they were a comment about her husband.

The leaders were cognizant of this, and they acted as catalysts and orchestrators to bring the issue to the fore and deal with it in real time in the group. It is interesting to note that in this situation Betty and Peter both felt tremendous relief in sharing their feelings and fantasies, and they did not act them out. Once the feelings were exposed the excitement was experienced, and the need for action was reduced.

In this case, the content and nonverbal messages were secondary to the implied relationship between members. The leaders' understanding and acknowledgment of the interactions between members made it possible to deal openly with the issue.

Leaders' Personal Feelings

Of all the sources of input, the most predominant spur to direct action is the leaders' emotions. Most individuals generally act more out of what they feel than what they think. Group leaders are no exception. If a group leader feels angry or happy or sad in a group setting, his interactions with members may reflect this. Consequently, it is essential for leaders to know well their personal triggers and sensitivities. If emotions are generated within the group process, leaders can use their own emotions as a highly tuned pickup system. If, during a group session, a leader suddenly starts feeling anxious, he must search around the group to discover the source of this anxiety. Is it something a member is saying? Is it a feeling in the room because of what members are not saying? Is it that the topic has much unresolved conflict for the leader?

Two Crazy yet Utilitarian Assumptions

Each leader makes two heuristic assumptions in a group setting that reflect otherwise indefensible beliefs.

1. My feelings are an accurate and in-depth index of the group process.
2. Whatever I feel is due to something that is going on in the group.

If leaders are to be guided by such assumptions, they must be aware of their own needs, expectancies, weaknesses, and reactions, and they must have a clear understanding of any non-group-related pressures they are carrying. If the leader had a fight with his spouse before coming to the group session, his reactions to members may be more a reflection of those feelings than of anything actually occurring in the group.

One example of an extra-group experience occurred in a group where one of the co-leaders had an important romantic relationship painfully end at 3 A.M. prior to a 9 A.M. marathon group. By the time the group began he was feeling hurt, sad, lonely, and frightened. In this position, his emotional receptors for such feelings in others were hypersensitive. As is so frequently the case in such situations, a member of the group had similar problems, and the leader was exceptionally empathic, extra-perceptive and effective in helping her through a 5-year emotional block. Because the situations were so similar—rejection, feelings of loss, and helplessness—he was almost brilliant in this intervention and helped the member substantially.

When the co-leader, who was aware of the entire situation, invited the troubled leader to share his grief, the latter appropriately declined but was unable to continue effectively in a leadership role for several hours. Fortunately, the group could treat him as a quiet observer, and the co-leader could take charge. Had the co-leader not been fully aware of the situation, and had the outside problem not been the clear generator of all these feelings, misunderstanding, and confusion could have resulted.

Leaders frequently rely on their feelings. They assume that if they are responding in a certain way to an individual, significant others may be responding similarly, and this may be a clue or manifestation of an individual client's problems. To keep this sensory channel clear, leaders must be self-aware and understand their own sensitivities.

Theoretical Understanding

From our perspective, a theory provides a leader with several essential qualities necessary to make sense out of the apparent chaos of group interactions. Theories operate as filters, letting in relevant (understandable) data and blocking out irrelevant stimuli. They increase the amplitude of the primary signal and reduce others as noise. In addition to pointing out where the leader should look, theories provide sets of constructs that explain what the data mean when the leader finds them. They also provide a manner of response so that the therapist, having discovered and interpreted the data, has clear options for interventions.

Thus, leaders use their theories to tell them what is important, why it is important, and what to do about it. Without a theoretical or interpretive understanding of group behavior, a leader is confronted with a wide array of uncoordinated data, no consistent means to understand it, and no step-by-step plan of action. In short, without a theory, a group leader will respond spontaneously, inconsistently, and ineffectively. The particular theory that group therapists hold seems relatively less important than congruity with values, consistent application, and awareness of its limitations for identifying, classifying, and acting on diverse data. The theory applied must also be a good fit with the clients' needs in the group.

One Piece of Group Process

The way a group therapist uses these five systems (verbal content, nonverbal messages, the context in which the message occurs, leaders' personal feelings, and theory) and applies them to the leadership roles is shown in the following example and process analysis. The group focus is "working on relationships." They are in the therapy or Working Phase. The 10 group members are briefly described as follows:

- Agnes, 39 years old, divorcee. Very angry outwardly, seems to direct anger at men in general. When not speaking, seems depressed.

- Barbara, 30 years old, married, two children. Describes herself as happy but unfulfilled. Husband reportedly treats her as an object of his own gratification rather than understanding her needs.

- Betty, 29 years old, military wife, husband away for 9 months. Working on her B.A. at a local university. Regularly has affairs while husband is away.

- Charles, 48 years old, psychiatrist. He has been an effective private practitioner for several years. Divorced and living alone. Tends to be more "therapeutic" than intimately involved in equal relationships with others.

- Karl, 41 years old, dentist, married, five children, Has been sexually involved with several women in his practice. Very concerned that wife or professional colleagues will find out. Reportedly anxious to end this "addiction."

- Ray, 26 years old, married. Very athletic, engages in various sports at least three nights a week. Presents a strong machismo image but appears very sensitive underneath it. Currently his wife is very angry with him, threatening to leave him; he is confused about this.

- Sandy, 28 years old, nurse, cohabitating with 49-year-old lover for 5 years. Not happy with relationship but frightened of moving.

- Susan, 29 years old, successful, high-paid model. Unsure of life goals, very unsure of relationships with men. Aware that she presents herself sexually but resents it when men relate "only to my body." Looking for permanent relationship. Divorced twice and had an eating disorder in her teens.

- Toshio, 34 years old, immigrated to United States when 5 years old. Very quiet and polite, seems accepting of others. Painfully unable to request anything for himself.

- Willie, 32 years old, single. Describes himself as a swinger and has been in untold number of relationships. Proudly revealed that he doesn't use "safe sex" and that he had slept with 70 women in one year. In the group, he says all the right-sounding things, but they seem somehow disconnected from him. Has been in every "growth" experience to hit town in past 5 years.

This event occurs during the early stages of the therapeutic phase of the group. The scenario is first presented in entirety, and then a process analysis is provided in tabular form. Note that the entire sequence is described as if we were inside the leaders' heads.

SUSAN: There's something that is bothering me that I'd like to talk about.

FAY (Leader 1): Go ahead.

SUSAN: I just ended another relationship this weekend. He's a good guy, too.

FAY: (Expectantly) But …

SUSAN: It's like all he's ever interested in is sex. I like sex too, but it's like my body is all he wants.

RAY: Well, you do have a really nice bod.

SUSAN: Yeah, I know, and I feel good about that, but I'm more than just big boobs and a piece of ass.

FAY: You'd like him or anyone to appreciate your body, but also to appreciate the inner parts of yourself.

SUSAN: (Weeping) Yeah, I need to know if he loves me.

AGNES: Your body won't last forever and as soon as you start to sag, he'll take off and find some other honey who's younger. You know, Susie, most men are bastards like that.

(There is a 30-second silence.)

KARL: I don't think that's fair. There's so much more that's important than a woman's figure.

SANDY: Sue, I know what you're talking about. I think a guy like that is better off gone.

SUSAN: Yeah, but what if they're all like that?

WILLIE: (Smiling and looking at Susan) You just need to find another kind of man.

SANDY: Easier said than done.

RAY: Like Willie?

CHARLES: I wonder, Susan, if you attract only those kinds of men.

AGNES: (Sarcastically) Right, it's always the woman's fault—She didn't get raped, she led him on.

CHARLES: Your anger is really getting in the way. I feel that perhaps Susan is attracting these kinds of guys either because of where she looks, because of what she does with them, or maybe as a subconscious way of proving that all men are no good.

BETTY: Do you think that's possible?

SUSAN: Yeah, I've screwed up two marriages, and sometimes think I married bastards as a defense against letting myself be intimate.

LARRY (Leader 2): Sandy, can you verbalize that?

SANDY: (Tearfully) That just hits home.

LARRY: You're in a similar situation?

SANDY: (Nods).

LARRY: Can you tell Susan?

SANDY: You know Bob, the guy I live with … well, he's a good man, but he's just insensitive to my needs. Maybe I won't let him try, but it's just that he won't listen to any really deep feelings.

FAY: That really hurts.

SANDY: God, it's like there's a part of me that's too ugly for anyone to live with.

(During the silence, both women are crying now, and Larry moves over to where Barbara is sitting and puts his arm around her shoulders. She also begins to cry).

RAY: (With trembling lips) That's not only true for women.

LARRY: You've felt that also.

RAY: (Nods).

LARRY: I've experienced a feeling of not being understood also. It really hurts when you pay attention to it.

CHARLES: You've got to pay attention to it. If you understand it, you can come to grips with your humanity.

WILLIE: That's the asshole way. You just experience it as that's the way it is, and it's okay.

KARL: What does that mean?

WILLIE: (Condescendingly) It's all the same. It is what it is. You can't take responsibility for anyone else.

FAY: Susan, where are you now?

SUSAN: Feeling hurt and scared.

FAY: Talk about the fear.

SUSAN: I'm scared I just drive all men away because I'm not open. But if I open up I get clobbered. It's like if you're a model, only one kind of man approaches.

LARRY: Barbara, can you share your feelings with Susan?

BARBARA: (Very tearfully) It's not (related to) being a model. Bill and I have been married 8 years and I really love the guy, but I use sex to avoid sharing really intimate parts of me. I started to get involved with Charley, just to have someone I could tell those things to, but it started to get sexual and I pulled out.

FAY: If you got involved that way with Bill, you'd be vulnerable to hurt, but if you don't open up with your husband, you need a relationship on the side, which has even greater problems.

BARBARA: Really!

FAY: That hooks into Susan's feelings of frustration also.

LARRY: Karl, you look like someone kicked you in the stomach. What are you feeling?

KARL: It's like something really important is being said and I've got to face some stuff, too.

LARRY: You've gone the route of an affair also?

KARL: Several.

Leadership and Group Process

As shown in the process analysis at the end of this chapter (Table 6.1), the leaders respond verbally to only a fraction of the data they take in. For each comment they make, they must process their observations and feelings and incorporate them within their theoretical framework. The resulting interventions will be most potent when they are delivered with proper timing. Such skills take training and extensive supervised practice. Groups do not always move smoothly or in a linear fashion. The process ebbs and flows, and leaders must be prepared for substantive variability within this process model.

Note that the leaders frequently respond verbally to nonverbal messages, interactions between members, and their own feelings. Both leaders choose carefully the content of their interventions and employ one of the leadership roles for delivery. Their goal is to help the group members move consistently to deeper levels of interactional involvement and to be more nurturing for each other. They participate, model, reinforce, catalyze, and orchestrate in such a way that the group becomes increasingly therapeutic. Realize, however, that not every intervention by the group leader has an immediate (or any) therapeutic impact. Often, apparently well-timed, accurate, and meaning-laden leader statements have little to no noticeable corresponding response by the group members. Learning and behavior change in group therapy occurs as it does in other settings; it requires time, practice, and repetition.

Summary

An effective group leader plays many roles and performs many functions concurrently and sequentially. A continuum of leadership orientation from intrapsychic to interpersonal is presented as a backdrop for five major leadership roles. Strategic and tactful employment of levels of intervention, intrapsychic and interpersonal orientation, and leadership roles provide a fertile ground for group members' growth and learning. In addition, a number of personality characteristics enhance therapeutic success when they are present.

A leaders' ability to use both an intrapsychic and an interpersonal orientation increase flexibility and effectiveness within a group. The intrapsychic orientation provides depth of individual learning as well as integration of historical with present interaction. The therapist is largely active and is a catalyzer and interpreter of intrapsychic processing. The strengths of this approach are that it engenders effective problem solving and can move the group to greater depth more quickly. The interpersonal orientation focuses on relationships within the group. The focus is on the here and now of group interactions that is often more anxiety-provoking than exploring more serious personal problems outside the group. The therapist with primarily an interpersonal orientation is more of an orchestrator with less direct involvement in providing answers for members. The strength of this orientation is the increase in self-esteem afforded members through their altruistic and successful attempts to help each other.

Five major roles of the leader are identified and paired with specific stages of group process. The role of information disseminator is largely employed during the preparation and termination stage. During these two stages the leader needs to disseminate expert knowledge that helps members prepare for therapy as well as later integration of specific insights and skills. Another role primarily associated with the preparation stage and also with the transition stage is the role of reinforcer and environmental manipulator. The leader must maintain an awareness of the level of anxiety within the group and be responsible for intervening to optimize members' learning and growth. In a group setting there is an inverse relationship between anxiety and structure and a curvilinear relationship between anxiety and learning. The leader modulates anxiety and optimizes learning through the judicious application of structure.

Acting as orchestrator, the group leader connects needs with resources within the group. During the therapy phase, the leader encourages members to share similar experiences; this provides an awareness of universality, cohesion, and altruism between members. The role of catalyst is used to focus the energy of the transition stage to address directly the challenges to the leadership. In the therapy phase, the role of catalyst is used to deepen interpersonal and intrapsychic work. However, it is during the termination stage when the role of the catalyst is most important. The therapist is responsible for initiating and completing the termination process.

Termination is often avoided by the group as a whole and must be actively structured by the group leader. The role of model is used throughout the group and perhaps provides the most subtle and sophisticated learning for members.

The personality traits that a leader might aspire to model would include honesty, integrity, patience, courage, flexibility, warmth, empathy, intelligence, timing, and self-knowledge. The optimal group leader would have the maturity of an integrated self. In other words, honesty is tempered by warmth and empathy. Patience is balanced with courage, and both are guided by an intelligent use of timing. Self-knowledge allows the leader to be true to his/her own values while being accepting and flexible in his or her approach to others.

Table 6.1 A Process Analysis

Content	Nonverbal Messages	Interactions Between Members	Leader's Feelings	Leader's Thoughts/Theory	Leader's Role
Susan: There's something that is bothering me.	Susan's lips trembling. No large affect in others.		Comfortable, anticipatory.		
Fay: Go ahead.	Eye contact between Fay and Susan.	Everyone tuned in to Susan.	Anticipatory.	Probably something to do with men.	Catalyst
Susan: I just ended another relationship this weekend. He's a good guy, too.	Looking down, sad. Sandy avoids eye contact.	Sandy leans toward Susan. Willie tries to make eye contact.	Sadness about end of relationships in personal life. Caring for Susan.	Wonder what she does to pull men close and then push them away.	Model-participant (listening)
Fay: But …	Fay leans forward.	Everyone looks expectantly at Susan.	Caring for Susan.	I'd like to get her to share this openly.	Catalyst
Susan: It's like all he's ever interested in is sex. I like sex too, but it's like my body is all he wants.	Susan close to tears. Fay/Larry very tuned in. Sandy looking down.	Agnes seems to be sitting above Susan. Ray, Karl, Charles all seem close and open to her.	Caring for Susan. Fear that she will stop halfway. Confidence that group can deal with problem.	Want to keep her talking and avoid interruptions of other members.	
Ray: Well, you do have a really nice bod.	Ray looking at Susan's breasts. Susan turns red, smiles.	Willie, Ray, Karl looking at Susan's body. Agnes glaring at the men.	Fear this will sidetrack. Slight initial anger at Ray for his lack of sensitivity.	Ray broke the tension. He probably tried to do something nice. It should backfire. Susan is embarrassed. Wonder if she'll be angry or seductive.	Model-Participant

Content	Nonverbal Messages	Interactions Between Members	Leader's Feelings	Leader's Thoughts/Theory	Leader's Role
Susan: Yeah, I know, and I feel good about that, but I'm more than just big boobs and a piece of ass.	Susan looks embarrassed; sticks out breasts while she talks about them.	Seduction, comptetion.	Attraction to Susan's body; competition.	She's being seductive. Could be an example of what she's describing—men treat her as sex object because she presents that part when she's emotional.	
Fay: You'd like him or anyone to appreciate your body but also to appreciate the inner parts of yourself.	Fay looks empathic. Susan about to cry. Agnes looks angry.	High anxiety. Each member seems to be focusing inward.	Tenderness toward Susan. Understanding of both needs.	See the fear reaction—seduction. See how she needs both caring for inner self and attractiveness to physical self. Wonder about confronting. Want to see group reaction.	Catalyst Reinforcer
Susan: Yeah. I need to know if he loves me.	Susan crying. Sandy near tears. Barbara pale. Agnes moving around a great deal.	Most seem to be focusing inward: little contact. Willie looking at Susan.	Tenderness toward Susan. Recalling personal hurt feelings.	Susan is at point of crying and feeling better temporarily versus going fully into the pattern. Decision to push her into greater awareness. Still waiting for group reaction.	Model-Participant (listening; nonverbal encouragement to continue).

Content	Nonverbal Messages	Interactions Between Members	Leader's Feelings	Leader's Thoughts/Theory	Leader's Role
Agnes: Your body won't last forever and as soon as you start to sag, he'll take off and find some other honey who's younger. You know, Susie, most men are bastards like that.	Agnes talking through clenched teeth, pressured speech, loud tone. Others pull back.	Attention focus shifts from Susan to Agnes.	Anger, disappointment, anxiety at this turn of events.	Agnes is anxious, expressing it as anger. Pulls process toward herself—interesting form of seductiveness. Wonder if anyone will fall for it and make political feminist response. Wonder if I/my co-leader should intervene or let group do it.	Model-Participant (nonverbally looking at Susan; away from Agnes). Environment Manipulator
[30 second silence]	Agnes glaring. Karl staring at Agnes. Susan weeping.	Karl staring at Agnes. Barbara looking at Susan. Others looking down.	Tense.		
Karl: I don't think that's fair. There's so much more that's important than a woman's figure.	Karl looks like he's holding back anger with "calm." Barbara looks anxious.	Lot of head nodding. Barbara looking at Susan with caring.	Disappointed that Karl opened door to Agnes.	Resolve to get focus back to Susan. Avoid Agnes's anger until more appropriate time.	Environment Manipulator
Sandy: Sue, I know what you're talking about. I think a guy like that is better off gone.	Turned toward Susan—back toward Karl who is staring at Sandy. Agnes taking a prone position.	Sandy obviously not reacting to Karl.	Confused; a bit uncomfortable. Interest in process.	Wonder about Sandy's cutting off Karl. Desire to refocus on Susan or unhappy with what he said? Could she have some feelings or history with Karl?	

(continued)

Table 6.1 A Process Analysis (*continued*)

Content	Nonverbal Messages	Interactions Between Members	Leader's Feelings	Leader's Thoughts/Theory	Leader's Role
Susan: Yeah, but what if they're all like that?	Agnes sits up. Sandy shakes head.			Sounds a bit facile. Will wait it out—too easy a response.	Participant
Willie: You just need to find another kind of man.	Willie smiling, looking directly at Susan. Agnes turning red.	With Willie's seductive approach, Charles, Sandy, Karl, Agnes all pull back.	Angry at Willie's seductiveness. Jealousy.	Unhappy with Willie's seductiveness. Okay, here's a chance for enactment. Susan can deal with problem here and now.	
Sandy: Easier said than done.	Ray grinning. Susan showing little affect.	General negative reaction to Willie.		Waiting to see how group reacts.	
Charles: I wonder, Susan if you attract only those kinds of men.	Speaking quietly.	Group attention turning to Charles.		Charles is in his familiar junior therapist mode. Wonder if he should be confronted or will he offer Susan/group something?	
Agnes: Right! It's always the woman's fault. "She didn't get raped, she led him on."	Sarcastic tone.	Group almost audibly groans.	Sad she's maintaining that stance. Wonder about source of her anxiety.	Mental note to get back to Agnes's anger and anxiety. Have to keep it out now—bad time to deal with it.	

Content	Nonverbal Messages	Interactions Between Members	Leader's Feelings	Leader's Thoughts/Theory	Leader's Role
Charles: Your anger is really getting in the way. I feel that perhaps Susan is attracting these kinds of guys because of where she looks, be-cause of what she does with them, or maybe as a subconscious way of proving that all men are no good.	Charles leaning forward. Looks confident.	Group looking at Charles and Susan.	Glad he's doing it. Wondering if there'll be a leadership challenge.	He sounds like he's on to something for Susan to con-sider. Hope it's concern for her and not defensiveness or self-aggrandizement.	
Betty: Do you think that's possible?	Looking at Susan, who seems sad.	Many members focusing inward.	Concern for Susan and Sandy.	See if Susan will respond or pass it off.	
Susan: Yeah. I've screwed up two marriages and some-times I think I married bastards as a defense against letting myself be intimate.	Susan has tears in eyes. Sandy very pale.	Group moving toward Sandy.	Concern for Susan and Sandy.	Want to connect Susan and Sandy.	
Larry: Sandy, can you verbalize that?	Sandy apparently in pain.		Concern for Sandy.		Catalyst

(continued)

Table 6.1 A Process Analysis (*continued*)

Content	Nonverbal Messages	Interactions Between Members	Leader's Feelings	Leader's Thoughts/Theory	Leader's Role
Sandy: That just hits home.	Begins to cry. Susan looks at Sandy.	Group moves toward Sandy.	Comfort in process.	Want to connect Susan and Sandy and work on fear of intimacy for them and in this group.	
Larry: You're in a similar situation.	Sandy nods. Susan gets teary.	Group looks at Susan and Sandy.		Now need to connect them.	Catalyst
Larry: Can you tell Susan?	Sandy nods. Susan looks expectantly.		Comfortable.	Need to get her to explain content.	Orchestrator
Sandy: You know Bob, the guy I live with? Well, he's a good man, but he's just insensitive to my needs. Maybe I won't let him try, but it's just that he won't listen to any really deep feelings.	Sandy's eyes are clear. Susan crying. Barbara looks sad. Ray avoiding eye contact.	Cohesiveness developing. Focus on Sandy.	Bit anxious to bring out more feelings, but believe it's necessary.	Want to bring feelings to a head now and facilitate their going deeper.	
Fay: That really hurts.	Said with caring and understanding.		Relief for saying it. Caring for them.	Bring arousal to optimal levels. Will have to support members.	Catalyst Model-Participant

Content	Nonverbal Messages	Interactions Between Members	Leader's Feelings	Leader's Thoughts/Theory	Leader's Role
Sandy: God, it's like there's a part of me that's too ugly for anyone to live with.	Looks very hurt and angry. Susan crying. Barbara looking very sad.	Barbara, Charles, Ray, Susan all moving closer.	Empathy, hurt. Concern for Susan and Sandy.	Desire to make support physical. Better if Susan does it. Barbara also needs help.	
[Silence]	Susan and Sandy embracing and crying. Larry puts arm around Barbara's shoulders and she cries. Ray's lips trembling.	Susan and Sandy holding each other. Larry supporting Barbara.	Sadness, concern, anxiety about boundaries.	Have to ascertain members' reactions.	Participant, Reinforcer, Catalyst, Orchestrator
Ray: That's not only true for women.	Lips trembling.	Women look to Ray with support.	Concern for Ray, personal sadness.	Ray's sensitivity coming through.	
Larry: You've felt that also.	Ray nods.		Sadness about rejection.	Important to support Ray.	Reinforcer, Catalyst. Participant
Larry: I've experienced a feeling of not being understood also. It really hurts when you pay attention to it.	Larry's eyes are moist. Susan, Sandy, Barbara weeping.		Sadness, concern, anxiety.	Reaching out to Ray. Good contact.	Model-Participant

(continued)

Table 6.1 A Process Analysis (*continued*)

Content	Nonverbal Messages	Interactions Between Members	Leader's Feelings	Leader's Thoughts/Theory	Leader's Role
Charles: You've got to pay attention to it. If you understand it, you can come to grips with your humanity.	Crying stops.	Members pull back, look to Charles quizzically/skeptically.	Negative about Charles's interruption.	Assume Charles is uncomfortable with the intimacy being expressed. Changed tone to be safe in "expert" mode.	Participant
Willie: That's the asshole way. You just experience it as that's the way it is, and it's O.K.	Willie smiling, but looks pressured. Interpersonal group distance increases.	Members pull back further. Willie is somewhat isolated.	Fear of loss of control.	Charles reduced anxiety enough for Willie to issue challenge. Expect a strong reaction from group.	
Karl: What does that mean?	Question posed in challenging tone. Susan withdrawing.	Most of sadness changed to detachment. Little closeness.	Glad for Karl's challenge. Sad to lose Susan and Barbara.	Karl is challenging Willie. Need to get back to Susan, who seems to be withdrawing.	
Willie: It's all the same. It's what is. You can't take responsibility for anyone else.	Almost detached. Speech seems like recitation. Susan staring at ground.	Group becoming more distanced.	Anger at Willie. Impatience with his "est" speech and detached language.	Need to return to main process and get away from this.	
Fay: Susan, where are you?	Relief from group to focus on Susan. Agnes looks hurt.	Focus on Susan. Charles looks approvingly at Fay.	Comfort with intervention. Anxious to get Susan back to her feelings.	Susan could pull out now. If we don't get her to focus on her feelings of hurt and fear, it could be another rejection/failure experience.	Catalyst Model-Participant Environment Manipulator

Content	Nonverbal Messages	Interactions Between Members	Leader's Feelings	Leader's Thoughts/Theory	Leader's Role
Susan: Feeling hurt and scared.	Group focus on Susan. All look calm and involved except Agnes—still appears angry, and Willie smiling almost condescendingly.	Barbara and Sandy very tuned in to Susan.	Comfortable. Anxious to get Susan working with her feelings.	Pressing in on Susan. This is the time for her to open with Sandy and Barbara's support.	Catalyst
Fay: Talk about the fear.	Susan fidgeting.	Attention on Susan.		Encourage Susan. Be aware of effect on other members.	
Susan: I'm scared I just drive all the men away because I'm not open. But if I open up I get clobbered. It's like if you're a model, only one kind of man approaches.	Susan fidgeting, Barbara shaking her head negatively.		Glad she's beginning.	Keep her focused on this. Key is her fear of involvement-commitment and possibly that this fear manifests itself in behaviors that are contrary to her desires.	
Larry: Barbara, can you share your feelings with Susan?	Susan looking to Barbara who is tearful. Almost detached. Speech seems like recitation. Susan staring at ground.	Attention shifting to Barbara.		Trying to get Barbara to share obvious feelings with Susan. Provide/get support for Barbara and Susan.	Orchestrator

(continued)

Table 6.1 A Process Analysis (*continued*)

Content	Nonverbal Messages	Interactions Between Members	Leader's Feelings	Leader's Thoughts/Theory	Leader's Role
Barbara: It's not being a model. Bill and I have been married eight years and I really love the guy, but I use sex to avoid sharing really intimate parts of me. I started to get involved with Charlie just to have someone I could tell those things to, but it started to get sexual and I pulled out.	Barbara and Susan talking and looking at one another. Others looking at Barbara Willie still smiling.	Barbara talking directly to Susan.	Comfort with intervention. Anxious to get Susan back to her feelings.	Interesting. Barbara is sharing her own identical fear—covered other fears of intimacy by increasing sexual activity.	Catalyst Model-Participant Environment Manipulator
Fay: If you got involved that way with Bill, you'd be vulnerable to hurt, but if you don't open up with your husband, you need a relationship on the side, which has even greater problems.	Barbara looks scared. Susan nodding her head. Karl becoming pale.		Anxiety that they could lose Susan, but wanting to support Barbara.	Try to tie Barbara's problem with husband to Susan's problem with men. Concern for Sandy and Karl.	Catalyst
Fay: That hooks into Susan's feelings of frustration also.	Barbara and Susan looking at each other. Karl more pale.	Barbara and Susan mutually supportive.	A bit confused, generally comfortable.	A lot of things going on simultaneously. Need to pick up most critical. Worried about nonverbals from Karl.	Orchestrator

Content	Nonverbal Messages	Interactions Between Members	Leader's Feelings	Leader's Thoughts/Theory	Leader's Role
[15-second silence]	Willie smiling. Karl very pale.	Leaders making eye contact for support.	Anxious about introducing Karl into this mix.	Decide to include Karl.	
Larry: Karl, you look like someone kicked you in the stomach. What are you feeling?	Karl exhales loudly.	Focus on Karl.		Hope Karl is in with Susan and Barbara. Want to keep this together and on topic of intimacy.	Catalyst
Karl: It's like something really important is being said and I've got to face some stuff too.	Karl agitated. Others focused on him.	Focus on Karl.	Anxiety about Karl's "secret."	He's probably had an affair also—related to Barbara's earlier statement.	Catalyst Participant (listening)
Larry: You've gone the route of an affair also?	Karl exhales noticeably.	Others look nervously at Karl, admiringly at Larry.	Fear of being wrong.	What if I'm wrong? Either way, have to keep the topic on fear of intimacy.	Catalyst
Karl: Several.	Karl exhibiting several emotions: fear, pride, relief, etc.	Focus on Karl.	Interest.	Want to be careful about curiosity. Is he being seductive? What's his affect?	

CHAPTER 7

Group Leader Training

P roper preparation of professional group leaders is such an essential component of ethics, that we have devoted a separate chapter to training issues. In Chapter 8, we explore the other major ethical concerns. Each of the guidelines for proper training described in this chapter is consistent with ethical standards of the American Counseling Association, American Group Psychotherapy Association, American Psychiatric Association, American Psychological Association, and Association for Specialists in Group Work.

Training

Two essential statements can be made about the availability of qualified group leaders:

1. With the tremendous increase in the use of groups in a wide variety of settings, there is a great need for qualified group leaders.
2. Group leadership skills are complex and varied.

Given these two conditions, the training programs for group therapists must address a wide variety of needs. Effective group leaders must understand and work with the group process. They need to be aware of individual intrapsychic phenomena, interactions between people, and group-level phenomena. They need to have a working theory of psychotherapy, an understanding of normal and abnormal behavior, and respect for diversity and individual differences. They must have a working understanding of their own personal dynamics and their strengths and weaknesses.

Training

Training programs for the most part have been fairly haphazard. In most graduate mental health programs, trainees have received instruction in individual psychotherapy and only informal instruction in groups, usually in a practicum setting. Although Hollis and Wantz (1990) describe a steady, consistent growth of university courses and practicum offerings, it has occurred primarily at the undergraduate and masters level.

Indeed, two reviews (Shapiro, 1996, 2001) of curricula of graduate programs nationwide indicate that in both psychiatry and clinical psychology doctoral programs, no courses in group therapy are required. Most masters programs have a single-term course required for students who will be practitioners. Burlingame, Fuhriman, and Mosier (2003) and Markus and King (2003) exploring psychiatric, psychological, and social work programs and clinical internships concluded that group leader training was overall insufficient. These and other studies consistently report that extant group counseling and therapy training programs are longer on knowledge of research on groups and short on experiential learning.

More complete training is scattered and somewhat rare, reflecting the generally held illusion that expertise in group therapy arises naturally from expertise in individual therapy or family therapy. Many individuals, without training in group dynamics have been thrust prematurely into group leadership roles in practica and internships, only to find their individual counseling skills insufficiently effective in such settings. After one such experience, a psychiatric resident commented, "This isn't therapy … It's chaos." A psychologist with many years of expertise in individual therapy was struck by the "interruptions at the most inopportune moments, and the inability of people to wait their turn." Similarly, family therapists may have difficulty adapting to the group's shifting systems and members' unwillingness to act as a unit.

Because of these factors, many practitioners have a negative view of group therapy: an opinion they are too willing to share with potential patients.

This is communicated both consciously and unconsciously. Frequently overheard are statements such as, "We don't have an individual therapist available for you now. I suppose we could put you in a group." Such an indication that group counseling or therapy is suboptimal or a fallback position will affect clients' willingness to enter a group and to be less hopeful once enrolled.

Although some of the individual and family therapy skills are common in group therapy, the reality is that group counseling and therapy are different from other forms of mental health delivery. That is its strength. Because of such differences, specific training in group therapy is *essential*. Although practitioners have known this for decades, change has been slow to develop (cf. Kaplan & Sadock, 1971).

The group leader programs that do exist seem to have certain core elements (cf. Alonso, 1993; Conyne & Bernak, 2004; Corey, Corey & Corey, 2014; Dies, 1980; Jacobs, Masson, & Harvill, 2009; Shapiro, 2010; Toth, Stockton, & Ervin, 1998):

1. Theory and skill learning
2. Personal group experience as a member
3. Observation of professional group leaders
4. Supervised practice as a group leader, with extensive feedback

In addition, personal individual, group psychotherapy, and continuing education in group methods are frequently recommended (Corey, Corey & Corey, 2014; Glass, 1997; Yalom & Lescz, 2005).

Supervised Practice

In any profession, the learning-by-doing approach seems central to mastery. The group therapy situation is so variable and the interactions between unique combinations of participants so unpredictable that preparing a novice group leader adequately for all contingencies is not possible. All leaders must learn, in part, through on-the-job training. However, trial-and-error learning without immediate and accurate feedback commonly leads only to repetitive errors. *Supervision* of the practice is the element that makes the difference. Supervisors must be able to observe the interactions between group members. They must also be able to offer suggestions and alternatives in such a way that trainees can listen nondefensively. Supervisory suggestions need to be integrated into the leader's repertoire and applied as they fit the situation, rather than simply mimicking the supervisors' words or actions in the next session. Feedback from several sources is helpful—from co-leaders as well from supervisors. Another important source of input is less-trained observers (videotape operators, students in training, group members, etc.); their observations and "naïve" questions can often be remarkably helpful. The most effective means to provide accurate and sensitive feedback that we have employed over the past 30 years is delivered when the supervisor observes the group through a one-way mirror or by videotape playback.

Parallel Process

During supervisory sessions, the interactions that occur between the leaders and supervisors are often the major topic of discussion. Frequently the blocks that inhibited interactions in the group sessions are reproduced in the supervisory hour. Competent supervision thus involves both the sharing of knowledge and a form of individual or group psychotherapy. The competent supervisor can use his or her group leadership skills in the supervisory hour and almost simultaneously serve as a teacher, a therapist, and a model of effective therapy.

Alonso (1993) strongly suggests that supervision of group leaders be done in supervisory groups—a method that certainly reinforces the supervisors' faith in the group method. She underscores the importance in such group supervision of mitigating shame for errors and faults, providing peer and supervisory support, affording opportunities for vicarious learning from peers and experts, encouraging healthy intellectual experimentation and competition, expanding the capacity for empathy, and reducing problems of projective identification common in trainee groups.

Observation of Professional Leaders

Learning by imitation is exceptionally powerful when the model has attained a desired level of achievement (Bandura & Walters, 1963). In most trades, the rewards of apprenticeship have included the opportunity to practice developing skills under the supervision of a master craftsman and the experience of being in the presence of that craftsman in action. Watching a professional group leader is a similar opportunity for a trainee to obtain a realistic view of the true nature of group leadership. Observing such a therapist, trainees can view successes and failures, begin to discover areas for improvement in their own developing skills, and see the results of particular therapeutic interventions in specific situations without feeling personally threatened. Hence they can maximize personal time spent in trial-and-error learning and can get some feeling for the scope of a therapist's duties.

For optimal learning, the observation may be paired with feedback sessions in which observers can discuss with the professional leader events and choices made in the group meeting. During these sessions, questions can be asked, various solutions can be discussed and evaluated, and a great deal of mutual learning can take place.

Professionals also benefit from such feedback. Even the most seasoned professionals can benefit from such feedback and questioning. Yalom (1975), for example, states, "I have always found the reflections and feedback of observers, regardless of their level of experience, to be personally helpful to me and thus to the functioning of the group" (p. 504).

Indeed, the National Training Laboratories (NTL) groups that have provided such a spur to the use of groups in business and clinical settings date much success to feedback sessions in which group participants observed the process and commented on the group leadership team's evening meeting (Bradford, Gibb, & Benne, 1964). In the group training programs we have led, students are able to view video recordings or live group therapy through two-way mirrors and then to ask the therapists what they were thinking when they made a certain intervention or declined to respond to something in the group. Graduate students often report that such interactions are a highlight of their training.

Not every professional will be comfortable with being observed. It is important, for training purposes, to find group leaders who do not become overly defensive in discussing aspects of their groups and who are open to a variety of solutions to problems, not necessarily their own singular method.

Personal Group Experience as a Member

For trainees to learn about the effects of a group in nonacademic, nonintellectual ways, they must experience a group as a member (ASGW, 2000; CACREP, 2017; Caffaro, 2001, Coche, 2001; Corey, 2015; Jacobs, Masson, & Harvill, 2009; National Training Laboratories, 1970; Shapiro, 1978, 2001; Yalom & Lescz, 2005). The group experience is emotionally powerful. Unless a leader can empathize with the intense pressures and fears of membership, his understanding of members will be subsequently diminished. The better group leaders understand group phenomena affectively and sensorially as well as cognitively. They can then more fully comprehend what it is like to be vulnerable in a group. Before requesting self-disclosure by members, leaders should realize the level of anxiety and courage such action entails. They must know in a firsthand way what the fears of nonacceptance and peer pressure can be like. In this way, leaders learn how to make better informed and more timely requests for members' participation.

Empathy is only one component of this aspect of training. As a member, trainees also have another opportunity to see an experienced leader in action concurrent with their own higher levels of affect. This is different from pure observation, in which trainees can view the group action more dispassionately. Trainee members in such a group can also observe the coordination between co-therapists and the maximum use of each co-leader's special strengths.

Finally, these training groups are often therapeutic for members. Trainees can discover their personal strengths and weaknesses in such a group and take corrective steps. Typically, training groups are not designed for deep therapeutic intervention, and members with deep-rooted or pervasive psychological problems are encouraged to resolve them in separate individual or group psychotherapy. Less severe problems can be effectively addressed in training groups once competitive defensiveness is reduced.

In developing a training group, three cautions are mandatory. These involve (1) political, (2) personnel, and (3) competitive considerations.

Political. Even in an era of "enlightened" acceptance of alternative paths and solutions to problems, administrators, practitioners, and faculty members are likely to be threatened by the use of groups. Often these individuals are very persuasive in developing support against any such nontraditional innovations. In developing training programs in several locations, founders of group training programs are regularly accused of "forcing psychotherapy onto students," "having personal needs for intimacy met in group settings," "forcing students into nervous breakdowns," "playing with fire," "creating unemployable trainees," "opening the university to inevitable lawsuits," and even "introducing students to communism (or God-lessness)." Despite a lack of information and the absence of truth in any of these statements, the harassment, threats, and pressures to terminate group training programs continue to this day. This sort of difficulty seems relatively universal and must be confronted in almost any setting in which a group training program is instituted. Despite one of the most successful and extensive group training programs, we have had to defend the program against some extraordinary and unfounded claims in every decade during its 50-year existence. We have never been in real jeopardy, but vigilance and clear documentation has been a necessity.

Personnel. The best paper program or plan of action in the world cannot withstand the effects of inappropriate personnel. In this age of technical expertise, the critical component in virtually every personal equation remains the human one. In a group leadership training program, proper staff is the critical requirement. Because the trainees will imitate their trainers, these leaders must have high levels of technical skill and integrity, follow the ethical standards of the profession, and be personally well-adjusted and nondefensive. Regardless of theoretical orientation, these group leaders should be process-centered and integrative with their expectations of member behavior. For example, Yalom (1975) believes "that the trainee's first group experience should not be one of a highly specialized format (for example, TA or Gestalt)" (p. 511).

The particular profession of the leaders is less important than their skills in conducting these very difficult groups. In fact, having group leaders from a different profession than the one for which the students are training is often valuable. This mix helps build necessary interdisciplinary respect.

Competitiveness and Role Anxiety. Training groups are difficult to lead. Members are sometimes highly anxious and competitive with one another and the leaders. After co-leading psychology intern training groups for a number of years, we believe that we have experienced every possible manner of challenge. Because of the competitiveness, criticism of leadership, and desire to practice the therapist role along with a contrasting anxiety about their emerging role as therapists, training group members sometimes open up cautiously and slowly by comparison with members in other groups. They take fewer personal risks, and a large part of the leaders' job is to enhance interpersonal trust, cohesion, and cooperation among members. The earlier in the training these groups are instituted, the easier it is to develop a cooperative, rather than competitive spirit. By the time trainees are clinical psychology interns, psychiatric residents, or last-semester master's students, the task is massive because of their ego threatening fears of professional incompetence. Normally, once students know what is expected of them and establish trust in the group, they are ready for a meaningful personal group experience.

One additional strategy may help diminish the anticipated competitiveness and suspiciousness regarding the use of material that emerges in the group. This involves the employment of nonfaculty members from the professional community as group leaders. Using such clinicians has several additional positive effects: greater confidentiality; reduced worry about being graded for content of self-disclosure in the group; exposure to working clinicians whom students may emulate; and enhanced connection between the professional community and the training institutions.

Theory and Skill Learning

The emphasis on the psychological needs of group leaders should not in any way lessen the importance of academic competencies. Jacobs, Masson, and Harvill, (2009) adapted a microcounseling approach (cf. Ivey, 1994) to skill development. Several skills are mandatory. Group leaders must be able to perceive, understand, and articulate group dynamics, group process, and content (Stockton and Toth, 1996). They must have an active knowledge of normal and abnormal behavior patterns, including principles and theories of learning and motivation. They must also have a working theory of behavior (Corey, 2015) and a solid understanding of the ethics of their profession. In addition to exemplary individual psychotherapy skills, group leaders must have an understanding of the effects of groups on individuals and the power of interaction matrices.

Skills Unique to Group Treatment. In addition to the skills required of all therapists, some capabilities are necessary in effective group counseling or thera-py. Among these skills are the capacity to connect people and ideas (universality) and disconnect them (autonomy and individual growth). Early in a group, the leader may emphasize similarities between members and later (in the therapy phase) turn the focus toward individuation.

For example, a leader might comment, "Lashonda, as you describe what you are experiencing, I am struck by how similar that might be to what Jason was saying last session." By contrast, she might respond, "you are all describing what it's like to be in school together and the pressures of school, but Bonnie also is a single mom with three children. That seems like an added burden."

Therapists need to attend to a host of nonverbal cues between members and leadership and members and each other. Group counseling and therapy involves the ability to scan and observe members' behavior (especially those who are not being verbal at the time).

> **TRINA (Leader 1):** Rob, stay with that experience that you were describing when you went home last week to visit your parents.
>
> ROB: Well, it's never good. I feel like my dad criticizes me for everything and no matter how much I accomplish, it's constant

put downs. I don't even know why I go. Between him and my stepmother, it's not very pleasant. Just an obligation.

CAM (Leader 2): (Watching the rest of the group while Leader 1 is focused intrapsychically on Rob) Trina, let me check in with Katie and Don for a moment. (Then turning to them) You both seem distressed, what's happening for you right now?

DON: Well, I'm not sure about Katie, but it sounded like Rob was at my house with my mom.

Another skill involves maintaining focus on one member when another member's anxiety gets expressed by their breaking into an ongoing process.

Keeping focused in the presence of an interruption may be essential. In a group of teens at a high school, the leader was working with Carlo, a high school junior who was describing his near-terror of not getting into a college. Another member jumped in and asked a question, "My friend told me that I should take the PSAT over, because my score might go up." Then turning to the leader, she asked, "What do you think about redoing the PSAT?" The leader avoided the interruption by responding, "Let's address that question in a bit. Right now I am interested in Carlo's anxiety."

One of the most difficult skills to master for people who are drawn to the helping professions is also one of the most important: rudeness. Group leaders may have to cut off a member, not waiting for them to finish before verbally interceding. The cutting off of unfocused, rambling, repetitive, or insulting monologues is essential in maintaining control over a group in which there may be members who verbally dominate the group time.

In the course of a lengthy monologue during the group, the following interaction demonstrates this point.

MARY: So like I was saying before, the way I keep getting treated by my boss is horrifying. She is constantly on my back and she doesn't even know what we are doing on the project. Like yesterday she came in during our coffee break and …

LEE (Leader 1): Sherry, you seem to be having a reaction to what Mary is saying. Would you be willing to share that?

MARY: You are cutting me off.

LEE: I am cutting you off. At the moment I think what you said had an influence on others and I am interested in their reactions.

MARY: But I was getting to the most important part.

LEE: And we may have time soon to get back to that. Sherry, what is happening for you?

The capacity for drawing out a quiet or reticent group member is also of significant value. In individual therapy, waiting the client out until he or she is ready to address an issue is usually a successful approach. In group, however, a client who is reticent may inadvertently cede their time to other more verbal members, and in the process never get the chance to receive the help they are seeking.

> **LEADER:** Will, last week you made a commitment to consider talking to your friend about how she treats you. I wonder if that came up this week.
>
> WILL: Yeah. Sorta. I mean not that much.
>
> **LEADER:** Please say what happened.
>
> WILL: Not that much. It's probably a bad example.
>
> **LEADER:** Bad examples are my favorite. What happened. Begin by saying when this occurred.
>
> WILL: Well, we were supposed to meet for lunch at noon at this restaurant. I was there on time, but she came in 30 minutes late and no phone call or nothing. She just showed up like nothing was wrong.
>
> **LEADER:** I can see that several people here are having a reaction, but before we ask them, what did you want to do or say.
>
> WILL: Well, after I went through the worry that something happened to her, I got irritated (this is not the first time she has done this), I started to think …
>
> **LEADER:** Say what you were thinking, even if you'd never do those things.

Finally, the ability to summarize an entire group process and connect members around a theme or issue may be particularly appropriate.

> **LEADER:** I am struck by something that's been occurring for the last hour in group. Everyone has been describing in one way or another a sense of being alone and not understood. Yoko, you said that it was hard to be the only person from Japan in group and felt that you didn't express yourself as well in English. Carmen, you talked about the danger of deportation for your undocumented family members. Walt, you said that you felt alone when you were with your wife. Lisa, you reported on what it's like to be the only person in the office working on a difficult project. And Lu described feeling lonely as a single person. It seems

that our group theme is a sense of isolation, disconnection, and loneliness.

Theories of Group

Almost every individual theory of counseling, psychotherapy, and social work has been adopted by group leaders. In addition, there are a few group therapies that stand on their own such as group-as-a-whole therapy (i.e., Ettin, 2000; Garcia, Lindgren, & Pinton, 2011; Rubel & Okech, 2006).

Schaffer and Galinsky (1974) offer a compendium of a dozen theories of group. These include psychoanalytic, group-dynamic, existential-experiential, psycho-drama, Gestalt, behavior therapy, Tavistock, social work, T-groups, encounter, theme-centered, and self-help. Corey (2015) focused more on groups in counseling offers 11 theories of group including psychoanalytic, Adlerian, psychodrama, existential, person-centered, Gestalt, transactional analysis, cognitive behavioral (CBGT), rational emotive (RET), choice theory, and solution-focused. Emotion-focused therapy (Compare, Tosca, Lo Coco, & Kivlighan, 2016), attachment theory (Marmarosh, Markin, & Spiegel, 2013), motivational interviewing (Wagner et al., 2013), and acceptance and commitment (ACT) (Cosio & Schafer, 2015) are also finding increasing use by practitioners working with specific populations of clients. In a special issue of the *International Journal of Group Psychotherapy*, Shay (2017) introduces 18 models of group treatment, up from the 10 described by Dies in 1992.

What is a novice group leader to do with the array of contrasting group theories and models. To what extent is pluralism, integration, or a single theory to be chosen? In his 1992 paper, Dies described the proliferation of models as "polymorphous diverse" (Dies, 1992a, p. 2).

It is our position that each theory offers practitioners tools with which to observe, comprehend, and intervene in a group. The particular model is less important than the "fit" with the leaders' values and the clients in the group. We recommend that graduate students sample different theories as they learn to find what suits them. Subsequently, the integration will occur with leaders' maturity and experience in the field. You may find yourself quite aligned with one approach or you may find yourself shifting with group experience. Wampold and Imel's (2015) and Norcross's (2011) works and the "dodo bird" effect (Luborsky, Singer, & Luborsky, 1975) inform us that all theories work if they are attuned to the therapist and client values and styles of change (Shapiro, 2016b).

We believe that the core to all group treatments is an understanding of the generic trajectory of group process, basics of group dynamics, opportunities to observe experienced group leaders, personal experience as a group member, and careful supervision. One aspect of being in an experiential training group is to help students discover, elicit, and articulate their core values and related personally embedded theoretical orientation and approach to practice. Their awareness and development of a theoretical base and style that is congruent supports their integration of person and technique.

A Model Training Program

The model group leaders training program presented here emphasizes the relevancy of courses in personality and counseling theories, psychopathology, individual training in counseling and psychotherapy as well as family therapy, and a variety of listening and research skills.

In describing a model NTL training program, Appley and Winder (1973) delineated five developmental stages: *participant* (no experience necessary), *beginning trainer* (two labs of experience), *intermediate trainer* (20–25 labs required), *trainer of trainers* (lab experience, senior trainers, and current practice), and *consultant*. This program is quite similar to the group leadership training program that Shapiro designed and headed at the University of Hawaii in the 1970s and at Santa Clara University in California since the early 1980s. Similar progressions were described during the same period by Foulds and Hannigan at Bowling Green State University in Ohio, Corey and his associates at California State University at Fullerton, and Yalom at Stanford University Medical School. The Shapiro (1993) model is a four-term 2-year program during which group leader trainees experience a variety of roles associated with group leadership. The curriculum for the four terms outlined in Table 7.1, is described below.

Table 7.1 Model Group Training Program

Stage I	Stage II	Stage III	Stage IV
Group Work	**Group Work**	**Group Work**	**Group Work**
Membership in interpersonally oriented experiential training group. Led by (external) licensed professionals and advanced student co-leaders in program.	Membership in second training group; one that is more intrapsychically oriented. Serve as video operators and observe Stage I groups and supervision. Class in practice, process and procedures of group leadership	Serve as apprentice co-leader in counseling or psychotherapy group with clients in a community agency. Take an advanced group leadership class in which trainees are members of a group that is co-led by professional leaders and video recorded. Class involves reviewing leaders' actions during group.	Co-lead Stage I groups under direct supervision of professional co-leader and attend supervision with all group leaders and co-leaders. Observe real-time supervision of a group and contribute to running audio track supervision
Adjunct Work	**Adjunct Work**	**Adjunct Work**	**Adjunct Work**
Training in basic therapeutic communication skills. Supervised individual counseling/psychotherapy practicum. Review group video recordings between sessions.	Continue individual practicum in community agency. Take classes in counseling, assessment, and psychotherapy.	Review video replays. Review video replay with stereo audio of real-time supervisory comments.	Complete internship or practicum equivalent in supervised professional setting, including consultation, individual and group therapy and participating in in-service training.
Remedial Work	**Remedial Work**	**Remedial Work**	**Remedial Work**
Consolidation of knowledge in theories of psychotherapy and psychopathology, multi-cultural counseling.	Engage in individual or group therapy as needed.	Engage in individual or group therapy as needed.	

Stage I: First Term

Potential group leaders are enrolled in an interpersonally oriented personal growth group (Group 1) provided by the training institution. The groups are led by a professional licensed practitioner from the community and co-led by an advanced (fourth term) student in the training program. All group leaders are supervised by another experienced community group leader.

Group sessions—which run for 2 hours weekly, with one 8-hour marathon session approximately midway—are video recorded in their entirety. Members are encouraged to view the videos after each session. The recordings are held for the week between sessions and are available only to members of the group and the co-leaders. In addition to their membership in the group, trainees learn basic communications, listening, and counseling skills and (in some programs) engage in a supervised individual psychotherapy practicum. During this first term, trainees are expected to consolidate their knowledge in two adjunct areas: psychopathology and theories of counseling and personality.

Stage II: Second Term

Potential group leaders take an extensive course in the practice and procedures of group leadership containing the curriculum presented in this text. In addition, trainees are required to be members of a second training group in which the leader has a different orientation (i.e., more intrapsychic, Gestalt, client-centered) and encouraged to volunteer at an agency where they might observe or assist in a counseling or psychotherapy group led by a professional group leader in the community.

In addition, trainees also serve as video camera operators in the first-term group for the next group of new trainees. In this role, they have the opportunity to observe a group without being personally vulnerable or responsible. They are also included in the supervision sessions that follow each group session. During this term, trainees are expected to be engaged in study of individual counseling, family therapy, and assessment classes.

Stage III: Third Term

Trainees are enrolled in an advanced group leadership seminar and in practicum in the community. In the latter, they are encouraged to participate and to lead under supervision any groups in their placement that are appropriate.

In the advanced group seminar, students are again members of a training group with professional co-leaders. The group sessions are video-recorded and the leadership is explored in weekly class sessions. During these classes, member behavior is not open for discussion, but the leaders are available to describe their interventions, timing, rationales, and theory in a give-and-take format. The video recordings are explored in depth as are alternative interventions. The essential component in this stage is the leaders' willingness to be open and vulnerable. The effective seminar leader is willing to respond to student questions with theories, rationales, and concerns and is willing to admit to a lack of ideas, missed opportunities, and openness to alternatives.

In one such interchange, a class member asked, "I've been wondering why you chose not to intervene at this point with an interpretation of the process between, Charles and I." Was it better to focus on what was [relevant] in my past instead?" The professor replied, "You know, if I had thought of it at the time, I would have preferred what you are suggesting. Let's compare the relative merits of each intervention."

This interaction in class, honored the student's perception and recommendation, encouraged her to be more active in class, and served to model to all students that professionals are imperfect and can learn regardless of how senior they may be. It made future interactions in class far more creative and interesting.

Stage IV: Fourth Term

Trainees co-lead a first-term group with an accomplished licensed community group leader under direct supervision by that leader and also by the group leaders' supervisor. They meet the group for weekly 2-hour sessions and one 8-hour marathon session. Each session is electronically recorded. Prior to and immediately after each session the leader and co-leader meet for debriefing and supervision. In a supervisory session of all the group leaders and the professional supervisor, leaders are required to view the video recordings and to present the parts they found most difficult to handle. During these weekly supervision meetings, issues and problems in leadership and specific incidents in the groups are discussed. Trainees are expected to review the audio or video recordings at least once during the week.

Alternative Supervisory Procedure

When trainees are advanced in a doctoral program or are already licensed at the master's level, two trainees may lead the first-term group. The professional leader from the community becomes a supervisor and observes the group from behind a two-way mirror. All sessions are video-recorded as above, but here an audiotape is also made.

These audio recordings make special use of stereo channels. During the session, in addition to the video, an audiotape recording is also made on a stereo cassette. Track 1 contains the conversation in the group meeting, and track 2 contains simultaneous process comments made by the trainees' supervisor in real time, while she or he is observing the group. As soon as the session is over, trainee leaders meet with the supervisor for feedback and analysis of the session, consulting the videos as appropriate. They also review the audio recordings with the real-time commentary during the week between sessions. In this model, both trainee leaders and the supervisor attend the master supervisory sessions in which trainee leaders and supervisors from all concurrent groups meet with a professional expert.

During this term, trainees are also expected to do practicum or intern-level work under supervision at a mental health or counseling center and to co-lead a community group with a mental health population.

Throughout this training, extra care must be given to maintaining the highest possible standard of confidentiality. Group members' identities must be protected, and except for extraordinary circumstances normally governed by law, their names should not be part of supervisory discussions. It is the leadership concerns, dilemmas, and strategies that serve as the focus of discussion. Of course, at no time is the content of group performance to be graded.

Beyond the Model: Fifth Term

After trainees complete their degrees and become licensed, they are invited to be professional group leaders and supervisors for subsequent populations of students. This builds in a continuity and ongoing connection between alumni and the training program. It also provides the program with relevant expertise. To avoid inbreeding and a lack of critical discussion, a good strategy is always to have a mix of people from various backgrounds as leaders.

The Group Training Sequence

During the entire model group leadership training program, appropriate reading is assigned, and trainees take adjunct courses to fill in related deficiencies. Trainees are also encouraged to undertake individual and group therapy as clients, for both training and personal concerns.

Review Table 7.1 to observe how trainees move through this group training sequence from member, to observer, to leader, to supervisor. Each succeeding stage is built on successful completion of the previous one, and each represents a building block for the next. Success in each stage requires a major effort and increasing responsibility. By the conclusion of the sequence, trainees must demonstrate competence in the identification and use of the group process. They must be effective group leaders, capable of using and transmitting the ethical values of professional leaders, and they must be aware of their own personal dynamics and limitations. Each trainee must also be able to work independently as well as part of a co-therapist team.

We believe that a 2-year intensive program is necessary to accomplish all these goals. Individuals with broad background in mental health may not need to go through as extensive a group therapist traineeship as described here, but the total amount of training in this program is not excessive for a novice in a mental health discipline. If your own training does not contain similar components, it is useful to seek out additional supervised practice and continuing education.

Summary

In this chapter, four universal components of group leadership training have been identified. Training begins with the individual's personal group experience as a group member. The experience provides emotional learning as well as a foundation for empathy with future clients. Training groups are often a student's first experience with formal "therapy" and ideally a beginning of increased self-knowledge and continued growth—both vital to effective leadership.

Although theory and skill development can be accomplished within a didactic setting, observation of professional group leaders is necessary for modeling of the complex behaviors and attitudes necessary for therapeutic groups. Ideally, at least one academic term would be devoted to group process and another to group leadership. Finally, supervised practice as a group leader, with individual feedback integrates theory with practice.

CHAPTER 8

Ethics

Professional Issues in Group Leadership

The therapist should operate in a way that is comfortable and natural. Nevertheless, there is an etiquette of professional group leader behavior and parameters to which we must adhere. In life we must follow many conventions. We do so, maintaining our uniqueness while adjusting to various situations and environmental demands.

We play different roles on the street, on the beach, with in-laws, at a party, and in the office. If we were to act in precisely the same manner, regardless of the context, we would demonstrate an unacceptable rigidity or inflexibility. The same is true for the group therapist. In this chapter, we describe appropriate leader behaviors. These are presented as guidelines to be integrated with the leaders' values, and professional standards, while respecting the rights of group members.

Ethics

Professional ethical standards exist to protect clients, the public, and practitioners. A clear set of rules, regulations, and guidelines would be germane to meeting that goal. In fact, each of the major associations: American Psychological Association (APA) (2002), American Group Psychotherapy Association (AGPA) (2002), American Counseling Association (ACA) (2014), Association of Specialists in Group Work (ASGW) (2008), National Association of

Social Work (NASW) (1999), National Training Laboratories (NTL) (1970), whose members conduct group treatment have issued sets of guidelines to govern the practice. For the most part, these coordinate fairly well. However, sometimes they conflict and the ethical standards are regularly in flux (i.e., Corey, Corey, & Callanan, 2010).

In fact, ethical standards are increasingly more demanding and cautious for mental health practitioners. Standards that recently seemed clear, safe, and fixed have been called into question and altered by forces and institutions that are outside professional or practitioner organizations. A litigious society, required changes in professional ethical guidelines regarding marketing of services by the Federal Trade Commission, previously unknown dangers of certain therapeutic procedures, potentially contrasting demands of "best practice," third-party (i.e., insurers) constraints, and the general influence of economics on therapeutic practice all combine to make ethical mental health practice far more challenging and complex than ever before.

Many ethical issues can arise in therapeutic groups, and whereas a well-intentioned person of any background may potentially deal with them adequately, a leader who has had professional training in proper behavior with patients and current standards in the field will be able to meet them more satisfactorily.

A core precept of the Hippocratic Oath taken by physicians is the duty to do no harm. So it is for group leaders. We are there to assist and enhance processes that promote the members' mental health and well-being. To be most effective, leaders enlist members' cooperation and confidence. We must be scrupulously careful not to misinform clients or to misrepresent or exaggerate the benefits to be derived from the group.

Group leaders are there to help members, but at what cost? It is not unusual, for group members to want to discuss matters with which the therapist feels uncomfortable. For example, group members may wish to criticize the therapist's supervisor or other staff at the institution in which the groups occur. Leaders also may be asked personal questions about themselves, other patients, or other people. Some of these are questions the leaders shouldn't answer; other may be considered unethical to answer. What is the leader to do if one member makes sexual overtures to another? What are the ethical requirements when the problem goes beyond the active group participant, when it also involves the leader, the group, the other members, the institution, even the counseling or psychotherapy profession? When does the member's need supersede the leaders'?

Is it appropriate to refuse to answer any particular query? Such a refusal may affect the group. Is it more beneficial for members to have more complete openness, or limits that will offer greater security? What if a member requests something unprofessional or reveals something illegal? None of these queries is easy to answer.

We take the position that therapists' ethical responsibility is to protect members by establishing clear limits in the group interactions. As the group unfolds, leaders must act in conformance with their consciences, their capabilities, the ethics of the profession, and the laws of society. Normally, this will not inhibit or interfere with effective group progress. However, such limits must come from adequate self-knowledge. Every therapist has personal limitations. Leaders who are unaware of their personal "blind spots" may not set appropriate limits and thereby create risk for themselves and their clients.

One question that arises with some frequency after graduate students view a video in which a leader reaches out and puts her hand on the arm of a group member is whether such touch may violate the ethical standards. Is touch always inappropriate? Does it destroy the "frame" of therapy? Is it to be viewed sexually? What about humor? What if the leader makes a joke about the nature of the human condition? All therapists may agree that it is never acceptable to have a member as the butt of a joke, but what if the leader responds with humor with no target but him- or herself.

There are several ethical issues that require understanding and a clear focus. In addition, training and qualifications described in the previous chapter, familiarity with the client population, use of exercises or techniques within the group, dual relationships, confidentiality and informed consent, and cultural/diversity issues are all grounds for clear ethical guidelines.

Basic Ethical Standards for Group Leaders

The "prime directive" of all professional therapy is never to practice beyond the scope of one's training. The dictum, "A little knowledge is a dangerous thing," is particularly germane to group leadership. A very strong argument for requiring graduate school training for professionals is that graduate school is the setting in which the ethics and mores of functioning professionals are learned. Untrained leaders often get into ethical binds, or never see the ethical side of the issue at all. They may try to be very well-meaning as leaders, but they may inadvertently still do grievous harm to group participants.

An untrained or poorly prepared leader who does not understand the full scope of ethical responsibility can naively apply a few simplistic guidelines or procedures to all group situations. In the "pressure cooker" group situation, techniques for opening difficult issues abound. The ability to use them properly and to know how to contain sensitive issues is far more complex and is akin to a surgeon who can open a wound and remove or repair a failing body part, but who does not know how to suture or successfully close the incision.

One commonly misunderstood example of the importance of attending to members' vulnerability is the manner in which locus of responsibility is addressed. It's an issue that many encounter group leaders give primary emphasis (and one that may have unintended cultural consequences). Schutz (1973), for example, argues that health and success for members are contingent on the extent to which they take responsibility for their actions—a very strong precept of individualistic cultures. In this view, the following are all examples of irresponsible behaviors: "The devil made me do it," "I just can't do this," "You make me feel so sad," "If only my karma was better," "My Enneagram or Myers-Briggs is opposite his. There's no chance of understanding," or "I'm a Gemini, that's why the Pisces guy hates me." Schutz's belief is that if individuals will own their feelings and actions, they will be able to be more assertive and more effective in their day-to-day interactions. This, of course, presumes that all members of the group share this value system.

Employing this belief ethically and responsibly within a well-delineated theory of personality can be extremely valuable. Within such parameters, responsibility-taking is defined clearly, modeled by the leader, and developed in concert with other skills. However, an unprofessional therapist may employ this construct as a standalone "mandate" without placing it into a network of related constructs. Such misuse is often characterized in nonprofessional "pop psychology." These leaders characteristically have mastered reasonably effective skills for opening up an individual emotionally, without the necessary capabilities to help the individual integrate or close.

In one such group, the leader led the group on a guided fantasy and hypnotic regression to open the third group session. As this regression approached its end, he gave the following suggestions:

> … Now you're feeling totally relaxed … totally open to your experience… and now as I count backward from 10 to 1 you'll get younger and younger. You'll actually be ten years old and you'll feel all the 10-year old feelings. 10, 9, 8 … you're getting sleepy and open; 7, 6, 5 … you know what it's like to be 10 years old; 4, 3, 2, 1 … now be 10, act 10, feel 10. Now you see your parents. Look at them … feel the helplessness you feel with them … how much you need their love and how they never give you enough …

At this point, one member burst into tears and began mournfully crying out, "Don't leave me; please don't leave me."

> **TY (Leader):** Okay … let's hold this exercise. (Turning to the crying member) What are you experiencing, Ben?
>
> BEN: I don't want to lose her.
>
> **TY:** Your mother?

BEN: She died when I was 10. She had no right to leave me alone like that.

TY: *You* didn't believe *she* had a right to die.

BEN: She made me so lonely.

TY: You mean you felt lonely when your mother died.

BEN: I can't help feeling so scared now and sad.

TY: You're choosing to feel sad and scared.

BEN: I'm *not* choosing; you're setting me up to experience these things and I do.

TY: I'm not willing to take responsibility for your feelings.

Not only does this leader fail to confront the emerging clinical material, or provide necessary support for a regressive experience, but he is also a poor model. While instructing Ben to take responsibility, the leader is himself being personally irresponsible. Furthermore, instead of empathizing with Ben, he constantly restructures Ben's words to fit into the leader's own nascent theoretical language. In this case, a single dictum regarding the concept of "responsibility" is guiding the leader's total interaction to the detriment of all members. As the late Charles Schultz noted in his *Peanuts* cartoon: "There's a difference between a bumper sticker and a philosophy of life."

A professional training program is a hedge against a "bumper sticker" approach. If students learn anything, they must learn the ethical guidelines of their profession.

The American Psychological Association has separate but related sets of guidelines for group therapists (2010) and growth-group leaders (1973). The American Group Psychotherapy Association (2002), The Association for Specialists in Group Work (2012), and the American Psychiatric Association (1994) have issued single sets of guidelines for all group leaders. Relevant portions of all these professional standards are summarized below.

Similar guidelines are observed by members of the medical, nursing, and family therapy (AAMFT, 1988); social work (NASW, 1999; ASGW, 2012) professions; and the National Training Laboratories (NTL, 1970).

The following guidelines are common for licensed counselors and therapists:

1. Group therapists are committed to acting objectively and with integrity, maintaining the highest standards in professional practice. They must not violate accepted moral and legal codes of the community or misrepresent their qualifications.

2. Group therapists are mandated to preserve confidentiality and protect the integrity and welfare of the individuals. In cases of conflicts between

co-leaders or leaders and institutions, the group leaders' primary concern must be for the members' welfare. This includes the situation in which the leader believes that there is no reasonable expectation that a certain individual will benefit from the group. In such a case, termination of this member from the group is required.

3. In every group, leaders must receive *informed* consent from members regarding any and all group endeavors.

4. Administration of services, treatment diagnosis, or personalized advice can only occur within the context of a professional relationship. It is appropriate to offer only those services that may reasonably be expected to benefit members in the group.

5. Creating exaggerated notions of success in clients is improper.

6. Financial and interprofessional matters must be in accord with community standards, and respect for other professionals and clients is expected.

7. Clients' right to privacy and nonparticipation are to be protected.

Several similar guidelines have been written for growth-group leaders.

Participation in a growth group should be voluntary. Explicit information regarding group purposes, procedures, goals, fees, availability of follow-up training, educational qualifications of leaders, issues of confidentiality, and any restrictions on members' freedom of choice must be available. Screening is necessary for both inclusion and exclusion of members and for exploration of terms of the contract. Client welfare must be considered more important than research or experimental concerns. Any evaluative, experimental, or other research procedures should be fully disclosed and evaluated publicly, and the relative responsibility of group leaders and members specified. It is expected that regardless of the leader's professional discipline, leaders will hold these ethical concerns as primary.

In general we subscribe to the "best practices guidelines model" (ASGW, 2012; Rapin, 2014). We see these as aspirational, because, for the most part, these ethical guidelines are professionally and morally if not legally binding.

Informed Consent

Entrance to a group does *not* constitute a carte blanche acquiescence to anything that might follow. Members must be informed of their rights to participate or not and the ramifications of refusal to engage in any particular group activity. Members of groups must be informed of the group goals, procedures, purposes, and costs.

They must give their consent to participate, and they must have the right to refuse to participate in any specific group activity. Their right to leave the group is guaranteed. They must be honestly assured that their welfare will be safeguarded as much as possible and that the leader will not exploit clients for political, special interest, or personal reasons (cf. Pinney, 1983).

Some examples from recent groups include the following:

- A member's right to decline if the group leader decides that breaking a heterosexual couples group into temporarily separate male and female subgroups would enhance group communication.
- A member's right to not participate or protest the leader's belief that a prayer at the end of each session is proper.
- A member's right to refuse participation in an exercise in which a level of physical contact is recommended in the group to enhance self-acceptance.

Members who exercise such rights, should not be pressured to acquiesce. However, the question of giving "veto power" to any member must also be addressed. Entering a group without having these issues specified is dangerous.

In the following transcript from a group of adults who are having difficulty with being open and transparent, the leaders recommend that a member try an experiment. When she declined, the following occurred.

> **CARY (Leader 1):** Brianna, I wonder if you'd be willing to try a little experiment in here?
>
> BRIANNA: (With a hesitant look) What do you have in mind?
>
> **CARY:** You have been describing how difficult it is to be open about your feelings of sadness and anger with your husband. I wonder if you might try to express either of these to Bryce (a member of the group who has been very supportive of Brianna).
>
> BRIANNA: I don't think I can.
>
> **CARY:** Would you like to try?
>
> BRIANNA: Is it okay if I don't?
>
> **CARY:** Of course it is. What is coming up for you now just thinking of it?
>
> BRIANNA: I am shutting down inside. It's just too much for me right now. I don't want to do it now. Maybe some other time.
>
> BRYCE: You know, Brianna, I am okay with this if you want to try.
>
> **CARY:** So, Brianna is clear that she doesn't want to try it now, but that's a good offer if she does want to in the future.

Here a member is not consenting to participate in a particular leader sug-gestion. The leaders not only allow her the right to decline, but protect her from having the issue reopen with another member's offer to help.

Most leaders have the "rule" that if a member says "no" or "I don't want to do …" That is sufficient to stop the activity. In addition, the leader will refrain and also keep other members from asking a series of "why not" questions, that is likely to reopen the discussion and violate the "No means no" dictum.

It is our experience that when members are given these rights and protected in this way, they are far more likely to feel safer and deal with personal issues with greater depth later in the group. Regardless of this potential therapeutic benefit, however, it is the ethical way to proceed.

Involuntary Groups. One complication to informed consent is for involuntary groups. This may include incarcerated populations, other court mandated partic-ipants, hospital inpatients, students, military, or workers on some jobs. With the change of increasing incarcerations, particularly for minor drug offenses, there has been a shift to court-mandated participation in group counseling (Riordan & Martin, 1993).

In involuntary groups, leaders often allow considerable time for griping and ventilating angry feelings about being forced to participate. Because the mandat-ed client is legally coerced, he has less control over the outcome or implications of his participation and loses to some extent confidentiality rights, customary in voluntary groups. The group counselor's ethical obligation, and treatment plans, shift from one exclusively focused on the client to a dual responsibility to the justice system and the client. To some extent this represents formidable limits to confidentiality. The courts may also mandate the theoretical approach, away from person-centered and toward leader-centered or team-centered with other professionals.

In general, both the clinical and ethical guidelines recommend that all group members become at least "nominal" volunteers. This is most often characterized by statements such as "as long I have to be here against my will, I suppose I'll try to see what I can get here." Members who bring their bodies to the group, but leave their consciousness elsewhere are unlikely to gain much from group counseling and they are likely to inhibit trust-building and work of others. Often, leaders need to inform members that attending sessions without participating may not fulfil the necessary requirements.

One of our former students had one of the most stressful jobs related to groups. Prior to her entering graduate school, as a person with a B.A. in psychol-ogy, she was responsible for weekly meetings with court-ordered drivers who had been arrested for "driving under the influence." They were diverted to the group instead of jail. Needless to say, her group members were quite involuntary. When she came into her first class in group counseling in her masters program, she said that she never wanted to do group counseling and related "war" stories of her experiences with what seemed like "acting out angry teenagers."

Confidentiality, Privileged Communication, and Secrecy

Group leaders must treat members' activity within the group as confidential communication within limits set by law and professional ethical standards. Most of the content of any client's revelations in group should be kept confidential as is any such material in individual therapy. To safeguard members' privacy, confidentiality must be a group norm. For members to disclose very personal information without some sort of agreement that their secrets will not be made public is absolutely essential. There is no justifiable rationalization to violate this precept save those required by law (potential danger to self or others, child or elder abuse, etc., or a violation of other ethical responsibilities). Any breach of confidentiality can have serious consequences in members' lives. Potential members need to be forewarned about any possibility that confidentiality may not be honored. If the issue is not specifically discussed in the group, the probability of such a violation increases.

Although confidentiality is necessary, secrecy is severely discouraged. Group procedures and processes must be able to stand the test of scientific research. If a group leader does not wish to allow his or her methods to be open for public or professional scrutiny, the reasons for such secrecy should be seriously questioned. Although such secrecy may enhance in-group cohesion by supporting a dichotomy between group members and those who are not in the group, strong exclusive allegiances to group leaders and other members and a corresponding sense of elitism may make transfer of training extremely difficult and reinforces alienation from any people in their lives who are "uninitiated." Such a situation more resembles a cult than a professional therapeutic endeavor. The result of secrecy about methods and procedures thus is the precise opposite of the group goal of enhancing life outside of group.

There is a potential group-specific significant risk to clients. As Welfel (2010) indicates, in counseling and therapy groups, clients are encouraged to disclose personal information with one another and to serve as helpers for one another in an environment that is often characterized by high levels of affect and less control by group leaders. However, the other members are not mental health professionals and not obligated to abide by ethical standards. Indeed, they may be completely unaware of these. It is essential that group leaders educate and try to impress on all members the necessity for keeping others' personal information confidential.

One group leader broaches this topic by invoking a long-time, popular advertisement for Las Vegas. He says, whatever is said in this group, stays in this group. It is nevertheless wise to warn group members that individual members (who are not bound by professional ethical responsibilities) may be fallible and can leak information to outsiders. To attempt to handle this problem by forcing a compact of silence is probably imprudent. However, it is our experience that confidentiality is regularly maintained by group members. Corsini (1957), concurs, citing his 10-year experience with groups in prisons, "Only one case of revealing of information came out—and it was reported by the guilty one himself!"

As Ware and Taylor (2014), summarizing work on confidentiality with children (i.e., Corey, Corey, & Callanan, 2010; Gerrity & Delucia-Waack, 2006; Stone & Isaacs, 2003) indicate, this issue is compounded further when working with minors. The screening process with children also involves additional considerations (Hines & Fields, 2002) with parents, guardians, schools, and other agencies.

Internal Confidentiality. A related question emerges when members of the group meet outside of group. Do they have the right to discuss matters or other members from the group (Lasky & Riva, 2006)?

With regard to this concern, Yalom (1990) cautions that in his experience, members of the group will almost always discuss group matters out of group sessions. Instead of trying to prohibit "the inevitable," his solution is to request that these members report to the group what was discussed outside.

No Time Limits. It is important to express that confidentiality applies beyond the duration of members participation during the group. Although it is harder for members to adhere to a permanent confidential status, it is the leaders' responsibility to emphasize that exposing another person's private information is unacceptable even years after the group has concluded (Gladding, 2012).

Screening

Whenever possible, screening of members for inclusion (described in detail in Chapter 2), is an ethical right of group participants. Clients have the right to be placed in the most therapeutic possible situation. This extends to the mix of people in the group and the avoidance of isolates (i.e., Riva, Lippert, & Tackett, 2000).

Members have a right to know in advance the limits of any group in dealing with their symptoms or needs. The ethics of leadership include avoidance of group mixes that could be toxic or otherwise dangerous for any individual. For example, had the group leader known of the ardent "right-to-life" stance of the member and of another member bringing up an abortion (Chapter 2), they would have been wise to keep them in separate groups. As Corey, Corey, Callanan, and Russell (2014) state, "Leaders want to keep in mind that all groups are not appropriate for all people" (p. 47).

Jacobs, Masson, and Harvill (2009), Shapiro et al. (1998), and the ethical guidelines of the ASGW (Thomas & Pender, 2008) and ACA (2014) recommend that screening be done in an individual interview by one of the co-leaders. This is the most time-consuming, but as Shapiro (1978) indicates, the time spent up front will pay back large dividends if the right people are screened into and out of a particular group.

Whether or not they do personal interviews, some leaders (i.e., Corey et al., 2010) often use the initial session for continuing screening. They often officially form the final membership after viewing them together in the first group meeting. In one such group at a college counseling center, a young man was referred to a far more appropriate group for him after he seemed quite overwhelmed by the level of expressed affect during the first session. When the leaders, following professional ethical standards, recommended that he be placed in a more appropriate group, he expressed considerable relief and thanked the leaders profusely. It wasn't that he was not suited for a group. It was just not this group.

Without screening, there can be no control over membership. Individuals can end up in thoroughly inappropriate groups. The profit motive or organizational convenience seem the most likely justifications for failure to screen potential members. This may be a special problem in the current economically centered mental health environment. Patients are more likely to be assigned to a group by time, location, or cost criteria rather than clinical suitability. Often a preferred provider organization (PPO) or health maintenance organization (HMO) offers a single group or a small selection of groups to anyone needing group treatment in their cachement area or system. In addition, practitioners, faced with decreasing availability of clients are more prone to stretch the range of clients screened into a particular group. When dealing with one's mental health needs, personal beliefs, values, or behaviors, profit and convenience are uniquely inappropriate decision criteria.

Dual Relationships

The ethical standard for psychologists (APA, 2010) is as much as possible to avoid dual relationships whenever possible. In most cases, combining personal or business relationships and therapy relationships is problematic and likely unethical. It is also unethical to create income by encouraging clients to be engaged in additional services offered by the therapist. This may be especially difficult in group treatment. Some therapists commonly serve as therapists for individuals in individual therapy and group therapy simultaneously. This can create a dual relationship.

One common such situation is the professor/group leader role common in training programs (Gladding, 2012). In this situation, members of the group are simultaneously students in a class on group theory and process. Thus there is a risk that what they disclose in a group setting may affect class grading. This possibility may also have a chilling effect on what members choose to disclose in group. As described in the last chapter, we strongly encourage training programs to separate these two and have outside professionals lead the experiential groups whereas professors teach the classes. Goodrich (2008) notes that these situations have been inadequately studied to make firm judgments and rules, but that the best practice guidelines are to try to avoid even the possibility of a conflict of interest, dual-relationship situation.

It is important to note that the proscription against dual relationships may be very difficult when one practices in a small or rural community. A counselor in a small community may have as her client a physician, who is the sole ophthalmologist in the area. Similarly, one's children may be in a school with the children of clients and they may have activities together. There is no easy way to explain why the children might not be on the same soccer team for fear of violating confidentiality.

In these situations, most people learn to compartmentalize their activities. In addition, it is essential to discuss the outside connections during confidential therapy sessions and come to a mutual agreement as to how such associations will be treated. One of these occurred regularly when the senior author was working in a small community and led a group of therapists in the same community. It was impossible to avoid outside professional meetings. Thus discussions of the multiple contacts and appropriate behavior in the group and outside became a significant early issue.

Credentials

A degree from an accredited graduate training program in one of the mental health fields is no guarantee of ethical leadership, but lack of such credentials is considered a negative indicator. There is a greater probability that a nonprofessional leader will be unaware of, or fail to conform to, ethical standards, than will a professionally trained leader. If the leaders themselves are not yet licensed professionals, they should be supervised by a recognized professional expert. It must be noted that a license to be a group counselor falls well short of being able to do so knowledgably and ethically.

Consider this 2017 advertisement for a group sponsored by a well-regarded hospital in the San Francisco Bay Area. The text appeared in a neighborhood paper.

> The [Medical Center] in conjunction with the Eating Disorder Clinic has scheduled a support group for those struggling with eating disorders 7–8:30 P.M. Tuesdays in Conference Room X at the Hospital. [Mary Helso-Field], a volunteer with the Eating Disorder Clinic and an eating disorder survivor leads the group.

The group leader had no credential, no stated professional education or competence in dealing with a very serious range of mental health disorders, often co-morbid with other psychiatric disorders, and her only knowledge stated about them was as a fellow survivor. This is, to be fair, described as a "support" group, but the public is relatively unaware of differences between support and counseling. Ms. "Helso-Field" is not required by law to live up to appropriate ethical standards or best practices, because she is not a professional. However there are serious dangers to members of such a group and a shocking obliviousness of liability for the hospital. No screening was indicated.

Advertising

Although rulings by the Federal Trade Commission in the 1990s eliminated the former professional restrictions on advertising, the wise consumer and professional are advised to be wary of immodest claims of success, promises of dramatic life changes, or suggestive inducements in newspapers, websites, bulletin boards, or public magazines. Professionals normally advertise groups via referrals, modest brochures to other professionals, members of a self-selected mailing list, word of mouth, and reputation. Public advertising should include the leaders' credentials and experience and offer a pregroup free screening interview.

Group Size

Groups of fewer than 6 or more than 14 members are often inappropriate except when dealing with certain specific patient populations. In a too-small group, cliques can form and the likelihood for scapegoating may increase. Each member may be pressured to produce an uncomfortable level of verbalization, often at a faster rate than is desirable. In a too-large group, process cannot be effectively monitored, trust is difficult to develop, cohesion is limited, and often members who are shyest and most in need of attention can get lost in the shuffle.

As a general rule, *as pathology increases, the group size decreases.* Thus a group of 10 to 12 "normal-neurotic" outpatients is quite appropriate as is a group of 6 or 7 schizophrenic inpatients. Similarly, groups for young children tend to be quite a bit smaller than groups for older individuals. It would be unusual for example, to have a therapy group of more than 4 to 6 preschoolers.

Costs

The average rates for group work vary little in most settings, usually being set by professional consensus, insurance or agency coverage, and population served. Groups that are offered for token low payments or excessively high costs should be carefully investigated. Sometimes groups are offered at very low cost because they are subsidized by other funds, occur in an agency, or competent professional leaders offer services at a reduced rate as they are trying to build practices. Sometimes professionals charge very low fees as part of their *probono* (charity) work. By contrast, other leaders charge low rates because that is all their services are worth. That is not a true bargain.

Group leadership is difficult work, and when professionals put in time and effort, they have a right to adequate remuneration. Yet, some group leaders charge excessively high rates for their work. They rationalize that the more people pay, the more they will get out of the experience. This seems irresponsible to most professionals. Often, members pay for elaborate settings, resort costs, catered meals, and so on; these amenities may be desirable, but they are certainly unnecessary to successful group therapy. Sometimes these high-priced group leaders are on a workshop circuit; they come into town for a short time period and leave promptly afterward—taking the money and leaving no provisions for follow up.

In 2016, such a group leader with a theoretical specialty came into the San Francisco Bay Area, between similar appearances in Las Vegas, Los Angeles, and Palm Springs. Group sessions were held in a first-class hotel and attracted most participants from high-income Silicon Valley company employees and spouses. Although many thought it a good experience, others considered themselves casualties of the "concert circuit" approach. At least two people who participated in the weekend group had to be hospitalized soon thereafter. Organizers of the events determined that those individuals actually benefitted from the experience, "because they realized that they needed help."

Such excesses need to be moderated by screening for different populations for therapy and growth-oriented groups and follow-up care.

Follow-Up Services

Ethical responsibilities do not end with the termination of the group per se. Group counselors and therapists have an obligation to members to help them deal with issues that are generated in the group, but that hibernate and come into fruition only after members have left the group setting. This does not mean that the leader engages in follow-up therapy with each member. It is important, however, for the leader to be available for consultation and referral, at least for issues that are group-engendered. Some groups, often those that are part of research, schedule a follow up for data collection and consultation.

If a group leader does not provide some level of follow-up services, group members can miss the opportunity to maximize important group learning. Even worse, they can be left in a new wilderness, opened by the group, without adequate survival skills. If the leaders are not available for referral or postgroup therapy services, a major safeguard against casualties is neglected.

Culture

Since we first entered the field, and perhaps because our earliest practice was in Hawaii, ethnicity and culture has been a very salient aspect of ethical treatment. In the 21st century, cultural diversity is a given in North American society. Providing ethical standards to clients of varied cultural backgrounds and particularly minorities may be an additional challenge.

The ethics of all related mental health professions require increased understanding and sensitivity to those whose backgrounds are different. It also demands a careful personal assessment and awareness of gender issues, personal values, attitudes, and biases. Psychology has long struggled with the –emic (member of a culture) and –etic (outside observer) perspectives and conflicts between group membership and individuality. The exploration of diversity goes to the heart of how an individual experiences her- or himself. The factors include matters of ethnicity, race, culture (both macro and micro) age, sex and gender (as self-defined), socioeconomic status, religion, lifestyle, disability, primary language, political leanings, and so on.

The very belief in therapy and its capacity for change involves a cultural bias. It may strive to be value free or value neutral, but the forms of group therapy in which we engage are very Western in orientation. Failure to acknowledge cultural value differences is likely to result in underuse and lesser impact of group counseling (Sue & Sue, 2016) and premature termination (Leong, 1992).

Three strongly held group values can be problematic with diverse populations:

1. Mediterranean and some other Western European cultures for example often revere speaking up and expressing feelings in group. By contrast, members whose ancestral culture is more East Asian, Latino, or Native American may be reticent to speak until a request is given for participation (Sue & Sue, 2016). For these members, hesitancy to speak up may be more a sign of respect than avoidance.

2. Group treatment often favors a culture of individualism and self-growth over members whose primary cultural values are more collective (Chung, 2015; Pederson, 2000; Ratts & Pedersen, 2014).

3. Shame cultures versus guilt cultures (Benedict, 1934; Creighton, 1990). Groups are characteristically far more oriented to issues of guilt than of shame. Methods and procedures that elicit and work through guilty feelings (either for something done or not done) may be far less effective when addressing core issues of shame (usually something experienced as humiliating and disgraceful), which may extend to a sense of letting down an entire family or community.

Gender norms and other deeply embedded assumptions also manifest in groups. In most parts of the world, including North America, there are expectations that women take a back seat to men when it comes to expressing strongly held or contrary opinions. The danger of professional ethnocentrism or gender bias may be mitigated by awareness of the differing styles of members of a group. It is not unusual for leaders in a group to ask members about their preferred style of interacting and subsequently to approach them using that framework.

In a recent group of very diverse graduate students, a woman, born in Korea said that her goal for the group was to speak up more. The following is how the leader responded:

> **MO (Leader 1):** That sounds like it is not easy for you to do so.
>
> SOO: No, it's not what is expected in my culture and my family.
>
> **MO:** (Turning to the group) I wonder who else shares Soo's challenge.
>
> AYDA: (A woman in the group, wearing a hijab) That would be me for sure, especially if the men here were dominating.
>
> BRAD: Well, I may be one of those men, but I pretty much learned "not to speak until spoken to."
>
> **MO:** What I am hearing is that at least for some folks in this room initiating is difficult and seems unnatural, and I am aware that a few others didn't even join in here to speak up. So let me ask Soo to talk briefly with Ayda and Brad about what they could do together to support each other in this very real challenge to achieve a fairly unfamiliar goal and also what the rest of the group could do to support them.

Another approach that has been successful for us when there is a small minority, who feels that speaking up would be unseemly or inappropriate unless they were specifically asked include for example, giving blanket permission for them to try out this new behavior for a short period of group time.

In this situation, the leader offered special permission to verbalize to a very reticent Japanese woman, who he saw as having a lot of emotions that she kept to herself. After a particularly heart-wrenching discussion about personal loss had occurred in the treatment phase of the group, the client was visibly affected by others' responses, but verbally quiet. The leader turned to her and said, "Yoshiko, this discussion seems to be very emotional for you. Is there something you'd like to express verbally?" When she replied that it was hard for her to speak of such intense emotions and besides what others had said was more important, the leader smiled and replied, "I am going to try something unusual here. For the rest of our two hours today only, I am going to declare a special no-shame option for Yoshiko alone. If you want to blurt out anything, appropriate or not, you and you alone have permission to do so until the group ends today."

Finally, recently in a training group, Li, a member self-described as "Asian" said, "we don't express ourselves openly." The leader, a Chinese American woman herself reflected, "When I am in a mixed group like this, I tend to keep more of my reactions to myself, but when I am with my friends, I am a bit of a chatterbox." Li nodded and affirmed that she was like that also. At which point the Leader said, "I'd like you to try something today. I'd like you to imagine that the group was made up of your friends and everyone is an Asian woman and act as if that were so. Would you be willing to try that sometime today?"

In each case, the person's self-identified culture is respected and honored, while encouragement is given to try a small experiment with moving toward a self-determined goal.

It is not possible for most counselors and therapists to be aware of all cultural differences in our ever-increasingly diverse population. A leader may know a great deal about African Americans and far less about Hmong Americans. We may understand Catholicism far better than Islam. A leader who has come from the Philippine Islands or studied there may comprehend both the language and culture of *tagalog* speakers, and know far less about those who speak *Ilocano*. In India alone, there are more than 2,000 dialects (and microcultures), each somewhat different. People whose culture is "Asian" may be very different. After all, people from Kazakhstan, Korea, and Israel all have Asian roots, but very different cultural backgrounds. Finally, knowing about Americans from New York, doesn't necessarily make one knowledgeable about people from El Paso. We are also very aware that within-group differences may dwarf between-group differences. One of the most underlooked divergence in North America is socioeconomic. The culture of poverty crosses many racial and ethnic lines. Values, life orientation, family constellation, and effect of prejudice all affect individuals dramatically.

Comas-Diaz (2014) uses the term "cultural competence" to encompass knowledge of self and others, openness to and comfort in honoring differences, and awareness of one's personal prejudices and limitations. Comas-Diaz (2014) identified characteristics of culturally competent therapy. These include an ability to shift between cultural frameworks within a single group, openness to the intersectionality of members' experience (the variety of mixed influences), a pluralistic sensitivity, and to encourage empowerment to address issues in the group, especially for minority populations who have experienced long-term oppression or lack of privilege.

In discussing approaches to couple therapy, Shapiro, Patterson, and SooHoo (2017) reported that it is by definition cross-cultural and any counseling or therapy has to be multicultural to be successful. This is especially salient in group treatment. Each person comes from a unique background and set of influences. It is essential for group leaders to be sensitive to broader cultural trends as well as respecting each person as a minority of one.

In one group, a member described herself as, "I have no ethnicity. I am just white." She didn't say this in a self-deprecating manner but was describing a sense of having a diffuse identity. Although the group originally let it pass and moved on, later the leader asked, "what is it like to be 'just white?'" The member responded, "Well I don't know. We are from Minnesota, fourth generation, and my family is Scandinavian." Understanding that to still be a very large categorization, he persisted, "Where in Scandinavia? My grandfather came from Finland." She replied, "Swedish 100%. I don't think anyone from my town in the Iron range was from Finland, only Swedish and Norwegian. It was actually a big deal when I was engaged to my husband because he is Norwegian."

The leader asked, "Do you think anyone here shares your background?" This opened a discussion for all group members to begin discussing their own cultural backgrounds and to begin encountering similarities and differences.

Sensitivity to and awareness of differences and the ability to accept plural ways of being, allows members to work within their own ethnocultural framework to get what the group has to offer. Leaders' abilities to recognize significant differences in processing from their own preferred styles go a long way to enhancing both safety and effectiveness in group.

Up to now we have been discussing situations when group members come from different backgrounds than the leader. Yet one of the most dangerous tendencies comes from those who seem very alike. This problem of *assumed similarity* can fool group leaders into cultural errors as well. In fact, it is likely that when a member comes from a significantly different background, there is an almost automatic desire to learn about the differences. By contrast, when members look like you, talk like you, have parents that seem the same as yours, have the same religion, and so on, there is a contrasting tendency to assume that they are in fact similar. This can set off an obliviousness to real differences.

As one of our students remarked, "I figured that another African American, lesbian, from San Francisco was someone I knew all about. As it turned out, she resented me for assuming I knew her and spent two sessions trying to prove that I didn't have a clue. Indeed, I did not. We might have looked alike and knew similar communities, but we are really different."

Special Dangers in Group

Scapegoating. Scapegoating, which originated as early as biblical times (Leviticus, 16:8–10), is an ancient practice of shifting blame for sins onto (often human) others, whose punishment absolves those sins. In group therapy, the phenomenon occurs when one individual is treated as the object of projection and blame by others. A majority of group members (denying some unpleasant aspects of themselves) see those negative traits instead in a "group-determined victim." Because the blaming is an unconscious projection, attacking him or her is a way for the group to feel better about themselves by disowning those troubling personal attributes.

Because members are not obligated to follow professional ethical standards, they might act in ways that cause harm. The scapegoat is usually an easy target for criticism or blame and a convenient object for others who would more easily externalize a personal problem than face it directly.

In one such adult counseling group, there was a man in the group who fully lived up to his self-description as a "computer geek." He spoke initially in objective terms, was far more interested in finding solutions than exploring personal feelings and was fairly inarticulate talking to others in the group.

LEADER 1: Ryan. You seem more reserved than normal today. Where are you?

RYAN: I'm here in the group. Just tired from not too much sleep this week. Big project at work.

FRAN: You are never present! Last week, when Lisette was talking about her failing marriage, you just said she should get out with no feeling for her.

LISETTE: Yeah, I wondered why it sounded like support, but it left me cold. It's like you just don't care about anyone but yourself.

ELLEN: I know. It's like he says the right thing, but it's so off-putting.

LEADER 2: (Interrupting and trying to cut off the ganging up on Ryan.) Ryan, you seem to be catching a lot of criticism. What's going on for you?

RYAN: You know I am used to people misunderstanding my motives. I feel like I am being misrepresented here.

FRAN: You know you may think you are being helpful, but you are always hurting others, particularly the women In the group.

With this escalation to sexism and the term "always," Fran is attacking Ryan and essentially inviting others to join in. In many groups, without firm leadership intervention, this could evolve into potentially harmful scapegoating.

LEADER 1: (Turning the focus back on the attacker) Fran hold on a minute. You seem very angry at Ryan now. What is coming up for you?

FRAN: Well he just is always attacking women and I'm sick of it.

LEADER 1: How is Ryan attacking you right now?

FRAN: Well, he's just so unemotional. Just like my ex and this guy at work.

LEADER 1: This seems important, what about people not showing their emotions is dangerous for you?

Only after Fran's reaction is brought into the group can the leader return to Ryan and begin to explore his personal pattern of inadvertently inciting others' anger at him.

This example of a group going "off the rails" is possible under conditions of anxiety pulling members away from facing more intimacy or other relational unknowns. Haeseler, (1992) citing Buys (1978) warns about deindividuation, diffusion of responsibility, pressures toward uniformity, and group think. This kind of loss of personal responsibility and demand for uniformity in a mob has been well studied in psychology, since the dawn of the 20th century (Freud, 1981; Le Bon, 1895; Rousseau, LeBon et al., 2017).

Under the guise of helpful feedback, an insecure group operating less as individuals than as a unit can subject members to destructive criticism or attack and demand conformity. There is no question that such pressure (often for inappropriate or premature self-disclosure) can be damaging.

As Lakin (1991) notes, groups that are designed to be helpful could be experienced as tyrannical, constricting, and bigoted. For Lakin, leadership determines whether a group will be perceived as positive or negative.

He cautions leaders to be aware of pressures for premature cohesion, the group being excessively swayed by powerful (tyrannical or domineering) members, and pressure for increasing expressiveness. The last has also been described as a mandate for increasingly embarrassing confessions.

Leaders must recognize that there are powerful forces in a group that a leader cannot fully control and instead must focus on how they may be harnessed. It may be a little like using electricity or as one trainee once opined, "I feel like I am riding an elephant." To comply with and enforce the ethical best practices standards, group leaders must be willing to interrupt a process and have the courage to protect all group members. It requires focusing on extant process, sensitivity to members ego strength, awareness and willingness to address the consequences of members' interpersonal interactions, and navigating the waters between becoming authoritarian (overcontrolling) or laissez-faire, allowing the group to control the ship's rudder as well as its engine.

Atypical Group Goals and Procedures. Each group has methods and value systems that are tied to its goals. Members need to be made fully aware of the intent of the group before they can make an educated decision to join. Hidden agendas of group leaders often lead group members into directions they would not have chosen had they been better informed. An example of this occurred in 1997 with a group leader who believed very strongly that members had to reject all aspects of their childhood, including their parents and relatives, before they could be totally functioning adults. However, he advertised his group as a place where members would "come to know themselves more fully, become freed of blocked energy, and gain a fuller connection with their past." Needless to say, his way of accomplishing this aim involves a series of procedures that many potential members would reject if they were informed of them in advance. Once participants are in the situation, group pressure may influence their compliance.

Groups as Parts of a Movement. Whenever the leader has a particular philosophy to sell or an "axe to grind," group members can get lost in the process. Groups are designed for individual growth in directions determined by the individuals themselves. When individual needs become subjugated to other, often hidden designs, the individual may suffer. A member of a group led by a self-appointed "guru" can find acceptance only within a certain framework. He must conform to role expectations of a larger body and his development is limited to the lines sanctified by the movement. In such a situation, individual freedoms frequently are set aside. This is not to suggest that belonging to an organization larger than oneself cannot be a rewarding experience.

However, group therapy or growth work are not the appropriate places for this type of leadership. One man's mission can be another man's destruction. A men's or women's group leader who is sexist and promotes the "war between the sexes" as a way of supporting a personal angry agenda may be a poor guide for members who wish to comprehend differences, honor their own gender and connect with the other sex.

Psychological movements may be as influential and dangerous as political ones. Frequently, diagnoses and treatments, particularly in the pop psych culture have a "du jour" quality. In the mid-1990s, for example, some leaders seemingly held beliefs that the vast majority of their clients had undiscovered multiple personalities, were sexually abused as children, or suffered from adult attention deficit disorders. When they promote these beliefs as group leaders, members may be at risk. Unless members are aware of such prejudices or fads, they may be influenced to perceive all their life difficulties as the result of some unique cause, or may develop symptoms that will fit with the leader's proselytizing.

Jargon. Each group, of necessity, has its own language system and theoretical orientation to highlight and describe various aspects of the group process. However, language systems can be used to obfuscate and mask differences as well as to delineate issues. If a member finds people speaking in a manner he does not comprehend, he is in a high-risk circumstance. This situation is compounded when a group employs commonly understood words, but in a way that has special unique meaning. One example of this is the word *experience*. In some groups, this word describes the sum of all input for an individual. In another group, it refers only to emotion or feelings, and, in a third, experience means compliance. Thus, if a leader is not easily understood, or if the group employs an unfamiliar or confusing language system, the group should be avoided.

Treatment Groups and Growth Groups

Without guarantees of safe practices, group members are left unprotected and can be seriously hurt by the machinations of an unprofessional group leader. In a series of articles and textbooks, Lakin (1969, 1972) elucidates critical concerns for leadership. He contrasts the psychotherapeutic intent in groups from the growth motive: "The therapists' mandate is relatively clear—to provide a corrective experience for someone who presents himself as psychologically impaired" (1969, p. 924). On the other hand, in a training group, Lakin explains, "There is no way for a participant to know in advance, much less to appraise intentions of trainers, processes of groups or their consequences for him" (p. 924).

Lakin also made a distinction between participants of the early growth and later training groups. Early participants were mostly psychologically sophisticated, mainly professional, and in general, they had intellectual understanding as their goal. In contrast, since the late 1960s and early 1970s vast segments of the general public became participants. When members are generally less sophisticated and more psychologically disturbed, they are most often seeking a cathartic rather than an intellectual experience. Furthermore, Lakin added, there are a great number of inadequately prepared group leaders.

Many authors decry the lack of adequate screening and group preparation for both members and leaders in growth groups and workshops, and a corresponding lack of follow-up or posttraining. Beymer (1969), Coulson (1972), Dreyfus and Kremenliev (1970), Lieberman, Yalom, and Miles, (1973), and Shostrom (1969), as well as Lakin, have all warned against the ethic of high drama in growth groups. The tendency to view the value of an interaction as linearly related to the amount of affect expressed is far too common. Techniques and exercises designed to bring members to high levels of emotional arousal are easily acquired and frequently used.

In such an environment, leader and peer pressure in a group can push members to levels of emotion and affect-induced behaviors that are not easily reincorporated into their lives. It is inappropriate for any group leader to create such drama and subsequently absolve himself of responsibility by rationalizing that patients who are harmed are "choosing" to lose control.

These rationalizations are simply not defensible with unscreened, unsophisticated clients. Lakin (1969) and Shapiro (1975) point out that the *caveat emptor* principle is professionally indefensible. The "consumer" may in fact agree to an implied contract that he really does not understand. Lakin (1969) says, "It cannot be assumed that the participant really knows what he is letting himself in for" (p. 926). At the request of a powerful leader, or with group pressure, members may engage in affectionate, aggressive, personally revealing, or sexual behavior in the group that they will regret later and that may have subsequent negative repercussions.

A leader who is unaware of the power she wields or of the nature of transferences formed in a group setting can tread on sensitive ground and create a condition of vulnerability in members that she cannot or will not handle effectively. Even more dangerous is the leader who accepts this position of power as a means of self-enhancement. Instant "gurus," people with a mission or point of view to sell, and those who are insecure may comfortably bask in the facile glory of group leadership. Such self-aggrandizement may come at a high cost to members.

Shapiro (1978) reported on such an individual who was operating in Hawaii during the 1970s. He falsely claimed to be a clinical psychologist. In the course of his weekend-long marathon group meetings, which consisted of approximately 10 to 12 regulars and 2 to 3 new members (initiates), each member was to take the "hot seat" and tell the thing that was most upsetting to him or her. In one case, a psychology graduate student was accused of "not owning" his latent homosexual fears. The student in question seriously examined himself and after a time denied any homosexual leanings. The leader, with intense emotional support from the group, then "worked" with this student *for 6 consecutive hours* to get him to accept his homosexual feelings. When the leader suggested a scary exercise "to help get him more in touch with his repressed feelings," the student fled the room. In a state of panic and questioning whether he did the right thing to leave, he called his professor-advisor to ascertain whether or not this procedure was acceptable "therapy." He was advised not to return to that group and to explore in personal psychotherapy the feelings that resulted from the marathon session experience.

This particular student had considerable ego strength to sit through 6 hours of this kind of treatment and to leave the room to make a phone call. A group member with less strength could have suffered much more serious harm. The group leader was himself subsequently hospitalized after several similar incidents, and a credentials check brought him under the jurisdiction of the authorities.

By modern-day standards, even for growth groups, it is appropriate to inform members of proper standards for group leader behavior; to inform them of their rights to decline or leave any particular component of group, and for redress; and to provide information about appropriate state consumer protection and professional boards.

The public should be protected from excesses such as those described here and forewarned of the possible dangers of participation in certain types of groups. Leaders should take care to provide answers to all of the concerns a reasonable, consumer may have. The ethical guidelines for potential group members, delineated here, is but a bare minimum, designed to increase the probability that ethical, responsible group principles will be applied. There is, of course, no guarantee that any group will be effective for any given individual. These criteria are intended to function as warning signals. To the extent that groups fail to conform to these indices, the probability of unethical, irresponsible, and dangerous leadership is increased.

Summary

A group experience can be very powerful, and entering into such a situation should not be done impulsively. The decision to enter a group should be weighed; each individual should be aware of their goals for participation. Several group approaches can be examined and a choice made that corresponds to an individual's goals and abilities, if possible after consultation with trusted others.

To help the individual evaluate various groups, the ethics and standards of the group leaders must be clearly specified. These ethics are inextricably woven with the extent and quality of their training.

General principles of ethics for psychotherapists are applicable to the group setting with certain specific considerations and adaptations. The principle of competence was most directly addressed in the previous chapter with the authors' proposed model educational program for group leaders. The importance of awareness, knowledge, and skills specific to the group modality are stressed. The group therapist needs to model integrity, respect, concern for others, and social and professional responsibility.

Ethical considerations specific to group psychotherapy include screening, informed consent, the rights of group members, and understanding of diversity and confidentiality.

Screening for a therapeutic group consists of matching an individual with a compatible group composition and goals. One advantage of HMOs and other large mental health contract providers is a large patient pool from which to form appropriate groups. Groups ideally would be homogenous in ego strength, developmental level, and goals; the group would also have a short-term focus on the presenting problem.

Informed consent involves a two-way communication where the leader is responsible for determining the prospective group members, understanding and agreement regarding group goals, procedures, and leader qualifications. Members' rights and agreements should be communicated verbally and in writing. An initial and intermittent discussion of the limits and importance of confidentiality is another ethical responsibility of group leadership.

Finally, provision for follow up after any group is advised.

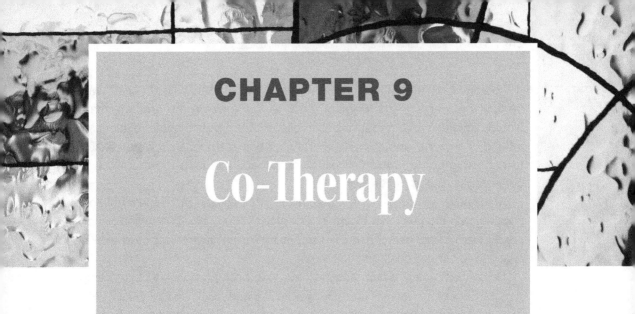

CHAPTER 9

Co-Therapy

In most examples presented in this text and in the model training program, the groups all have two leaders. We believe that every group can be conducted best by more than one therapist. For the most part, clinical practice and some research also support the use of co-therapists for both training and therapy. Rosenbaum (1971) suggests that the presence of a co-therapist increases the validity and intensity of specific interpretations, helps root out and break through therapeutic impasses, helps neutralize or clarify neurotic problems of the therapist, increases the depth and movement in therapy, allows for simultaneous probing and support, and aids transference. Corey (2015) includes the advantages of the different perspectives of life experiences and insights of two therapists, the combined strengths of a complementary leadership team, and re-creation of early family experiences with a male and female co-leader. The leaders may also gain in knowledge by observing and working with another professional and by splitting the work load in the group. Thus while one leader focuses intrapsychically on an individual, the other may focus on group process and attend to other members' reactions.

Not everyone agrees with the use of co-therapists. In times of economic cutbacks and restriction of mental health services, using two leaders is almost anathema to cost-cutting health management. However, we believe that co-therapy is sufficiently more effective that it actually will result in long-term cost saving.

Economic reasons are not the sole arguments against co-therapy. For many years, the notion of using more than one therapist was directly discouraged on theoretical grounds. Classic psychoanalytic theorists were particularly averse to the addition of a co-therapist on the grounds that it would severely and negatively complicate the transference relationship. Indeed, concerns about multiple transference relationships were reasons to eschew group treatment at all. General cautions about co-therapy were consistently issued by Slavson (1964).

Many have also argued that personal factors between the leaders will complicate group progress. For example, Cooper (1976), Corey (2015), and Shapiro (1978) warn of dangers when the leaders fail to maintain an effective working relationship or have conflicting theories.

By contrast, many group theorists have long been proponents of co-therapy groups. Early proponents of co-therapy were Hadden (1947) and Whitaker (1949), who used co-therapy as a training device; Dreikurs (1950), Grotjahn (1951), and Hulse (1950; Hulse, Ladlow, Rindsberg, & Epstein, 1956), who investigated the use and implications of multiple therapists in a group setting; and Lundin and Aranov (1952), who have provided a lengthy description of their use of two therapists in groups of schizophrenics receiving insulin treatment at Chicago State Hospital. Later work (e.g., Dick, Lessier, & Whiteside, 1980; Diamond & Shapiro, 1973; Harari & Harari, 1971; Levine, 1980; Napier & Gerstenfeld, 1983; Rosenbaum, 1971; Shapiro & Diamond, 1972; Shapiro, Marano, & Diamond, 1973; Yalom, 1995/2005) all support the use of co-therapists in a variety of group settings. Delucia-Waack (2006) favorably explored the use of co-leader teams in psychoeducation groups with children and adolescents.

Two predominant reasons were given to support the use of co-therapists in the early work. Dreikurs (1950) and Hulse (1950) and his associates (Hulse et al., 1956) favored co-therapists for their value in reproducing a "family setting" within the group therapy context. Hulse et al. (1956) also recommended the use of male and female co-therapists to stimulate this "family" reaction. Several articles have reported on investigations of the transference phenomena in such a setting for husband-and-wife co-therapy teams (Harari & Harari, 1971; Low & Low, 1975), father-and-son teams (Solomon & Solomon, 1963), and interracial leader teams (Shapiro, 1976). The conclusion is that the generated transference provides a great deal for the group to explore.

In addition to the family simulation, the early use of co-therapists for training was frequently reported. Whitaker's (1949) early work training physicians and Hadden's (1947) training with interns and residents are excellent examples. Anderson, Pine, and Mae-Lee (1972), Gans (1957), Rosenbaum (1971), and Yalom (1995/2005) have also indicated the value of a co-therapy model for training. Two forms of co-therapy can be used in training: an egalitarian model (Getty & Shannon, 1969; McGhee & Schuman, 1970) and an apprentice model (Shapiro et al., 1998).

For maximum therapy impact, many authors agree with Yalom (1975) who states "a co-therapy arrangement of anything other than two therapists of completely equal status is, in my experience, inadvisable" (p. 420).

In the egalitarian model, the leaders are generally equal in ability and are held out to the group as equals. In the apprentice model, there is a clear leader and an assistant co-leader. Each model has obvious advantages and disadvantages. However, the apprentice model is especially useful in training. The co-leadership relationship is a powerful, intimate liaison. Shapiro (1993) has suggested that the same level of scrutiny be put into finding a co-leader as one gives to finding a close friend, personal therapist, or life partner. Issues of power and status must be worked out as well as stylistic and theoretical differences. Such adjustments take patience and flexibility. Because we are dealing with group leaders, however, we expect tolerance and a give-and-take approach. Usually, problems of co-leadership can be resolved. Generally, only therapists whose personal styles mesh and whose theories coordinate will be effective as co-leaders. Thus it is not surprising to find co-leader teams in which one has an existential orientation and another, an object-relations orientation. The primary issue to which they will have to adjust is to the centrality of exploring the present (existential) or history (object relations) and the more active approach and greater self-disclosure of the existential orientation.

However, it would be less likely for a cognitive behavior and an object relations-oriented leader to be effective partners. Here the focus on behavior before insight versus insight-first orientations may be a larger chasm to transverse.

A Few Basic Rules for Co-Leaders

Co-leaders are wise to sit across from one another, not side by side. They need to be able to see each other and to signal nonverbally when appropriate. In a new group, co-leaders will mark carefully their seats before members enter the room.

It is best when co-leaders do not follow one another in verbal interaction. Thus when one leader intervenes in some way, it is recommended that members speak before the next leader chimes in. Sometimes, group members experience leaders following one another as "piling on," and will become more resistant to speaking themselves. Corey et al. (2014) see this as particularly likely during the transition phase of a group.

It is essential that the group goal and methods are set and that both leaders are on the same page. Any unknown or secret agendas are anathema to leadership and the group (Riva, Wachtel, & Lasky, 2004).

Competition regarding interventions, theoretical interpretations, or cutting one another out is very deleterious (Luke & Hackney, 2007). These issues are best addressed and resolved before or between sessions; not worked out in the group. Differences of opinion may be discussed in group, but cooperatively rather than competitively.

Co-leaders need to maintain a good working relationship, in which differences may be aired, discussed and resolved for the benefit of the group functioning. Okech (2008) and Okech and Kline (2006) focus on the need for co-leaders to have an ongoing commitment to address interpersonal relationship issues. This includes particularly any issues of diversity, be they cultural or theoretical.

Advantages of Co-Leadership

Although training and transference-family simulation issues were the early reasons for co-therapy, several other excellent reasons have been advanced as co-therapists have worked together. These include better coverage for the group, mutual support for the leaders, feedback mechanisms, opportunities for better interactional fit, lower effect of powerful countertransference, self-therapy, on-the-job learning, greater opportunities for role flexibility, modeling, easier termination for leaders, reduced chance for burnout, and greater effectiveness.

Better Group Coverage and Greater Effectiveness. Even the seemingly omniscient group therapist is not infallible. In every group, an individual leader's attention will be focused on some members and not on others. Whether because of theory, personality, or the interaction between leader and members, each leader will tune in to some members and some processes in a group while missing others. Every individual therapist has blind spots. The addition of a second leader with unique perceptions, theoretical orientation, and personal reactivity to members helps reduce the number and size of these blind spots. Where one leader cannot empathize with a particular member, the second leader may, and vice versa. In this way, co-leaders provide greater coverage.

As one leader opined after a recent group, "I couldn't for the life of me understand what was driving this one member and found her not only difficult, but off-putting. To my pleasant surprise, my student co-leader was quite well tuned in to her and made a couple of terrific interventions. Even in supervision, when he described how he understood the member, I could understand, but not connect fully."

Commonly, each therapist has preferences in terms of the members with which she or he works most effectively. With two leaders, the effects of negative preferences can be minimized. Thus, more voluntary and effective treatment can be offered to each individual.

Mutual Support and Self-Therapy. In addition to being able to fill in for each other, co-therapists work together. When co-leaders support the same perception, it is more difficult for members to resist. Rosenbaum (1971) notes that, "Patients are more prone to accept two interpretations that are constant than one solitary interpretation" (p. 501). Similarly, when one leader makes a tentative response and finds support from the co-leader, he or she can then follow up with less fear of being totally off the track. If co-leaders disagree, they can negotiate and find an adequate alternate path, with less tentativeness by either. In this way, co-leaders check and balance one another.

There is also tremendous personal value in a co-therapy situation. When people are consistently in a highly charged emotional climate like that of group therapy, they need someone to talk to about their own feelings and reactions to group members and process. Group members regularly deal with basic human conflicts. Group leaders share these life strifes and are not immune to personal response. The perfect partner for discussing these problems is another person who was subject to identical stimuli—the co-therapist. Each co-therapist serves as a reality-based sounding board and therapist for his or her partner. There is also the advantage of being able to discuss the group without a chance of inadvertently violating confidentiality.

For these and other reasons, the choice of a co-leader is a major decision not to be taken lightly. Co-leaders who have a personal as well as professional relationship may be mutually therapeutic, a connection that is especially important immediately following a turbulent group session. The co-leaders also serve as peer diagnosticians, for each other. Often a co-leader's responses in the group meetings will be an indication of certain psychological blocks or problems. It is the other leader's job to observe and relay such information back to the partner.

Interactional Fit, On-the-Job Learning, Role Flexibility, and Modeling. Frequently in a group setting, a member will need to confront personal issues and to feel support at the same time. Co-therapists are ideally positioned to do this. Instead of having a single therapist engaging in both challenging and supporting behaviors, a very complex therapeutic task, each of the therapists can choose a single role. One of the leaders can provide enough support so that the members feel safe enough to drop some of their psychological defenses and hence be more receptive to otherwise threatening feedback from fellow members or the other leader. In this way, members can experiment with new behaviors in a supportive environment.

Often these co-therapist roles switch, depending on the nature of the inter-actional matrix of the group. Thus, one leader may be the supportive therapist with some members and the confronting therapist with others. When groups are co-led by a male and a female therapist, members often see the female as warm and loving (mom) and the male as authoritative or authoritarian (dad). In the breaking down of such stereotyped projections, many members revisit experiences with their parents and experience significant therapeutic breakthroughs.

In the course of a group, co-leaders will, of necessity, disagree. Sometimes, it's a time to trust the co-leader and go with whatever he or she is doing. Sometimes, however, the disagreement as to what to do may be more major. If they can express this disagreement openly in the group and negotiate a settlement, they serve as powerful role models in effective conflict resolution.

THERAPEUTIC CONFRONTATION

It may be important to describe confrontation in therapy and particularly in a group. Effective confrontation typically does not involve challenges to the person's position or beliefs or an "in-your-face" ambiance. Instead, it involves offering the members a chance to look at discrepancies in their statements and behavior or incongruities between verbal and nonverbal expression. These confrontations might be among the more powerful:

LEADER: You know Richard, I am confused. You are describing something that seems very sad and yet you are smiling as you talk about the end of your marriage. Can you help me understand better what you are experiencing?

Another direct confrontation occurred recently in a group of people who work in the computer industry. This confrontation was very cognitive in this highly cognitive group:

LEADER: Lindsey, I am confused here. Earlier today you said you were a software person and your goal at work and at home was to solve problems. Just now you said that what was happening in your relationship with your sister was "fate," and that there was nothing to do about it. I am confused by what seems a contradiction. Can you help me understand better?

A more emotional confrontation occurred in a group of immigrants, who were discussing the difficulties they had with feeling accepted. One member was saying that he was angry at his roommate, who couldn't understand him at all. While he reported this his eyes were watery and he was sniffing back tears.

LEADER: Yuri, you look very sad. I wonder where the anger is at being dismissed so often.

Harari and Harari (1971) discuss the value of a husband and wife co-therapist team fighting fairly to resolution as a valuable component of the co-therapy approach. Naturally, co-therapist problem sharing should be kept to a minimum and dealt with only once the group has evolved far enough to deal with such conflicts. In terms of our group process model, Phase III should be well underway before such leadership problems are shared. If too many co-therapy conflicts are publicly resolved in the group, members can become wary, lose their faith in the leadership, and develop feelings that the group is not equipped to deal with their own problems.

It is not unusual for example for one leader wanting to focus on a group level interpretation, while the other is more intent on an intrapsychic approach with one member. The following discussion is from a training group of graduate students, led by two professional leaders.

GENE (Leader 1): Carli, you seem stuck between wanting to go deeper into something or to avoid it entirely.

CARLI: Yes, that's the story of my life.

GENE: I wonder if you'd be willing to try something by focusing a bit on that incident you described earlier when you were a teenager with your stepdad.

They began the exploration, but little movement was occurring. As the co-leader looked around the room, she noticed that other members seemed withdrawn and not focusing on what Carli was saying.

KARA (Leader 2): Gene. I'm wondering what you have in mind right now.

GENE: (Getting the signal that his co-leader was focused elsewhere in the group) I was thinking it might be beneficial to Carli to make a (intrapsychic) connection between a fairly deep dynamic in her life and what's happening in the group. What do you have in mind?

KARA: I was primarily focused on what is going on (group level) in the group. I see different people look like they are shutting down.

GENE: I'm okay with either. What's your preference?

KARA: If it's okay with you Carli, I'd like to check in with the group before we proceed on any specific issues.

Carli rapidly gave her consent and the leaders focused at the group level. What is most important is that the leaders had different desires at the moment. They discussed it openly and came to a resolution in front of the group. This demonstrates both transparency and a method of conflict resolution without any major battle.

Of course, sometimes the conflict is larger and the leaders may feel much more strongly about their approach, but as long as they are willing to negotiate and seek resolution, it is good modeling for members. As one member of a couples group said when the leaders differed, "Jeez. That was amazing. Mommy and daddy disagreed and didn't end up in a fight!"

Other Values of Co-Therapy. Co-therapy provides for personal growth (Benjamin, 1972) of the leaders. It is also convenient when one therapist is sick or on vacation (Rosenbaum, 1971), and economical in terms of better coverage, more therapeutic resources per hour, and so on.

Dangers of Co-Therapy

All the dangers in a co-therapy situation seem to be a function of inappropriate selection, a dependent or conflicted interpersonal relationship, and/or competitiveness. Corey et al. (2014), Heilfron (1969), Luke and Hackney, (2007), MacLennan (1965), and Yalom (1995) have all addressed the problems inherent in a co-therapy relationship.

Competitiveness in the co-therapist situation can be devastating. In no case can one co-leader work to further himself at the expense of his partner and still have an effective group. A crucial test of their cooperativeness comes during the transition phase test of the ceiling where a challenge is issued to one of the leaders. If the co-leader comes to the support of the challenging member(s) at the expense of the co-leader, an almost unclosable gap can ensue. Actually, the nonchallenged leader's proper role in this situation is to support both and focus on process. In any case, vying for the members' affection can be as destructive in a group as it is in a family when parents fight for children's affection.

Competitiveness seems especially prevalent in groups of advanced students where the status dissimilarity between the leaders and members is not apparently great, such as groups of psychology or social work interns or psychiatric residents. Having the co-leaders simultaneously be members of another training group usually reduces such competition.

Selection of a co-leader is an important decision; one leader should never feel like he or she is "stuck" with a partner's judgment. It is best when co-leaders have complementary skills and styles rather than identical ones. Most authors agree that a male-female team or a culturally diverse team is good, but physical characteristics are outweighed by skill and mutual sensitivity. It is also important that co-therapists be clear about their own personal relationship. If co-leaders have a dual relationship (professional and personal), it is essential for them to be explicit with regard to these roles and in agreement as to the relative place of each. It has been somewhat common for a married couple, both licensed therapists, to form a co-leader team. Co-leaders must also be able to work at relatively equivalent speeds to keep the group process moving consistently.

Although there has been considerable clinical observation, there is little empirical research on co-leadership (Riva, Wachtel, & Lasky, 2004). Miles and Kivlighan (2010) working with intergroup dialogue groups explored similarities and dissimilarities in teams and reported that it was most effective in group when group co-leaders "share cognitions (theoretical perspectives) about the group but are dissimilar in terms of their skill sets and behavior within the group" (p. 114).

At least in these groups of undergraduates, as group leaders are more similar in approach and values, there is less conflict within the group, particularly early in the group process. Researchers also found some evidence that when there were more dissimilarities between leaders, there was less conflict over time. They concluded that this effect was related to the co-leaders bringing complementary skills to the group. This process study did not measure treatment groups or group outcome. However it is consistent with multiple observations about co-leader teams.

When Co-Leaders Are "Too Expensive"

Despite all the compelling arguments favoring co-leadership, a practitioner may well be in a situation where immediate cost is paramount and/or the third-party payer simply refuses the extra cost of another professional. Even though we might prefer an equal partner, there is much to be gained from an apprentice co-leader who is less trained or experienced. We strongly recommend that practitioners regularly contact graduate mental health programs and give opportunities for advanced students to be co-leaders in any group. This certainly serves the profession as well as clients. There is also the benefit of having one's work viewed though a novice's eyes. Not atypically, a student's perception will be fresh and on the mark, uncovering surprises that trained eyes might miss. We can learn from their perceptions and from the questions we professionals are forced to answer when working with trainees.

It is important to note that despite the apparently obvious advantages and recommendations of many publications on co-leadership in groups (i.e., Corey, Corey, & Corey, 2014; Deluccia-Waack, 2006; Yalom & Lecsz, 2005), there has been precious little research on the processes or outcome of group co-leadership. Until more attention is paid to comparative outcome research, we can rely on clinical observation and experienced leaders to suggest that it is a superior model of leadership.

Summary

The co-therapy model for group leadership offers many benefits. It allows training and modeling to occur within the leadership dyad. In both an equality and an apprentice co-therapy model, mutual feedback, support, and personal growth are available.

Although a co-therapy arrangement offers emotional support and supervision to each therapist, it is the group members who benefit most from the presence of two therapists. A co-therapy team is a more effective therapeutic agent within a group setting. Two therapists working together can provide better coverage of the three levels of group process; group, interpersonal, and intrapsychic. The therapists can provide mother and father transference figures and contribute a greater repertoire of therapeutic resources to the group.

Despite the benefits of a healthy co-therapy relationship, there are dangers inherent in two therapists sharing the leadership role in a group. Similar to a marriage, problems of inappropriate selection and or competitiveness within the co-therapy relationship can result in more harm than good for the group. Leaders need to pay as much attention to the foundation of their co-therapy relationship within the group as they do to the emerging group process.

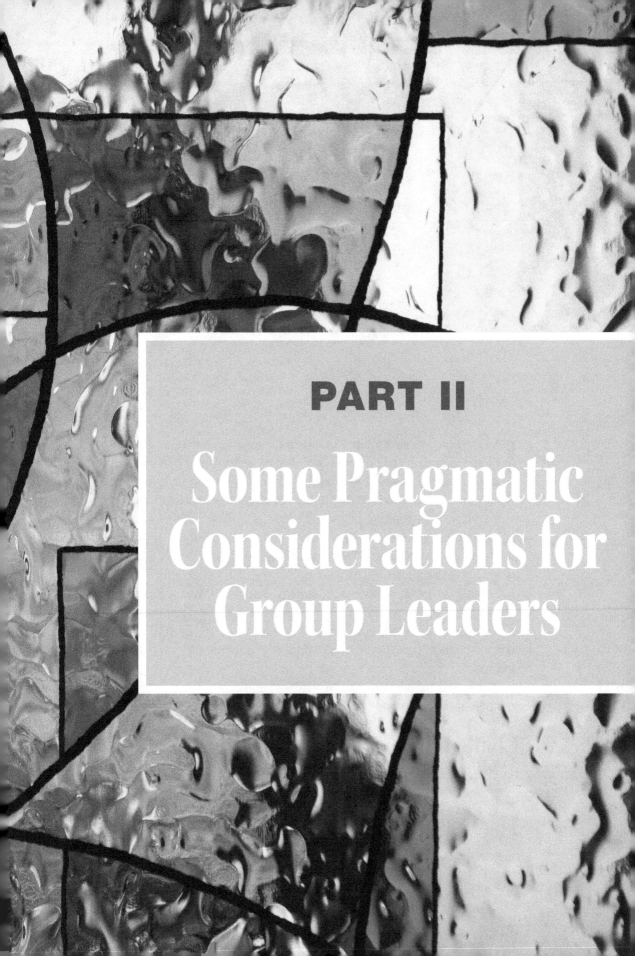

PART II

Some Pragmatic Considerations for Group Leaders

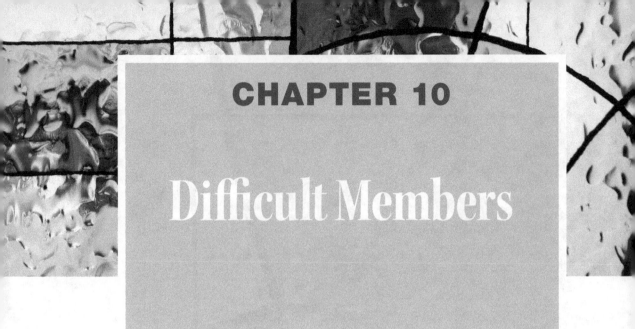

CHAPTER 10

Difficult Members

E verybody wants a toolbox or recipe book, just in case …
Regardless of one's level of skill or expertise, it can be daunting at
times sticking with the group process and having faith that everything
will all work out for the best. It's understandable that leaders of all skill levels
would wish for a toolbox or recipe book as insurance against difficulty or
disaster. Most novice therapists at one time or another, envy apprentice
plumbers who carry around tools that make those reassuring clanking sounds
as they go out on jobs.

Sometimes basic recipes *can* be invaluable to provide a model for effective action in the face of challenging circumstances. Appropriate application
of techniques coupled with the group leader's ability to tailor the "recipe"
to immediate circumstances can support and enhance group process and
progress.

In this chapter and the next, we explore some purely pragmatic aspects of
group treatment: challenging situations and useful techniques.

Challenging Client Behaviors

Many novice group leaders become alarmed that a problematic member may
have an extremely negative effect on the group or a fantasy that he or she might
even destroy it. Until a leader gains enough clinical experience to understand
that difficult or negative member behaviors are often self-limiting, will likely be
mitigated by the responses of other members or may be useful with the correct

"Aikido-like" group leadership to move the group to deeper levels of interaction, she or he will be more likely to try to lean on specific techniques to cope with the unfolding process. We encourage instead a renewed focus on process and only very judicious use of specific tools and techniques.

Every group leader inevitably encounters members who present challenges, evoke anxiety, and call into question the competence of the leader to work successfully with particular behaviors and issues. Leaders often become most frustrated when they try to do everything right while nothing changes or the situation worsens.

For many novice group leaders, these few members seem to have an extraordinary influence on the overall group. In addition, until a leader gains enough clinical experience to have a comfortable grasp on the limits of client behavior, it is useful to consider some methods that address some of the most common difficult and mind-bending problems that may arise in group. Almost every group leader we have supervised has asked, "What can I do?" with a specific member behavior in group. Or as one experienced therapist opined, "I get the most frustrated when I do everything as planned, but it doesn't work."

As we contemplate intervention as the leader, with particularly challenging members and situations it is useful to consider five progressively more involving steps:

1. Allow the group space and time to give each other helpful feedback and learn how better to develop effective ways to work together.

2. Help the group work with a particularly challenging member through attention to nonverbal cues in the group and encourage members to give feedback about the challenging behavior (domineering, loquacious, junior therapist) and the effect it has on them personally. The leader can support using "I" statements of feelings. This may be an opportunity for authentic dialogue between members, promoting trust and cohesion by modeling and encouraging compassionate assertiveness.

3. If a constructive dialogue seems remote or too daunting to address in the time available for members, the leader may intervene directly by exploring the group process.

4. Should that fail, the leader can intervene directly with the member in question with respectful therapeutic interventions along with appropriate limit setting.

5. Finally, if none of these methods work and the challenging behavior continues or escalates, the leader will have to manage the situation with direct limit setting or possibly referral to an alternative treatment.

The following exploration of commonly encountered disruptive behaviors provides understanding, guidance, and options to cope with disruptive behaviors that weren't discovered during screening. These situations may range from the annoying to obstructive, and in extreme cases, dangerous.

Resistance or Refusal

Before discussing the specific challenges, it is important to distinguish between *resistance* that arises from (1) internal ambivalence to change and (2) conscious, deliberate noncompliance, such as refusal and oppositional rejection.

Psychological resistance is defined here as an internal, unconscious struggle between the pull of the status quo, which provides the benefit of avoiding substantial anxiety; versus risk in the service of change, which offers the benefit of increased flexibility and symptom reduction (Shapiro, 2016a). Refusal, which may also be fueled by fear of change, constitutes a conscious rejection of therapeutic efforts. Both may be activated in the group environment where self-reflection, disclosure, and interaction are encouraged. The group norm of experimentation with novel thoughts and behaviors further raises the possibility of elevated levels of anxiety.

Facing those fears in new ways activates both healthy anxiety (from facing the unknown) and neurotic anxiety (avoidance and pulling for the status quo). The major difference is that with internal resistance, the client is attempting to change but is being blocked by a need for security, even if the familiar is aversive. The nature of the reticence to face the fears of the unknown is often a strong indicator to the therapist of the defensive strengths of group members. Understanding those strengths is a key to being able to join him or her as a supportive partner in coping with the need to make changes.

Group members presenting behaviors such as overtalkativeness, overcontrolling behavior or avoidance by taking a role as a junior therapist in a group, are best approached from a therapeutic or clinical perspective. We make three heuristic assumptions:

1. that clients defend with strengths rather than weaknesses,
2. true resistance is a message from the client's unconscious mind requesting aid, and
3. the nature of the resistance is a GPS indicator to the best bridge across the anxiety-filled moat.

Often, when the therapist joins the client more fully in his or her avoidance of the feared changes by supporting and understanding the status quo (and need for security), it paradoxically opens the door for the client to feel safer exploring more fully his or her existential anxiety and confronting the neurotic anxiety (Shapiro, 2016a).

As a rule of thumb, it is important to determine the underlying anxiety that drives disruptive behaviors and the consequences of those actions. Awareness of those will go a long way toward being able not only to survive the behavior, but to use it for the group advantage. The model we use is a bit like therapeutic Aikido—using the attacker's energy and redirecting it for better purpose. For example, incarcerated or otherwise involuntary group members may develop cohesion around their shared desire to not be forced to be in the group. Once this connection and some trust is established, the group can become supportive and foster authentic dialogue and problem solving.

By contrast, clients who externalize their anxiety and consciously refuse to participate or disrupt other members' participation, initially may be approached clinically, but the group leaders may eventually also have to manage their behavior. Sometimes, behavioral management interventions are required earlier in the group trajectory. Thus in a group of adolescents, particularly those "in the system," the fear of change or the peer, social benefits of acting out may be so great, that counseling or therapy must take a back seat to getting their anxiety-driven oppositional or noncompliant behavior under control.

Posthuma (2002) lists several crucial leadership skills including attending and listening, objectivity, genuineness, empathy, warmth, respect, flexibility, creativity enthusiasm, humor, clinical reasoning and acumen, responsibility, self-confidence, and therapeutic use of self. Corey (2015) and Shapiro et al. (1998) add reframing, normalizing, confronting, refocusing, and providing feedback that enhances self-awareness.

Some challenging client behavior for supervisees and experienced therapists:

1. The domineering member or incessant talker

2. The distractor or joker

3. The intimidator

4. The "junior therapist"

5. Negative competition

6. The silent person

7. The hyperemotional (anger, sadness, crying, etc.)

8. Those who may be hostile to other members and the leaders

9. Those with an unknown outside relationship

10. Those whose pathology inhibits the group and who may need to be referred to a more appropriate treatment (i.e., those with psychotic, sociopathic, severely borderline, or narcissistic personality disorders)

In dealing with difficult client behaviors in group, some therapeutic assessment is essential. For example is a person being excessively loquacious because they want to gain something from the therapist or other members, or conversely, because they want to avoid something? What are the consequences of their actions in the group and potentially elsewhere? Are they being disruptive as a way to push for more attention or to keep the group from going to a deeper level of interaction? What are the evident and potentially unconscious fears behind the behavior? Does this behavior require control or empathy from the therapist and how do we know which is which?

Although some leaders naturally rely on analytical/cognitive skills to inform their assessment, others rely more on their own emotional responsivity and processing. We like to think of neither of these as the best one or even as distinct. Instead we consider them as two tracks on the same stereophonic music. Both contain relevant data. Mixing both tracks together provides a dimensionally richer experience as each related yet different track adds to the overall experience. When we leaders "listen" to the combined cognitive and emotional data in the group situation, we go beyond our natural style as we gain a much fuller appreciation of what is occurring. When co-leaders possess complementary styles, therapeutic assessment can be accelerated and enhanced.

With each of the challenging examples that follow, group leader engagement and facilitation of the therapeutic process will win out over group member management. However, there are exceptions in which security must be achieved before therapy can occur.

As a group evolves, anxiety increases at certain stages. When it becomes uncomfortable, members engage in previously learned behavior to effectively reduce, rather than face the anxiety. For example, when it becomes uncomfortable, some members become quiet, scope out the situational ambiance, and slightly withdraw. Others get chatty. There is no particular universal best level of verbalization, but when avoidance of anxiety gets extreme, the behavioral expressions of that anxiety block progress and may do so in quite intense ways. These can be difficult to address and stand out as problematic for group members and leaders.

In this chapter we are exploring those problematic behaviors that reflect neurotic anxiety—that which pulls for the status quo and avoids facing fears of the unknown. In all of these, we begin with identifying and using process, moving to intrapsychic exploration and finally to management as needed.

The Incessant Talker

In many groups, a person or two may appear to be talking all the time, commenting on every statement made by other members and leaders. They are garrulous in group, with tendencies to ramble, repeat, loop back to their own earlier statements, fail to move to deeper levels, and often "fill the airwaves", preventing others' participation. At certain points in the group trajectory, others may welcome the distraction and reduction of pressure to do their own work or conversely feel cut out from the benefits of the group. They may tune the person out, withdraw, or confront the member or the leaders (usually with some frustration or irritation).

When the relentless talker is apparently using verbalization to avoid the anxiety of silence or of others bringing up threatening subjects, the goal of the leaders is to find ways to address the anxiety, move past the obstruction, and move into deeper levels of interaction. One method is to help reduce the person's level of anxiety by providing additional security/structure. This may be done at the group, dyadic, or intrapsychic level.

Another possible motivation for the "talker" may be that she or he is trying to be the "good" client and trying to meet perceived expectations by incessantly talking in group. When the goal is to meet others' supposed desires, the talker is often characterized by long, drawn-out, repetitive, irrelevant, and often boring stories that truly do not engage other members or even permit them access. Frequently, this verbal "rambler" seems unaware of the audience and is talking to satisfy personal internal needs—often to be "a good kid" while paradoxically ensuring an opposite effect on the group and its leaders.

A third motivation for excessive talkativeness is related to anxiety around self-esteem. This often takes the form of "showing off" to the group. Such a person may name drop, try to demonstrate expertise, take over as a "junior leader," or act to curry favor with the leader as the "best member" or "star patient." This person may well be exceptionally worried about being ignored or abandoned. Hyperverbalizers frequently have underlying concerns that unless they are somehow better, they will be judged as inferior. The competitive quality of this behavior may be problematic in a group where members are primarily seeking support.

Leadership with the Overtalkative Member. Observation of the individual and the group is essential before intervention. Leaders must ponder a number of questions and usually between sessions, co-leaders will discuss their understanding of individuals, their impact on others, and how best to approach them in the group.

Questions arise about whether the talker is self-serving or obliging the group by being unconsciously elected to take an anxiety-reducing role by slowing down group progress, instead of pressing into unfamiliar, more fertile ground.

Leaders will have to explore the length and breadth of the talker's expression, the impact on others and the extent to which it can lead to movement in the group process. Relevance of the comments and their role in the group should be noted. For example, if the group is presumably moving into the treatment phase and a member is rambling on about the food in the cafeteria or his or her particular take on some recent news story, but not looking at himself or herself, the leaders must intervene. Of course, if one person is using up a majority of the air time, the leaders need to help others get some time also.

Process interventions can be made at any level. For example, at the group level, the leader may request that each member express their thoughts or feelings or restate a ground rule, often also adding a change in direction.

> **LEADER:** Karl has been describing his questioning about whether or not he should get a second cat because now he is away from home many hours a day and he thinks his cat may be

lonely. I know most of your concerns may not be about a pet and so I am wondering what others are thinking and feeling about the larger issues of caretaking and loneliness.

Here the leader has taken a small part of the content of what Karl has been discussing somewhat obsessively, deepened it, and turned to the other group members with a request that they address larger personal issues. She has also given Karl the message in a noncriticizing manner that it is no longer his time for talking.

Another group-level intervention may be to state something like the following:

> **LEADER:** Karl has been saying quite a bit and it's a lot to take in all at once. I'd like to hear from others about what is important to them. It's important that everyone gets a turn for some group time.

Dyadic or interpersonal approaches may also work. For example, the leader may ask another member to chime in or invite two or three other members to discuss this between themselves.

> **LEADER:** Karl has been discussing a dilemma that has to do with caretaking and loneliness. Robert, earlier in the group you were also discussing feelings of loneliness. Could you tell Karl what it's like for you?

Or alternatively, the group leader could take Karl out of the interaction:

> **LEADER:** In describing his dilemma about his cat, Karl has brought up an important issue for many people, the relationship between caretaking and loneliness. Robert, earlier you talked about how taking care of your younger brother was a way that you might have avoided feeling lonely after your divorce. Could you say more about that to Jasmine?

The leader may also approach this from an intrapsychic position:

> **LEADER:** Karl you seem to have a double dilemma here. Would you be willing to speculate what you think you'd have to deal with if the dilemma with your cat didn't exist?
> KARL: It's a real problem.

> **LEADER:** I know and it's not easy to deal with. So I am wondering, what would it be like if this problem was not present? When I ask that what are you feeling?

The intrapsychic level of inquiry will vary depending on the stage of the group process. In the treatment phase, it would be wise to look for depth with Karl, even if he might not be able to go there, because it serves as an invitation to others to respond at greater depth. If Karl can process the anxiety that is likely to arise when he doesn't have to worry about his cat, the therapy can continue. However, if he cannot, it's an opening for others.

In response to the question about his feelings, Karl might insist on restating the problem from square one.

> **LEADER:** (Cutting Karl's monologue off quickly) Excuse me Karl, I am wondering what others here are feeling now, particularly about what it would be like to be without a particular problem that blocks them. How about you, Bev?

Managing the Incessant Talker if Process Fails. Our experience is that going to process is the best option in promoting overall group development and enhancing the therapeutic impact. However, there are times when the focus on process does not work.

At those times, the leader needs to manage the situation and reduce the member's impact on the overall group development. There are several ways to proceed from distraction to direct confrontation. Each of these methods provides at its core, structure and security.

The least confrontation necessary to accomplish a shift is usually the most desirable. In the group with Karl, the leader may impose structure by specifically requesting that Karl listen without speaking.

> **LEADER:** Karl, I am going to cut you off here. I am really interested in what Bev has to say about her own loneliness. I am asking that you listen closely to what she has to say. Later, I want to get back to you for your reflection about that. Bev …

Sometimes a leader must be forceful and use an important skill for all therapists—rudeness. It is sometimes necessary to be impolite and to interrupt others, especially when they are rambling on.

> **LEADER:** (Interrupting one of Karl's stories) I am going to interrupt you for a while, Karl. Robert, I am interested in how the loneliness Karl is anxious about impacts you.

KARL: You are cutting me off again.

LEADER: I am! I am noticing that Robert is reacting to what you are saying. Robert, could you go ahead?

More directive and confronting ways, if necessary, include the direct reflection:

LEADER: Karl has been talking for a while. I'd like others to have a chance, or Karl, I'm aware that when you don't seem comfortable or know exactly what to do, you begin to get talkative. I am wondering how others deal with their anxiety (looking toward group).

Of course this is easier when a co-leader can also redirect and provide structure.

LEADER 2: I wonder if other members in the group can give Karl feedback on what it's like for them when he is talking.

When such feedback is offered, it is important to help the loquacious member to mitigate defenses that might become activated if he feels attacked. Structure with support for new reactions is a very important leader responsibility. To do this effectively, leader must monitor and intervene if feedback isn't constructive.

The model of process before management is the best approach for most of the problem clients in a group.

The Dominator

Sometimes, a member can be a dominant figure in the group, but not necessarily through excessive verbalization. They maintain control by intimidating others in a variety of ways. The dominator defends against his or her anxiety by trying to exercise control over the group process and other members. They may enforce group rules or try to set their own standards for the group. Most of the time, leaders assume that the person who has to control situations and others' behavior is responding to an internal need to avoid feeling out of control.

This may be expressed by being ever-critical, or by expressing disgust at others' struggles. Often this is accompanied by denial that much can be personally gained from the group. As one member in a group opined about a dominating member, "Jesse always has some comment about anything I say or others say. It's like he's the cop and to slight him in any way leads to retribution." Other manifestations include pushing the leaders to do something different and to point out flaws in their theories or interventions. As Jesse replied during transition, "You two should be using scientifically proven methods. Your theories are just that.

They are untested and maybe unsafe. Could you provide some literature to inform us about your theory?"

Although much of the intimidation may be verbal, it may also be conveyed by an imposing presence or other nonverbal signs. For example, the dominator may sit too close to someone or talk in a louder than normal voice. One woman in a group we led came to the meetings at the last minute, laden with food and a beverage, in violation of group rules. She always seemed on the verge of spilling something on the carpet or furniture—something that created distraction and apprehension for one of the leaders.

The best therapeutic approach to the dominator is to recognize and indirectly address the fear of being out of control. This might be accomplished by adding structure to the group, reducing pressure on the identified dominator by relieving him of the focus of the group's attention or to facilitate the need to be in control by requesting assistance.

> **LEADER:** Jesse, you seem to be particularly sensitive to everything in group being on the up and up. I wonder if you'd be willing to send me an email each week after group, letting me know your thoughts about how you might be able to describe what you want in the group, but doubt you will get.

Or the following:

> **LEADER:** Jesse, you have a finely tuned sense of how things should go in group. I'd like to offer you a challenge for just 30 minutes this evening. Would you be willing to let go of your critical eye and try to see what might be useful for you in this group, even if it is quite imperfect?

Sometimes, direct structuring is necessary. In the situation with the member who broke the group rule about eating or drinking in group, the leader chose to confront her directly:

> **LEADER:** Nina, I am guessing that you rushed here and didn't have time for lunch, but your tippy drink cup and the salad perched on your knee is distracting me. I ask you in future meetings to eat before you come into the group room.
>
> NINA: You are just more worried about a spill on your precious chair or carpet than you are about people.
>
> **LEADER:** There are two things that I am concerned about. If I am distracted for whatever reasons, I cannot do my job as well

as I'd like, and I want an agreement that you will follow the group rule about not eating during meetings.

In some extreme cases, such as work we have done in correctional facilities or other in-patient facilities, domination can extend beyond the group or be so disruptive that therapeutic work is severely compromised. This may call for the group therapists to meet outside with the member to either help him or her to focus on the anxiety base of their actions, or in the case where other members may be justifiably intimidated, to drop a person from the group.

The Distractor or Joker

Some people avoid anxiety by distracting from deeper levels of interaction primarily through sidetracking the group or turning sometimes serious matters into jokes. This "class clown" phenomenon functions in three ways: it reduces the tension in many situations, it enhances the comedian's status and popularity, and it gives the joker a special role in the group, similar to the royal fool, who is not subject to the standard rules.

Another form of diverting the group attention is distraction while another person is talking. For example, Lara, a member of a training group, had the habit of thrusting her legs into the middle of the group room and slowly removing the leggings over her tights while others were talking. In another group, one member with a severe visual impairment, would get up and move close to another person who was speaking. As she moved around the room, she interfered with eye contact between the leader and the member who was working verbally on some issue. In this situation, the leaders, aware of her disability were loath to do anything that could seem prejudicial or insensitive, yet they were being inhibited from their work. They could not determine whether she was moving about because of her visual impairment or because of her anxiety about the topic.

For leaders dealing with distraction, there are three basic approaches: (1) ignoring the behavior, hoping that without reinforcement it will diminish; (2) confronting in the group with structural interventions; and (3) talking to the person between sessions about the distracting behavior.

In many groups, nonreinforcement of the behavior and ignoring it is sufficient for its reduction or extinction. Sometimes this approach will not be effective when a distracting jokester is truly funny and the other group members laugh in appreciation. Group members temporarily may be seduced or co-opted through humor. In one group, a member was a professional stand-up comedian. His comments were creative and often hilarious. He never made fun of others in the group but when he focused his humor on himself or on politics, he was both insightful and hilarious. Attempting to extinguish the behavior by ignoring it was impossible. Thus the leader turned to confronting the member in the group.

> **LEADER:** R.T., you know you often see right through to the core of an issue and then say some hilarious things about it. For example, when you were describing your Saturday evening dinner, your analogies between the conversation and the food was great.
>
> R.T.: Well, thanks I'm glad you appreciate it.
>
> **LEADER:** You are a talented comedian. Here's my concern. When you make fun of the dinner you had or of the reaction you had in here when Margie made that comment about how elusive you could be, you partially deflected the disquiet or pain of those events. As humorous as you made the dinner sound, when you talked about the discrepancy between what you had hoped for and what you actually got, it seemed painful to me and frankly at some level, more tragic than funny.
>
> R.T.: You got me Doc. That's what I do. I make fun so I get to avoid the misery.
>
> **LEADER:** Well it seems to work for you professionally, but I always think that everybody works with that old TV character, Ed Norton. Do you know that Art Carney character? (R.T. looked a little puzzled; the leader, laughing, continued.) That's me being a dinosaur, eh. He worked in a sewer. Bottom line is that things that are very good in your stand-up work setting may fail in another. Right now, as much as I might enjoy your humor, I care about your sadness.
>
> R.T.: Well, it was sad last weekend and it was also hard to hear what Margie said.
>
> **LEADER:** Would you be willing to tell her what about her comment made you sad—without a joke?

One of the interesting components of this intervention is that the leader used R.T's characteristic actions, distraction to an obscure reference, to enhance the power of the message.

In most situations these first two interventions work fairly well. When they fail, a conversation outside of group might be appropriate, indicating that as leader you can see how R.T., for example, avoided feelings and distracted with humor and that it also interfered with other members being able to work on serious concerns.

Similarly, Lara, the lady who removed her leggings in group, can be ignored, or can be confronted in group:

> **LEADER:** Lara, I think you come here after working out and your leg warmers apparently get uncomfortable while you are sitting in group. I'd prefer if you removed them prior to the group or when you are talking, because it can be distracting when others are the center of the group's attention.

With the visually impaired group member, the leaders decided to talk to her outside of group and asked that when she had to move to be able to see better, that she be careful not to block others' vision. When she said she wasn't very aware of that, they compromised by saying that if she was blocking sight lines, they would ask her to move over to the right or left and she would do so.

The Junior Therapist

One potentially difficult client is a member who acts as much as possible as if she or he were an assistant group leader. This is especially common in training groups in mental health training programs. For many who are naturally drawn to the helping professions, offering care may serve three functions: altruism toward other members, enhancement of the junior therapist's self-esteem, and avoidance of facing one's personal issues.

Because altruism is so desirable, it often takes several sessions to detect the negative personal consequences for the junior therapist and other group members when used as a defense against personal anxiety or a lopsided attempt at self-enhancement. Once group leaders comprehend that a particular member freely offers help, but is reticent to or avoids receiving it, they need to view the behavior as resistance to facing personal fears. This form of resistance is best approached therapeutically.

In a group of mental health professionals, Betty was an active member often offering caring to others. Through the first several sessions, she made a number of therapeutic comments, showed empathy for fellow members' pain, frequently offering understanding and assistance. Whenever, someone asked her about her personal concerns, she deflected and redirected attention to someone "more in need." At one point, other members insisted that she have some time to talk about her challenges in group and in life. When it got postponed to the next session, she began the session by offering everyone homemade chocolate-chip cookies before the session began.

> **LEON (Leader 1):** Betty, we ran out of time last week when you were about to talk about some personal issues. I want to be sure we set aside time for you today.

BETTY: It's okay. Actually, I was worried about what happened for Carly, when she went home last week to talk with her partner.

(As the group turned to Carly anticipating that she would begin speaking, Leon interrupted.)

LEON: Carly, I want to be sure we have time for you also, but if it's not urgent, I'd really like to know what's going on for Betty.

BETTY: I am okay.

LEON: You are very good at showing kindness and caring for others here. Even today, when we scheduled time for you, you took the time and effort to bake cookies for everyone. I want to ask you a question. Since you are so prone to helping others, when do you get a turn?

BETTY: I really don't need one now.

SANDRINE (Leader 2): May I try something here? Betty may I put my hand on your shoulder? (Getting assent, she continued) I'd like to speak for you for a moment and respond to Leon. Leon, I appreciate what you are doing, but I am much more comfortable when I give help than when I receive help. I guess it's my many years as a mom. In fact, when you offer me time for myself like this, it makes me more anxious. (Turning to Betty) How close is that?

BETTY: Yeah. It's what I am feeling.

LEON: Sandrine, what is the anxiety like for Betty?

When Leon asks his co-leader, Sandrine about Betty's anxiety, they are working together, suggesting an important path for Betty to explore, by asking it of his co-leader. They are using Betty's penchant for deflection from herself to others, by putting the revelation in Sandrine's hands; action once-removed from Betty. From here, Sandrine may involve Betty by requesting assistance. She is asking Betty for help, but maintaining a focus on receiving rather than giving.

SANDRINE: Help me out here Betty. Can you say what is so threatening about being the recipient?

The other group members then joined in and talked about frustration of not feeling equal to Betty in a give-and-take way.

Another intervention with the "junior therapist," provides much more direct structure. As soon as Betty deflected attention to Carly, Leon may have intervened:

> **LEON:** Betty, I am aware that you have a penchant for helping others. It's probably why you are a good therapist and mom. I am going to ask you to try an experiment today only. I want you to do nothing to help anyone else in the group, but when others try to help you, you may accept the help or you may tell them you are too anxious when you accept help. If you follow your natural tendency to help anyone else, Sandrine and I will interrupt and focus attention back on you.

Yet another approach was offered in a training group of prospective graduate students approaching licensure.

> **LEON:** Betty, you seem to get a great deal of pleasure and satisfaction from offering help to others. I would like you to consider that you are so good at it, you make it hard for anyone else to get that same rush.

In our experience, the "junior therapist" rarely needs management. Instead, because they are so eager to please, they are willing to comply with the leaders' interventions. For most people who are primarily helpers, being noncompliant would essentially involve being a poor member and would be ego-dystonic; contrary to their ways of being.

You Think You Have a Problem? The Other Competition

The goal of competition in group is to somehow gain a larger share of the support and help from the leaders and other members. It may be that the most helpful person wins this competition, albeit at the cost of a loss of chances to deal with personal issues. An opposite competition may occur, one where the "winner" is the most needy person in the group, and therefore has the greatest right to whatever group support and attention is possible.

One example of this is the "help-rejecting complainer," described as a process issue during the transition phase, in Chapter 3. The "unsolvable problem" is most effectively perceived as one of the tests of leadership. It is best resolved by the group through the process of developing trust and establishing limits on what the group can do.

A more problematic form of this is more enduring and can be found is each phase of the group trajectory. It occurs frequently when other members describe problems in their lives and want to work on them. The needy person quickly indicates that he or she either has the same problem, only worse, or a much bigger problem that requires immediate group attention. The competition here is triage for attention as the person most requiring assistance. Contrary to winning honor and respect as the healthiest person in group, victory is to be seen as the least healthy person and therefore the most deserving. Often, these individuals grew up in families of origin in which the contest for power was always won by the sickest person.

In one group for example, a 55-year-old woman began talking about her guilty feelings about convincing her aging father to move from his home of many decades into a retirement community. As she was describing how hard it was to convince him to move and the painful interaction she had when she and her brother took away their father's car keys, the "neediest" member chimed in and went into a lengthy description of his parents developing Alzheimer's dementia and their subsequent deaths. Group sympathy (although not empathy) quickly shifted to his tragedy.

Similarly, when a man in the group was struggling with a difficult decision about whether he and his wife would be trying to have a child, Liz, another member, began describing the horrors of in vitro fertilization and of having triplets, one of whom survived birth and her lengthy postpartum depression. Later in the same group, a woman in the group was describing her debilitating chronic back pain and how it was difficult to remain at work or to do the household chores. Liz played her "trump card," saying that she had the exact same problem and that it was an ordeal to just make it to the group each week.

So it went, week after week. Liz often seemed to be suffering from the same or a worse disorder than each other member. It was a challenge for the group energy; either pay attention to the most poignant problem expressed, or to support others.

Usually, as with the help-rejecting complainer, the group will begin to understand the process and either proceed with others' concerns despite the neediest person's escalations, or they will confront the person as someone who always has the worst problems. The leaders can also support this action by refocusing the group away from that individual. Sometimes a member will experience several "tragedies" during the course of the group. These individuals are usually less than pleased to share the limelight with other members who have "smaller" problems.

During the treatment phase of the group, Charley, a man in his late 50s began talking about his worry about a positive PSA test, indicating a possible prostate cancer. He had spoken to a urologist who recommended surgery and minimized the risks, because they caught it early. Paul responded with caring and advice.

> PAUL: Did you have only the one PSA test? They are notorious for false positives. Be sure to have at least one biopsy and maybe also try that new test of urine to be certain.
>
> CHARLEY: I didn't know about the other tests and they will be doing a biopsy in two weeks.

PAUL: Please also be sure to get a second opinion about treatment. There are lots of options now and the risks of side effects are lower.

LEADER: Paul you seem to be both knowledgeable and very caring toward Charley.

PAUL: Yeah. I had a prostate cancer scare a few years back and went through all the confusion, anxiety, and decision making. It was really awful and I am sorry Charley is going through that now.

CHARLEY: If it's not too much to ask, what did you do?

PAUL: Well, because my cancer was a certain type, I got the radioactive seeds. There's a specialist at the University Hospital who laid out all the options. I'll give you her name if you'd like.

CHARLEY: Thank you. May I ask how it worked out for you?

LIZ: You know I know what you are feeling, I had some lumps on my last mammogram and I think I may need a mastectomy. There's a lot of cancer in my family, so I know what it's like to be afraid of surgery. Just last month, my sister-in-law …

LEADER: (Refocusing back to Charley and Paul) Liz, hold on for a moment. What you are saying is important, but I am interested in Paul's answer to Charley's question. Paul, please go ahead.

PAUL: I was very lucky. It's been almost 6 years since the treatment and I have had no problems. I don't think that's the solution for everyone, but it has been good for me. None of the scary side effects of incontinence or impotence at least so far.

LEADER: What's it like to hear that, Charley?

It was important for the leaders to stay with the ongoing process and keep Liz from taking over as the most hurting patient in the room at the moment. It will be useful to check back in with her, but not during the time when Charley was vulnerable and getting support from at least one other member.

In this example, the leader supported the ongoing group process to keep the focus on Charley and Paul. Sometimes she or he will have to intervene more directly. Statements focused on process are almost always the most desirable. Thus, a more direct confrontation might focus more intensely on Liz's behavior, once the work with Charley was complete.

LEADER: Liz, I'm aware that when someone else is describing some personal difficulties, you tend to jump in with your own experiences that are often worse than others. In this case it was a possible breast cancer, which seems terrifying. Earlier you talked about your parents' Alzheimer's, postpartum depression, and chronic back pain.

LIZ: Well, they are all real.

LEADER: I don't doubt that. I am just wondering if you feel you can be most helpful by identifying and empathizing with others' pain? It's almost like you have to share the experience to relate.

At this point, the group and leader may explore what it's like for others. Some members may feel empathy when another relates a similar or worse experience. Others may feel cutoff or overshadowed by a bigger tragedy. It is likely that the whole group can explore family-of-origin experiences and what the consequences are to be average, rather than most or least hurt.

The Painfully Silent Person

Earlier we described natural differences in level of verbalization during the group and as a reaction to anxiety. Whereas some members get overly chatty, others become very quiet and withdrawn. Having a range of such reactions is both normal and helpful in a group. However, just as the overtalkative person can be disruptive, so can the person who offers "a loud silence" in the group.

It is important to distinguish between a person who is just naturally quiet and person's whose silence pervades the group. It is also important to recognize that some members of a group will learn more vicariously than directly in a "hands-on" manner. For such people, silence may be productive, especially when they are processing internally ongoing interactions in the group. By contrast, others may be withdrawing because they are afraid to speak or behaving punitively by giving the group "the silent treatment" out of anger.

As we described earlier, quieter members of the group are commonly identified and requests for their verbal participation is made by members or leaders. This most frequently occurs during the transition phase where inclusion and confronting differences are dominant themes and during treatment, when mutual help and problem solving are central. In some groups those interventions are sufficient for each member to find his or her natural place in the level of verbal communication offered.

In addition to these adjustments to each other, there are some far more serious silences that demand the leaders' attention. Some individuals use silence in a group to express either fear or disapproval. In these situations, interventions are advisable. Sometimes invitations to speak are all that is necessary. However, leaders need to take caution about pressuring silent members who are anxious. With a member who used silence to handle internal anxiety, pressure will likely increase both the anxiety and resulting withdrawal.

Dealing with the Quiet Member. We approach silence in the same way we approach most challenging situations in group. First we allow time and space for the group to solve the problem. Invitations and confrontations from the group are usually less anxiety provoking than leader attention. Secondly, we help the group confront the member. This often takes the form of observing verbal and nonverbal cues from more active members. We then ask one of these members to verbalize their thoughts and feelings to the quiet person. We then support engagement between the two.

> **LEADER:** Marla, would you share your feelings about this with Diane.
>
> MARLA: (Turning to Diane, the quiet member) Okay. So Diane I was saying that I am very stressed out right now with my supervisor. I just feel like no matter what I say or do, I am always wrong. Even if something goes right, he gives credit to someone else.

If Diane remains silent, but looks at Marla and shows any signs of listening, the leader may assist the interaction.

> **LEADER:** Diane, I wonder if you could tell Marla if you have ever felt that way?

Because that is close to a universal experience in school or on the job, it should be possible for Diane to respond to Marla. Even if she reports that she has never had that happen, the leader might ask her to give Marla advice on how to avoid it.

Another method to include the silent member is for the leader to go to a group-level intervention and request that each person in turn respond to some common group concern. For example, "could we go around and each one of us relate to Marla's comment about her work situation." As each member makes a comment, the leader may compliment them in turn for their willingness to share. Another is to have a standard check-in and check-out for each session in which each person is expected to say something about where they are emotionally and cognitively. One leader has each person verbally assign themselves homework between sessions based on what they would like to have happen in group. If these methods do not yield the desired results, the leader may directly and gently request more verbalization from the member. One approach is to join with them by giving permission for them to speak at their own pace.

During the early sessions, leaders need to assess the consequences of the person's silence. Is it protective and if so, from what threat? Does it provide control? Does it express anger? Is it seductive, requiring others to work hard to get something? Each of these requires a different approach.

For example, if it is about control, the leaders can explore with the individual whether it is self-control or other control. The former may result from overwhelming anxiety, shame, a fear of intimacy, painfully low self-esteem, shyness, or a history of betrayal or abuse in prior relationships. This may involve the leaders carefully drawing the person out and working through the issues of concern. It might also represent a screening failure and worthy of private meeting with the painfully silent person to determine whether the issues fit within the group's capability.

By contrast, if is related to control of others, as in passive aggressive behavior, the leader may want to give extra time for the group to reach their tolerance levels, become frustrated and move on as if this member was only an observer rather than a participant. Paradoxically, it's at this point that the painfully silent member may make his or her first verbal foray into the group.

When the Whole Group is Silent Later in the Process. During early transition, silence is a significant aspect of the group development. However, later in the trajectory, particularly at the beginning of a session or after some particularly intense work, the whole group will be silent. The best approach here is to recognize and take control of the silence. One of the most effective methods is to sanction the silence, "Let's take a few moments to center ourselves and focus inward, before we start talking." Then the leader can break the silence by asking, "what was your focus during the silence?" then regardless what emerges, there is an expectation that the group members will discuss their inner dialogues and engage with one another.

The Over-Emotional Member

In some groups, there are members who are challenging because of their extreme affective responses. They frequently express their emotions often at quite intense levels. One form of this is the member who always seems to be sad and crying. It is, of course, normal for group members to cry during a group session, especially when they are dealing with something very sad in their own lives, or are touched by another's experiences or struggles. However, there are also members who present a challenge to the group leaders because they are weepy or crying very frequently.

When a member cries in group, it naturally brings them to the center of the group's attention. In most situations, tears and weeping call out for caring from others. It seems insensitive to ignore such expressions of emotion for both the individual expressing the emotion and to others. Yet it also represents a situation wherein a member can dominate the group by expressed emotionalability or fragility.

It is natural to focus attention on a crying person and ask for them to verbalize their current experience. It is also important to be aware of any inability to respond verbally or on the impact of the tears on others. Sometimes, a person cries be- cause they are sad. Sometimes, however, the tears reflect more an inability to express other emotions such as fear or anger. Occasionally, the tears are a way to control or stop group process.

If the crying member does not engage with the leader or another member who tries to be supportive or helpful, others in the group have to deal with their experience of being in the presence of tears and not being able to assist or comfort the person. Those feelings of helplessness will in time give way to frustration. The leaders' roles during such times are to support all members and to try to keep other members from asking a host of probing questions about the cause of the tears.

THE TISSUE ISSUE

Most of the time when a member begins to cry, tissues emerge suddenly from leaders or members of the group. Often, a box of tissues is handed around to the person who is crying. Leaders differ on their interpretations about the tissues. Some believe that the tissues are an expression of sensitive caring and an invitation for an individual to continue to work on whatever issues are occurring. Other leaders believe that the offering of tissues represent a subtle request to dry one's eyes and stop crying. Of course, there is no debate if the tears involve a running nose or smeared mascara.

Dealing With Crying

The challenging client is the one who cries frequently, but does not attempt to deal with the underlying emotion or issues that seem to elicit the tears. In the unusual situation when the group cannot move on in the presence of emotional lability of a member, the leaders may need to intervene directly. This intervention requires both support for the person and an open expression of one's own feelings.

> **LEADER:** (Looking toward the crying member) Connie, I need your help here. I am experiencing two different feelings now: a caring for you with a desire to comfort you and a sense that you would prefer not to be comforted. So I am stuck in the middle. Which of those would be your choice?

When the level of emotional intensity is considerably inconsistent with the extant emotional expression in the group, particularly early in group process, leaders may have to redirect or truncate it to avoid setting a new norm for tears and angst that frightens other members. This is done by acknowledging the level of evident pain, cautioning the individual that there may not be sufficient trust and support in the group at this time, and going to other members to comment on what they are experiencing.

When Members Are Hostile or Insensitive to Others

Sometimes in a group, a member may be unreasonably insensitive to another's perspectives, ways of being, or culture. In such cases, there may be a need for the leaders to protect the member under attack without waiting too long for the group to deal with the issue. Among the most common issues to emerge are culture, politics, and religion. There is no problem for members to disagree on such issues, but when the dispute turns aggressive, hostile, or demeaning, the leader has to step in. As a general rule, intervention is necessary whenever name-calling may occur. Usually, in groups the potential for such difficulties are mitigated by screening or the general respectful group ambiance. Nonetheless, such problems may occur, particularly when in facilities in which group entrance is automatic.

In one group of very intelligent, but agitated teenagers in a hospital psychiatric ward an issue arose around religion. One 19-year-old who was hospitalized after going off his medication for bipolar disorder began talking about how he got arrested and sent to the hospital ward:

> TERRY: When I had my fall from grace that got me in here, I was just out there you know, like really out there. I didn't know where to turn, so I just hung out at the JC and was bumming for change. I got drunk and picked up by the cops and was sent back here.
>
> CAL: You know Terry if you were to give your life to God, those things wouldn't happen so much. I was born again and when I get out of here, I'm going to get more involved in my faith. I know it will work and keep me straight.
>
> MELINDA: Cut the crap Cal! You just hang on to religion because you can't think things through on your own. Karl Marx said, "Religion is the opium of the masses," You think you can switch from oxycodone to Saint whatever and it'll be all right.
>
> SARA: Mel, you are being tough on him, if that's Cal's answer let him be. I go to church with my family sometimes and my mom is a real believer.
>
> MELINDA: (Interrupting) I don't care if you go to church or not. I just don't like it when Cal pulls his holier than thou card and tells us all what we should do. If there was a God, we would not be in here miserable with so many problems.

At this point the group is working on the issue and the leader is carefully observing. If it gets any more challenging, he or she has to break in and redirect the discussion to more internal concerns.

> CAL: So I know I am going to heaven and maybe I can help Terry get there and maybe if Sara went to church more often, she could too.
>
> MELINDA: (Showing some anger) You hypocrite. You are going straight to hell. You just don't know it yet. You are a fool for putting your hopes on some old white guy with a beard in the sky. Shit, if you are so holy, why are you always coming on to me on the ward.
>
> **LEADER:** Mel, you seem to be really upset now, what is happening inside?
>
> MELINDA: Oh it's just that Cal is so dangerous with all his …
>
> **LEADER:** (Interrupting) What is going on with you right now?
>
> MELINDA: I just don't like phonies.
>
> **LEADER:** I understand that you don't like it, but something seems to be hitting you in a very sensitive place. Do you have a sense of what makes you so vulnerable now?
>
> MELINDA: I grew up with all that prayer and religion and basically it was just a way for my parents' sadism to come out and punish us … One day I was locked in the cellar to think about my sins and they just forgot me there—great holy people right!
>
> **LEADER:** So when Cal brings up his faith, it conjures up terrible memories for you and it looks like you are reliving what sounds like terror even now.

Notice that whenever a member is approached in a demanding or hostile manner, the leader needs to break in and turn the energy and focus of attention back on the attacker, *not on the target.*

In groups in high-tech areas such as Silicon Valley, the stereotypic engineer, "nerdy" young male may be an easy target. When such an individual expresses himself in very cognitive ways, he may be accused of being unfeeling or insensitive to emotions in others. Often, he will not be comfortable with anger directed at him, especially by women and might respond by asking for examples. If these are given, he will pick areas of the example to prove that he is not insensitive. That will only exacerbate the negative projections.

In one such group, Annie, a woman was describing an abusive experience with her ex-husband. Others in the group jumped in to support her and to show distaste for the described husband. She portrayed him as an "absent husband and father who had no time for me." In response to a question as to whether he also had affairs when he was on the road (from a person who later admitted that she had actually regularly engaged in such behavior), Annie replied derisively, "maybe with his computer!"

As the discussion intensified, a member turned to Arthur, who looked very much the part of engineer with heavy rimmed glasses, his shirt buttoned up to the top, pocket protector, and new "smart" watch connected to his smart phone.

> SHEILA: What do you think about this Arthur? You look like you could be Annie's ex.
>
> ANNIE: (Laughing) No. Arthur just looks the part. He isn't the type I'd be involved with.
>
> SHEILA: Me either.
>
> **LEADER:** Arthur seems to be getting a lot of heat, primarily because of his work and appearance. What is generating such negativity toward him?
>
> SHEILA: Well. He doesn't seem very concerned for Annie and last week he told Beth that he thought she was being unfair to her partner. He just doesn't get it.
>
> **LEADER:** Sheila, you seem angry at Arthur, because of what he represents to you. That seems important. What button is being pushed for you?
>
> ANNIE: I think Sheila was just being sensitive to my hurt.
>
> **LEADER:** Sheila, would you agree with that? (After an affirmative nod) So how could you be supportive of Annie without jumping on Arthur?
>
> SHEILA: She knows I care about her and what she went through. I also had an ex who was a bastard. He even stole from me when he split.
>
> **LEADER:** So you have some real understanding of Annie's pain. What button is Arthur pushing that makes your negative energy go toward him?

Only after the group discussed what was going on for Sheila and to some extent Annie and another person in the group that had been critical of Arthur and how he was an easy target for their projected anger, the leader turned to Arthur and asked, "What's it like for you to be such a target?"

Stereotyping can lead to prejudicial interactions and the leader must interrupt any scapegoating and direct attention toward the attacker, not the target.

Assumptions about a person related to some identity they share, whether it's race, religion, gender, national origin, or occupation can be troubling even if they seem positive on the surface. Sometimes, these can be experienced as "micro-aggresions" (Sue, 2010).

In a recent group for example, Ryan was told that he looked very well educated, because he was Chinese American. The speaker likely meant it as a compliment, but the internal reaction of others was far from positive. The member replied, "I know that Asians are very into education and Ryan here just seemed smart." Then the leader of the group turned to Ryan and asked, "What's it like to be considered well educated based on how you look?" Ryan said it troubled him and felt like he was being put into an "Asian box." This led to an interesting discussion of what it's like to be categorized, despite it being a positive description. This allowed a professionally dressed woman in the group to start describing how she always felt judged by her appearance and was often pigeon-holed as being available in ways she was not intending. It also allowed a member who is gay to describe the prejudice he experienced regularly.

Anger, hostility, and categorization are all ways of increasing distance and restricting intimacy. This is anathema to the group goals of breaking down barriers and developing more intimate personal connections. Anything that goes in an opposite direction is problematic and requires quick and clear intervention.

Members Who Have an Undisclosed Outside Relationship

Sometimes, members in a group are known to one another in ways that could impede group progress. These include those with a personal friendship, romantic relationship, occupational relationship, or past connection that is unresolved.

In our experience this is usually a type of screening miscue that can present intense challenges. Here are a few examples:

1. Two people working for the same company were vying for a promotion, while being in the group. Not only were their vulnerable feelings affected, but the whole group was inhibited.

2. In a training group for graduate students, a romantic couple joined the same group, hiding the information of their relationship. That created two problems: an in-group of two and a progressively failing relationship that dominated group time.

3. Despite rules to the contrary, two members of a group became a couple without telling the other group members or the leaders, creating hidden agendas.

4. Three long-time friends joined the same group, forming a protective subgroup.

5. One group of singles included a divorced couple.

6. Two men who had been long-time adversaries both ended up in the same counseling group. Although their professed goal was to come to a better relationship, their prior experience with one another was a real block in group development.

7. A boss and her subordinate were screened unknowingly into a group working on work-life balance.

Sometimes problems such as these emerge in process in the group, especially when members' behavior is out of line with the events occurring in group. Sometimes they confess their outside relationships or one of them does. When the issue does come to life, it is essential that the group have an opportunity to discuss it and share their feelings about the impact of the subgroup within the larger group and a sense of betrayal.

For leaders, discussion within the group is only one part of their dilemma. It is often necessary to separate the folks with prior relationships. Several questions include, does one person in the subgroup get referred out and if so, which one? Is it better to keep them both in the group and monitor any collusive behavior? Do both have to be referred?

Members with Atypical Ego Strength or Pathology

Although every effort is made to discern equivalent levels of pathology in each group, sometimes errors are made. When a person in the group shows signs of being a true outlier and potential danger to self or others in the group, the leaders have to privately meet with the person and refer him or her to a more appropriate treatment.

These consults, which are never easy, should be done with both co-leaders. Additional careful discussions must be made to explain to the group any reasons for the person's future absence, without violating any confidentiality. A generic, "we spoke with Regis and we decided that another treatment was better suited to his needs," is usually best, but will nonetheless likely lead to other members' fears of rejection.

Members with sufficient pathology to be asked to leave a group are often the most difficult to convince of the necessity of such a move. Patients who suffer from sociopathy, ongoing addictions, or severe personality disorders are especially resistant and it takes some real courage on the part of leaders to make and keep the necessary decision.

Summary

In this first of two chapters on pragmatic concerns for new group counselors and therapists we focus on members with particularly challenging behaviors. Ten difficulties for group leaders are highlighted. These include members who dominate verbally or intimidate, distract, focus on others' needs instead of their own, are noticeably silent, compete for the role of worst-off person, are hyperemotional or hostile, and have secret relationships or more serious psychopathology.

The process for dealing with these challenges involve five steps that progress from no intrusiveness to major intervention: (1) allow the group to handle the problems; (2) assist the group through support, encouragement, and feedback with a focus on process; (3) direct careful, sensitive intervention in the group; (4) direct intervention with the member that is both therapeutic and limit-setting; and (5) manage the situation outside the group.

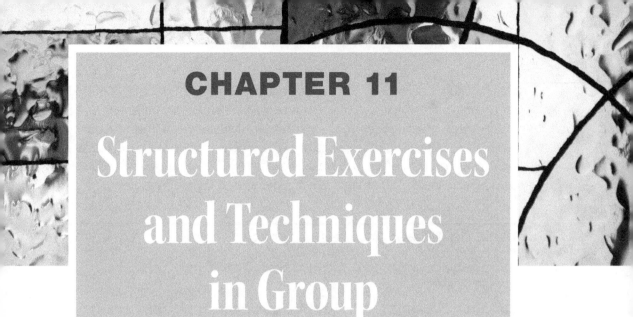

CHAPTER 11

Structured Exercises and Techniques in Group

T o the novice therapist, discovering a recipe to alleviate anxiety about minimal experience as a group leader, or perhaps an entire cookbook containing a compendium of techniques seems very appealing. Indeed, when the lay public and novice counselors and therapists think of groups, they often think of structured exercises they may have experienced personally in various workshops or retreats. Some of the techniques, such as the ones described at centers such as the Esalen Institute and popularized in the press can seem pretty dramatic or radical. In contrast to extraordinary techniques and exercises, this chapter focuses on the normal and ethical use of group techniques in a counseling, therapy, training, or growth format with professional leaders.

Structured exercises have a legitimate place in group treatment. Many group therapists have been recommending certain structured exercises to facilitate group process and outcome almost as early as writing about group counseling and therapy began in earnest. In 1971, Russell recommended exercises to supplement the natural spontaneity of the group members. Cooper and Bowles (1973) described how techniques could reduce the barriers between members and increase their willingness to self-disclose. Verny (1975) stressed their value in facilitating openness and Pfeiffer & Jones (1972–1980a) described how techniques provided flexibility in the levels of structure employed by the leaders.

Denny (1969, 1972), discussing art therapy groups, showed that art materials facilitated the release of feelings, promoted self-understanding, and led to constructive action. Since the mid-1930s, play therapy has been advocated in groups of children (Axline, 1947, Beiser, 1955, Bender and Woltmann, 1936).

Moreno and his associates (Moreno & Moreno, 2011), and Bobula (1969) used psychodrama techniques to break down barriers in hospitalized patients.

Several excellent compendia of techniques are available and will not be replicated here. For listings and descriptions of a wide variety of group exercises, readers are encouraged to investigate the resources listed in Table 11.1. These resources provide more than 1,000 different structured exercises for use in groups.

TABLE 11.1 17 Selected Compendia of Group Techniques

Cohen, A. M., & Smith, R. D. (1976). *The Critical Incident in Growth Groups.* La Jolla, CA: University Associates.

Conyne, R. K., & Crowell, J. L. (2007). *Group Techniques: How to Use Them More Purposefully.* Upper Saddle River, NJ: Prentice Hall.

Corey, G., Corey, M. S., Callanan, P., & Russell, J. M. (2014). *Group Techniques* (4th ed.). Pacific Grove, CA: Brooks Cole.

Fehr, S. S. *101* (2010). *Interventions in Group Therapy* (Rev. ed.). New York: Taylor and Francis.

Fehr, S. S. *101* (2016). *Interventions in Group Therapy* (2nd. ed.). New York: Taylor and Francis.

Hills, C., & Stone, R. (1970). *Conduct Your Own Awareness Sessions.* New York: Signet Books.

Jones, J. (1992). *Icebreakers: Sourcebook of Games, Exercises and Simulations.* London: Kogan Page.

Lewis, H., & Streitfeld, H. (1972). *Growth Games.* New York: Bantam Books.

Newmeyer, M. D. (2010). Group techniques. In R. K. Conyne (Ed.), *Oxford Handbook of Group Counseling.* New York: Oxford University Press.

Otto, H. A. (1970). *Group Methods to Actualize Human Potential.* Beverly Hills, CA: Holistic Press.

Pfeiffer, J. W., & Jones, J. E. (1975a). *A Handbook of Structured Experiences for human relations training* (Vols. 1–5 and Reference Guide). La Jolla, CA: University Associates.

Pfeiffer, J. W., & Jones, J. E. (1975b) A handbook of structured experiences for human relations training (2nd ed., Vols. I–VI and Reference Guide). La Jolla, CA: University Associates.

Pfeiffer, J. W., & Jones, J. E. *Annual Handbooks for Group Facilitators, 1972–1975.* (1972–1980a). La Jolla, CA: University Associates.

Russell, J. (1971). Personal growth through structured group exercises. *Voices: The Art and Science of Psychotherapy, 7,* 28–36.

Schutz, W. C. (1967). *Joy: Expanding Human Awareness.* New York: Grove Press.

Schutz, W. C. (1972). *Here Comes Everybody.* New York: Harrow Books.

Zweben, J. E., & Hamman, K. (1970). Prescribed Games: A Theoretical Perspective on the Use of Group Techniques. *Psychotherapy Theory Research and Practice, 7*(1), 22–27.

Used judiciously and employed moderately with a clear purpose, techniques and exercises can spur an entire group to action, reduce defensiveness, provide the group leader with valuable information for subsequent action, and reduce the total time necessary for the group to accomplish its predetermined goals.

What are Techniques in Group?

It would be easy to define as techniques any overriding theoretical approach or style employed by the leaders. Indeed, almost any repetitious leader behaviors could be construed as such. Some of these behaviors such as honesty, integrity, patience, courage, flexibility, warmth, empathy, timing, and so on, are considered more global characteristics and more a function of good therapy than as techniques per se. However, in this text we are exploring activities that fit within the purview of a group leader's theory, manner, and to some extent his or her personality. These are structured exercises that are used by a group leader to change the group process in some particular manner. It is expected that a well-trained, ethical leader who employs structured exercises will do so with honesty, integrity, empathy, and excellent timing.

For current purposes, we are defining techniques as structured exercises that are *relatively short-term, voluntary* group experiences that are *instituted or sanctioned by group leaders* for a *specific purpose.* These experiences *must be well timed* and must have *clearly determined starting and ending points,* and their effects must be *debriefed in detail* as soon as they are concluded.

Relatively Short Term

For each of the structured exercises described in this chapter (and many more that are presented in the bibliography in Table 11.1), the total group time expended is less than the length of a given session. Frequently the exercises, especially the nonverbal ones, are completed in moments and most in less than 15 minutes. Debriefing of group members' reactions, however, may take up to several hours of group process.

Voluntary

Group members should have the right to refuse to participate in any exercise, as they do for any other individual component of the group. Often novice group leaders get so caught up in completing the exercise that group members are pressured into participation, which they resent, resist, and from which they gain no benefits. Such resentment and violation of members' rights and trust can seriously affect subsequent learning in the group. The group therapist should remind members of their rights to refuse to participate in any group activity.

Instituted or Sanctioned by Group Leaders

These exercises are employed by group leaders to accomplish a specific goal. Often, in the course of a group, a member will recommend that the group try a particular technique. Unless the leader agrees to its application, such a suggestion cannot be considered as being within the purview of this definition, although it is almost always worth discussing.

Specific Purpose

Perhaps the most important factor in determining the value of a technique is the extent to which it fulfills a specific need in the group process. Group leaders may institute a particular technique to increase or decrease the level of anxiety or comfort extant in the situation, to provide the leader with important (diagnostic) information to elicit members' feelings, to clarify a particular piece of group process, to generate a different level of discussion (quantity or depth) to shift or deepen the focus of members, to offer opportunities for experiential learning, to increase the level of trust and sharing in the group, and even to make the learning more enjoyable (Jacobs et al., 2016; Shapiro, 1978). Unless the leader has a particular goal in mind before employing a technique, he or she can develop a tendency to throw in a technique at any point where the group process is not understood. Such casual and extravagant use of exercises can undermine the group process and increase members' dependency on the leader. The worst time to try to accelerate the process with a technique is when the leaders are unmindful of the extant group process.

Well-Timed

It is extremely important that exercises be presented in such a manner as to enhance group process. Poorly timed, a technique can cut off the natural process of the group and be destructive. It is very important for a leader to be aware of the ongoing process for the group and for each member before introducing a shift in the group that a new technique might bring. There also must be enough time available to complete the exercises and discussion of members' reactions during the sessions in which they are introduced. Indeed, it can be dangerous to members if time runs out in the middle of an exercise. Similar to preparing a special meal, carefully attending to the dish as it cooks and seasoning only as needed and at the right time in the process make for a far better meal.

Clearly Determined Starting and Ending Points

It is important for group leaders to make it clear that a technique is beginning and to request members' participation. Termination of a technique is marked by the leader's invitation to members to discuss their experiences during the exercise.

Discussion/Debriefing

Perhaps the most important aspect of participation in an exercise is the group members' reactions to this participation. To integrate the experience into a larger personal framework, members must verbalize their feelings, thoughts, and sensations; hear reactions of others who have shared their experiences; and then incorporate their new learning into their experiential insights, cognitive maps, and behavioral repertoire.

Types of Techniques

Techniques in a group may serve two, sometimes opposing functions: Because they add structure, they may reduce ambiguity and decrease the anxiety in the group. By contrast, when they challenge members to stretch in their abilities and to try something new (and perhaps unexpected) they are pushing members into greater anxiety, facing fears of the unknown, that comes with such deviation from expected norms.

In general we view techniques to fitting into two categories: those that are primarily diagnostic, providing information about individuals' strengths and needs and those that are more oriented toward treatment and change. Some exercises provide both or begin with an exploration of strengths and needs and evolve into experiments with different manners of thinking, feeling, and behaving.

Jacobs et al. (2016) delineate structured exercises into 14 activity types. They relate each to the population and needs of group members and specific phases of group. In the chart below, we have added eight additional categories, to provide a sense of the wide range of available techniques (see also Corey, Corey, & Callahan, 2010; Nitza, 2014).

The number and variety of structured group exercises is nearly infinite. They range from verbal to nonverbal, from active to passive, from observation to direct participation, from humorous to serious, from giving verbal feedback to making physical contact, from reacting to management simulations and high-level cognition to children's games. However, many beginning group therapists find discovering techniques and employing them somewhat daunting. One way to increase comfort is being a group member and trying out some exercises personally. In addition, as a way to increase one's repertoire and for some uniquely creative ideas, we actually recommend befriending a kindergarten teacher. They seem atypically knowledgeable about discovery, creativity, and techniques that work with all ages.

Table 11.2 Categories of Structured Exercises

Introduction techniques	Termination techniques
Subgrouping: Dyads or triads	Written exercises
Exercises for children	Exercises for adolescents
Rounds	Common reading exercises
Feedback exercises	Trust exercises
Creative props	Arts and crafts exercises
Movement exercises	Projective exercises
Moral dilemma exercises	Group-decision exercises
Fantasy exercises	Meditation, guided imagery, altered states
Personal skill building	Interpersonal skill building
Touching exercises	Intimacy building exercises

When Techniques "Go Off the Rails"

Before describing techniques, and how we recommend using them, it is essential to discuss the dangers of such techniques and what happens when the intended technique doesn't work as planned. Sometimes a technique that seems particularly appealing to the leader, does not gain acceptance by the group.

In one group the leader was trying to establish what each person's "growing edge" was for the next few sessions. She chose the reincarnation example (below), in which each member would state what they would like to be if they were reincarnated as an animal. After she explained the exercise, the following occurred.

> ALEXA: You know, I feel very uncomfortable with this idea. It would be inappropriate for me to be involved in this.
>
> LUIS: Oh come on. Try it. It'll be fun. I'd like to come back as an eagle.
>
> ALEXA: I really do not want to do this.
>
> PETE: Why not? What's your objection?
>
> ALEXA: In my religion, we are taught that God made man as having dominion over the animals and that only man is created in God's image. It seems like blasphemy for me to believe in reincarnation and especially as a lower life form.

> **LEADER:** Alexa, you certainly do not have to be part of anything that you feel would violate your beliefs. I wonder how others feel about this?
>
> DANA: Well, I don't feel that way. I think man is no more special than any being. I'd like to do this.
>
> **LEADER:** (after several others chimed in saying they wanted to do it) So we have a disagreement in the group. Alexa will not participate and others want to do so. How might we deal with this?
>
> KELLI: Why don't we vote on it?

When others agree, Alexa indicates that she will not be swayed by a vote "even if it's everyone against me."

> LUIS: So can we do it and you will just not participate?
>
> ALEXA: I don't think I should be present. I'll have to leave until it's over, but I don't want the group to think badly about me.

In this situation, it is clear that the group is stuck vis-à-vis completing the exercise. If they go ahead, they are banishing a member. If they don't, they are giving anyone in the group veto power over group activity. They don't have an agreement that a majority vote would be binding or any other agreement on how group decisions may be made. How will the leader respond? The fact that religion is involved further complicates the matter. What are they to do?

Although refusal to do a technique like this is fairly rare, it illustrates a very important issue for the group. We call this the "golden rule for structured exercises." This rule makes the very important point that the process is central and the only way that the group has a true dilemma is if the leader is ego-invested in getting her suggested technique to work.

THE GOLDEN RULE FOR STRUCTURED EXERCISES

It is far less important to complete the exercise than to deal with whatever behaviors and feelings are generated by the exercise or the suggestion of the exercise. This is the principal rule to be followed in presenting structured experiences to a group.

The disagreement within the group and any resultant conflict, perhaps from members who do want to do it is a far more important process issue than getting the exercise done as proposed. The well-run group has to face several issues about how decisions are to be made here including how to protect each person and how to make it useful to everyone.

Consistent with our perspective throughout this text, we believe that the greatest benefit to individual members and the group as a whole occurs when leaders attend to the unfolding group process. Thus, we recommend utilizing choice techniques judiciously and sparingly. Applying such exercises might be compared to the use of appropriate condiments in the culinary arts. They work well to enhance the main dish but work horribly as the main dish itself.

Dangers of Techniques. Because structured exercises have the capacity to accelerate and deepen process in groups, they have built-in potential for problems as well. The greatest dangers involve triggering members to deal with sensitive issues prematurely, losing the ongoing process, breaking an implicit contract with members regarding expected group activities, diminishing trust, creating overdependence on leaders, restructuring the relationship between members and between members and leaders, creating excessive drama at the expense of quiet reflection and using precious group time in irrelevant pursuits (Corey & Corey, 1992; Jacobs et al., 2012; Nitza, 2014). Kottler and Englar-Carlson (2014), Lakin (1969), and Shapiro (1978) among many others express concern about leaders using showy techniques to open members up with little consideration of the ensuing events. Corey et al. (2010) also makes a particular distinction between techniques that are appropriate for the group members needs and those of the leaders. Although this is more often the case for nonprofessional leaders, technique excesses are not complete strangers to those professionals who are unaware of group process.

In their classic study of encounter groups, Lieberman, Yalom, and Miles (1973) concluded that leaders who used large numbers of structured exercises were significantly less effective on outcome measures than those who used fewer such exercises. Paradoxically, high exercise frequency leaders were generally viewed as more competent and effective by members on subjective measures. However, the more the leader structures the group experience, the more the leader is considered a "star," the less chance members had to develop progressively toward meeting-workable therapeutic goals and the more likely the group was to have increased numbers of "casualties" (members who got worse as a function of their group membership). Verny (1975) expressed the dangers of technique-centric leadership as "creating a time bomb without diffusing it" (p. 142). He and others have noted the potential for a member to feel shaken and need additional support when the leader is not present. Such negative out-of-group or postgroup events can result in therapeutic setbacks.

Procedures before Instituting a Specific Technique. As a check against the use of techniques without sensitivity for the ongoing group process, we recommend a series of questions for leaders to consider prior to recommending a particular structured exercise.

1. What's happening now in the group process?

2. What would I like to have happen?

3. Am I looking to change the level of group functioning for my personal comfort or something needed by the group members?

4. If I did nothing different, what would occur?

5. How long before these issues would naturally emerge?

6. Is it appropriate to *this* group? Techniques that are perfectly fine in some groups are inappropriate to others. If there would be a shock reaction by members, it is usually not a good idea.

7. Is it the right time to do a structured exercise? Any intervention that seems either divinely inspired or "off the wall" is usually an idea best left unverbalized.

8. Which technique will I recommend?

9. What is the likelihood that the group will be willing to participate?

Only after all of these questions have been considered by the leaders should an exercise be recommended to the group. The group leader, much like the individual psychotherapist, needs to be well-practiced in the theoretical, emotional, and cognitive aspects of therapy as well as sensitive to process variables and flexible in using intervention strategies. As early as the mid-1970s, Pfeiffer and Jones (1972–1980a) discussing the optimal use of structured experiences, recommended a five-stage process: experiencing, publishing reactions to the experience, integrating the sharing with other participants, generalizing from the experience, and behavioral application. This formulation very much follows our own recommendations for all group process and is valuable as a means of incorporating structured experiences into the group.

In summary, we recommend that leaders look first to the group process, providing space and time for group members to work effectively on the issues that brought them to the group. Second we recommend enhancing the process by judicious supportive and mildly confrontive interventions. When those are insufficient, the leaders might well decide to introduce a structured exercise that is timely, appropriate for the group and consistent with the theoretical approach being followed. The technique must fit within the ongoing process, not the reverse where the process is disrupted and follows the results of structured exercises.

Selected Structured Exercises

In the next several pages we are providing some examples of structured exercises that have been used successfully in our groups. It is essential that each is instituted at a time appropriate to the group stage of development.

Introductory Exercises

Almost every group leader begins their groups in characteristic ways, during the early transition period. The goals of introductory exercises is to allow for the beginning of inclusion for members, sets a tone for the group members, expresses the expectation that they will participate verbally, and reduces initial anxiety. We recommend that leaders take brief notes during these introductions and write down what each person says about their goal for the group.

Standard Introduction Exercises. These exercises are usually done after leaders give their names and go over the ground rules that were described in screening:

> **LEADER:** Let's start by giving your names and saying briefly why you are here. (Turning to the person on immediate left or right). Please say what you hope to get out of the group and what you fear might occur. Could you begin?
>
> - (Option a): Some leaders (i.e., Corey, Corey, and Haynes, 2014) don't set up a sequential introduction. Instead they allow members to enter as they wish. Of course, the leaders keep track and call on anyone who does not volunteer.
>
> - (Option b): This option is particularly for people whose names are well known and/or want additional anonymity:
>
> **LEADER:** There are name tags in front of you. Please choose a name you'd like to be called during this group and print it on the name tag. It can be your actual name a nickname, or something you've always wanted to be called. Don't tell why you've chosen this name or whether it's your actual name. Sometime later, we may ask what the name means to you.
>
> - (Option c): This exercise allows for an alliterative introduction and the practicing of others' names:
>
> **LEADER:** Please say your first name and provide an adjective about you that begins with the same letter, such as "Serious Sadie," or "Anxious Arnie." Each person will then say the names and adjectives of each preceding individual, in reverse order. For

example, "I'm 'Happy Harmon' and this is 'Serious Sadie,' and this is 'Good Guy' and so on." Introductions end when the last person gives the names of all others.

Introduction for Shy People. Public speaking is often quite threatening. For some people it is their greatest fear. When there are people in a group that are relatively shy, we recommend techniques that mitigate slightly those social anxieties. For such people it is usually far easier to talk with one person, so we start them off introducing themselves in a dyad.

> **LEADER:** Please choose a partner. Somebody here you don't know or someone you would like to get to know better. (When everyone has paired off, leader continues.) Okay, now decide who will talk first and who will talk second. The person who will talk second is to interview the first person for 10 minutes. When you're the interviewer, try to get to know the person in a personal way, not just status or occupation, but values, attitudes, feelings, likes, dislikes, and so on. Be sure to have time for both of you to be interviewed. When this is done you'll be asked to introduce your partner to the group.

After everyone has introduced his or her partner, each individual is allowed to correct, elaborate on, or agree with the information regarding himself or herself. Discussion frequently focuses on problems of choosing a partner or waiting to be chosen (avoid rejection, but take a chance on not getting whom you want), the embarrassment or comfort of having someone else talk about you, and so on. Often successful with groups of administrators, businesspeople, and school teachers, this technique usually generates much discussion in the early there-and-then stages. If the members are particularly anxious, the group can move from dyads to groups of four, eight and so on, until everyone has met in a group smaller than the total group.

Nonverbal Introduction. Some leaders are fond of breaking social patterns early in a group. Rogers (1969), a therapist who is rarely associated with techniques, frequently began growth and encounter groups by asking members to stand up and mill around. They were then instructed to make eye contact silently. "As you meet others, find someone you would like to communicate with nonverbally." The group then broke into dyads. "Now, using only your hands, say hello to this person" (approximately 30 seconds). Some leaders also add additional instructions such as "express competition with this person" (30 seconds). "Now express cooperation with this person" (about 30 seconds). "Okay, now express cooperation with one hand and competition with the other" (30 seconds). Now, nonverbally express what this contact has meant (30 seconds), and now say good bye.

This technique is not recommended with groups of children and adolescents or with individuals dealing with more severe pathology.

Hard Introduction Technique. With certain populations and sufficient environmental control, some group leaders try to get members to jump into the group rather than ease their way in. One of our colleagues, experienced in working with those who have been sexually abused, other severely traumatized clients, and those recovering from addictions, takes this approach. Approaches like this involve exposure, prolonged exposure or flooding methods (see Tran & Gregor, 2016).

Her rationale is embedded in her opening statements, explaining that strength is built through risk-taking that will ultimately facilitate a greater sense of safety and competence. Thus she begins groups by immediately immersing group members in situations that push them to go deep before lightening the tension.

Termination/Closing Exercises

At the other end of the group, termination also often calls for special structure to ensure that group members deal with separation and loss and transfer of training. Because these issues are often complex and underscore much of what has occurred in the group to date, group leaders are careful to allot sufficient group time for them to come to fruition.

Standard Termination. This technique is an excellent, natural way to bring matters to closure. Our typical, multisession approach was described in Chapter 5. Shapiro (2017) offers a five-part version with vertically linked stages. An announcement of the remaining time, a request for unfinished business, an invitation to describe what was learned and how it will fit in members' out-of-group lives, follow-up information, and a formal saying good bye.

> **LEADER:** Well, we've only got two sessions left after today. I'd like to recommend that we spend a little time reflecting on this experience. Before we do that, I wonder who in here has any unfinished business, unresolved feelings, feedback, requests that you'd like to bring up at this point. Now would be a good time.

Although members may initially ignore the rapidly elapsing time, they do often accept this invitation and proceed to discuss their considerations. When this unfinished business is completed as well as possible, given the time restraints, the first phase of this exercise ends. The leader then continues:

> **LEADER:** Let's go around the group and describe what you will be taking home from this group and how you will use it in your ongoing life outside this room.

It is important to note that sometimes members' plans to institute their group behavior into their back-home lives may require considerable discussion and role plays to ensure that their plans do not cause harm. It may be useful to review the examples described in Stage 24 of the group process in Chapter 5. After the group addresses the transfer of training considerations, the leader often requests their feelings about the group experience and about its ending.

> **LEADER:** Let's go around the group one more time, and one-by-one share our feelings about the group and our feelings about it ending. Who'd like to begin?
>
> When this is completed, the group normally says its good byes and terminates.

Extended Termination. Often, during the termination period, leaders like to increase the level of trust in the group. One simple structured exercise allows for both trust-building and emerging transfer-of-training issues.

> **LEADER:** Well, our time is rapidly running out, and I'm aware that we only know certain parts of each other's lives. To get a fuller picture, I'd like to recommend an exercise in which as we go around the group, each of you share something about yourself that you'd like us to know, but there's been no reason to bring up in the group till now.

This exercise often yields a wide variety of responses and allows members to express conflicts they previously thought were inappropriate. In one such group, one woman took this opportunity to share the fact that she'd had a surgical procedure between the fifth and sixth group sessions and was unsure about its relevance for the group. Sometimes, the disclosures are light. One very dour man in the group disclosed that in his spare time, he did stand-up comedy at a local club. A woman in the group described her passion for work in third world countries and her summers building homes in Africa. Another woman revealed that now that she was an "empty-nester" she has decided to return to school and pursue a long-desired master's degree. Their revelations are often excellent ways to help connect the group with their larger life experiences. It leads well into the descriptions of what was learned and how it will be used.

Another extension of the termination process is in closing rituals. Some leaders like to mark the end of group with a symbolic closing. A few of these were described in Chapter 5 and many others are common. Kaphan (2017) describing termination in open groups, has each member hear a "eulogy" in which the other members describe what he or she has meant to them personally, and how the group will be different without the member. Other leaders, offer parting gifts (Shapiro, 2002) or prayers, hope, and wishes.

Introductory and Closing Exercises in Each Session

Many group leaders have structured experiences to open and close each session. These usually include a check-in and check-out. Kottler and Englar-Carlson (2015) describe an opening ritual for their sessions that involves an opening short meditation or moment of silence to help members make the transition from out-of-group lives to being more present in group. This is followed by a "check-in," during which each member describes briefly the current state of their being and issues they'd like to address in the group. They also ask members for progress updates on working on the concerns they previously discussed.

The check out, usually involves members in turn, disclosing feelings about the session and discussion of what each person learned in the meeting and a description of plans to work on between group meetings.

Artwork and Other Projective Techniques

Many group techniques focus on diagnostics. It is particularly useful for leaders to learn members' strength and growing edges. Art work provides opportunities for members to demonstrate these in ways that might be much more difficult verbally. The techniques can give insights into individual members and also group hierarchies and ways of relating.

Almost any medium can be used and there is a substantial literature devoted to art therapy, including *The Journal of Art Therapy* that has been in existence for more than 30 years. (Art materials have been used therapeutically in a multitude of group settings, i.e., Erford, 2016; Rankanen, 2016; Schwartz, 2017; Weinberg, 2010.) Among the populations with which art therapy has been shown to be of particular value are those who are less verbal or for whom English is not a primary language, multicultural, refugee (Kaimanowitz & Ho, 2016) and immigrant populations (Rosal, 2016), clients suffering from posttraumatic stress disorder (Lobban, 2016; Visser & du Plessis, 2016), psychosis (Parkinson & Whittier, 2016), the elderly, university students (Boldt & Paul, 2011), and of course children and adolescents.

Any art materials can be used in creating the artwork. It is useful to have art supplies available, such as large pads of construction paper, butcher paper and paints, crayons, and so on. When using paints, smocks or having members bring old clothing are often useful.

The Group Drawing. After laying out a large piece of paper and a large box of crayons, the leader suggests that members do group drawing:

> **LEADER:** Please use these crayons and draw a picture of the
> group. I know that you may feel that you are not a good enough
> artist, but this doesn't have to be a masterpiece. Just try your

best. You'll have 20 minutes to complete the drawing. Please begin now."

- (Option a): The group need not work together on this task. Often leaders prefer to have each member work independently and then have all members look at the drawing as a whole and at the component parts.

- (Option b): The group need not draw itself. Requesting that they draw whatever they like can produce much diagnostic information. There is also a cathartic effect to free drawing that can be of great value in certain group settings.

Process Value. In all the diagnostic exercises, the production is far less important than the process by which the group takes to the tasks. A tremendous amount of information may be gleaned from how group members participate in this exercise. The leader can observe for later use in the group discussion, the nature of members' cooperation, competition, passive and active aggression, compliance, hierarchical work structures, intragroup alliances, ego needs, and work styles. The salience of process observations is of course true in all group work, but art and other projective materials bring the observations into bold relief.

For example, as members begin drawing the group, who takes charge? Who works cooperatively? Who competes with whom? Who sidetracks? Who resists the work? Do any of the members not follow the instructions or do some individual side project? Does anyone make it difficult or impossible for others?

In one group of adults in their 30s and 40s, one of the members took several crayons and drew a separate rendition of the group in a corner of the paper. Although it seemed far more artistic, it led to both group conflict and later discussion of how this member always had to strive for perfection, at the cost of several personal relationships.

In another group two members got into a hearty (and quite obsessive) discussion of the color names on the crayons, but did not use them to draw. In some groups, one person self-appoints herself or himself as the supervisor, defines others' roles, and gives instructions for their compliance. In others, an art critic emerges, commenting on the lack of skill of fellow members.

Some more dramatic examples have occurred, such as in a group of outpatients at a mental health clinic, one man took all the crayons and doled them out carefully to others at his whim. In a couples group, a husband criticized his wife's drawing ability, choice of colors, inabilities to use perspective and shading, and overuse of the materials. She agreed with him on each count and then accidentally spilled coffee on the paper and, in cleaning it up, tore it in half. This entire episode was accompanied by profuse apologies.

In a group of adolescents in a school-based group, originally started for awareness and reduction of bullying at the school, one boy drew a picture of another boy, exaggerating certain physical characteristics. He then proceeded to show several other members this caricature. Their subsequent teasing and laughter precipitated a pushing fight between the "artist" and his "victim."

It is easy to see how such behavior can lead to significant process discussions and a great deal of material for the group in debriefing and subsequently. As usual in groups, the events themselves are less important than the meaning and interactions between members. It was easy to focus the "bullying" group on how teasing and bullying were related, and the inevitable consequences of criticizing others. Dealing with the accidental spill centered around how no matter how critical the husband was, he did not get what he apparently wanted. These issues are of great value for group exploration. In fact, one of the prominent aspects of learning that occurs is that being in charge more often results in a loss than a win.

If You Build It. The following set of art-related techniques are primarily focused on use of building materials. Most common today are Legos, blocks, or similar tools from past generations such as Erector Sets, Lincoln Logs, and Tinkertoys. The exercises offer views of interactions and of ongoing group process.

The techniques most common are presented here in three related phases, but each of the phases can be instituted independently with success. In Phase 1, the leader introduces the exercise: "I'd like to try an exercise. Now, could I have X (number of) volunteers (approximately half the number of members in the group)?" Frequently one or two members volunteer immediately, then several moments can pass before the requisite number is obtained. As soon as there are enough volunteers, the first phase of the exercise is completed and debriefed. The reasons why some members volunteer and others refrain provide valuable information as to members' receptivity to new experiences, trust in the leader, and choices between freedom and security in an unstructured situation. Common responses are: "I thought it'd be fun and I figured you wouldn't ask us to do anything too weird" and contrastingly, "I want to know what I am volunteering for, before I commit."

Phase 2 begins when the volunteers are brought into an inner circle. The leader empties a box of Legos, Tinkertoys, or similar items on the floor or table in front of the inner circle. Addressing the volunteers, the leader says, "Your task is to build something with these materials. You have 10 minutes to complete the task." Addressing the outer circle, the leader says, "While they do this, your job is to observe and try to understand better the group process."

When the building time is completed, members' feelings regarding participation or nonparticipation, styles of approach to the task, teamwork, observations, and analysis of the observers are discussed. This section can take several minutes. When this is completed, the leader proceeds to the (optional) third phase.

LEADER: Now let's change places. Those of you who were in the inner circle switch to the outer circle, and those in the outer circle switch into the inner circle. (Once the move is made.) For you in the inner circle now, your task is to alter the structure in whichever way you like to improve it. You have 10 minutes. You who are now in the outer circle, please observe the group process for later discussion.

Some of the issues that can be highlighted by this exercise are cooperation versus competition, work styles, ego needs ("I made this and they changed it; therefore, that's a criticism of me"). Some of the more interesting diagnostic information can be depicted by the following examples:

1. In a group of "hyperactive" adolescents, one member took all the round parts (wheels) and built his own movable designs, oblivious of the rest of his group.

2. In a group of military personnel, one member took charge and assigned each member a task. He then supervised and critiqued their progress.

3. In a group of businesspeople, one member dismantled the entire structure and began to rebuild it, with less than a minute under the time limit.

4. In another group two members got engaged in a discussion of the right color scheme for the bulk of the group time.

5. In a group of firefighters, the members of the second group discussed the merits and admired what the prior group had done, instead of changing it.

Such behaviors, and observations of their effects on the group process, often provide a vivid perspective on ongoing group hierarchies, roles, and process and sometimes can have a great impact on individuals in the group. When disquieting behaviors occur, other members learn how to deal with them more effectively by practicing and observing tentative solutions.

101 Techniques in a Small Package. For therapists starting out on a limited budget, a whole host of exercises can be accomplished with inexpensive, easily transportable, and safe alternatives such as a deck of playing cards. The same three phases of the building technique can be done with the leader handing the volunteers a deck of cards and requesting that they play a game.

With this exercise, the hierarchical roles in the group come to the fore quickly. Who gets to suggest the game that is finally agreed to? Who wants a different game and holds out? Who has to win whatever game is played because of a fear of losing? For example in one group of fourth graders, one girl took all the aces and picture cards, then dealt out the remainder to the other members for a game of "war." In debriefing, she reported that being a loser was terrifying at home or school and she had to always win.

One of the most particularly interesting aspects of this exercise is the holder of the control in the group and the impact of passive power. In many groups using this or similar techniques, one member cannot for the life of them learn the proper rules. Their inability makes the game unplayable and retains maximum control for whomever is most incompetent. It also leads to significant group discussion about the nature of power and control and their frustrations.

Wet Materials. Using messier art materials can reveal some characteristics that are less likely with cleaner ones. Silly putty, clay, and finger painting have all been used in group with some success. When some members dive in, possibly making a mess, and others may be reticent to "get their hands dirty," it can lead to productive discussions.

Water color paints or finger paints are sometimes used in art exercises. Painting something together (sometimes the group itself) is similar to the crayon drawings. However, paints do add that dimension of messiness and what it means to members.

There are special concerns in using finger paints with younger members. The senior author recalls his last use of these materials while leading a group of fifth and sixth graders in a mental health clinic. After using a finger paint exercise one afternoon, he received a phone call from a distraught mom following the group. She related, "I sent a black child to school today and got a blue one back after your group." Recalling how her son had taken the pail of colored water and dumped it over his head—he looked like a smurf on leaving—the leader apologized, and offered to take care of any cleaning. She responded, "No. I got it covered. I appreciate your apology, but I hope you will never use those paints again." The group occurred in 1969. He permanently switched to crayons that day!

Group Sculpture. We have found that use of clay and other tactile materials are particularly useful in inpatient and elderly populations. A related diagnostic exercise that seems to work particularly with higher-functioning groups is sculpting. It may take several forms and some require physical touching by members, and thus is contraindicated if this could be problematic.

Self-Sculpting. In addition to using sculpting materials like clay are methods where the members use themselves. This group of techniques begins with a brief diagnostic and moves quickly to a therapy intervention. In self-sculpting, the leader may notice for example that a member's posture or manner of sitting may reflect a particular emotion. One of the methods that may be used is to request that the member in question either hold that position or exaggerate it and then alter it in ways recommended by the leader. In one group of adult professionals, a member was slouched down into his chair as he talked about a general lack of energy in his work and home life. When he asked that the group help him with this, the following interaction occurred:

LEADER: Marco, to get the help you want, would you be willing to try a small experiment?

MARCO: Sure. Anything that might help.

LEADER: First, I'd like you to notice your posture right now, don't change it, just be aware of the way you are sitting in the chair. Okay, now please try to slouch down a little more. Just slightly and notice what that feels like.

MARCO: That's uncomfortable. Can I go back to the way I was sitting?

LEADER: Yes. Of course, but this time, I'd like you to go further than how you were before. Please sit up more straight and see what that feels like.

When he does that, and replies that the new position was also not particularly to his liking, the leader continued:

LEADER: Okay. If you'd be willing to hold that position for just 2 minutes, I'd like you to take four or five deep breaths, hold them, and let them out. What are you aware of now.

MARCO: This seems weird, but I feel lighter a little more energized.

LEADER: What do you make of that?

MARCO: I don't know. Maybe I should breathe deeply more often.

At this point, the leader asked for others' reactions. A few members commented that they had done the same thing as Marco and had a similar reaction. Other members told Marco that he seemed more approachable when he sat up and looked more energized. As one member offered, "Marco, the way you were sitting before made you seem unapproachable, like you had not time for me or interest. Right now I think I could reach out to you."

The sculptured body positioning was an effective tool to change his outlook and make him less foreboding in his albeit slumped-over manner.

Process Sculpting. One of the promising techniques comes from the family therapy literature. It is a diagnostic exercise in which members make the group process become real by placing each other in ways that describes their place and process in the group.

In a training group of interns, there was a very competitive process between a man and a woman for control of the direction of the group. After a few sessions in which the competition became increasingly disruptive, and a lack of ability by the group to discuss the competition directly, the leader suggested,

> **LEADER:** I think we could understand the process better if we could see it. (Turning to a member who generally understood and responded to ongoing relational process). Pris, would you be willing to move people around in such a way as to make a statue out of them that would depict the process? I'd like everyone to let Pris direct their positions.

Pris began tentatively and slowly, but as other members allowed her fuller direction, she placed the group members into a small cluster. Then she had the two competitors out in front, each pointing in a different position and trying to pull the group to follow. Once she was done, the leader asked her to comment on her work, while the group members held their positions. Finally she asked the members of the group to comment on Pris's handiwork. They all agreed that the group felt like the statue. That they were being pulled in two directions and that the two competitors were trying to lead the group in different ways.

In this group, discussion followed and the issue of competing became a prime subject for exploration. Generating process-level interaction is one way to use the diagnostic value of the sculpture. Another is to use it therapeutically by having others modify the sculpture to make it feel better to them.

Interaction Statue. When two or more people in a group profess to desiring closer communication, but consistently seem blocked, the leader can choose the more frustrated of the pair and ask him or her to create a picture of the interaction by posing the other one.

> **LEADER:** I wonder if you two would be willing to try something to break this impasse (After gaining consent from both parties.) Okay, Patti, would you be willing to create a statue of your relationship with Marvin? Move him into a position that depicts his relationship to you. (As soon as they begin.) What material are you using—clay, granite, wood, or what?

The type of material chosen often reveals how malleable or intractable the sculptor thinks it is. Once the statue is complete, both the sculptor and the living statue are asked how they feel about the work and their positions. After they and other members respond, the leader then requests the following of the sculptor:

> **LEADER:** Patti, would you now place yourself into the statue assuming a position that represents how you perceive the relationship between the two of you? (As soon as this is done.) Please hold that pose for a moment and check out your feelings about it. Any alterations? Okay, let's discuss it.

Discussion centers on different perceptions of the relationship by the two individuals, feedback from the group, and the difficulties of maintaining the relationship in its current form.

In one instance, a male member of a co-ed group of people in their early 20s sculpted a female member into a pose with one knee up, one arm extended with fingers spread, and the other hand formed into a fist in front of her chest. When he placed himself into the statue, he rested his groin just above her uplifted knee and her outstretched hand and fingers against his neck. He was also leaning backward, cowering away from her.

She responded to this by suggesting another statue where the roles were reversed. She then placed herself on the floor with his foot on her throat and his fists beating his chest, as if in victory. The resultant discussion of these two perceptions allowed the participants to begin talking about how when they feel attraction, they perceive attributes in the prospective relationship that mimic their prior experiences and fears of being hurt.

One particularly interesting facet of this exercise was that the other group members were able to acknowledge that *both* statues seemed accurate. It also broke along sex lines, with the men feeling like the sculpture the male member made and the women feeling more like the one the female member made. This was a major impetus for the entire group, including the two sculptors to discuss their fears of being hurt in a new relationship and their projections of past experiences onto new people. One of the interesting pieces of feedback was when a woman in the group said, "When you curl your lip after you say something, it is just like my ex and I start feeling scared and angry."

Group sculpture exercises involve some physical contact between members. Group members or leaders who are uncomfortable with such contact may find it too threatening.

Trust Techniques

One of the larger categories of structured exercises is designed to enhance the levels of trust among members in a group. There are a vast array of such techniques and many have been used in human resources and other business-related workshops, retreats, and institutes. Because of this, some have become normalized and don't have the impact they had when they were unique to groups in the 1970s. We will describe a few of these briefly, but most we find to be unhelpful in any serious therapeutic manner.

Trust Fall. The essence of this exercise is that participants are believed to develop trust in others by allowing themselves to fall backward into another's arms. Members are asked to choose a partner of approximately similar size. With both facing in the same direction, one behind the other, the person in front closes her/his eyes and holds out their arms parallel to the floor. Then as they feel themselves begin to sway, they allow themselves to fall backward, to be caught under their outstretched arms by the partner. The roles are then reversed.

Although this relatively simple exercise is a favorite among workshop enthusiasts, and can be a good classroom exercise it has little effect on deeper levels of trust in a group. There is a significant difference between trusting someone to be sure that your head does not hit the floor and self-disclosing.

Rocking or Lifting. Many group members remark that this exercise is reminiscent of someone being carried around in a mosh pit at a rock concert—albeit drug free. This exercise is used primarily in training and growth groups.

In this exercise, the leader asks one member of the group who feels left out or mistrustful to volunteer for an experiment in trust-building. Once the volunteer agrees, the group leader continues: "Would everyone be willing to form a close circle facing inward and would you (identified member) stand in the middle, close your eyes, and let your body fall toward other members of the circle?"

Often members keep moving the central person from one to another until they gently lower him to the floor. Then the group gently lifts the person to the waist, shoulder, or above head level and supports and rocks him.

This exercise is more complex than the trust fall and has greater potential for impact on the volunteer. It does seem to help a member open up to being touched nonsexually and to feel more central in the group's attention. This technique is strongly contraindicated for therapy groups in which the physical contact may be threatening. Once again, the type of trust that has people assured that they won't be dropped may be substantially different from the type of trust that involves sharing of the kinds of feelings, attitudes, and thoughts, necessary for patients in a therapy group.

Blind Walk. Like many other physically oriented trust exercises, the blind walk also requires that members use more of their senses. This is an exercise that leaders are advised to observe, rather than participate. When a leader or members become aware of a less than optimal level of trust in the group, she or he may recommend this exercise. Usually seen in encounter, training or growth-oriented groups, it is inappropriate with groups in which there is unexpressed anger or individuals with more severe pathology.

Group members pair off into dyads. Each pair is given a blindfold and the following instructions:

> This exercise is called a blind walk. It is designed to help people get in touch with senses besides seeing. Choose which partner will be blindfolded first. Place the blindfold across the eyes of one person. From now on there should be no verbal communication until the entire exercise is completed. Your task is to lead the blindfolded person around, giving him or her as full a sensory experience as you can, safely. Each person will lead for

20 minutes. Everyone should be back in this room in 40 minutes and we'll discuss this experience.

Debriefing is usually active, and members generally seem able to express a variety of feelings. Emergent themes often include the relative comfort of leading or being led (*dependence, independence*), fears of being inadequate, concerns about being responsible for another person, and so on. Although primarily a diagnostic exercise, there is also therapeutic benefit in the participants' enhanced levels of trust.

Sometimes, fairly dramatic experiences may occur during this exercise. In one dyad, the person without the blindfold, took her partner to the kitchen, opened the refrigerator, and treated her partner to aromas and tastes while blindfolded. During debriefing, many group members applauded her for her creativity and caring for her partner. This was a particularly powerful experience for the blindfolded person who described himself as reticent to try new things and for the caretaker who saw herself as fairly unimaginative and suffering from low self-esteem.

In another group, in which the exercise was clearly ill-suited, one of the participants came back with light scratches on his arms and face after his "caretaker-partner" had walked him into some bushes. This led to some useful expressions of anger during the debriefing, and questions about personal safety.

Trust and Universality Exercises

Some techniques in groups serve more than one purpose. They are characteristically treatment focused and occur most commonly later in the group process. The techniques involving personal secrets often fall into that category: involving development of greater trust in the group and also an enhanced sense of universality. As George Bernard Shaw famously opined, "If you can't get rid of the skeleton in your closet, you'd best teach it to dance."[1]

Secrets in a Hat. The most common way this technique is done is each person is asked to write down a secret about themselves on a slip of paper. The slips are then placed in a receptacle and drawn out one by one and read anonymously. The group then comments on each secret. Leaders who use this method frequently report that individuals feel less alone, because everyone has secrets and also experience some defusing of their personal secret.

Because of inadvertent blushing and other nonverbal indices, we feel that the anonymity of the individual secrets is less secure than desirable. We have had some success with a much more prolonged method.

I've Got a Secret. This extended technique may take a considerable amount of time and can expand to an entire session. We have often used it during marathon sessions of several hours. It has five interlinked components.

---

1   Retrieved from http://www.imdb.com/name/nm0789737/bio

LEADER: I'd like each person to think of a secret; something about yourself that you've never told anyone. You will not have to tell us your secret. Just keep it in mind. (Once each person has a secret in mind, the leader continues.) Okay, beginning with (indicating a member to the immediate right of the leader and going counterclockwise), I'd like you to indicate who in the group would be most critical of you if they knew your secret.

Members and leaders in turn choose that member (or leader) they feel would be most critical of them. This is then discussed, and feedback regarding reasons for selection is encouraged. After this discussion is terminated, the leader continues:

LEADER: This time we'll go around clockwise (turning to member on immediate left). Indicate the member you feel would be most accepting of you if they knew your secret:

Members and leaders indicate their choices, and feedback as to reasons for choices is again requested. In addition, members are asked to express their feelings about being (or not being) chosen. After this discussion is terminated, the leader continues:

LEADER: Now, being careful not to divulge your secret, please indicate why you have kept it a secret. Let's begin with Joe (indicating a member located halfway around the group from the leader).

Members will give a variety of reasons for keeping secrets. Most frequently they involve shame or discrepancy from an image they like to keep. Occasionally, the response is something like "if people knew, they'd lock me up and throw away the key." When a member simply says "I don't know" or "I never got around to telling anyone," the leader must ask the member to explain further until they share a more real feeling or concern. There may also be a brief discussion of reactions to this phase of the exercise.

LEADER: This time let's go around and choose one person in the room whose secret you'd most like to know. We'll begin with Mary (another member who has yet to go first).

This stage frequently elicits a lot of laughter and joking. It also has some diagnostic value. People often choose someone they want to get to know better outside the group or engage in a childlike game of "I'll tell you mine if you tell me yours."

After this phase ends, the leader asks, "Would anyone like to share their secret?" Depending on the group and the nature of the secrets, somewhere between zero and 60% of the members share secrets. After the sharing, discussion of the entire technique should include members' feelings about their secrets (often dramatically different) and about other members. Often members' secrets lose their negative valence through this exercise. Frequently, the secret a member began with morphs into a different secret.

The key to this technique, as with most others, is the debriefing interspersed with the structured components of the exercise. The impact of being chosen as accepting or unaccepting (critical) by one or more fellow group members can be substantial. The impact of not being chosen can be equally powerful.

In one group, all the other members chose one woman as the person who'd be most "critical." When questioned about her feelings, the following was her response:

> LOUISE: It doesn't bother me. We're used to that sort of reaction.
>
> **LEADER:** We?
>
> LOUISE: All narcs. I was undercover for many years.

The group responded to her by telling her that they hadn't known her profession, but she seemed always to be taking mental notes and evaluating others in the group. She came to understand that she was maintaining her professional behaviors in her personal life and alienating people she wished to befriend.

Incidentally, Louise's personal secret was that she had a twin sister who died when she was 13, and she'd never had a close friend she felt she could trust since then. The obvious connection was very helpful to her in developing both insight and behavior change.

The content of the secrets that people do share is interesting. The greatest percentage (more than half) of all reported secrets is extramarital affairs. This is followed in frequency by aggressive and illegal secrets, and so on. One secret we've heard only once was a man who confessed that he was a priest. He kept this secret in the group because he feared others would react to him differently, if they knew.

The subsequent dialogue indicated his perception was accurate:

> KEITH: Well, my secret is that I'm a Catholic priest.
>
> SUE: Really? I never would have guessed that.
>
> KEITH: I just wanted people to react to me as Keith, not as Keith in my religious role.

As quickly as a fervent "Amen" to a particularly moving prayer, Patrick replied, "How could you think that Father?" The rest of the group burst into laughter at that point, leaving the confused Patrick a few minutes to figure out what he had said that was so humorous.

Another unique response was a fellow in the group who said after the exercise, "You know, I have kept this secret from my wife for more than 25 years. I am going to go home and tell her." The group drew in their collective breath, imagining dire consequences and asked Thomas to work it out first in group. Thomas replied, "No. I want to tell her; not anyone else."

At the beginning of the next session the following occurred,

CAMILLE: Thomas, did you tell her? What happened?

THOMAS: (Smiling) Oh. She knew all along. She didn't know it was a secret.

CAMILLE: So what was the nonsecret?

THOMAS: I wanted to tell my wife. I don't want to tell it here.

The group rewarded him with applause and the leaders underscored how Thomas had successfully brought group learning home. However, they also issued a caution that others may want to try things out in group before attempting them outside.

Role Playing: The Grandfather of the Techniques

Role playing is so ubiquitous in group therapy that it deserves a separate category. Although it qualifies as a technique, role playing and its partner, psychodrama, can be an entire method of group treatment; one supported with considerable research and clinical data.

Johnson and Johnson (2009) describe role playing as an opportunity for group members to experience situations concretely, gain insight into current behavior, and try out alternative behaviors. Because role play is imaginary, it is often less threatening and more easily accomplished than facing personal fears directly. Gladding (2012) describes one form of role playing when members "set up an imaginary life situation and ask others in the group to play certain parts" (p. 128) that are prescribed. Another form of role play, also seen in the closely related empty chair technique (Glass, 2010), is to have a member have one part of herself speak to another part (often imagined sitting in an empty chair).

Role playing and psychodrama have a lengthy history, dating back to the 1930s. Corsini (2010), Corsini and Cardone (1966), Bennis (1964), and Shapiro (1978) state that although role playing requires an "as-if" quality, it demands considerable personal involvement, making it an especially useful set of techniques in group treatment. Working with college student groups, Gibb (1952) demonstrates that adding role playing to a T-group experience enhanced self-reported gains in self-insight by comparison to those in T-groups alone. Gibb adds that there were also nonsignificant trends in role flexibility and ability to conceptualize roles.

Shapiro (1970) also showed augmentation of encounter group effects by use of role playing as a group technique, in comparison with control group subjects who did not role play. In a comprehensive review of extant literature, Siegel (1969) concluded that there is strong evidence to suggest that role playing as a technique produced both attitudinal and behavioral changes. Indeed, the more active and emotional the role-playing procedure, the greater the impact (Mann, 1967).

Two early empiracle studies were generally influential (Janis & Mann, 1965; Mann & Janis, 1968). In these studies, subjects in the role-playing group showed significantly greater reduction in smoking than did an equivalent group of subjects who listened to tapes of other subjects' role-playing sessions.

Role playing today is so accepted that one would be hard pressed to find a theory or practice without role playing (Corsini, 2010). Indeed many texts of group therapy theories have a role play section within each theory.

Role playing has some significant advantages over direct conversation and often provides some unexpected options. For group members, it allows for creativity and potentially fun to emerge. They can rehearse emotionally and behaviorally from a presumed safer distance. Group members can have "as-if" conversations with significant others in their lives without risk of severely negative consequences. They can act out another person's perspective. Given an opportunity to "act" in an unfamiliar role, whether as self or other, new ideas can be uncovered, different emotions may be experienced, practice may lead to actual or revised sets of behavior, and atypical approaches may be tried.

Role playing can be done with one or more individuals in a group or with the entire group as a whole. The most fascinating phenomenon of the role-playing procedures is the rapidity with which members become truly emotionally involved. Members quickly project their own affects, values, and attitudes into their roles, and in a sense, become the character they're playing. In this emotion-laden state they are more susceptible to rapid learning.

As a set of techniques, these role-playing procedures provide members with a means of viewing their maladaptive behaviors in cognitive, affective, and sensory ways. This occurs in a supportive environment in which reinforcement is readily available. In this way these techniques can help to maximize learning in the group setting.

Psychodrama

Role playing is a close and mutually nourishing cousin of psychodrama (Moreno, 1970; Moreno & Moreno, 2011). According to Corsini (1957), formal psychodrama is different than using psychodramatic techniques within a host of group therapeutic modalities. The major difference between the two is that formal psychodrama is a method of using theater and drama per se as therapy, whereas role playing is seen as a technique within other therapies to provide both diagnostic and therapeutic actions.

Role Playing Significant Others

One of the most common forms of role play involves the members of the group taking on the personae of significant others in a person's life to help bring the actual interactions to life and also to work through them in a relatively safer environment. Thus, a member of the group may feel a need to confront a family member but is worried about the repercussions. In the group they have an opportunity to try out potential confrontations without the evident danger. The most frequent role plays of this type are family-oriented.

> **LEADER:** I'd like to suggest that we try something different now. Lin has been saying how difficult her childhood was, and I'm having a hard time grasping the current situation. I would like to ask members of the group to act like your family, Lin. Who here is like your mother? Your father? Your twin sister?

After the member indicates other group members who remind her of these significant family members, the leader asks those others if he or she would be willing to role play the family members. Once the roles are set, Lin is asked to instruct and inform each player in the intricacies of his or her role, and the representative family scene is played out:

> LIN: Well it's actually my stepdad not my father that's the big problem.
>
> **LEADER:** Okay, address your stepfather (played by Henry). What do you want to tell him?
>
> LIN: I am 26 years old and even though I am still living at home, I want you to stop treating me like a teenager.
>
> HENRY: (As stepfather) As long as you are under my roof, you will behave properly, or you can move out.

After the leader checks with Lin that Henry's response is accurate, she recommends that Lin continue.

The role play may take several "takes." Lin will be asked to do what she usually does with the responses from the other role players and also what she'd like to do differently to get a different reaction from her stepfather. She will also be asked where her support will come from in the group and in her family and include those roles. In doing this, Lin may get a chance to work through her feelings and come to a new approach that may work better for her needs.

Acting As If

This technique is designed to help individuals behave in ways that are atypical and difficult for them. In one group, Connie was pressured by other members to speak up for herself. She continually demurred and claimed that she was very conflict-averse and believed that saying what she wanted could precipitate a huge fight. The leader here recommended that Connie try it in a make believe setting as an experiment.

Earlier, she reported that when Gwen, another group member asked her to lunch after the last meeting, she went, even though she didn't want to go. She said that she preferred to eat alone and reflect on the group meeting. She quickly added, "It isn't about you Gwen. I am just so introverted, I need a lot of private time to figure out what just happened."

> **LEADER:** So what was it like to do what you thought Gwen wanted instead of what you preferred?"
>
> CONNIE: Oh, it's what I always do. It was okay. Lunch with Gwen and Barb was pleasant.
>
> **LEADER:** Let's try something different in here. Instead of just going along, could you let the part of you that wanted to be alone, respond to Gwen. Would that be okay with you, Gwen?
>
> (When Gwen assented, the leader asked Connie to try.)
>
> GWEN: Barb and I are going to lunch after the group, would you like to join us?
>
> CONNIE: This is really hard.
>
> **LEADER:** Just focus and tell her what you want.
>
> CONNIE: (In a very soft voice) Thank you, Gwen, but I really need to be alone now.
>
> **LEADER:** Please try saying that again and this time say it louder and tell Gwen, you *want* to be alone.
>
> CONNIE: Thank you, Gwen. Maybe some other time. Right now I want to be alone to process the group for myself.
>
> **LEADER:** How does that feel?
>
> CONNIE: I am scared at what she might think.
>
> **LEADER:** Ask her!
>
> CONNIE: Gwen, are you insulted that I declined your invitation and was just being selfish?

GWEN: No. I admired your taking the extra time for yourself. It's something I often deny myself.

LEADER: What do you hear?

CONNIE: That Gwen isn't insulted and that she thinks it's good for me to be me.

LEADER: That's what I heard also. Would you be willing to try an experiment for the rest of today's meeting? Would you speak from your assertive side and see what happens, just while we are together today?

Role Reversals

This role-playing technique is especially effective in groups of families, couples, and other natural groups. It is particularly dramatic when two or more members have a difficult time listening to each other and communicating openly. With married couples the husband is asked to role play the wife, and vice versa. The most amazing thing is that they can do it so well.

> **LEADER:** Jim, I'd like you to try something. Be Judy. Act like you are her. Present her point of view, her emotions, everything. And Judy, you be Jim. Use his words, his gestures, etc. Try it now.

Both members of the couple are now confronted with a little example of what it's like to deal with the impact of their own behavior. They typically respond as emotionally to their own behavior as they did to that of their partners. This experience often leads to greater understanding of each other's feelings and thoughts and motives, and greater communication ensues. It is useful to note that members of couples are usually very good at portraying their spouses.

Behavioral Rehearsal

One particularly utilitarian and common procedure in the transfer-of-training phase of group therapy is behavioral rehearsal. This procedure, particularly in groups with a CBT frame, involves practicing for outside realities by simulating newly acquired behaviors in the safer group environment and receiving feedback from the other group members and leaders. Thus members are requested to role play their next discussion or confrontation with their boss, spouse, parents, and so on. One example of this was described in the discussion on the termination phase (Chapter 5):

> **LEADER:** Let's try the situation where you share your feelings with your boss. Who will play the boss? Okay, describe the

setting, situation, and so on, and then tell him how you feel (what you're thinking, wishing, etc.).

In one group, a member was distraught that he couldn't get his insurer to authorize eight more sessions of the group. He had made several calls and had hung up when placed on "interminable holds with elevator music." He was afraid that he'd have to drop out of the group. Other members had some ideas as to how he might get through to the one person who could say "yes." The leader recommended that they role play for him (allowing him vicarious learning). One other member showed very straightforward assertiveness beginning when the person at the insurer asked may I put you on hold. He replied, "NO! Do not put me on hold again. I only want you to forward my call to the person who can authorize additional sessions. Please put me through to that person directly or give me the correct phone number to reach him or her." In the rehearsal, the first time, the person was disconnected. On the third try, she actually got through by beginning with, "Please tell me your name again. … Thank you, Al. Please do not place me on hold, my phone disconnects when I am on hold. I really need your help now."

The person with the problem then tried it in group. Each time, the other members empathically reflected his frustration even while they threw hindrances at him in the practice phone calls.

Empty Chair Technique

One form of role playing, uses an unoccupied physical chair for an individual to project interactions with others or self. In group, this is primarily an intrapsychic approach found in the treatment phase of the group.

There is some dispute as to the therapeutic origins of the technique. It is likely something that could be found in various forms in psychodrama. Gestalt therapists (Glass, 2010; Woldt & Toman, 2005) following Perls, have used the procedure for decades and it has become a staple of Emotion Focused Therapy (Greenberg, 2016; Greenberg & Goldman, 2008). According to Glass (2010), if a client has conflicting desires and behaviors (i.e., a desire for high achievement, paired with procrastination), the client can place each side in a separate chair. As he inhabits each chair, he talks from the voice of that side of the conflict. "As the interplay between these polar opposites is heightened and thereby more fully experienced, integration through greater self-acceptance becomes possible" (p. 381).

Another common scenario is when an individual provides the group with only one side of their personality, such as the caregiver or always nice person. The individual may be asked to express their nice person presentation from one chair and their angrier, more critical part in a second chair and express that side to each other group member.

In addition to using the empty chair to hold the disowned parts of self, a member may be asked to place a significant other in the chair and have a conversation with him or her. In one group Jeff, a 55-year-old man repeatedly reported holding himself back from relationships and job opportunities, claiming that his now 80-year-old mother had instilled in him a fear of anything new when he was a child and her influence continues to this day.

> **LEADER:** Go ahead and put your mother in the empty chair and tell her what has come of her anxiety as you experience it. Tell her directly, don't beat around the bush. It can't hurt her, she's not in the group.
>
> JEFF: (With great hesitancy) You know Ma, I never knew the Great Depression and I haven't really had to suffer much my entire life, but I am still always scared to do anything new.
>
> **LEADER:** Give her an example and express the feelings.
>
> JEFF: When this woman I am dating wanted to go on a hot air balloon ride in Napa, I made so many excuses, she must have thought I was a neurotic mess. I guess that may be right, but as anxious as that made me, I wanted to try it. I just felt like I had to hold back because it's the sort of thing our family never did. Joanie (sister) does the same thing.
>
> **LEADER:** Stay with your own feelings, don't try to rationalize.
>
> JEFF: I don't know. I just feel like I am letting you down if I do anything risky.
>
> **LEADER:** Okay, come over here to the mom chair and be your mom. Respond to your son.
>
> JEFF: (As Mom) Hot air balloon! That is very dangerous. It's the Hindenburg all over again. People die from that all the time.
>
> **LEADER:** Jeff, come back and respond to her.
>
> JEFF: Mom, the Hindenburg was hydrogen, these are helium.
>
> **LEADER:** Instead of explaining to try to convince her, tell her again what it's like for you.
>
> JEFF: Mom, you're not listening. I am feeling stifled in my whole life because of things that happened in our childhood before I was born. I want to be free to do some different things than be a CPA 24/7.
>
> **LEADER:** Okay be mom here again.
>
> JEFF: (As Mom) Who is this woman? Do I know her? She sounds dangerous.

When the leader indicated that he respond from his first chair as Jeff again, he said, "yes that is what she would say. There's no winning with her."

> **LEADER:** Check out what Pedro is experiencing. He seems to be smiling a lot.
>
> JEFF: Pedro, you look like you are ready to laugh.
>
> PEDRO: I can't tell if it's your mom or mine and if it isn't mine it does seem funny that two 50-something guys are still trying to please unpleasable mothers as if we were 5 instead of 50. Mine would actually tell me not to go out with the new woman.
>
> **LEADER:** Jeff, what's your reaction to what Pedro is saying?
>
> JEFF: (Begins to laugh and then continues) I've got to get her out of my head or give up having my own life. Any ideas?" (directed to the leader).
>
> **LEADER:** Who here has some ideas about how Jeff could do a critical mother-ectomy?

After the group members laughed, each one began talking about how they are being influenced by extraordinary cautions from childhood and how whenever they went ahead and tried something new despite the anxiety, they had more real experiences—sometimes positive and sometimes negative. Lani, mentioned that her internalized mother was much more strict and cautious than her actual mother or grandmother.

The empty chair technique in this group not only helped Jeff confront his own demons, but also opened the whole group to a deeper discussion of security and freedom and facing the fears of the unknown, both in the group and in their everyday lives.

Doubling or Alter Ego

One special form of role playing that comes directly from psychodrama involves the use of an external alter ego. In this technique, a leader or member of the group can speak for another person. This is especially helpful if the individual in question is having difficulty expressing some powerful feelings or blocking feedback from other members.

In one example, Candy, a 33-year-old woman, was talking about her recent divorce very indirectly and in vague terms. At one point, Jolene, another member questioned her:

> JOLENE: You know Candy, from how you are describing it, I can't tell what you are feeling, anger, sadness, or what.

CANDY: Well it's complicated. I don't feel okay bad-mouthing Jake and I know that I'll be okay … just not feeling that so much now.

LEADER: Jolene, what is your sense of what Candy is feeling under the politic concerns for others?

JOLENE: I think she's probably scared and angry.

LEADER: Candy, would you be okay if Jolene put her hand on your shoulder and spoke those emotions for you? (When Candy assented, Jolene got up, stood behind Candy, and placed her left hand on Candy's right shoulder.)

CANDY: I am really pissed at Jake for cheating on me and I am scared of my future.

The leader addressed Candy and asked how close that was. Candy nodded and replied that it was somewhat accurate. The leader then asked Jolene to continue in her role as Candy addressed the group.

CANDY: Jake is the only man I was ever with sexually and now the world is daunting.

JOLENE: I am scared half to death that nobody will want me now. Jake found some other woman and I am feeling so unappealing.

JAVIER: (An older man in the group responded) Candy, I was in your place a few years ago, and it makes sense that your self-esteem is in the toilet now. Mine was and the whole dating scene is really scary, especially when my self-confidence was low. For what it's worth, you are a smart, attractive woman and once you believe that again, things will get better.

CANDY: I hope so. Thank you for saying that. How did you turn it around? Did you try online dating?

JOLENE: (*doubling*) I just worry that anybody I met would betray me like Jake and besides, if I told you all how pissed off I was with Jake, I think you'd want to reject me too.

At this point Candy burst into tears and acknowledged the depth of her fear of rejection and the "unattractive sides" of herself like her anger. The group responded by sharing similar experiences of presenting a more polite than real face.

By presenting the underlying emotions, Jolene was able to speak Candy's truth through her touch and doubling. It allowed Candy to deal with the reality of her world instead of perceived expectations. In many groups, members may not be able to double effectively. A co-leader may be a most effective emotional alter-ego.

Hand Puppets

One interesting variation of role playing can be found in the use of other objects that can speak for an individual. Hand puppets do this particularly well, and members usually get somewhat playful using the puppets. Some group leaders have several animal puppets that can be placed on a hand and speak the unspoken, like other role-playing exercises.

The leader suggests that members "choose a puppet to speak for you. Which animal would be best to say what you'd like to say?" The actual choice of a hand puppet may be a useful indication of the emotions or thoughts that are being suppressed. Thus when a person chooses a lion or a bear, it may be to express a need for power. A bird may indicate a perceived need for freedom or a cuddly animal a request for nurturance.

Guy had been a quiet supportive member of the group through the early sessions. When he was confronted by another member, he agreed with her and backed down. After a few more similar incidents, the leader asked him to choose a hand puppet. He chose a shark. When the leader asked the shark to speak for Guy, his mounting irritation emerged.

> GUY: (Holding the hand puppet on his right hand and moving the shark mouth up and down) You know, I am sick of always being a good guy. I have sharp teeth and when I smell blood in the water, I want to attack.
>
> **LEADER:** What would that look like?
>
> GUY: Not like me.
>
> **LEADER:** Okay would you be willing to speak from the shark parts only.
>
> GUY: Okay, here goes. I was upset, no really angry (growls) when you made fun of me last week (addressing the woman in the group who had confronted him). You don't know what's going on inside me. You know sharks can be wounded too.

This led to a more real confrontation between the two in which she told him that she liked him better as part shark, part "good guy." That was important information for him. Historically, he had always tried to be close to others, particularly women by being a best friend. It was very important for him to hear that he couldn't be a big brother or be sexy. He had to do both.

Reincarnation. A related imaginary technique that is primarily diagnostic asks the members to choose an animal they'd like to be in another life. Despite the example of refusal given above, this is a relatively nonthreatening technique that is also typically very enjoyable for the participants. A leader might introduce the exercise as follows: "If you were to die and come back as an animal, what would you most like to be? Let's each describe the animal we chose and say a few words about why we made this particular choice." The instructions for children and adolescents are simpler. "Choose an animal you'd like to be."

After each person chooses and describes his or her choice, the leader can inquire as to whether the animal represents a growing edge for the person. Chosen animals tend to reflect desires/needs for power (elephants, rhinos, lions, sharks), appearance (leopards, minks, purebred show dogs), affection (koala bears, puppies, my own dog or cat), freedom (eagles, hawks, jaguars). In discussing these "growing edges" members can often begin to examine in a less threatening manner their desires for changes in their lives. The leader may sometimes ask a member to be (role play) the chosen animal and reflect the growing edge in the group.

> **LEADER:** So Sam, what would the eagle in you do right now as you are talking to Bea.
>
> SAM: Actually, I'd tell her that she is mind-reading and I just want out of her thinking she knows what I am thinking.
>
> **LEADER:** Speaking as your eagle, tell her here.

The exercise may also be done with inanimate objects. People's choices again represent similar themes of strength, longevity, beauty, or meaning to an individual, and so on.

Depth Exercises

These exercises have primarily therapeutic functions. They are primarily used in the treatment phases of the group, can be dramatic, and require excellent timing and closing skills. Some can be done at the group level, but these techniques are primarily intrapsychic approaches that may open up one or two individuals to greater depth, but except for vicarious learning, they have less breadth. They often resemble individual therapy in a group context.

In these exercises, there is an expectation of regression, leaders suggesting images, thoughts, and feelings while members are in a state of heightened receptivity, relaxation, or a mild altered state of consciousness. In each of these techniques, the member is asked to relax and then to accept direction of his or her mental images from the leader. The approaches are designed to enhance awareness, repressed memories, or insight into the unconscious mind,

At the lighter end of the scale are often group-level exercises such as focusing (i.e., Gendlin, 1982), centering, or meditation. A related technique is a guided fantasy, in which the leader takes members on a trip in their minds to discover something that may be useful. Often the relaxation component is followed by a journey with physical sensations down a path of discovery (a hidden object, a wise elder, something glittering in water). The member brings back the message/discovery offered to the group for discussion.

More intrapsychic and deeper exercises involve regression to an earlier stage of psychological development and addressing precursors of a current problem. Members are encouraged to recreate the feelings that existed at that bygone time. Such experiences are frequently highly affect-laden and similar to the Gestalt "hot seat," characteristically facilitated with individual members rather than the group as a whole. Insights from regression fantasies may be diagnostic, but these techniques are primarily employed for treatment.

Hypnotic trances have also been used by some leaders. The leaders inductions may be formal, but more often are informal and permissive (Erickson, 1975). Systematic desensitization (Wolpe, 1969) and Jacobsen (1925) relaxation procedures have also been used, particularly in groups dealing with anxiety.

The Rule of Parsimony

Each of the structural exercises presented above can be skillfully and effectively applied if it is used in a timely manner. Like most tools in a craftperson's kit, they can be used to assist or to deter the group process. Each leader must make hard decisions regarding the use of techniques, with reference to the considerations recommended earlier.

The Exception. One major type of group needs to be far more technique-centric. These are groups for children and young adolescents. There are several reasons for this. First, the normal avenue of communication for children is not sit-down conversation. Children communicate through play as well as through language. Second, most children who are referred to groups have limited attention spans. Third, children are often intimidated and less natural when they are forced to play a game with adults' rules. It is much easier for younger group members to have rules that suit their natural tendencies.

Activity groups and play therapy have long been the preferred approach with younger clients. With children and adolescents, it is essential for leaders to provide a vast array of relevant stimuli with some structure to keep motivation in the group at optimal levels.

Groups for children and adolescents may use effectively many of the techniques described above and hundreds of others. We have had success in adolescent groups with physical activities such as dance, movement, and short sport exercises preceding conversation. Having members bring in their favorite music and describing what it means to them has also been very useful. It is also very important to remind ourselves of the "golden rule of exercises" in groups with younger members: What's important is how they react to the suggestion.

A Sample Mixed Exercise Process

As a way to better understand the use of techniques in a real-life group, we are concluding this chapter with a multiuse series of techniques that intertwine and build on one another in a closed men's group. It is a demonstration of how techniques in groups may evolve as the members become more ready for changes in group process. The vignette is designed to demonstrate flexibility in application rather than a particular formula or guideline. Notations in brackets will depict the techniques.

The events occurred (slightly revised, compressed, edited for time, and fictionalized for confidentiality) in a 12-session group of eight men ranging in age from 24 to 66 years with no outliers. Three members and the leader were veterans; one with combat experience.

Session 8

As the group was in the therapy phase, the youngest member, Lenny, remained engaged but limited in his range of expression of affect. One of his stated reasons for being in the group was to deal with the loss of his father, who was killed in combat 13 years prior. In the group to date, Lenny's feedback to others and statements about himself were always accompanied with a smile.

A technique began to emerge when Jamal called Lenny "ever-smiling cheerful one" when Lenny offered happy-faced sympathy to Jamal about losing his job. When another member remarked that Lenny's smiling about something so troubling was "weird," the leader intervened: "Ask Lenny to say it again without smiling."

> JAMAL: Thanks oh cheerful one. I wish I was as light hearted as you about this.
>
> LENNY: I feel for you buddy, but I just don't want to bring you down. As I've said before I like to keep a positive attitude about things. I'm trying to help.
>
> **LEADER 1:** It seems that your support that should be valuable isn't getting through as intended. I'd like you to try an experiment if you're willing, Lenny.
>
> LENNY: (With a big smile) Sure thing. That's why I'm here.
>
> **LEADER 1:** Okay. Repeat what you said to Jamal without the smile.
>
> LENNY: (With feigned soap opera seriousness) I'm sorry you lost your job Jamal *and I know you'll find another one.*

At this point Lenny broke out laughing as did the group, except for Leader 2.

LEADER 2: (After making eye contact with Leader 1 and getting a nonverbal, green light to go ahead). So Lenny, let me be the bad cop here. I'm going to push you. Try it again. (*rehearsal*)

This time, Lenny did a little better. Two takes later he was yet to approach normal congruent affect. Discussion was opened up to the principal participants about their experience and then other group members weighed in. Lenny continued to lapse into inappropriate smiling mode, but with his agreement to practice, he tried to accept reminders to shift to more appropriate affect when called upon.

For the leaders, it was important to help Lenny increase the risk of being congruent. There are several approaches that can be taken here: Remind Lenny to say things like he means them; by contrast, ask Lenny to increase his light affect when it inappropriately occurs to give him a sense of ability to regulate it (*acting as if*); use a doubling technique help Lenny experience more of the unpleasant emotions; create a role play to help Lenny express his emotions more easily in a once removed manner; or get Lenny into more personally emotional issues and helping him face them directly, without the use of humor (*intrapsychic*).

Aware of the ego strength of the participants and because the first option had only minimal success, the leaders decided to approach the matter with increasing intensity. They began to consider a more difficult and sophisticated exercise, designed to facilitate processing the core issues that motivated Lenny's fierce dedication to exhibiting only a sunny disposition.

Lenny had spoken about his dad on many occasions. His death when Lenny was 11 years old led the boy to idolize his fallen hero. Unfortunately, in the process he detoured around the necessary and healing process of grief.

LENNY: (Smiling broadly) I'm really glad that Mark, Jon, and Stan are veterans. When I talk about my dad in the group, I think you guys (looking at the three) get what I'm trying to say about him; like you could have been maybe one of the troops out there with him.

LEADER 2: Stan, Could you give Lenny some feedback? In your own words, what did you just hear him say?

STAN: Well, I heard him say he's happy we warhorses are in the group.

LEADER 2: Do you believe what he's saying?

STAN: Funny you should ask that, I do and I don't.

LEADER 2: Say more about the do and don't?

STAN: Yeah (looking at Lenny). On the one hand you're telling me you're glad, but when I look in your eyes, they're spooky, man!

LEADER 2: Can you describe how Lenny's eyes are spooky?

STAN: I've seen that look a lot out in the field, especially in young troops. Sort of like a deer in the headlights.

LEADER 2: Can you name the feelings inside that look?

STAN: You look scared shitless man.

LEADER 2: Anything else?

STAN: I don't know. I just know that when you look at me like that, I want to cry and I DO NOT like to go there!

LEADER 1: Lenny, every time you talk about your dad, lightness appears in your words but heaviness appears in your eyes. I want you to try something to give your words the backup power they deserve to send a clear message. Will you give it a go?

LENNY: Well, you know me. I'm always game to try things out in group but give me a break doc (big smile), and let me know what you have in mind.

LEADER 2: Good for you; not just going along. (Then shifting affect to a more somber tone.) Pick Mark, Jon, or Stan and tell him one thing you want to share about your dad.

Treat what you say with the importance of the words that might be spoken at the ceremony when he was posthumously awarded the Purple Heart. Make the person you choose get what you're trying to say. Use your words, your face, your body, your mind, your feelings, all of you to get through. I also would like the two unchosen vets to stand beside you as you speak and help you to get the message through. (*technique described*)

(The leader gains assent that the three vets were willing.)

LENNY: (Smiling) Well "here's the deal" for me. I do feel happy when I remember my dad. Why are you trying to take that away from me?

LEADER 1: Keep that happiness with you and don't lose it. Imagine putting it in your back pocket while you do the exercise. As soon as it's over, I'm going to ask you about the treasure in that back pocket, and I may very well encourage you to take it out and use it a lot for the remainder of the group. On the other hand, I'd sure like you to be able to share your sadness, hurt, anger, fear, confusion, frustration, and a whole lot of other feelings so that other people really understand them and get you. Let's see if you can get heard fully, understood and deeply appreciated. Besides, the group deserves to receive what you have to offer. (*explanation of technique*)

LENNY: Geez Louise, you sure are making a mountain out of a mole hill but what the heck. I've come this far and you senior citizens seem to know what you're doing, so okay (winks).

The leader asks Lenny to come to the middle of the group circle along with the member he's chosen to talk to and with the other two veteran members to stand alongside as he speaks (*setting the stage*):

LEADER 1: Okay. Lenny. Just say, face-to-face with Stan (combat vet) what you said before about Mark, Jon, and Stan being in the group.

Lenny states his appreciation in exactly the same cheerful way as before.

STAN: Say it like you mean it!

LENNY: I do (still smiling).

At this point the leaders believed that Lenny's underlying fragility did not require any special caution.

LEADER 1: Lenny, take a minute to connect with 13-year-old Lenny (2 years after his father died). Remember that kid? Think about where you lived then. Get a picture of the neighborhood, your school, your house, or apartment. Imagine yourself at 13. See your neighborhood in your mind's eye. Remember the school that you went to; your house; your room. Imagine the family sitting around the dinner table. Remember who was in your family and remember where your dad used to sit at that table before he went to war. (*regression*)

Leader 1 was closely monitoring nonverbal levels of Len's affect. Had it been possible for Lenny to directly deal with the incongruity between his feelings and his smiling, they could drop the exercise and continue directly. This was not the case with Lenny. Meanwhile, Leader 2 was scanning the other group members looking carefully for nonverbal signs of discomfort (to be addressed later) and connecting with members in nonverbal support as the exercise unfolds.

LEADER 1: Now choose one of the men behind you to give an alternate "you" voice to that 13-year-old. He will say some things just as if you had said them. Some things will fit, some might not. Don't worry about that. Just keep communicating with Stan. We can go over what "alternate you" said later. Also, the other man standing beside you will be there to support you (replicating the sense that his dad was his early protector) as you say these important things about your dad to Stan. (*doubling or alter ego*)

LENNY: I want Jon to be mini-me and Mark to be my support buddy.

The foregoing was said with appropriate affect. Len's humorous tone only slightly covered a more vulnerable affective state. The leaders did *not* address this directly.

LEADER 1: Len, please tell Stan anything you want to say to him about you and your dad.

LEN: He was a great dad.

MARK: (As Len) I really miss him.

LEN: He was fun, smart, a good soldier. He was also really moving up fast.

MARK: I was only 11 when he died. I was just a kid. It's not fair.

LEN: (Looking annoyed) I want to be just like him.

MARK: I want my dad.

Because several group members appeared very sad and close to tears with this interaction, the leaders decided to focus at the group level, broadening the scope and reducing the stress on Lenny.

LEADER 2: Let's pause here a minute. Len would you be OK in coming back to the group and take your seat in the circle?

LENNY: (Looking relieved) Sure.

LEADER 2: Jon, how about you coming back to the circle also?

Jon agrees and moves back to the circle.

LEADER 1: Mark and Stan, are you okay in staying with this a little longer? (If yes, the leader continues. If not he considers volunteers to take their place.)

LEADER 2: Anybody who wants to be with Mark and say some things as an 11-year-old. Lenny, please come up now in support of that 11-year-old child.

As others were able to be involved, Len was free to experience his feelings out of the spotlight. The grief and feelings of abandonment affected several members and led to considerable work in subsequent sessions.

Between Session Leadership Meeting

After this session, the leaders met to review what had occurred and consider how to proceed. Both agreed that Stan, a retired combat military officer, had done yeoman's work as requested. They determined that he deserved some time to debrief as the next session unfolded. Stan's emotional debriefing was facilitated using the empty chair technique. As is common, co-leader debriefing involves each checking in emotionally and theoretically and a review of the unfolding process to inform the next steps in Session 9.

LEADER 2: We've been talking about our experience and what the exercise with Lenny meant to us personally. Stan, your role was to be silent during the exercise and to listen as Lenny talked to you about his dad. I wonder if there's anything you want to share about how that was for you.

STAN: It was okay. You know I'm used to being there for the people under my command and this was kind of like that. Len had some things to say and I was there for him. That's what I'm trained for. That's what I do.

LEADER 2: You mean, in general?

STAN: Well it's not like I don't have feelings or don't care, I just can't go there. You break down in combat and you're dead. Not a great career path.

LEADER 1: I've got a dilemma here that you can help clarify. We have a clear ground rule if anyone stated that they didn't want to get into something in group, we would back off and stop. But you just said you "can't go there" which sounds like an invitation to help. I hear that you want some help to express your feelings without losing the rest of you in the process. Just man-to-man. What's your preference?

STAN: (After a long pause) I don't even know where to start.

LEADER 2: Well if you're willing, could you say some more about the young men you saw in combat that had that haunted look you noticed in Lenny last week?

STAN: There really isn't any more to say. That touchy feely stuff is just too risky. If I lose my edge and get soft ... I have all kinds of responsibilities; to my wife, my kids, my command ... feeling more is a luxury I can't afford.

MARK: It sounds like you're living your life like you're at DEFCON 1. Don't you ever take a break?

STAN: (Chuckling) I used to hate R&R. I could never relax on furlough; always thinking about my troops; always somewhere else but on the beach watching the palm trees. Hell, I didn't even notice them. (Looking at the leaders in turn.) I guess it's really hard for me to "be here now" as you gurus like to say. It's like my head and protector-self won a battle with my heart. I really want to be present and closer to people, but what if I lose me in the connection.

LEADER 1: Who do you want to be closer to?

STAN: Well it has to be my wife, first and foremost. She's my best friend, but no matter how hard I try to give her what she wants, she says I won't open up to her. We have a comfortable lifestyle; money in the bank. She shouldn't have a care in the world but she says that I move away. I think it's true.

LEADER 2: Let's go back to what you want.

STAN: I want to show her how much I love her but I don't know how else to give.

LEADER 2: I have an idea about how to proceed.

STAN: Well, if I could keep the starch in my collar and still loosen up a little I'd be willing to give it a try.

LEADER 2: Good enough. You are in charge of this exercise. I'll just ride shotgun with you since I'm familiar with some of the terrain. We'll stop any time you say.

STAN: Fair enough. What do we do?

LEADER 2: It sounds like you have two sound tracks going on inside you. One track takes care of business at hand and is both dominant and successful. The other is a feelings track. Let's try to deal with both instead of one at a time. I'm going to set up an empty chair that will represent the feeling Stan. The chair you are now occupying will be the Stan that speaks to the feeling Stan in the other chair. Then I'll ask you to move to the feeling chair and speak to you from that position, and back and forth. Got it?

STAN: (With a tone of resignation) Okey dokey.

LEADER 2: How about giving "Feeling Stan" a name?

STAN: Let's call him Walter.

LEADER 2: Why Walter?

STAN: Why not?

(Everybody laughs, including Stan.)

STAN: Okay. I'll just call him Stanley.

LEADER 2: Let's start by saying anything you want to Stanley.

STAN: I know you're always there inside me. I don't trust you (pauses). You show up at all the wrong times. Just when I need to focus, you distract; you yammer; you nag me while I have work to do. You're a little dangerous as a distraction.

LEADER 1: Observes the group and considers who might also be included in the exercise as it unfolds.

LEADER 2: So Stanley really makes you feel uncomfortable and unfocused.

STAN: Yes, but I see what you're doing. You just slipped in a feeling.

LEADER 2: Good point. Can you move over now to Stanley's chair? Speak to Stan from the feeling position. Your performance objective is to make a good case for a feeling you.

STAN: (In a weary monotone voice) You need me. Your wife is walking on eggshells around you as if you were an IED (land mine). She doesn't know what's going on inside you and is starting to give up trying. Meanwhile you live your life like an observer from the outside.

LEADER 1: I think Stanley could use some help. Will someone volunteer to add some strength to Stanley's point of view?

At this point Roger, a middle manager who had been working out his issues with authority in the group, volunteers.

LEADER 2: Stan, return to the other chair and Roger, take a seat in Stanley's chair. Express your feelings and his in an emotional way.

ROGER: Look Stan, I happen to have a lot of heat on this but you don't see me ripping you a new one or losing it. You need your feelings and more than that, you deserve them. You act like feelings are on a toggle switch; on full blast or off. Listen to me! You can just notice when you have feelings and you try to express 10%, 20%. You don't have to blow people away or shut down—more like a rheostat!

LEADER 2: Thanks Roger. (Motioning him back to his seat.)

STAN: I'm really uncomfortable with this.

LEADER 2: Can you say why?

STAN: (Looking pale and shoulders slumping) I don't think so.

LEADER 2: Are you okay to keep going?

STAN: I don't know what to do.

LEADER 2: (Gently) That's really unlike you. I'm guessing something is going on.

STAN: This is really hard for me. I have something to say to Roger.

LEADER 1: Roger, are you willing to come back and this time stand behind Stanley's chair?

(Roger returns.)

LEADER 2: Stan, just talk to the chair and look at Roger if it helps.

STAN: I don't know how people will react to my feelings. They might not like me.

LEADER 1: Roger, can you give a name to any feelings you're picking up from Stan.

ROGER: You sound scared, Stan.

LEADER 2: We need a volunteer to double for Stan. Are you willing to help?

TOMMY (the most empathic member was chosen): I sure am willing to help (Stan is avoiding eye contact).

LEADER 2: Please stand behind Stan and speak as if you were him. Talk to Stanley while giving Stan your best support.

TOMMY: You don't know what it's like. I remember when I met Betty. We were close. We were in love. We were free. Since then I've seen a lot of ugliness, felt a lot of pain and even caused a lot of pain. You want to talk about feelings? How about all the friends I've lost. All the times I had to suck it up and just press on. It's easy to talk about feelings but don't make me feel them. It's too hard.

(Leader 1 noticed Lenny sitting in the circle with tears running down his cheeks and moved across the circle to sit next to him.)

STAN: (Looking over at Lenny) Thank you Len. Maybe I'll get there in time. For now I understand that maybe I can try to share my ugly feelings. You have a lot of courage.

Lenny's tears were the first sign to the leaders that he could begin the very necessary grieving process for his loss of his dad. Stan's connection with him at the moment was an unfreezing for him as well. The process continued with each other member relating how they were similar to Lenny and Stan.

In session 11, Lenny asked to talk to his dad in the empty chair, with both support and doubling by others. Lenny had a conversation with his dad as the son and as the father (*role reversal*).

Summary

Group techniques (structured exercises) are defined as relatively short-term, voluntary experiences, instituted or sanctioned by leaders for a specific purpose. To be effective, they must be well-timed, with clearly determined starting and ending points. Their effects must be debriefed by members and leaders immediately upon conclusion. They serve two functions: diagnostic and treatment or change.

Used judiciously and employed moderately with a clear purpose, techniques and exercises can catalyze the group process, provide alternatives to direct confrontation, uncover otherwise hidden information and effectively reduce group time spent in achieving predetermined goals.

An emphasis is placed on the importance of group leadership training and the value of the highest ethical principles as they relate to the employment of structured exercises.

The dangers of employing techniques in the group setting are highlighted and the golden rule for structured exercises is articulated: *"It is far less important to complete the exercise than to deal with whatever behaviors and feelings are generated by the exercise or the suggestion of the exercise."*

A pre-employment procedural checklist is offered as a means to insure sensitivity to the ongoing group process before instituting any technique. To be effective, any chosen exercises should be aligned with the group members and the extant group process. There should be a good reason for applying them. It is almost always a bad idea to use a technique as a substitute for a process focus. We recommend a three part process to use technique or exercises: 1) Attend to and nurture the unfolding group process, 2) Enhance the process with supportive and confrontive interventions, and 3) Employ the chosen structured exercises cautiously when appropriate for the unfolding process.

In general, we recommend eschewing structured exercises in favor of tracking group process. However, groups for young children, adolescents, and less verbal clients, characteristically, are more technique-driven.

Examples and descriptions of a small sample of structured exercises are presented and correlated with evolving group phases. Specific modalities described include artwork and other projective techniques, trust techniques and several role-playing-related exercises.

The chapter concludes with a case study in which several interrelated mixed-depth exercises are employed to deepen the process at intrapsychic, dyadic and group level interactions. As it unfolded, it facilitated both personal work for individuals and an enhanced bond between members.

PART III
The Future

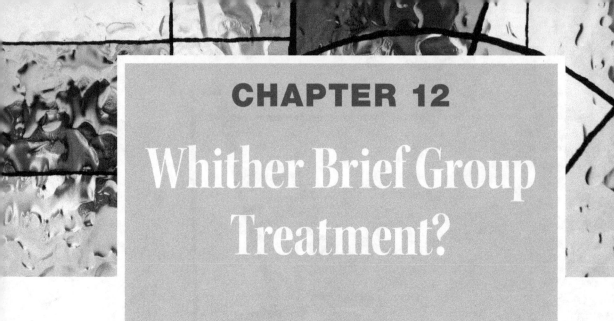

CHAPTER 12

Whither Brief Group Treatment?

C haracterizing the events of one's own times is always a dubious enterprise. Even more questionable is predicting confidently the future of one's field of expertise. Nonetheless, in this chapter we will extrapolate from our understanding of the times, the historical realities of the field, research, and practitioners' intuition to project a course. If at times, we seem to be too involved with trees, those who join us on our journey will have to presume the presence of a forest.

Historical and Recent Trends

From Pratt's (1906) early work with tuberculosis patients involving ministers, Marsh's (1931) early experiments with what later became known as *milieu therapy*, and Moreno's (1932) classification of the "group method" to the present, group work has paralleled social needs and changes. For most of its history, group work has been particularly responsive to the interaction of personal and social needs. Not only has the content of group discussion followed social trends, beliefs, myths, and feelings, but group solutions have typically been predicated on changes in contemporary ways of responding to dilemmas in individuals' lives.

Thus, with apologies to stereotypical characterization of large bodies of time and numbers of people, we explore the interaction of social trends and corresponding individual needs. The 1950s, following the immediate postwar period was seen as a time of personal conformity and economic growth. In those years, people could get ahead by "playing the game." Correspondingly, group work was primarily centered on *adjustment to broader social norms* with members focused on becoming "team players": Socio-psychological approaches centered on an understanding of the process of the group and its application to a wider environment. Group research was primarily descriptive and theoretical, dominated by psychoanalytic thinking; it involved the application of individual psychological approaches to the group setting.

The decade of the 1960s (1964–1973) can be viewed as the period of rebellion. In the West, it was an era of political unrest, marked by a diminution of trust in established authority, and considerable questioning of traditional values. Groups during this period focused on questions of power, social integration, and alternative (Eastern) philosophies. Encounter groups emphasized unorthodox rather than traditional solutions to social and interpersonal problems. Therapy groups began to incorporate social, as well as intrapsychic and physiological diagnoses and treatments. The political theme of the 1960s was confrontation between peoples of different cultures (e.g., Black vs. White, "cops" vs. "hippies," young vs. old). Group work responded by attempting to develop *bridges between people* based on common ground and mutual learning. Research was primarily limited to descriptive and "black box" (outcome) studies.

The decade of the 1970s (1973–1982) labeled by many as the "me" generation, had *self-actualization* as a primary social focus. The sexual revolution, popularization of mind-altering substances, and other means of self-exploration and/or escapism all represent part of a greater consumerism that often followed the maxim, "If it feels good, do it." As usual, group work addressed the needs of the times. Primary themes in groups were *identity* and *self-esteem*.

Gender became a dominant theme in the 1970s as well. Based partially on the civil rights movement, and reproductive freedom that followed easy access to birth control methods, the women's movement became a significant social catalyst, influencing mores, values, attitudes, and behavior in virtually every realm of Western society. Attention to and consideration of gender and equality issues occurred in group work also. Curiously, not until the late 1980s did men's groups emerge, spurred by women's group outcomes and the popularity of authors such as Robert Bly (1990, Bly & Moyers, 1989) and Sam Keen (1991).

Group technology also found its way into the workplace, salesroom, and classroom to a much greater extent. The small group format and technology often gave way to larger groups (e.g., community groups, "est" seminars) or to different settings (classrooms, sales enhancement classes, limited partnership sales), but the technology that had developed in the small group was still dominant. In research, the beginnings of comparative outcome studies and serious studies of group process appeared in greater numbers.

In the 1980s family roles were examined in new ways. Women's roles in particular, were reconsidered and expanded. As the "baby boomer" generation progressed through their 30s they began to add *family* to *career* and *self-actualization*. The resulting combination produced a "we can do it all," attitude among an expanding middle class. Women's and minority considerations were powerful themes in the culture in general and in groups. Along with a revision of women's roles came a greater awareness of a multiplicity of family formats. Group work commensurately took a giant turn in that direction by incorporating family therapy into the group literature, including family therapy research for the first time in the annual review of groups in the *International Journal of Group Psychotherapy*. The technology from natural groups, best exemplified by marital and family therapy and industrial psychology, were increasingly integrated into group work. In addition, considerations regarding family of origin have merged with more classical intrapsychic explorations in current therapy and growth groups. Research was increasingly process centered.

As the 1990s disappeared into the millennium, dominant social trends included single issue politics, predominance of fiscal over social considerations, a wider divergence between the "haves" and "have not's" and reduced availability and reliance on extended families and physical communities for support. Commensurate cutbacks in governmental economic support, medical coverage, and community props have propelled individuals and nuclear families to become the primary social entity. Within this framework, *diversity* and the need for personal *choices* became more central.

As these social forces coalesced to support individualism and disconnection with those who are in the same physical space, there was an increasing electronic connectivity with those who share specific interests, but who may be geographically quite distant. Each person now carries in his or her pocket or purse, a powerful computer with connectivity to friends, colleagues, and acquaintances who share interests, political views, and social perspectives regardless of physical proximity. Along with this is a snowballing loss of intimacy and privacy among cyber-strangers and a compensatory need for connection.

It became normative during meeting or university class breaks to see a dozen or more people sitting in close proximity, each absorbed in his or her separate lives with no acknowledgment or connection to those adjacent. It may seem like a joke, but it is common for people living together to text one another, rather than get up and meet in another room in the same abode.

Offering both diversity and personalized support, groups have focused more and more on specific needs of a host of diverse cultural and interest clusters. Specialty groups for people with similar interests, diagnoses, cultural backgrounds, and gender orientations represent the areas of greatest growth.

An outgrowth of this increasing specialization has been a growing realization that "we can't have it all" at least not without a perspective of the limits and value of time. Indeed, in the middle class, time, recognized as a limited commodity, is becoming a more dominant currency. Downsizing, a growing acknowledgment of the limitations of institutional support for the individual and a contrasting empowerment through the high tech revolution have all pushed individuals to make significant choices (i.e., time vs. money).

Managed Care

Nowhere is the impact of downsizing and choices more evident than in health care. Medical advances that allow for greater longevity present us with opportunities and choices. Longer life after the productive years produces an inevitable dilemma: Who gets the expensive, life-extending, and limited services? The field of medical ethics has grown dramatically. Even more evident has been the dramatic growth of managed health care, in which budgetary considerations play an increasing role in determination of what services are covered by third-party (insurance) payment and what are considered unnecessary and hence, unreimbursable. By providing cost-effective and specific solutions, theme-centered specialty groups are increasingly offered as a means to address managed care and client needs concomitantly.

Into the 21st Century

If the 1950s showed us the *individual in society;* the 1960s presented the *individual against society;* the 1970s gave us the *individual's conflict with self;* the 1980s saw the *individual's integration into the new family;* and 1990s showed *a growing realization of the price of individual freedom and choice,* it was expected that first fifth of the 21st century would involve reintegration of the individual in society in the *age of information.* That integration has yet to be found. Instead, the first decade and a half of the 21st century has seen greater sociocultural fractures. Special interest groups have proliferated and bonding has become increasingly insular. Most people live near, converse with, and share social media outlets with other like-minded individuals. With a proliferation of cable outlets, even news based on computer algorithms and identity politics, has become more partisan, building barriers to connection between electronic and cultural tribes. What is very evident in this world of in-groups and out-groups is a need for greater intimacy at the human level.

These evolving trends play into the expansion of group technologies in the foreseeable future. For the past 50 years, the extended family has been a diminishing resource. In addition, the positive, stabilizing influence of other traditional major institutions such as schools, churches, and government have been also less supportive to individuals.

Changes in the workplace exemplify and exacerbate these shifts. Decentralization, downsizing, extended hours for those who are employed, deterioration in benefit plans, people working remotely without "water-cooler" connection, and a general reduction of security and loyalty have ushered in a new era with new needs for individuals. As available information grows at a "geometric" pace, specialization becomes more salient. Individuals with computers, tablets, smart phones, and a high-speed Internet connection may do the work of entire companies.

Naisbitt and Aberdene (1990) in their *Megatrends 2000* concluded,

> The great unifying trend at the conclusion of the 20th century is the triumph of the individual. … It is an individual who creates a work of art, embraces a political philosophy, bets a life savings on a new business, inspires a colleague or family member to succeed, emigrates to a new country, has a transcendent spiritual experience. … Individuals today can leverage change far more effectively than most institutions" (p. 298).

Such individual power of course engenders greater social fragmentation and pressing psychological needs. If I can no longer rely on my job to guarantee my retirement and health care, if I can no longer count on the schools to educate well my children, if I cannot count on government to provide sufficient resources for everyone of my generation, I must rely on myself, my co-workers, my family, and my friends. Yet, extended families are no longer as omnipresent sources of security. Even the form of family has dramatically changed. If one is to believe middle-class clients in dual-earner families, there is decreasing time for friends, community, or even each other. Too much freedom without sufficient security or time is a prescription for certain unconscious fears of abandonment and isolation.

What are the antidotes to these fears? From our perspective, barring a sociopolitical revolution rivaling that of the 1960s in power and scope, the answer is intimacy in its broadest sense. Where may individuals find intimacy in the world of telecommunication, telecommuting, the Internet, and the isolated nuclear family? It is curious that one of the dominant themes to emerge from the worldwide web is its value in creating groups of people of similar interest and to find ways to connect them. Indeed, dating services have also been an integral part of the computer generation. Is this a way that individuals may satisfy yearnings for connection, albeit through telephone wires, Wi-Fi, texts, tweets, and modems?

In the therapy realm, group therapy may be much better suited than individual work to the needs of individuals who feel isolated. Although the intimacy of a transference relationship may promote greater self-understanding, it is the group interactions with peers that provide intimate connection between equals. Adolescents who are depressed or feeling isolated at school seem to respond much more positively to group interaction. Company CEOs and presidents who have no peer group at work similarly are offered special opportunities in a group of others who might understand their pressures and isolation.

It is a natural conclusion that as the individual becomes more independent, his or her needs for connection will move more to the forefront. Groups of individuals who share certain values or needs will be especially useful. This trend has already been in place for several years. The popularity of theme-oriented groups, self-help groups, and diagnosis-related groups has been burgeoning and is likely to continue.

This is all an argument that group counseling or therapy will be often *the treatment of choice*. Groups may provide both prevention and treatment for the alienation disorders of our times. Moreover, economic factors have also coalesced to make groups more desirable to those who pay for mental health treatment. Whether groups are to occur in a managed care system emphasizing cost containment, or paid for directly by consumers who will demand affordable effective treatment, brief groups are very likely to proliferate in the foreseeable future.

Professional Issues in Groups of the Future

In the May 1985 special issue of the *Journal of Specialists in Group Work* (Conyne et al., 1985), several experts in the field of group work predicted trends for the year 2001. The editors of this special edition of the journal summarized these contributions:

> For the most part, ... the future of group work seems robust to the authors. Groups will abound. They will become major forces for combating the increasing depersonalization and anomie that are likely to accompany the computer and "high-tech" revolution. As Gazda illustrates, group work will be directed much more extensively to the well population as a major means to prevent excessive life stress and situational problems and to promote life skills. Group methods will be used increasingly with families, with diverse populations, within organizations, and even, according to Klein, to achieve social change across all levels of systems: in groups, organizations, communities, regions, nations, and the world (p. 114).

Almost two decades into the new millennium has shown that most of the predictions remain on target. However, there are forces that continue to prevent group from becoming "the therapy whose time has come." Chief among these are the dilemma of adequate training for leaders, a need to better understand and respond to diversity and a dearth of compelling process research evidence.

The Clarion Call

Who will lead the groups that are necessary in the 21st century? The history of group therapy is littered with reports of well-meaning but untrained professionals applying individual therapy, family therapy, and education skills to group work. Historically, in many institutions, group treatment has been assigned to a variety of professional and paraprofessional staff members, often without regard to their background and training. Because it is the least understood of the therapy methods, and because individuals are least well trained in offering it, group treatments have often been denigrated. An unfortunate cycle ensues.

Once group treatment is considered an inferior form of care, many institutions consign group treatment to staff members with the least training. Thus, in a typical inpatient setting, it is normal to see a group led by nurses, aides, occupational therapists, and social workers on a rotating and irregular basis. Many groups have different leaders on consecutive days.

Furthermore, patient attendance is often not supported or is even sabotaged by staff. The groups run by leaders untrained in group process are then evaluated accurately to be inferior methods of treatment. The self-fulfilling prophecy continues with groups being further denigrated. Group treatment per se is *not* being judged; it is groups led by those with inadequate understanding and training in group methods. An unfortunate reality is that in untrained hands, the very tools that most produce growth in groups can be dangerous for members. Corey and Corey (1992), Haeseler (1992), and Lakin (1991) among others describe the potential for scapegoating, diffusion of responsibility, pressures toward uniformity, premature vulnerability, unreasonable demands for inappropriate affect, and promotion of impulsivity.

Group leaders of the future must be specifically trained in group process and group methods. Simply because an individual is licensed or has a staff position at an institution that holds groups is insufficient to qualify him or her as a group therapist. Indeed, there are serious ethical considerations in using untrained leaders. Each of the mental health professional organizations has a code of ethics that defines the scope of practice. In line with the "do no harm" injunction, is a demand that practitioners recognize the boundaries and limitations of their training and competencies. Individuals who are not qualified by education, training, or experience are in violation of ethical codes when they lead groups. Newman and Levant (1993) note that the generic practitioners' license is such that each individual counselor or therapist scope of competence is necessarily less than the scope permitted by license.

It is incumbent on each practitioner to obtain the requisite training, work under direct supervision of a qualified group leader, work with an experienced co-leader, or resist employer or economic pressure to practice group leadership when it is beyond the scope of his or her training. Equally essential is that well-trained group leaders educate their professional colleagues and the public to understand and appreciate the value of group process and professional leadership. Practitioners also need to address an unfortunate countertrend toward both leaderless groups and a proliferation of "psychoeducational" groups (classes) run by novice counselors hired by employee assistance programs and agencies subcontracted by managed care organizations primarily on the basis of economic convenience.

What is Appropriate Training? There is no current special credentialing for group leaders that has any *legal* standing. A licensed therapist is not specifically barred from practicing group therapy. Only ethical guidelines limit the scope of practice in this regard. At least one attempt for a national standard is being supported by the National Registry of Certified Group Psychotherapists in association with the American Group Psychotherapy Association. However, this is voluntary and the registry is a professional not a licensing organization.

In this text we have described what we believe to be *minimal* training for group leaders if they are able to use group process effectively. We believe that group training is best taught as a specialization in graduate training and continuing education classes. Certainly the training should include a basic course, extensive supervised practice, personal group experience as a member, observation and/ or co-leadership with experienced professional group leaders, and licensure. We also recommend strongly personal individual or group therapy and continuing education in theory and group methods. Such training could allow for a new group therapist specialization in mental health—one that would promote a higher status for group work and attract better qualified practitioners.

The goal of appropriate training is to produce leaders who are more master craftspersons than technicians. Particularly in an age so influenced by technology, the irreplaceable value of human interaction is what counters isolation and fosters growth. Leaders who know themselves and are courageous and ethical in bringing that self-knowledge to group interventions are best suited to have maximum impact on their clients. It is also important that leaders become aware of and sensitive to the personal backgrounds of members of their groups.

Diversity

In addition to training in group process, leaders need training in knowledge of diversity. Groups are made up of individuals who bring disparate personal histories and cultures to each meeting. In any group, there may be members with different needs, backgrounds, religions, races, ethnicity, and cultures. Leaders must be sensitive to, and aware of these differences.

In some ways, comprehensive knowledge of diversity is becoming increasingly complex. Commentaries on data from the 2010 U.S. census indicate that the percentage of ethnic minorities will dramatically increase and that by the year 2025, Caucasians will become a numerical minority. Doubtlessly, sociocultural value differences will mandate alternative intervention styles and possibly even group values. For example, the supremacy of independence that predicates many therapeutic interventions may be far less valued in some ethnic groups.

Immigrant groups with a variety of Asian, Hispanic, Muslim, or Russian backgrounds may need to be treated differently. It is insufficient to assume that a Chinese immigrant from Hong Kong will be similar to an Irish immigrant simply because they are both first generation. Indeed, it is equally important to recognize that two Chinese immigrants from Hong Kong may well have widely divergent needs and respond quite differently to the same intervention.

Sensitivity to diverse groups of individuals often does not come easily. Stereotyping and overgeneralization are as problematic as is assumed similarity. Thus, if the leader of the group is a 49-year-old African American woman with a degree in social work from a major university in New York, she must be cautious about assuming that a member of her group who shares all those anamnestic criteria will be like her. She must also be wary of assuming that the Samoan woman, African American man, or Japanese social worker in the group are different from her, similar to her, or like each other in some specific way.

Of course, individual leaders will never be able to fully know a host of cultures and the driving forces of cultural values within those cultures. It is essential to develop a sensitivity to cultural, ethnic, gender, religious, and lifestyle differences and to learn to approach within parameters offered by the members of the group.

There is little question that any counselor or therapist must constantly learn about the basic values and styles of behaviors customary in the diverse cultures of members. It is inevitable, for example, that members of a minority culture will view potential for change and influence differently than members of a dominant culture. It is also very important to recognize the differential value placed on traits such as independence in non-Western cultures. The differences between a "guilt" culture and a "shame" culture may have a large impact on the style of intervention required. Similarly, the power of nuances of language and emotion may be mitigated with clients who are engaging in the group using their second, third, or fourth language. Several authors have discussed the dangers of misunderstanding progress (Leong, 1992) or underutilizing group methods (Sue & Sue, 1990) in some Asian populations. Without understanding the interaction of cultural values and treatment method, a leader may easily misconstrue the behaviors, implications, progress, and meaning of groups with minority culture members (i.e., Pederson & Marsella, 1982; Brislin, 1990).

Dangers of a Diversity Focus. In addition to the great value a focus on diversity brings, there are also potential dangers to a diversity focus. One danger is to minimize the value of common human needs. In the rush to eschew stereotyping a group leader may also lose sight of the intrinsic similarities for affiliation, attachment, creativity, and suffering that surpass all boundaries. In addition, group members in any voluntary group will have subscribed at least partially to the group values or they wouldn't join at all.

A second danger involves the tyranny of political correctness. When form subsumes substance, political correctness may in some circumstances be used not as the protector of minorities, but rather as another form of intolerance. Any belief that a group member is correct because of skin color, gender, or national origin is prejudice. A group leader may be frozen into inaction or stuck in blandness because of an excessive fear of offending someone.

"I Don't Have a Culture, I'm From the Midwest." A delicate line separates true sensitivity to others with stereotypic limits of action that actually cheat members from much of what a leader may offer. To walk that line, a leader must be willing to be educated by each member of a group as to what particular intervention will best support change and to become increasingly aware of his or her personal cultural influences.

Perhaps the most significant culture a group leader will ever need to know is his or her own. Rappaport (1994) strongly urges therapists to acknowledge and explore their personal culture and value systems and to give up the notion that therapy is value free or neutral. What is important is awareness of the automatic, unconscious translations of input that provide meaning to the therapist, and to understand others' responses to one's self.

The leaders' values have a potentially powerful impact. In at least one study, Shapiro and Siu (1976) demonstrated how members of groups at least temporarily tended to take on behaviors, forms of speech, and cultural values of their leaders through subconscious modeling. From pretest to posttest, members showed a significant tendency to give responses more similar to responses of the leaders of their groups. Thus, when both leaders were Caucasian, the members of a multiethnic group developed values and responses more characteristic of Caucasians at posttest. Similarly, in groups led by co-leaders of Japanese and Hawaiian descent, the members' responses emulated more the values characteristic in those cultures. In groups led by co-leaders who were not of the same ethnic origin, less modeling of this kind was shown. An important note is that these value differences did not continue into the 6-month follow up.

Training for Diversity. The biggest problem to overcome is the "one size fits all" therapy. We need to develop instead a multicultural viewpoint. Such a perspective honors what actions, thoughts, and feelings mean to an individual within the context of culture, gender, and family of origin. This is a *true advantage for group treatment*. Each member can teach others about how a particular intervention might work for him or her.

Leaders are specifically encouraged to do the following:

1. To become informed about members' cultures but not try to be an expert.
2. To help members define how the group will fit and serve them personally.
3. To respect differences and break down stereotypes.
4. To focus explicitly on cultural issues; not to act as if culture is invisible.
5. To focus more interpersonally as multiculturalism increases.

6. To have a co-leader who is of a different gender or from a different ethnic group, especially when the members predominantly come from a similar ethnic background that differs from the leader.

Psychology has always been defined as the science of the individual. Clearly, psychologically based treatment cannot take a *one-size-fits-all* approach to groups even when group process is the cornerstone of that approach. Group treatment is ultimately treatment for *individual members.* Success cannot be defined by a group plan of action for all members. Each individual contributes something unique to the group process and each takes something personal away from the group.

The Issue of Research

There is a long history of research on groups of all types. Some of the studies are remarkably sophisticated empirically, whereas others rely more on the "your group made a new man of me, Doc" anecdotal data.

If brief group treatment is to claim (its rightful) eminence as a therapeutic modality, its rise will be supported by additional "hard data" process and outcome studies.

> Recent developments demonstrate that clinicians and researchers can no longer afford to maintain their mutual dissociation. Many experts have argued, in fact that the survival of psychotherapy as a profession depends on the active integration of research and practice (Dies, 1985, p. 72).

The challenges we face in the future are not new. Professional group leaders are in the best position to identify and evaluate the sophisticated process and outcome dimensions that will be fruitful to investigate. If we leave the empirical research to others, nonclinical factors, such as cost containment, theoretical insularity, so-called efficacy (laboratory-only studies), or conventionality may dominate future research. It is up to us to set up programs to study ongoing groups in private sectors, universities, and agencies and to press for appropriate grants to support more complex and expensive research.

Summary

In the 21st century, we will need to integrate the push for individualization and specialization in an information-age society with the corresponding human needs for affiliation. This will require greater sensitivity to increasingly diverse, multicultural memberships in our groups. We believe that groups provide an excellent antidote to feelings of isolation, disconnection, and alienation. By illuminating universal experiences and feelings, groups can help counter social fragmentation and polarization. To reach this goal, leaders must be well trained in generic group process, such as the one delineated in this text, and be ready to make adjustments for particular group populations. It is, after all, the *process focus* that allows therapeutic progress and crosses many clinical and socioeconomic barriers.

References

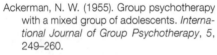

Ackerman, N. W. (1955). Group psychotherapy with a mixed group of adolescents. *International Journal of Group Psychotherapy, 5*, 249–260.

Alonso, A. (1993). Training for Group Psychotherapy. In A. Alonso & H. I. Swiller (Eds.), *Group psychotherapy in clinical practice* (pp. 521–532). Washington, DC: American Psychiatric Press.

Alonso, A., & Swiller, H. I. (1993). *Group therapy in clinical practice.* Washington, DC: American Psychiatric Press.

American Association for Counseling and Development. (1988). *Ethical standards of the American Association for Counseling and Development.* Alexandria, VA: Author.

American Association of Marriage and Family Therapy. (1988). *Ethical Guidelines.* Washington, DC: Author.

American Counseling Association. (2014). *ACA Code of Ethics.* Retrieved from https://www.counseling.org/resources/aca-code-of-ethics.pdf

American Group Psychotherapy Association. (2002). *Ethical standards.* New York: Author.

American Mental Health Counselors Association. (2015). *Code of ethics.* Retrieved from http://www.amhca.org/?page=codeofethics

American Psychiatric Association. (1981). *Code of Ethics.* Washington, DC: Author.

American Psychiatric Association. (1994). *Diagnostic and statistical manual of mental disorders* (4th ed.). Washington, DC: Author.

American Psychological Association. (2002, amended June 1, 2010). Ethical principles of psychologists and code of conduct. *American Psychologist, 58*(5), 377–402. Retrieved from http://www.apa.org/ethics/code/index.aspx

American Psychological Association. (1973). *Guidelines for Growth Groups.* Washington, DC: Author.

American School Counselor Association. (2016). *ASCA ethical standards for school counselors.* EthicalStandards2016.pdf, retrieved from https://www.schoolcounselor.org/asca/media/asca/Ethics/

Anderson, B. N., Pine, L., & MaeLee, D. (1972). Resident training in co-therapy groups. *International Journal of Group Psychotherapy, 22,* 192–198.

Andronico, M. (2001). Mythopoetic and weekend retreats to facilitate men's growth. In G. R. Brooks, & G. E. Good (Eds.), *The new handbook of counseling and psychotherapy with men.* San Francisco: Jossey Bass.

Appley, D. G., & Winder, A. E. (1973). *Groups and therapy groups in a changing society.* San Francisco: Jossey Bass.

Association for Assessment and Research in Counseling. (2016). *Resources.* Retrieved from http://aarc-counseling.org/resources

Association for Assessment in Counseling and Education. (2012). *Standards for multicultural assessment* (4th ed.). Retrieved from http://aarc-counseling.org/assets/cms/uploads/files/AACE-AMCD.pdf

Association for Specialists in Group Work. (2012). Retrieved from http://www.asgw.org

Association for Specialists in Group Work. (1990). ASGW professional standards for group work. Alexandria, VA: Author.

Axline, V. M. (1947). *Play therapy.* New York: Houghton Mifflin.

Bandura, A., & Walters, R. H. (1963). *Social learning and personality development.* New York: Holt, Rinehart & Winston.

Barlow, S. H. (2014). The history of group counseling and psychotherapy. In J. L. DeLucia-Waack, C. R. Kolodner, & M. T. Riva (Eds.), *Handbook of group counseling and psychotherapy* (2nd ed.). Thousand Oaks, CA: Sage.

Barrett-Lennard, G. T. (1962). Dimensions of therapist response as causal factors in therapeutic change. *Psychological Monographs, 76*(43, Whole No. 562), 1–33.

Battegay, R. (1989). Apparent and hidden changes in group members according to the different phases of group psychotherapy. *International Journal of Group Psycho-therapy, 39*(3), 337–353.

Bauman, S. (2010). Looking forward. *Journal for Specialists in Group Work, 35*(1), 1–2.

Beiser, H. R. (1955). Play equipment for diagnosis and therapy. *American Journal of Orthopsychiatry, 25*(4), 761–770.

Bender, L., & Woltmann, A. G. (1936). The use of puppet shows as a psychotherapeutic measure for behavior problem children. *American Journal of Orthopsychiatry, 6,* 341–354.

Benedict, R. F. (1934). *Patterns of culture.* New York: Houghton Mifflin.

Benjamin, S. E. (1972). Cotherapy: A growth experience for therapists. *International Journal of Group Psychotherapy, 22*(2), 199–209.

Bennis, W. G. (1964). Problems and vicissitudes in T-group development. In L. P. Bradford, J. R. Gibb, & K. D. Benne (Eds.), *T-group theory and laboratory method: Innovation in re-education.* New York: Wiley.

Berkovitz, I. H. (1972). On growing a group: Some thoughts on structure, process and setting. In I. H. Berkovitz (Ed.), *Adolescents grow in groups.* New York: Brunner/Mazel.

Bernadett, S. T. (1981). *Cross cultural counseling* [workshop]. Clark Air Force Base, Republic of the Philippines.

Bernard, C. P., & MacKenzie, K. R. (Eds.). (1994). *Basics of group psychotherapy.* New York: Guilford Press.

Beymer, L. (1969). Confrontation groups; hula hoops? *Counselor Education and Supervision, 9,* 75–86.

Blinder, M., & Kischenbaum, M. (1967). The technique of married couples group therapy. *Archives of General Psychiatry, 17,* 44.

Bly, R. (1990). *Iron John.* Reading, MA: Addison-Wesley.

Bly, R., & Moyers, B. (1989). *A gathering of men.* New York: Mystic Fire Video.

Bobula, J. A. (1969). The theatre of spontaneous man. *Group Psychotherapy, 8,* 47–64.

Boldt, R. W., & Paul, S. (2011). Building a creative-arts therapy group at a university counseling center. *Journal of College Student Psychotherapy, 25*(1), 39–52.

Bowen, M. (1971). Family therapy and family group therapy. In H. Kaplan & B. Sadock (Eds.), *Comprehensive group therapy.* Baltimore, MD: Williams and Wilkins.

Bradford, L., Gibb, I., & Benne, K. D. (1964). *T-group theory and laboratory method in re-education.* New York: Wiley.

Brislin, R. W. (1990). *Applied cross cultural psychology,* Huntington Park, CA: Sage.

Brooks, G. (2010). *Beyond the crisis of masculinity: A transtheoretical model for male-friendly therapy.* Washington, DC: American Psychological Association.

Brown, N. W. (2010). Group leadership teaching and training methods and issues. In R. K. Conyne (Ed.), *The Oxford handbook of group counseling.* New York: Oxford University Press.

Brown, S., & Yalom, I. D. (1977). Interactional group therapy with alcoholics. *Journal of Studies on Alcohol, 38,* 426–456.

Budman, S. H. (1992). Models of brief individual and group psychotherapy. In J. Feldman & R. Fitzpatrick (Eds.), *Managed mental health care: Administrative and clinical issues* (pp. 231–248). Washington, DC: American Psychiatric Press.

Budman, S. H., & Gurman, A. S. (1988). *Theory and practice of brief therapy.* New York: Guilford Press.

Budman, S. H., Simeone, P. G., Reilly, R., & Demby, A. (1994). Progress in short term and time-limited group psychotherapy:

Evidence and implications. In A. Fuhriman & G. M. Burlingame (Eds.), *Handbook of group psychotherapy: An empirical and clinical synthesis*. New York: Wiley.

Budman, S. H., Demby, A., & Randall, M. (1980). Short term group psychotherapy. Who succeeds? Who fails? *Group*, *4*, 3–16.

Burlingame, G. M., Fuhriman, A., & Mosier, J. (2003). The differential effectiveness of group psychotherapy: A meta-analytic perspective. *Group Dynamics: Theory, Research and Practice, 7,* 3–12.

Burlingame, G. M., & Krogel, J. (2005). Relative effectiveness of individual vs. group psychotherapy. *International Journal of Group Psychotherapy*, *55,* 607–611.

Buys, C. J. (1978). Humans would do better without groups. *Personality and Social Psychology Bulletin,* 123–125.

Caffaro, J. (2001). Group therapy training in a doctoral program. Unpublished paper presented at the American Psychological Association annual meeting, San Francisco, CA.

Capuzzi, D., & Gross, D. R. (1992). *Introduction to group counseling.* Denver, CO: Love Publishing.

Capuzzi, D., Gross, D. R., & Stauffer, M. D. (2010). *Group work* (5th ed.). Denver, CO: Love Publishing.

Carkhuff, R. R., & Berenson, B. (1967). *Beyond counseling and therapy.* New York: Holt, Rinehart & Winston.

Carroll, M. R., & Wiggins, J. (1990). *Elements of group counseling: Back to the basics.* Denver, CO: Love Publishing.

Cermak, T. L. (1985). *A primer on adult children of alcoholics.* Pompano Beach, FL: Health Communications.

Chung, R. C. Y. (2015). Critical issues in international group counseling. *Journal for Specialists in Group Work*, *40*(1), 6–21.

Coche, E. (1983). Change measures and clinical practice in group psychotherapy. In R. R Dies & K. R. MacKenzie (Eds.), *Advances in group psychotherapy: Integrating research and practice.* New York: International Universities Press.

Coche, J. M. (2001). Group therapy training with medical residents. Unpublished paper presented at the American Psychological Association annual meeting, San Francisco, CA.

Coche, J., & Coche, E. (1990). *Couples group psychotherapy.* New York: Brunner/Mazel Publishers.

Cohen, A. M., & Smith, R. D. (1976). *The critical incident in growth groups: A*

manual for leaders. La Jolla, CA: University Associates.

Comas-Dias, L. (2014). Multicultural theories of psychotherapy. In D. Wedding & R. J. Corsini (Eds.), *Current psychotherapies* (10th ed.). Belmont, CA: Cengage Learning.

Compare, A., Tasca, G.A., Lo Coco, G. & Kivlighan, D.M. (2016) Congruence of group therapist and group member alliance judgments in emotionally focused group therapy for binge eating disorder. *Psychotherapy,* 5(2), 163-173.

Conideris, M. G., Ely, D. F., & Erickson, J. T. (1991). *California laws for psychologists*. Gardena, CA: Harcourt Brace Jovanovich.

Conyne, R. K., & Bernak, F. (2004). Teaching group work from an ecological perspective. *Journal for Specialists in Group Work*, *29*(1), 7–18.

Conyne, R. K., & Crowell, J. L. (2007). *Group techniques: How to use them more purposefully.* Upper Saddle River, NJ: Prentice Hall.

Conyne, R. K., Dye, A., Gill, S. J., Leddick, G. R. Morran, D. K., & Ward, D. E. (1985). A retrospective of critical issues. *Journal of Specialists in Group Work*, *10*(10), 112–115.

Cooper, C. L., & Bowles, D. (1973) Physical encounter and self-disclosure. *Psychological Reports, 33,* 451–454.

Cooper, C. L., & Mangham, I. L. (1971). *T-groups: A survey of research.* London: Wiley Interscience.

Cooper, L. (1976). Co-therapy relationships in groups. *Small Group Behavior*, *7*, 473–498.

Corey, G. (1990). *Theory and practice of group counseling* (3rd ed.). Pacific Grove, CA: Brooks/Cole.

Corey, G. (2015). *Theory and practice of group counseling* (9th ed.). Pacific Grove, CA: Brooks/Cole.

Corey, G., & Corey, M. S. (1982). *Groups process and practice* (2nd ed.). Pacific Grove, CA: Brooks/Cole.

Corey, G., & Corey, M. S. (1987). *Groups process and practice* (3rd ed.). Pacific Grove, CA: Brooks/Cole.

Corey, G., & Corey, M. S. (1992). *Groups process and practice* (4th ed.). Pacific Grove, CA: Brooks/Cole.

Corey, G., Corey, M. S., & Callahan, P. (2010). *Issues and ethics in the helping professions* (8th ed.). Pacific Grove, CA: Brooks/Cole.

Corey, G., Corey, M. S., Callanan, P., & Russell, J. M. (2014). *Group techniques* (4th ed.). Pacific Grove, CA: Brooks/Cole.

Corey, M. S., Corey, G., & Corey, C. (2014). *Groups: Process and practice.* Belmont, CA: Cengage Learning.

Corey, G., Corey, M. S., & Haynes, R. (2014). Evolution of a group (2nd ed.). [DVD]. Pacific Grove, CA: Cengage.

Corsini, R. J. (1957). *Methods of group psychotherapy.* New York: McGraw Hill.

Corsini, R. J. (2010). *Roleplaying in psychotherapy.* New York: Routledge.

Corsini, R. J., & Cardone, S. (1966). *Roleplaying in psychotherapy: A manual.* Chicago: Aldine.

Corsini, R. J., & Lundin, W. H. (1955). Group psychotherapy in the Midwest. *Group Psychotherapy, 8,* 316–320.

Cosio, D., & Schafer, T. (2015). Implementing an acceptance and commitment therapy group protocol with veterans using VA's stepped care model of pain management. *Journal of Behavioral Medicine, 38*(6), 984–997.

Coulson, W. R. (1972). *Groups, gimmicks and instant gurus.* New York: Harper and Row.

Council for Accreditation of Counseling & Related Educational Programs. (2017). http://www.cacrep.org/wp-content/uploads/2017/07/2016-Standards-with-Glossary-7.2017.pdf

Cox, G. L., & Merkel, W. T. (1989). A qualitative review of psychosocial treatments for bulimia. *Journal of Nervous and Mental Disease, 177*(2), 287–301.

Creighton, M. (1990). Revisiting shame and guilt cultures: A forty-year pilgrimage. *Ethos, 18*(3), 279–307.

Cuijpers, P., van Straten, A., & Warmerdam, L. (2008). Are individual and group treatments equally effective in the treatment of depression in adults? A meta-analysis. *European Journal of Psychiatry, 22*(1), 38–51.

Darongkamas, J., Madden, S., Swarbrick, P., & Evans, B. (1995). Touchstone therapy group for women survivors of child sexual abuse. *Journal of Mental Health, 4*(1), 17–29.

Davenport, D. S. (2004). Ethical issues in the teaching of group counseling. *Journal for Specialists in Group Work, 29,* 43–49.

DeLeon, P. H., VandenBos, G., & Bulatoa, E. O. (1991). Managed mental health care: A history of federal policy initiatives. *Professional Psychology, 22,* 15–25.

DeLucia-Waack, J. (1997). A review and analysis of process outcome measures. *Journal for Specialists in Group Work, 22*(4), 277–293.

DeLucia-Waack, J. (2006). *Leading psychoeducational groups for children and adolescents.* Thousand Oaks, CA: Sage.

DeLucia-Waack, J., & Kalodner, C. (2005). Contemporary issues in group practice. In S. Wheelan (Ed.), *The handbook of group research and practice* (pp. 65–84). Thousand Oaks, CA: Sage.

Delucia-Waack, J., Kalodner, C.R. & Riva, M.T. (2014) *Handbook in Group Counseling and Psychotherapy.* 2nd Ed., Thousand Oaks, CA: Sage.

DeLucia-Waack, J. L., & Bridbord, K. H. (2004). Measures of group process, dynamics, climate, leadership behaviors, and therapeutic factors. In J. L. DeLucia-Waack, D. A. Gerrity, C. R. Kalodner, & M. T. Riva (Eds.), *Handbook of group counseling and psychotherapy* (pp. 120–136). Thousand Oaks, CA: Sage.

Denny, J. M. (1969). Art counseling in educational settings. *Personnel and Guidance Journal, 40,* 221–224.

Denny, J. M. (1972). Techniques for individual and group art therapy. *American Journal of the Art of Therapy, 11,* 3–11.

Diamond, M. J., & Shapiro, J. L. (1973). Changes in locus of control as a function of encounter group experiences. *Journal of Abnormal Psychology, 83*(3), 514–518.

Dick, B., Lessier, K., & Whiteside, J. (1980). A developmental framework for cotherapy. *International Journal of Group Psychotherapy, 30,* 273–285.

Dies, R. R. (1979). Group psychotherapy: Reflections on three decades of research. *Journal of Applied Behavioral Science, 15,* 361–374.

Dies, R. R. (1980). Current practice in the training of group psychotherapists. *International Journal of Group Psychotherapy, 30,* 169–185.

Dies, R. R. (1985). Research foundations for the future of group work. *Journal of Specialists in group work, 10*(2), 68–73.

Dies, R. R. (1992a). Models of group psychotherapy: Sifting through confusion. *International Journal of Group Psychotherapy, 42,* 1–17.

Dies, R. R. (1992b). The future of group therapy. *Psychotherapy, 29,* 58–64.

Dies, R. R, & Dies, K. R. (1993). The role of evaluation in clinical practice: Overview and group treatment illustration. *International Journal of Group Psychotherapy, 43,* 77–105.

Dies, R. R., & MacKenzie, K. R. (1983). *Advances in group psychotherapy: Integrating research and practice.* New York: International Universities Press.

Dinkmeyer, D. C., & Muro, J. J. (1971). *Group counseling: Theory and practice.* Itasca, IL: Peacock.

Dreikurs, R. (1950). Techniques and dynamics of multiple psychotherapy. *Psychiatric Quarterly, 24,* 788–799.

Dreikurs, R. (1951). The unique social climate experienced in group psychotherapy. *Group Psychotherapy, 3,* 292–299.

Dreyfus, E. A., & Kremenliev, E. (1970). Innovative group technique: Handle with care. *Personnel and Guidance Journal, 49,* 279–283.

Drum, D. J., & Knott, J. E. (2009). Theme groups at thirty. *International Journal of Group Psychotherapy, 59*(4), 491–510.

Durkin, H. E. (1954). Group dynamics and group psychotherapy. *International Journal of Group Psychotherapy, 4,* 56–64.

Egan, G. (1976). *Interpersonal living.* New York: Wadsworth.

Elkind, D. (1980). Strategic interactions in early adolescence. In J. Adelson (Ed.), *Handbook of adolescent psychology.* New York: Wiley.

Erford, B. T. (2011). Outcome research in group work. In B. T. Erford (Ed.), *Group work: Processes and applications* (pp. 312–321). Boston: Pearson.

Erford, B. T. (2016). Using activities and expressive arts in group work. In B. T. Erford (Ed.), *Group work in schools* (2nd ed.). New York: Routledge.

Erickson, M. H., Rossi, E. L., & Rossi, S. I. (1977). Hypnotic realities: The induction of clinical hypnosis and forms of indirect suggestion. New York: Irvington Press.

Erickson, R. C. (1975). Outcome studies in mental hospitals: A review. *Psychological Bulletin, 82*(4), 519–540.

Esman, A. H. (1983). *The psychiatric treatment of adolescents.* New York: International Universities Press.

Ettin, M. F. (2000). From identified patient to identifiable group: The alchemy of the group as a whole, *International Journal of Group Psychotherapy, 50*(2), 137–162.

Family Court Services, Santa Clara County Superior Court. (1993). Family Court Services Orientation Program, Santa Clara, CA.

Fehr, S. S. (2010). *101 interventions in group therapy* (Rev. ed.). New York: Taylor and Francis.

Fehr, S. S. (2016). *101 interventions in group therapy* (2nd ed.). New York: Taylor and Francis.

Fiebert, M. S. (1963). Sensitivity training: An analysis of trainer interventions and group process. *Psychological Reports, 22*(8), 829–838.

Finn, B., & Shakir, S. A. (1990). Intensive group psychotherapy of borderline patients. *Group, 14*(2), 99–110.

Forsyth, D. (2010). *Group dynamics.* Belmont CA: Wadsworth.

Foulds, M. (1971). Changes in locus of internal-external control. *Comparative Group Studies,* 293–300.

Foulds, M., & Hannigan, P. (1976). Effects of gestalt marathon workshops on measured self actualization: A replication and follow up. *Journal of Counseling Psychology, 23,* 60–65.

Frank J. D. (1961/1993). *Persuasion and healing: A comparative study of psychotherapy,* Baltimore, MD: Johns Hopkins University Press.

Frankl, V. (1963). *Man's search for meaning.* New York: Simon and Schuster.

Freud, S. (1924). *Collected papers* (Vol. II). New York: International Psychoanalytic Library.

Freud, S. (1981). Group psychology and the analysis of the ego. In J. Strachey (Ed. and Trans.), *Massenpsychologie und Ich-Analyse* [1921] (Vol. XVIII, pp. 67–143). London: Hogarth Press.

Gans, R. W. (1957). The use of group co-therapists in the teaching of psychotherapy. *International Journal of Group Psychotherapy, 9,* 618–628.

Garcia, C., Lindgren, S. & Pinton, J.K. (2011) Knowledge, skills, and qualities for effectively facilitating an adolescent girls' group. *Journal of School Nursing, 27*(6), 424–433.

Garfield, S. L., & Bergin, A. E. (Eds.). *Handbook of psychotherapy and behavior change* (3rd ed., pp. 627–670). New York: Wiley.

Gazda, G. M. (1989). *Group counseling: A developmental approach* (4th ed.). Boston: Allyn & Bacon.

Gendlin, E. T. (1982). *Focusing.* New York: Bantam.

Getty, C., & Shannon, A. M. (1969). Co-therapy as an egalitarian relationship. *American Journal of Nursing, 69,* 767–771.

Gerrity, D. A., & DeLucia-Waack, J. L. (2006). Effectiveness of groups in the schools. *Journal for Specialists in Group Work, 32,* 97–106.

Gibb, J. R. (1952). Effects of role playing upon a) role flexibility and upon b) ability to conceptualize a new role. *American Psychologist, 7,* 310–315.

Gladding, S. T. (2012). *Groups: A counseling specialty* (6th ed.). Upper Saddle River, NJ: Pearson.

Glass, T. A. (1997). Ethical issues ingroup therapy. In R. Anderson, T. Needles, & H. Hall (Eds.), *A practitioners guide to ethical issues in psychology specialty areas.* Springfield, IL: Charles Thomas.

Glass, T. A. (2010). The empty chair technique. In S. S. Fehr (Ed.), *101 interventions in group therapy* (Rev. ed.) New York: Taylor and Francis.

Goodrich, K. M. (2008). Dual relationships in group training. *Journal for Specialists in Group Work, 33*(3), 221–335.

Gottlieb, A., & Pattison, E. M. (1966). Married couples group therapy. *Archives of general psychiatry, 14,* 143–152.

Greenberg, L. S. (2016). *Emotion focused therapy* (Rev. ed.). Washington, DC: American Psychological Association.

Greenberg, L. S., & Goldman, R. N. (2008). *Emotion-focused couples therapy: The dynamics of emotion, love and power.* Washington, DC: American Psychological Association.

Grotjahn, M. (1951). Special problems in the supervision of group psychotherapy. *Group Psychotherapy, 3,* 308–313.

Grotjahn, M. (1971). The qualities of the group therapist. In H. I. Kaplan & B. I. Sadock (Eds.), *Comprehensive group treatment.* Baltimore, MD: Williams and Wilkins.

Grunbaum, H. (1986). Inside the group. In A. S. Gurman (Ed.), *Casebook of marital therapy* (pp. 742–775). New York, Guilford Press.

Gurman, A. S., & Kniskern, D. P. (1981). Family therapy outcome research: Knowns and unknowns. In A. S. Gurman & D. P. Kniskern (Eds.), *Handbook of family therapy* (pp. 742–775). New York: Brunner/Mazel.

Hadden, S. B. (1947). The utilization of a therapy group in teaching psychotherapy. *American Journal of Psychiatry, 103,* 644–651.

Hadden, S. B. (1955). Historic background of group psychotherapy. *International Journal of Group Psychotherapy, 5,* 162–168.

Haeseler, M. P. (1992). Ethical considerations for the group therapist. *American Journal of Art Therapy, 31*(1), 2–9.

Haley, J. (1963). *Strategies of psychotherapy* New York: Grune and Stratton.

Hall, Z. M. (1992). Group therapy for women survivors of childhood sexual abuse. *Group Analysis, 25*(4), 463–474.

Hansen, J. C., Warner, R. W., & Smith, E. J. (1980). *Group counseling: Theory and process* (2nd ed.). Chicago: Rand McNally.

Hansen, N. B., Lambert, M. J., & Forman, E. M. (2002). The psychotherapy dose-response effect and its implications for treatment delivery systems. *Clinical Psychology: Science and Practice, 3,* 329–343.

Harari, C., & Harari, C. (1971). The co-therapist encounter: A catalyst for growth. In L. Blank, G. B. Gottsegen, & M. G. Gottsegen (Eds.), *Confrontation.* New York: Macmillan.

Heilfron, M. (1969). Co-therapy: The relationship between therapists. *International Journal of Group Psychotherapy, 19,* 366–381.

Henry, S. (1981). *Group skills in social work: A four dimensional approach.* Itasca, IL: Peacock.

Hills, C., & Stone, R. (1970). *Conduct your own awareness sessions.* New York: Signet Books.

Hines, P.L. & Fields, T.H. (2002) Pregroup screening issues for school counselors. *Journal for Specialists in Group Work, 27*(4), 358–376.

Hollis, J. W., & Wantz, R. A. (1990). *Counselor preparation 1990–1992* (7th ed.). Muncie, IN: Accelerated Development.

Horney K. (1926). *Feminine psychology.* New York: Norton.

Horney K. (1935). The problem of feminine masochism. *Psychoanalytic Review, 22,* 241–257, 1935.

Horowitz, J. L., & Garber, J. (2006). The prevention of depressive symptoms in children and adolescents: A meta-analytic review. *Journal of Consulting and Clinical Psychology, 74*(3), 401–415.

Huston, K. (1986). A critical assessment of the efficacy of women's groups. *Psychotherapy, 23,* 283–290.

Hulse, W. C. (1950). The therapeutic management of group tension. *American Journal of Orthopsychiatry, 20,* 834–838.

Hulse, W. C., Ladlow, W. V., Rindsberg, B. K., & Epstein, N. B. (1956). Transference relations in a group of female patients to male and female co-leaders. *International Journal of Group Psychotherapy, 6,* 430–435.

Hymovitz, C., & Pollock, E. J. (1995, July 13). Cost cutting firms monitor couch time as therapists fret. *Wall Street Journal,* p. A1.

International Board for Certification of Group Psychotherapists. Retrieved from http://www.groupsinc.org/group/ethicalguide.html

Ivey, A. E. (1990). *Developmental strategies for helpers: Individual, family and network interventions.* Pacific Grove, CA: Brooks/Cole.

Jacklin, C. L. (1989). Female and male issues of gender. [Special issue: Children and their development: Knowledge base, research agenda, and social policy.] *American Psychologist, 44*(2), 127–133.

Jackson, J., & Grotjahn, M. (1958). Reenactment of the marriage neurosis in group psychotherapy. *Journal of Nervous and Mental Disorders, 127,* 503–510.

Jacobs, E. E., Harville, R. L., & Masson, R. L. (1994). *Group counseling: Strategies and skills.* Belmont, CA: Brooks/Cole.

Jacobs, E. E., Masson, R. L., & Harvill, R. (2009). *Group counseling: Strategies and skills.* (6th ed.). Pacific Grove, CA: Brooks/Cole.

Jacobs, E. E., Masson, R. L., Harvill, R., & Schimmel, C.J. (2012). *Group counseling: Strategies and skills.* (7th ed.). Pacific Grove, CA: Brooks/Cole.

Jacobs, E. E., Schimmel, C. J., Masson, R. L., & Harvill, R. L. (2016). *Group counseling: Strategies and skills* (8th ed.). Boston: Cengage Learning.

Jacobson, E. (1925). Progressive relaxation. *American Journal of Psychology, 36,* 73–87.

Janis, I. L., & Mann, L. (1965). Effectiveness of emotional role playing in modifying smoking habits and attitudes. *Journal of Experimental Research in Personality, 1,* 84–90.

Johnson, D. W., & Johnson, F. F. (2009). *Joining together* (10th ed.). Boston: Allyn and Bacon.

Jones, J. (1992). *Icebreakers: Sourcebook of games, exercises and simulations*. London: Kogan Page.

Kaimanowitz, D., & Ho, R. T. H. (2016). Out of our mind. Art therapy and mindfulness with refugees, political violence and trauma. *Arts in Psychotherapy, 49,* 57–65.

Kaphan, M. (2017). A ritual for termination. In S. S. Fehr (Ed.), *101 interventions in group therapy*. New York: Routledge.

Kaplan, H. I., & Sadock, B. J. (1971). *Comprehensive group psychotherapy*. Baltimore, MD: Williams and Wilkins.

Kaplan, H. I., & Sadock, B. J. (1983). *Comprehensive group psychotherapy* (2nd ed.). Baltimore, MD: Williams and Wilkins.

Keen, S. (1991). *Fire in the belly*. New York: Bantam.

Kemper, S., Kibel, H., & Mahler, J. (1993). On becoming oriented to inpatient addiction treatment: Inducting new patients and professionals to the recovery movement. *International Journal of Group Psychotherapy, 43,* 285–300.

Kirschenbaum, M. J., & Blinder, M. G. (1972). Growth processes in married-couples group therapy. *Family Therapy, 1,* 85–104.

Kline, N. S. (1952). Some hazards in group psychotherapy. *International Journal of Group Psychotherapy, 2,* 111–115.

Koss, M. P., & Butcher, J. N. (1986). Research on brief psychotherapy. In S. L. Garfield & A. E. Bergin (Eds.), *Handbook of psychotherapy and behavior change* (3rd ed.). New York: Wiley.

Kottler, J. A. (1982). Unethical behaviors we all do and pretend we do not. *Journal of Specialists in Group Work, 7,* 182–186.

Kottler, J. A., & Englar-Carlson, M. (2014). *Learning group leadership: An experiential approach.* Thousand Oaks, CA: Sage.

Kravetz, D. (1987). Benefits of consciousness-raising groups for women. In C. M. Brody (Ed.), *Women's therapy groups: Paradigms of feminist treatment* (pp. 55–66). New York: Springer.

Lakin, M. (1969). Some ethical issues in sensitivity training. *American Psychologist, 42,* 923–931.

Lakin, M. (1972). *Interpersonal encounter*. New York: McGraw Hill.

Lakin, M. (1991). *Coping with ethical dilemmas in psychotherapy*. New York: Pergamon.

Lasky, G. B., & Riva, M. T. (2006). Confidentiality and privileged communication in group psychotherapy. *International Journal of Group Psychotherapy, 56*(4), 455–476.

Laube, J. J. (1990). Why group therapy for bulimia? *International Journal of Group Psychotherapy, 40*(2), 222–235.

Le Bon, G. (1895). Psychology of Crowds. The Crowd by Gustave le Bon February. Retrieved from http://www.gutenberg.org/files/445/445.txt 1981

Leichter, E. (1962). Group psychotherapy of married couples group: Some characteristic treatment dynamics. *International Journal of Group Psychotherapy, 12,* 154.

Leong, E. T. (1992). Guidelines for minimizing premature termination among Asian American clients in group counseling. [Special issue: Group counseling with multicultural populations.] *Journal of Specialists in Group Work, 17*(4), 218–228.

Levin, S. (2015). Kaiser still violating mental health laws. Retrieved from http://www.eastbayexpress.com/oakland/kaiser-still-violating-mental-health-laws-clinicians-say/Content?oid=4580712

Levine, B. (1980). Co-leadership approach to learning group work. *Social Work with Groups, 3*(4), 35–38.

Lewis, B. (1978). An examination of the final phase of a group development theory. *Small Group Behavior*, *9*, 507–517.

Lewis, H., & Streitfeld, H. (1972). *Growth games.* New York: Bantam Books.

Lieberman, M. A., Yalom, I. D., & Miles, M. B. (1973). *Encounter groups: First facts.* New York: Basic Books.

Lifton, W. M. (1966). *Working with groups.* New York: Wiley.

Long, S. (1988). *The six group therapies compared.* New York: Wiley.

Lobban J. (2016). Factors that influence engagement in an inpatient art therapy group for veterans with post traumatic stress disorder. *International Journal of Art Therapy*, *21*(1), 15–22.

Low, P. & Low, M. (1975). Treatment of married couples in a group run by a husband and wife. *International Journal of Group Psychotherapy*, *25*(1), 54–66.

Lubin, B., & Lubin, A. L. (1987). *Comprehensive index of group psychotherapy writings.* Monograph. Madison, CT: International Universities Press.

Luborsky, L., Singer, B. & Luborsky, L. (1975). Comparative studies of psychotherapies: Is it true that "Everyone has won and all shall have prizes"? *Archives of General Psychiatry. 32*, 995-1008.

Luke, M., & Hackney, H. (2007). Group co-leadership: A critical review. *Counselor Education and Supervision*, *46*(4), 280–293.

Lunden, W. H., & Aranov, B. M. (1952). The use of co-therapists in group psychotherapy. *Journal of Consulting Psychology*, *16*, 76–80.

MacKenzie, K. R. (1987). Therapeutic factors in group psychotherapy: A contemporary view. *Group*, *11*, 26–34.

MacKenzie, K. R. (1990). *Introduction to time limited group psychotherapy.* Washington, DC: American Psychiatric Press.

MacKenzie, K. R. (1993). Time limited group theory and technique. In A. Alonso & H. I. Swiller, H. I. (Eds.), *Group therapy in clinical practice.* Washington, DC: American Psychiatric Press.

MacKenzie, K. R. (1994). The developing structure of the therapy group structure. In H. S. Bernard & K. R. MacKenzie (Eds.), *Basics of group psychotherapy.* New York: Guilford Press.

MacLennan, B. W. (1965). Co-therapy. *International Journal of Group Psychotherapy*, *15*, 154.

Mann, L. (1967). The effects of emotional role playing experience on desire to modify smoking behavior. *Journal of Experimental Social Psychology*, *3*, 334–348.

Mann, L., & Janis, I. L. (1968), A follow-up study on the long-term effects of emotional role playing. *Journal of Personality and Social Psychology*, *8*, 339–348.

Marmarosh, C. L., Markin, R. D., & Spiegel, E. B. (2013). *Attachment in group psychotherapy.* Washington, DC: American Psychological Association.

Marsh, L. C. (1931). Group treatment of the psychosis by the psychological equivalent of the revival. *Mental Hygiene, 15*, 328–349.

Markus, H., & King, E. (2003). A survey of group psychotherapy training during predoctoral psychology internship. *Professional Psychology: Research and Practice, 34*(2), 203–209.

McCallum, M., & Piper, W. (1990). A controlled study of effectiveness and patient suitability for short-term group psychotherapy. *International Journal of Group Psychotherapy*, *40*, 431–452.

McGhee, T. F., & Schuman, B. N. (1970). The nature of the cotherapy relationship. *International Journal of Group Psychotherapy, 20*, 25–36.

Miles, J. R., & Kivlighan, D. M. (2010). Co-leader similarity and group climate in group interventions: Testing the co-leadership team-cognition–team diversity model. *Group Dynamics, 15*(4), 326–342.

Moreno, J. L. (1911). *Die gottheit als komediant.* Vienna: Anzangruber Verlag.

Moreno, J. L. (1932). *Application of the group method to classification.* New York: National Committee on Prisons and Prison Labor.

Moreno, J. L. (1970). The Viennese origins of the encounter movement, paving the way for existentialism, group psychotherapy and psychodrama. *Group Psychotherapy*, *22*, 7–11.

Moreno, J. L., & Moreno, Z. T. (2011). *Psychodrama—Second Volume.* London: Northwest Psychodrama Association.

Morrison, A. P. (1986). On projective identification in couples' groups. *International Journal of Group Psychotherapy, 36*(l), 55–73.

Naisbitt, j. & Aburdene, P. (1990) *Megatrends 2000—Ten new directions for the 1990s.* New York: Avon.

Napier, R., & Gershenfeld, M. (1983). *Making groups work: A guide for group leaders.* Boston: Houghton Mifflin.

National Association of Social Workers. (1999). *Code of ethics.* Washington, DC: Author.

National Training Laboratories. (1970). *Personal growth and social change.* Institute for

Applied Behavior Science, Pamphlet 1–26. Washington, DC: Author.

National Union of Healthcare Workers. (2014). Retrieved from http://nuhw.org/nuhw-calls-justice-department-investigate-kaiser-permanentes-long-wait-times-paper-wait-lists-falsified-appointment-records/

Newman, R. & Levant, R. (1993) Proficiency certification: A useful tool in today's marketplace. *Independent Practitioner, 11*(4) 492–500.

Newmeyer, M. D. (2010). Group Techniques. In R. K. Conyne, *Oxford handbook of group counseling* (Chap. 16). New York: Oxford University Press.

Nicholas, M. W. (1984). *Change in the context of group therapy.* New York: Brunner/Mazel.

Nitza, A. (2014). Group techniques. In In J. L. DeLucia-Waack, C. R. Kalodner, & M. T. Riva (Eds.), *Handbook of group counseling and psychotherapy* (2nd ed.). Thousand Oaks, CA: Sage.

Norcross, J. C. (2011). *Psychotherapy relationships that work: Evidence-based responsiveness.* New York: Oxford University Press.

Norcross, J. C., Alford, B. A., & DiMichele, J. (1992). The future of psychotherapy: Delphi data and concluding observations. *Psychotherapy, 29,* 150–158.

Norcross, J. C., Pfund, R. A., & Prochaska, J. O. (1992). Psychotherapy in 2022: A Delphi poll on its future. *Professional psychology: Research and practice, 44*(5), 363–370.

Oesterheld, J. R., McKenna, M. S., & Gould, N. B. (1987). Group psychotherapy of bulimia: A critical review. *International Journal of Group Psychotherapy, 37*(2), 163–184.

Okech, J. E. A. (2008). Reflective practice in group co-leadership. *Journal for Specialists in Group Work, 33*(3), 236–252.

Okech, J. E. A., & Kline, W. B. (2006). Competency concerns in group co-leader relationships. *Journal for Specialists in Group Work, 31*(2), 165–180.

Orlinsky, D. E., & Howard, K. L. (1986). Process and outcome in psychotherapy. In S. L. Garfield & A. E. Bergin (Eds.), *Handbook of psychotherapy and behavior change* (3rd ed., pp. 311–381). New York: Wiley.

Otto, H. A. (1970). *Group methods to actualize human potential.* Beverly Hills, CA: Holistic Press.

Parkinson, S., & Whiter, C. (2016). Exploring art therapy group practice in early intervention psychosis. *International Journal of Art Therapy, 21*(3), 116–127.

Parloff, M. B., & Dies, R. R. (1977). Group psychotherapy outcome research, 1966–1975.

International Journal of Group Psychotherapy, 27, 281–319.

Pedersen, P. B. (2000). *A handbook for developing multicultural awareness* (3rd ed.). Alexandria, VA: American Counseling Association.

Pedersen, P. B., & Marsella, A. J. (1982). The ethical crisis for crosscultural counseling and therapy. *Professional Psychology, 13*(4), 492–500.

Pfeffer, A. A., Friedland, P., & Wortis, S. B. (1949). Group psychotherapy with alcoholics. *Quarterly Journal of Studies in Alcohol, 10,* 198–216.

Pfeifer, S., & Terhune, C. (2015, February 24). California again slams Kaiser for delays in mental health treatment. *Los Angeles Times.* Retrieved from http://www.latimes.com/business/la-fi-kaiser-mental-health-20150225-story.html

Pfeiffer, J. W., & Jones, J. E. (1972–1980a). *Annual handbooks for group facilitators, 1972–1975.* La Jolla, CA: University Associates.

Pfeiffer, J. W., & Jones, J. E. (1972–1980b). *A handbook of structured exercises for human relations training* (Vols. 1–8.) San Diego, CA: San Diego University Associates.

Pfeiffer, J. W., & Jones, J. E. (1975a). *A Handbook of structured experiences for human relations training* (Vols. 1–5 and Reference Guide). La Jolla, CA: University Associates, 1969–1974.

Pfeiffer, J. W., & Jones, J. E. (1975b). *A Handbook of structured experiences for human relations training* (2nd ed., Vols. I–VI and Reference Guide). La Jolla, CA: University Associates.

Pinney, E. L., Jr. (1983). Ethical and legal issues in group psychotherapy. In H. I. Kaplan & B. J. Sadock (Eds.), *Comprehensive group psychotherapy* (pp. 301–304). Baltimore, MD: Williams and Wilkins.

Piper, W. E., McCallum, M., & Hassan, A. (1992). *Adaptation to loss through short-term group psychotherapy.* New York: Guilford Press.

Piper, W. E., & Perrault, E. L. (1989). Pretherapy preparation for group members. *International Journal of Group Psychotherapy, 39,* 17–34.

Pollock, E. J. (1995, December 1). Managed care's focus on psychiatric drugs alarms many doctors. *Wall Street Journal,* p. A1.

Posthuma, B. W. (2002). *Small groups in counseling and therapy: Process and leadership* (4th ed.). Boston: Allyn and Bacon.

Powdermaker, F., & Frank, J. D. (1953). *Group psychotherapy.* Cambridge, MA: Harvard University Press.

Pratt, J. H. (1906). The home sanitarium treatment of consumption. *Boston Medical Surgeons Journal, 154,* 210–216.

Pratt, J. H. (1907). The class method of treating consumption in the homes of the poor. *Journal of the American Medical Association, 49,* 755–759.

Pratt, J. H. (1908). Results obtained in the treatment of pulmonary tuberculosis by the class method. *British Medical Journal, 2,* 1070–1071.

Pratt, J. H. (1911). The class method in the homes of tuberculars and what it has accomplished. *Transactions of the American Climatic Association, 27,* 87–118.

Pratt, J. H. (1934). The influence of emotions in the causation and cure of psychoneuroses. *International Clinics, 4,* 1–16.

Rachman, A. W. (1971). Encounter techniques in analytic group psychotherapy with adolescents. *International Journal of Group Psychotherapy, 21,* 317–328.

Rankanen, M. (2016). Clients' experiences of the impacts of an experiential art therapy group. *Arts in Psychotherapy, 50,* 101–110.

Rapin, L.S. (2014) Guidelines for ethical and legal practice in counseling and psychotherapy groups. In J.L. Delucia-Waack, C.R. Kalodner & M.T. Riva (Eds.) *Handbook of group counseling and psychotherapy.* (2nd Ed.), 71–83.

Rappaport, R. L. (1994). Culture, values and therapy. *Family Psychologist, 10*(2), 7.

Ratts, M. J., & Pedersen, P. B. (2014). *Counseling for multiculturalism and social justice* (4th ed.). Alexandria, VA: American Counseling Association.

Reicher, S. The psychology of crowd dynamics. In M. A. Hogg & R. S. Tindale (Eds.), *Blackwell handbook of social psychology: Group processes* (p. 185).. Malden, MA: Blackwell.

Reighline, P. B., & Targow, J. F. (1990). *Group psychotherapists handbook.* New York: Columbia University Press.

Ridley, C. A., & Bain, A. B. (1983). The effects of a premarital relationship enhancement program on self disclosure. *Family Therapy, 10*(1), 13–24.

Riordan, R. J., & Martin, M. M. (1993). Mental health counseling and the mandated client. *Journal of Mental Health Counseling, 15*(4), 373–383.

Riva, M.T., Lippert, L & Tackett, M.J. (2000) Selection practices of group leaders: A national survey. *Journal for Specialists in Group Work, 25*(2), 157–169.

Riva, M. T., & Smith, R. D. (1997). Looking into the future of group research: Where do we go from here? *Journal for Specialists in Group Work, 22,* 266–276.

Riva, M. T., Wachtel, M., & Lasky, G. B. (2004). Effective leadership in group counseling and psychotherapy: Research and practice. In J. L. Delucia-Waack, D. A. Gerrity, & C. R. Kalodner (Eds.), *Handbook of group counseling and psychotherapy.* Thousand Oaks, CA: Sage.

Rogers, C. R. (1969). *On encounter groups.* New York: Harper and Row.

Rogers, C. R. (1961/1995). *On becoming a person: A therapist's view of psychotherapy.* New York: Houghton Mifflin.

Rosal, M. L. (2016). Rethinking and reframing group art therapy: An amalgamation of British and U.S. Models. In D. E. Gussak & M. L. Rosal (Eds.), *The Wiley handbook of art therapy.* New York: Wiley.

Rosenbaum, M. (1971). Cotherapy. In H. I. Kaplan & B. J. Sadock (Eds.), *Comprehensive group psychotherapy.* Baltimore, MD: Williams and Wilkins.

Rosenbaum, M., & Hartley, E. (1962). A summary review of current practices of ninety-two group therapists. *International Journal of Group Psychotherapy, 12,* 194–198.

Rosenberg, S. A., & Zimet, C. N. (1995). Brief group treatment and managed health care. *International Journal of Group Psychotherapy, 45*(3), 367–379.

Ross I. (1977). The intuitive psychologist and his shortcomings: Distortions in the attribution process. In L. Berkowitz (Ed.), *Advances in experimental social psychology* (Vol. 10). New York: Academic Press.

Rousseau, J. J., LeBon, G., Mackay, C., Trotter, W., Martin, E. D., Lee, G. S., & MacDougall, W. (2017). *What is mob mentality? 8 Essential books on crowd psychology.* Retrieved from E-artnow.org.

Rubel, D. & Okech, J.E.A. (2006) The supervision of group work model: Adapting the discrimination model for supervision of group workers. *Journal for Specialists in Group Work, 31*(2), 113–134.

Russell, J. (1971). Personal growth through structured exercises. *Voices: The Art and Science of Psychotherapy, 7,* 28–36.

Rutan, J. S., Stone, W. N. & Shay, (2014). *Psychodynamic group psychotherapy.* (5th Ed.) New York: Macmillan.

Saunders, D. G., & Hanusa, D. (1986). The short-term effects of group therapy. *Journal of Family Violence,* (December), 357–372.

Schaffer, J. B., & Galinsky, M. D. (1989). *Models of group therapy and sensitivity training* (2nd ed.). Englewood Cliffs, NJ: Prentice Hall.

Scheidlinger, S. (1994). Nine decades of group psychotherapy—An overview. Paper presented at the annual meeting of the American Psychological Association, Los Angeles, CA.

Schutz, W. C. (1967). *Joy: Expanding human awareness.* New York: Harper and Row.

Schutz, W. C. (1972). *Here comes everybody.* New York: Harrow Books.

Schutz, W. C. (1973). *Elements of encounter.* Big Sur, CA: Joy Press.

Schwartz, T. (2017). Applying art therapy within group therapy. In S. S. Fehr, *101 interventions in group therapy* (2nd ed.). New York: Taylor and Francis.

Selzer, M. L. (1971). The Michigan Alcohol Screening Test: Quest for a new diagnostic instrument. *American Journal of Psychiatry, 127,* 1653–1658.

Shapiro, E. L., & Ginsberg, R. (2002). Parting gifts: Termination in group therapy. *International Journal of Group Psychotherapy, 52*(3), 319–336.

Shapiro, J. L. (1970). An investigation into the differential effects of a variety of sensitivity training procedures (Unpublished doctoral dissertation). University of Waterloo, Waterloo, Canada.

Shapiro, J. L. (1973, June 23). Encounter in Hawaii. *Hawaii Observer,* pp. 8–9.

Shapiro, J. L. (1975). Process, progress and concerns for encounter groups. Paper presented at Hawaii Association of Humanistic Psychology, Honolulu.

Shapiro, J. L. (1976). The use of videotape in group leader training. Paper presented at the World's Educators Conference, Honolulu, HI.

Shapiro, J. L. (1978). *Methods of group psychotherapy and encounter: A tradition of innovation.* Itasca, IL: Peacock.

Shapiro, J. L. (1992, March 21). Group therapy: The treatment of choice in the 90's. Workshop. San Francisco.

Shapiro, J. L. (1993). *Brief group treatment: A training manual for counselors and therapists.* Santa Clara, CA: Santa Clara University Counseling Psychology and Education.

Shapiro, J. L. (1994). *Brief treatment groups.* Workshop. Santa Clara University, Santa Clara, CA.

Shapiro, J. L. (1996). A semi-formal review of North American group training programs. Unpublished document.

Shapiro, J. L. (2001, August). Symposium. *Training for group therapists and counselors: Undergraduate, masters level, doctoral level and postdoctoral level.* Chair. American Psychological Association, San Francisco.

Shapiro, J. L. (2010). Brief group treatment. In R. K. Conyne (Ed.), *The Oxford handbook of group counseling.* New York: Oxford University Press.

Shapiro, J. L. (2016a). *Pragmatic existential counseling and psychotherapy: Intimacy, intuition and the search for meaning.* Los Angeles, CA: Sage.

Shapiro, J. L. (2016b, June 18). Therapists' and clients' mindsets. Do clients have theories: A five decade saga. Symposium for the Society for the Exploration of Psychotherapy Integration (SEPI), Dublin, Ireland.

Shapiro, J. L. (2017). A five-stage technique to enhance termination in group therapy. In S. S. Fehr (Ed.), *101 Interventions in group therapy* (2nd ed.). New York: Taylor and Francis.

Shapiro, J. L., & Bernadett-Shapiro, S. T. (1985). Group work to 2001: Hal or haven (from isolation)? [Special issue.] *Journal of Specialists in Group Work, 10*(2), 83–87.

Shapiro, J. L., & Diamond, M. J. (1972). Increases in hypnotizability as a function of encounter group training. *Journal of Abnormal Psychology, 79*(1), 112–115.

Shapiro, J. L., Marano, P. J., & Diamond, M. J. (1973). An investigation of encounter group outcome and its relationship to leadership experience. Paper presented at the 19th Annual Meeting of the Southeastern Psychological Association, New Orleans, LA.

Shapiro, J. L., Patterson, T., & Soohoo, T. (2017, August 5). Couple therapy minefields. Symposium. American Psychological Association annual meeting, Washington, DC.

Shapiro, J.L., Peltz, L.S. & Bernadett-Shapiro, S.T. (1998). *Brief group treatment: A practical guide for therapists and counselors.* Pacific Grove, CA: Brooks/Cole.

Shapiro, J. L., & Siu, P. K. (1976). Potential subtle modelling influences in group training: The impact of minority culture group leaders on members' identification and behavior. Unpublished paper. University of Hawaii, Honolulu.

Shay, J. J. (2017). Contemporary models of group therapy: Where are we today? *International Journal of Group Psychotherapy, 67*(1), S7–S12.

Shechtman, Z., & Toren, Z. (2009). The effect of leader behavior on processes and outcomes in group counseling. *Group Dynamics: Theory, Research, and Practice, 13,* (3), 218–233.

Shore, K. (1996). Beyond managed care and managed competition. *The Independent Practitioner,* 24–25.

Shostrom, E. L. (1969). Group therapy: Let the buyer beware. *Psychology Today, 2,* 36–40.

Shumaker, D., Ortiz, C., & Brenninkmeyer, L. (2011). Revisiting experiential group training in masters-level programs. *Journal for Specialists in Group Work, 36*(2), 111–128.

Siegel. J. M. (1969). Role playing: A review. Unpublished document. University of Waterloo, Waterloo, Canada.

Singh, A. A., & Salazar, C. F. (2013). *Social justice in group work: Practical interventions for change.* New York: Routledge.

Slavson, S. R. (1951). *The practice of group therapy.* New York: International Universities Press.

Slavson, S. R. (1964). *A textbook in analytic group psychotherapy.* New York: Grune and Stratton.

Solomon, J., & Solomon, G. (1963). Group therapy with father and son as co-therapists: Some dynamic considerations. *International Journal of Group Psychotherapy, 13,* 133–140.

Spotnitz, H. (1952). Group therapy as a specialized technique. In G. Bychowski & J. L. Despert (Eds.), *Specialized techniques in psychotherapy* (pp. 85–101). New York: Basic Books.

Stahmann, R. F., & Hiebert, W. J. (1980). *Premarital counseling.* Lexington, MA: Lexington Books.

Stice, E., Rohde, P., Seeley, J. R., & Gau, J. M. (2008). Brief cognitive-behavioral depression prevention program for high-risk adolescents: A randomized efficacy trial. *Journal of Consulting and Clinical Psychology, 76*(4), 595–606.

Stockton, R., Toth, P.L. (1996) Teaching group counselors: Recommendations for maximizing preservice instruction. *Journal for Specialists in Group Work. 21*(4) 274–282.

Stone, C., & Isaacs, M. L. (2003). Confidentiality with minors: The need for policy to promote and protect. *Journal of Educational Research, 96,* 140–150.

Stoute, A. (1950). Implementation of group interpersonal relationships through psychotherapy. *Journal of Psychology, 30,* 145–156.

Sue, D. W. (2010). *Microaggressions in everyday life.* New York: Wiley.

Sue, D. W., & Sue, D. (2016). Counseling the culturally diverse: Theory and practice (7th ed.). New York: Wiley.

Sue, S. (1984). Psychotherapeutic service for ethnic minorities. *American Psychologist, 43,* 301–308.

Sue, S., & Sue, D. W. (1971). Chinese American personality and mental health. *Amerasia Journal, 1,* 36–49.

Sue, S., & Sue, D. W. (1990). *Counseling the culturally different: Theory and practice* (2nd ed.). New York: Wiley.

Thomas, R. V., & Pender, D. A. (2008). Association for Specialists in Group Work: Best Practices Guidelines 2007 Revisions. *Journal for Specialists in Group Work, 33*(2), 111–117.

Thompson, C. (1941). The role of women in this culture. *Psychiatry, 4,* 1–8.

Thompson, C. (1942). Cultural pressures in the psychology of women. *Psychiatry, 5,* 331–339.

Tillich, R. S. (1973). Group therapy: A debate. Unpublished presentation. Hawaii Association of Humanistic Psychology, Honolulu.

Toch, H. (1988). Psychology of crowds revisited. *Contemporary Psychology, 33*(11), 954.

Toseland, R., Kabat, D., & Kemp, K. (1983). An evaluation of a smoking cessation group program. *Social Work Research and Abstracts, 19*(1), 12–19.

Toseland, R. W., & Rivas, R. F. (1984). *An introduction to group work practice.* New York: Macmillan.

Toth, P. L., Stockton, R., & Erwin, W. J. (1998). Application of a skill-based approach to teaching group counseling interventions. *Journal for Specialists in Group Work, 23,* 39–44.

Tran, U. S., & Gregor, B. (2016). The relative efficacy of bona fide psychotherapies for post-traumatic stress disorder: A meta-analytical evaluation of randomized controlled trials. *BMC Psychiatry, 16,* 266–287.

Truax, C. B. (1966). Therapist empathy, warmth and genuineness and patient personality change in group psychotherapy. *Journal of Clinical Psychology, 22,* 225–228.

Truax, C. B. (1971). Degree of negative transference occurring in group psychotherapy and client outcome in juvenile delinquents. *Journal of Clinical Psychology, 27,* 132–136.

Truax, C. B., & Carkhuff, R. R. (1967). *Toward Effective Counseling and Psychotherapy.* Chicago: Aldine.

Truax, C. B., Carkhuff, R. R., Wargo, D. G., & Kodman, F. (1966). Changes in self concepts during group psychotherapy as a function of alternate sessions and vicarious therapy pre-training, institutionalized mental patients and juvenile delinquents. *Journal of Consulting Psychology, 30,* 309–392.

Truax, C. B., & Mitchell, K. M. (1971). Research on certain therapist interpersonal skills in relation to process and outcome. In A. E. Bergin & S. L. Garfield (Eds.), *Handbook of psychotherapy and behavior change* (pp. 299–344). New York: Wiley.

Tseng, W., & Streltzer, J. Wampold, B. E., & Imel, Z. E. (Eds.) (2015). *The great psychotherapy debate: The research evidence for what works in psychotherapy* (2nd ed.). New York: Routledge.

Tuckman, B. W. (1965). Developmental sequences in small groups. *Psychological Bulletin, 63,* 384–399.

Tuckman, B. W., & Jenson, M. A. (1977). Stages of small group development revisited. *Journal of Counseling and Development, 64*(1), 52–58.

Vander Kolk, C. J. (1985). *Introduction to group counseling and psychotherapy.* Long Grove, IL: Waveland Press.

Vanicelli, M. (1982). Group psychotherapy with alcoholics: Special techniques. *Journal of Studies on Alcohol, 43,* 17–37.

Verny, T. R. (1975). *Inside groups: A practical guide to encounter groups and group therapy.* New York: McGraw Hill.

Vinogradov, S., & Yalom, I. D. (1990). *Concise guide to group psychotherapy.* Washington, DC: American Psychiatric Press.

Visser, M., & Du Plessis, J. (2015). An expressive art group intervention for sexually abused adolescent females. *Journal of Child and Adolescent Mental Health*, 27(3), 199–213.

Wagner, B. M., Compas, B. E., & Howell, D. C. (1988). Daily and major life events: A test of an integrative model of psychosocial stress. *American Journal of Community Psychology*, 16(2), 189–205.

Wagner, C. C.. Ingersoll, K. S., Downey, S. S., Johnson, W. R., Velasquez, M. M., Stephens, N. S., Drenner, K. L., Jasiura, F., Hunt, W., Martino, S., Santa Ana, E. J., Butterworth, S., Speck, L. Dunn, E. C., Hecht, J., Krejci, J., Carden, A., Farrall, M., Prescott, D. S., Ross, M., Feldstein-Ewing, S. W., Walters, S. T., & Baer, J. S. (2013). *Motivational interviewing in groups.* New York: Guilford Press.

Ware, J. N., & Taylor, D. D. (2014). Concerns about confidentiality: The application of ethical decision-making within group play. *International Journal of Play Therapy*, 23(3), 173–186.

Wampold, B. E., & Imel, Z. E. (2015). *The great psychotherapy debate: The research evidence for what works in psychotherapy* (2nd ed.). New York: Routledge.

Weinberg, H. (2010). Using art therapy technique in a psychodynamic group. In S. S. Fehr, *101 interventions in group therapy* (Rev. ed.). New York: Routledge.

Welfel, E. R. (2010). Ethics in counseling and psychotherapy: Standards, research, and emerging issues (4th ed.). Belmont, CA: Brooks/Cole.

Wender, L. (1936). The dynamics of group psychotherapy and its application. *Journal of Nervous and Mental Diseases, 84,* 54–60.

Whitaker, C. A. (1949). Teaching the practicing physician to do psychotherapy. *Southern Medical Journal, 42,* 899–904.

Whitaker, D. S. (1982). A nuclear conflict and group focal conflict model for integrating individual and group level phenomena in psychotherapy groups. In M. Pines & L. Rafaelson (Eds.), *The individual and the group: Boundaries and interrelations* (Vol. 1). New York: Plenum.

Woldt, A. L., & Toman, S. M. (2005). *Gestalt therapy: History, theory & practice.* Thousand Oaks, CA: Sage.

Wolpe, J. (1969). *The practice of behavior therapy.* New York: Pergamon Press.

Yalom, I. D. (1970). *Theory and practice of group psychotherapy.* New York: Basic Books.

Yalom, I. D. (1975). *The theory and practice of group psychotherapy* (2nd ed.). New York: Basic Books.

Yalom, I. D. (1980). *Existential psychotherapy.* New York: Basic Books.

Yalom, I. D. (1985). *The theory and practice of group psychotherapy* (3rd ed.). New York: Basic Books.

Yalom, I. D. (1990). *Understanding group therapy* [Video]. Pacific Grove, CA: Brooks Cole.

Yalom, I. D. (1995). *The theory and practice of group psychotherapy* (4th ed.). New York: Basic Books.

Yalom, I. D. (with Lescz, M.). (2005). *The theory and practice of group psychotherapy* (5th ed.). New York: Basic Books.

Yalom, I. D., Houts, P. S., Newell, G., & Rand, K. H. (1979). Preparation of patients for group therapy. In H. B. Roback, S. I. Abramovitz, & D. S. Strassberg (Eds.), *Group psychotherapy research: Commentaries and selected readings.* Huntington, NY: Krieger.

Yalom, I. D., & Lieberman, M. A. (1971). A study of encounter group casualties. *Archives of General Psychiatry,* 16–20.

Zweben, J. E., & Hamman, K. (1970). Prescribed games: A theoretical perspective on the use of group techniques. *Psychotherapy Theory Research and Practice, 7*(1), 22–27.

Index